Praise for Sinan Aral and **The Hype Machine**

Named one of the best books of the year by *Wired*

Longlisted for the Porchlight Business Book Award

"[*The Hype Machine*] might be described as prophetic. . . . At least two of Aral's three predictions have come to fruition."

—*New York*

"Eminently relevant . . . [*The Hype Machine*] offers hope that we can re-engineer social media to better serve society. [Its] biggest service, however, is to make us rethink our attitudes to big data and social media."

—*New Scientist*

"What Sinan Aral has achieved with his new book, *The Hype Machine*, is probably the most comprehensive and best structured presentation of social media's effects based on existing scientific studies and collective experience."

—*The Y Circus*

"Aral . . . takes readers on a wild journey to explore the role of social media in our lives. . . . [*The Hype Machine* is] timely for readers interested in important issues, such as data ethics, privacy, platform policies and regulations, the role of social media tech giants in our lives, and how these tools impact consumers' behaviors."

—*Library Journal*

"A useful, data-rich analysis of how we use social media—and how it uses us."

—*Kirkus Reviews*

"The scenario Aral describes should scare any technology leader, user of social media technology, or citizen within a democracy. . . . The urgency of Aral's message has only increased during the COVID-19 pandemic, when stay at home orders pushed even more people onto social media to keep in touch."

—Myles Suer, CMS Wire

"With his precision science and rollicking narrative storytelling, Sinan Aral, the director of MIT's Initiative on the Digital Economy, takes us on his fascinating twenty-year-journey as one of the first and most prescient scholars of social media. He explains how social media impacts our democracy, disseminates truth and lies, propagates hate and makes people fall in love, hooks us neurologically and emotionally, and connects us all, for better or worse. Is social media a boon for society or a curse? The answer is complex and you'll have to read *The Hype Machine* to find out."

—Richard Stengel, former U.S. Under Secretary of State for Public Diplomacy and Public Affairs, former editor of *Time*, and author of *Information Wars* and *A Long Walk to Freedom*

"It reads like a thriller, but it's all too true—a thoughtful, well-researched and timely look at how the structure of media changes the structure of our lives. It's time we took action and amplified the ideas that truly matter."

—Seth Godin, author of *This Is Marketing*

"Brilliant! Aral's masterful integration of science, business, law, and policy presents a powerful, accessible explanation of how social media affects all of us. Whether you simply want to understand the how and why, or need to make business or policy decisions, this is a must-read!"

—FOSTER PROVOST, NYU Stern School of Business,
author of *Data Science for Business*

"Sinan Aral is a scientist and an entrepreneur, and his unique perspective makes him the perfect guide to the world we live in today. From ads to fake news, *The Hype Machine* is the best critical foundation for understanding the connected world and how we might navigate through it to a better future."

—HILARY MASON, founder and CEO of Fast Forward Labs,
data scientist in residence at Accel, and former chief scientist at Bitly

"If you want the truth about falsehoods, real information about misinformation, and rigorous analysis of hype, this is the book for you. Nobody knows better than Sinan Aral how ideas spread online, and in these pages he's distilled a brilliant career into a fascinating read. Don't miss it if you care about how the Internet is changing our world."

—ANDREW MCAFEE, MIT, author of *More from Less* and
bestselling co-author of *The Second Machine Age*

"In this book, Sinan Aral, one of the world's leading computational social scientists, tackles one of the great challenges of our time: how to reengineer digital technology to better serve society. Authoritative, comprehensive, nuanced, and engaging, *The Hype Machine* is essential reading for anyone who wants to understand how we got here and how we can get somewhere better."

—DUNCAN WATTS, University of Pennsylvania, author of
Six Degrees and *Everything Is Obvious*

"*The Hype Machine* explains how social media changes who we know, what we do, and even how we think. As the world relies even more heavily on social media during the COVID-19 pandemic and the upsurge against racism and police violence, he helps us understand how digital technology will change our future, and what individuals, companies, and society should do differently to adapt and thrive."

—DAVID KIRKPATRICK, founder and CEO of Techonomy and author of *The Facebook Effect*

"The most important book of the year! Our friendships, economy, and society now depend on billions of social media connections around the world, and no one on the planet understands them better than Sinan Aral. In this lively, engaging masterpiece, drawing on his twenty years of pioneering research, Aral separates hype from reality, clarifies our most pressing challenges, and explains how we must respond."

—ERIK BRYNJOLFSSON, director of the Stanford Digital Economy Lab and bestselling co-author of *The Second Machine Age*

"In a sea of books about social media, this is the one to read. Sinan Aral understands the new social age like no one else, and *The Hype Machine* offers the single best examination of how social media works, what it does to us, and how we can make it better for consumers, citizens, and democracies. In short, it offers solutions for making social media 'social' again."

—CLINT WATTS, author of *Messing with the Enemy*

"Is social media a force for good or evil? Sinan Aral deconstructs the Hype Machine and takes us on a breathtaking journey through the economics, technology, and behavioral psychology that shape it. When lies spread faster than facts, how do we ensure the integrity of markets and elections? If you want to understand how we can capture the promise of social media and avoid its peril, read this!"

—MARIA RESSA, CEO of Rappler and a *Time* Person of the Year for 2018

"Everyone has a theory about social media, but Sinan Aral brings the science—and the storytelling. *The Hype Machine* is an immensely interesting, informative, and provocative look at the driving forces of some of the biggest technological questions of our time, and how they'll play out in the future of our democracy."

—ELI PARISER, bestselling author of *The Filter Bubble*

"*The Hype Machine* is a riveting story of social media's impact on how we vote, date, and shop—and thus how we live. With our democracy in the crosshairs, and tech companies controlling our screens, leading expert Sinan Aral pulls back the curtain on the digital tools used to direct the flow of influence in society. Part spy novel and part science thriller, it is an essential guide to ensuring our digital future."

—JONAH BERGER, bestselling author of *Contagious*,
Invisible Influence, and *The Catalyst*

"Full of rigor and insight, *The Hype Machine* tackles some of the most pressing policy questions of the Digital Age while keeping you on the edge of your seat (an unlikely combination). It's a must-read for policy-makers, business executives, and parents alike."

—DJ PATIL, former U.S. Chief Data Scientist

"*The Hype Machine* is a meticulous dissection of social media and how it affects our lives. Aral gives us a much-needed framework for understanding what happened in the 2016 election, and what will likely happen again if nothing changes."

—SCOTT GALLOWAY, bestselling author of *The Four*
and co-creator and co-host of *Pivot*

"In a timely and far-reaching book, Aral carefully and deftly examines the promise and peril of our social media environment, separating fact from fiction as well as offering thoughtful and practical suggestions for moving forward in our new world. *The Hype Machine* will be of interest to anyone concerned with building a healthy public sphere in the twenty-first century."

—ZEYNEP TUFEKCI, author of *Twitter and Tear Gas*

The Hype Machine

THE
HYPE
MACHINE

How Social Media Disrupts Our Elections,

Our Economy, and Our Health—

and How We Must Adapt

SINAN ARAL

Currency | New York

2021 Currency Trade Paperback Edition

Copyright © 2020 by HyperAnalytic, Inc.
Preface copyright © 2021 by HyperAnalytic, Inc.

Published in the United States by Currency, an imprint of Random
House, a division of Penguin Random House LLC, New York.

CURRENCY and its colophon are trademarks of
Penguin Random House LLC.

Originally published in hardcover in the United States by
Currency, an imprint of Random House, a division of Penguin
Random House LLC, in 2020.

LIBRARY OF CONGRESS CATALOGING- IN PUBLICATION DATA
Names: Aral, Sinan, author.
Title: The hype machine / Sinan Aral.
Description: First edition. | New York: Currency, 2020 |
Includes bibliographical references and index. Identifiers:
LCCN 2020012039 (print) | LCCN 2020012040 (ebook) |
ISBN 9780593240403 (paperback) | ISBN 9780525574521 (ebook)
Subjects: LCSH: Social media—Moral and ethical aspects. |
Information society. | Social interaction. | Propaganda. |
Misinformation.
Classification: LCC HM741.A73 2020 (print) |
LCC HM741 (ebook) | DDC 303.48/33—dc23
LC record available at https://lccn.loc.gov/2020012039

Printed in the United States of America on acid-free paper

crownpublishing.com

2 4 6 8 9 7 5 3 1

Book design by Simon M. Sullivan

To my parents—Thank you for every opportunity,
every conversation, and every hug.

To Kaya—May you always stay curious, creative,
and hungry for knowledge.

Contents

Social Media's Time of Reckoning

In 2021, a perfect storm of unfortunate but predictable events made it impossible for the world to turn a blind eye to social media's outsize societal effects. The unmistakable impact of what many once assumed was a childish technology built for mindless entertainment revealed itself to be so much more foundational and transformative. Social media is rewiring the central nervous system of humanity by algorithmically connecting, informing, nudging, persuading, mobilizing, and, yes, entertaining us. It's been doing so for years, with clear, measurable, and profound implications for our democracies, our economies, and our public health. And it's time we woke up to these realities.

It's essential that we understand how this technology works to promote and undermine our democratic ideals, to create and destroy economic value, and to enable and constrain the fragile public health infrastructure protecting us from growing pandemic risks. It's time to stop armchair theorizing about how social media works, and to instead get under the hood of these platforms, using science and evidence, to truly understand them. It's time we get past the debate about whether social media is good or evil (because the answer is yes to both) and get to the difficult business of designing, regulating, and using the technology in ways that harness its potential while avoiding its peril. That's why I wrote this book, and why I continue to work to steer social media's development today.

When I first published *The Hype Machine* in September 2020, I predicted that a groundswell of fake news would catalyze a contested U.S. presidential election to violence. Four months later, on January 6, 2021, we witnessed an unprecedented insurrection at the U.S. Capitol, motivated, legitimized, and coordinated in large part over social media. In the first edition of this book, I suggested that antivaccine misinformation could disrupt the COVID-19 vaccine rollout, aiding the resurgence of the deadly pandemic we all so painfully endured throughout 2020. Then, on January 30, 2021, we saw antivaccine protests, organized over Facebook, shut down one of the largest vaccination sites in one of America's largest cities, Dodger Stadium in Los Angeles. I predicted that social media would begin to sway equity markets with more regularity and with growing impact. Then, in late January 2021, GameStop's stock price jumped more than 1,700 percent, driven by retail investors coordinating over Reddit and other social media sites to put a "short squeeze" on hedge funds that had bet big on the company's demise. When these predictions came to pass, *New York* magazine called *The Hype Machine* "prophetic." But I don't consider myself an oracle; the consequences of this profound technology were entirely predictable. In fact, my colleagues and I had been warning about them for years.

The coronavirus pandemic of 2020 was a "black swan" event whose repercussions were felt throughout the world. We all remember where we quarantined, the relatives and friends and colleagues we could no longer see, and how we coped with the tremendous mental and physical strain the virus exacted. But another dramatic, albeit subtler consequence of COVID-19 was the abrupt shock it delivered to the world's global communication system—the system of digital connections that links our planet. Times Square, Trafalgar Square, and Tahrir Square became ghost towns. As the virus sent humanity scurrying off the streets and into our homes, it also pushed billions of people onto their laptops and smartphones, scrambling to get online. The world logged on to Facebook, Twitter, WhatsApp, Instagram, YouTube, and LinkedIn in record numbers, desperate for news, medical information, social support, human connection, and jobs. The day the offline world stood still, the online world ignited like a digital forest fire.

Demand for social media skyrocketed. Facebook Messenger, WhatsApp, and Facebook Live saw 50 percent increases in usage overnight. Voice calling over Facebook's apps doubled, while group calls in Italy grew by over 1,000 percent. As movie theaters closed, new downloads of Netflix jumped 66 percent in Italy and 35 percent in Spain. Netflix crashed under the weight of the demand. YouTube was forced to throttle their video quality to handle the deluge. And the Internet stuttered repeatedly. The already crowded ranks of social media grew massively during the pandemic, and now it's even more intertwined with our lives than ever before, simply because so many more are using it.

Social collaboration tools exploded with activity. Slack CEO Stewart Butterfield tweeted that "1,597 days after hitting 1M *simultaneously connected* users in Oct '15 we pass ten million. 6 days later: 10.5M, then 11.0M. Next day, 11.5M. This Monday, 12M. Today 12.5M." He attached a graph of the number of "newly created [Slack] work teams" to his tweet thread, which, after March 12, looked like a hockey stick with an extra-long handle pointing straight up. Digital natives were already on social media, but the coronavirus forced many digital Luddites to use social technologies for the first time. New users flocked to social platforms in droves, building armies of fresh profiles, wiring into what I call the "Hype Machine"—the real-time communications ecosystem created by social media. Describing their attempts to cope with the surge, Alex Schultz and Jay Parikh, Facebook's heads of analytics and engineering, respectively, wrote "usage growth from COVID-19 is unprecedented across the industry, and we are experiencing new records in usage every day." Facebook CEO Mark Zuckerberg was blunter: "We're just trying to keep the lights on over here," he said.

As the entire planet was denied physical contact for more than a year, the coronavirus altered our use and perception of social technologies in dramatic ways. Facebook, Twitter, WhatsApp, and Instagram became indispensable sources of human connection, timely medical information, social support, outreach, pandemic fundraising, free impromptu concerts, collaborative art projects, and real-time updates about the spread of the virus. Families played Monopoly over Facebook, friends attended cocktail mixers in live group chats, neighbors maintained vibrant WhatsApp groups, and many followed the news on Twitter. Group video kept families together. Hangouts kept work teams collaborating while the world stood still. Even my seven-year-old, who gets almost no screen time, connected with his friends and his first-grade class every day over Zoom and Messenger Kids.

Social platforms provided access to critical medical information about how to socially distance, whether to wear masks, where the hot spots were, and how to be safe at home. The platform companies got right to work, providing new services and data to model and mitigate the spread of the pandemic. Facebook used aggregate anonymous mobility data to create "colocation" maps of where people from different geographies were most likely to cross paths, which aided epidemiologists modeling where the pandemic was likely to spread next, from one geography to another. They spun up "disease prevention maps" that leveraged Facebook's mobile app data to help understand how people were moving and what that might mean for the spread of the virus.

As the director of MIT's Initiative on the Digital Economy, one of the largest centers researching the influence of digital technologies on our world, and head of MIT's Social Analytics Lab, a team of thirty MIT faculty and students studying the impact of social media on society, I felt we needed "all hands on deck" to address the crisis. We organized Zoom meetings to brainstorm how we could contribute to efforts to address the pandemic. While remembering to first do no harm, I reached out to my contacts at social platforms around the world to see how we could help.

With Facebook, we focused on modeling the effect of social distancing on the pandemic's spread. Facebook's disease prevention maps tracked aggregated, anonymous Facebook mobile app data on user location density, movement, and network connectivity, compared to pre-pandemic levels. We worked to combine this data with detailed records of the social distancing orders imposed on different regions, states, and cities around the world to estimate the effect of social distancing orders on the number of Facebook users present in public places within the region or city in which the order was imposed. But what we found was even more profound. As friends and families messaged each other from New York to Florida and from Texas to California, they also changed their COVID behaviors in response to the information they were receiving over social media. Our analysis suggested that the social communication happening over Facebook was actually governing how people responded to social distancing orders all around the United States. People's distancing behaviors in response to lockdowns in one state were significantly influencing the distancing behaviors of their Facebook friends in other, faraway states. This meant that there was a substantial cost—in resources and lives lost—to uncoordinated government responses to COVID-19 across the states, because social media's influence flowed so freely across state borders. We immediately called publicly for a coordinated national strategy, created "coordination maps" for the governors of all fifty states, and sent the information to the National Governors Association.

We also collaborated with Facebook and the World Health Organization (WHO) to create what became the world's largest longitudinal survey on COVID behaviors, norms, and perceptions. As of this printing, we've surveyed over 1.9 million people in 67 countries about their mask-wearing behaviors, their adherence to social distancing, their likelihood of visiting restaurants and other businesses, the impacts of the pandemic on their employment status, the economic hardship they were facing, and, of course, their vaccination intentions.

At the time, public health officials and the media were obsessed with vaccine hesitancy and continuously discussing how it could derail our vaccination efforts. So, as part of our survey, we created the largest longitudinal vaccine acceptance tracker in the world and ran experiments to understand how to increase vaccine acceptance. In one experiment, we found that giving people accurate information about the true rates of vaccine acceptance in their communities substantially increased their own likelihood of getting vaccinated. In other words, overstating or overemphasizing vaccine hesitancy could, by itself, have kept others from getting vaccinated. Public health communications should have instead been emphasizing the reality that large and growing majorities around the world were accepting vaccines, not rejecting them, and highlighting on social media the videos of influencers, like Barack Obama, being vaccinated. When we released the study, the White House reached out to us about it, and we advised them on how vaccine messaging could be improved.

COVID misinformation was also threatening to disrupt international pandemic containment efforts. So I called John Kelly and Camille François of Graphika, one of two companies commissioned by the U.S. Senate Intelligence Committee to investigate Russian interference in the 2016 and 2020 U.S. presidential elections, to brainstorm how we could track and fight the spread of COVID misinformation, as well as the growing threat of election misinformation ahead of the 2020 election. We decided to monitor, track, and publicly report on the automated software "bot," cyborg, and troll networks spreading misinformation about the coronavirus and the election around the world.

I also connected with Gustav Praekelt of the Praekelt Foundation in South Africa. Gustav and I had created an active, countrywide project using social media to fight the spread of HIV/AIDS in South Africa. When I asked him how we could collaborate on COVID-19, he told me he had repurposed the WhatsApp and Messenger tools we were using in our HIV project to disseminate official COVID medical information around the world. They had created something called COVID-Connect, an automated software robot that would field questions from the public and respond to them with the correct information from official sources over WhatsApp, Facebook Messenger, and text messaging. COVIDConnect had become the official engine of the global WHO WhatsApp channel and powered the automated national COVID response hotlines of South Africa, New Zealand, Australia, and ten other countries in Africa and Southeast Asia, amassing fifteen million users in just two weeks. It was fast becoming the go-to source for official information about COVID. But Praekelt and Facebook had a problem. They were worried about the spread of COVID misinformation on WhatsApp. It's hard to root out misinformation on an encrypted platform like WhatsApp, because messages can't be publicly tracked. So we got to work building a system to debunk COVID misinformation over the official WHO and national WhatsApp accounts.

The social platforms addressed the economic fallout from the pandemic as well. Small businesses used their Facebook pages to sell online. Live videocasts were hosted across social media to replace in-store events that usually generate foot traffic and boost sales. Stage shows were produced and aired over Instagram Stories and TikTok. Yoga classes, guitar lessons, and hairstylist sessions all transitioned to the Hype Machine. Facebook even set up a $100 million small-business relief fund to dole out no-strings-attached cash grants to keep small businesses afloat.

The people who make the social media industry tick are dedicated technologists. Many of them care about the future of our planet. They're wicked smart. And, as evidenced by their responses to the pandemic, most of them are committed to making the world a better place. But social media's impact on the world is not determined by intention alone. In October 2020, a plot to kidnap and kill the governor of Michigan, which was planned and coordinated over Facebook, was foiled by the Federal Bureau of Investigation (FBI). In January 2021, misinformation spreading over social media legitimized, mobilized, and organized an insurrection at the U.S. Capitol. As we all know, there have been dramatic missteps in building the Hype Machine.

Our enthusiastic embrace of social media in 2020 was a 180-degree reversal from 2019, in the weeks and months before COVID hit. Before the pandemic, social media had become a pariah. The #deletefacebook movement was gaining steam. The Cambridge Analytica scandal had forced Mark Zuckerberg to testify on Capitol Hill and in front of the European Parliament. Lawmakers were angling to break up the social media giants on antitrust grounds. Just weeks before the virus hit China, Sacha Baron Cohen called social media "the greatest propaganda machine in history." In his remarks before the Anti-Defamation League, he said, "Facebook, Google, YouTube, Twitter, and others . . . reach billions of people. The algorithms these platforms depend on deliberately amplify . . . stories that trigger outrage and fear. . . . It's why fake news outperforms real news, because studies show lies spread faster than the truth." The study Baron Cohen was referring to was one I published with my colleagues Deb Roy and Soroush Vosoughi in a cover story for *Science,* called "The Spread of True and False News Online." I'll return to it in the first two chapters of *The Hype Machine.*

But misinformation wasn't the only concern of social media critics before the pandemic. Facebook, Twitter, WhatsApp, Instagram, and YouTube were undermining our privacy, facilitating foreign interference in our democracy, threatening the integrity of our elections, promoting political lies for money, radicalizing terrorists, chilling free speech, and promoting hate speech. They spread genocidal propaganda; livestreamed mass murders like the one in Christchurch, New Zealand; promoted predatory lending to minorities; discriminated against women in employment advertising; tracked our every move; manipulated our emotions for revenue; and promoted political polarization.

Social media's promise and peril even played out in debates about the pandemic itself. Privacy debates took on new meaning during the COVID crisis as the threat of "surveillance capitalism" morphed into lifesaving "disease surveillance." Facebook filled gaps in inadequate national disease surveillance programs with scalable symptom surveys that identified the pandemic's spread. But social media was also a cauldron of misinformation about impending national lockdowns and false cures, nationalistic finger-pointing between the United States and China, and foreign interference designed to fan the flames of our fears. Google, Apple, and MIT developed Bluetooth-based contact tracing systems that would alert users who opted in if they had come in close physical proximity to the Bluetooth-enabled device of a COVID carrier. Privacy advocates listened in horror as the tech giants swore the system would remain anonymous. The perils of social media surveillance for privacy were sharply contrasted with the promise of social media surveillance for health. Some thought the surveillance was worth the privacy risk. Others thought the risks outweighed the benefits.

So which vision of social media is correct—the promise or the peril? Is the Hype Machine a force for good, for collective intelligence and solidarity? Or is it a scourge and a pariah? The global reach of Facebook, WhatsApp, Twitter, Instagram, and YouTube affects our communications, data, and privacy, as well as the flow of information around the world. It has the potential to be uniquely dangerous. But the pandemic reminded us how invaluable this far-reaching global communication network is to us, especially in times of need, and just how much we've come to rely on it for everything from news to job opportunities to entertainment to dating and relationships in our everyday lives.

The story of the Hype Machine as either the promise or the peril alone is one-sided. The truth is more complicated—it's sometimes uplifting and at other times depressing, sometimes shocking but always illuminating. My goal is to take you on a roller-coaster ride through what I've learned studying, building, investing in, and working with social media over the last twenty years. It's a harrowing journey with unbelievable discoveries and sordid scandals about how social media impacts our democracy; how it can disseminate lies even while connecting us to valuable truths; how it fights repression at times while promoting it at others; how it propagates hate speech while defending free speech; and, most of all, how all this works to hook us neurologically, emotionally, socially, and economically. The story not only reveals the business strategies behind social media, but also the relationship between social media's design and how it affects our society and our lives.

Can the promise of social media be realized without the peril? Or are they inexorably linked? We're at a crossroads. The decisions we make in how we design, regulate, monetize, and use social media today will determine which path we realize, now and for generations to come.

The Hype Machine

CHAPTER I

The New Social Age

*This is the whole point of technology. It creates an
appetite for immortality on the one hand. It threatens
universal extinction on the other. Technology is lust
removed from nature.*

—DON DELILLO

Human beings have always been a social species. We've been communicating, cooperating, and coordinating with one another since we were hunting and gathering. But today something is different. Over the last decade, we've doused our kindling fire of human interaction with high-octane gasoline. We've constructed an expansive, multifaceted machine that spans the globe and conducts the flow of information, opinions, and behaviors through society. This Hype Machine connects us in a worldwide communication network, exchanging trillions of messages a day, guided by algorithms, designed to inform, persuade, entertain, and manipulate us.

The object of this machine is the human psyche. It was designed to stimulate our neurological impulses, to draw us in and persuade us to change how we shop, vote, and exercise, and even who we love. It analyzes us to give us options for what to read, buy, and believe. It then learns from our choices and iteratively optimizes its offerings. As it operates, it generates a data exhaust that traces each of our preferences, desires, interests, and time-stamped, geolocated activities around the world. It then feeds on its own data exhaust, refining its process, perfecting its analysis, and improving its persuasive leverage. Its motivation is money, which it maximizes by engaging us. The more precise it gets, the more engaging and persuasive it becomes. The more persuasive it becomes, the more revenue it generates and the bigger it grows. This is the story of the Hype Machine—the social media industrial complex: how it was designed, how it works, how it affects us, and how we can adapt to it. And the story opens in Crimea.

Ten Days

On a cold day in February 2014, heavily armed gunmen surrounded the Crimean parliament building in Simferopol, Ukraine. They wore no sovereign markings but were later confirmed to be Russian special forces reacting to the deposition of Ukrainian president Viktor Yanukovych just days before. By all accounts, the gunmen were organized and professional. After breaking through the front door, they cut the building's communications, confiscated all mobile electronic devices, and systematically controlled who entered and exited the building, maintaining a tight perimeter and allowing no foreign journalists inside.

A few hours later, amid reports of heavy intimidation and fraud by the gunmen inside, the Crimean parliament voted to dissolve the government and replace Prime Minister Anatolii Mohyliov with Sergey Aksyonov, whose pro-Russian Unity Party had won only 4 percent of the vote in the previous election. Less than twenty-four hours later, similarly unmarked troops occupied the Simferopol and Sevastopol international airports and set up checkpoints on Crimean roads throughout the region. Two days later Aksyonov, who had earned the nickname "the Goblin" during his days as a businessman with ties both to the Russian mafia and to pro-Russian political and military groups, wrote a personal letter to Vladimir Putin, in his new capacity as the de facto prime minister of Crimea, formally requesting Russian assistance in maintaining peace and security there.

Before the Ukrainian government could declare Aksyonov's appointment unconstitutional, pro-Russian protests were whipped up throughout Crimea, developing a groundswell of visible support for reunification with Russia. The sentiment seemed one-sided, with many in Crimea expressing a strong desire to return to Russia. Within hours of Aksyonov requesting assistance, Putin received formal approval from the Russian Federation Council to send in troops. The Russian consulate began issuing passports in Crimea, and Ukrainian journalists were prohibited from entering the region. The next day Ukrainian defenses were under siege by the Black Sea Fleet and the Russian Army. Five days later, just ten days after the ordeal began, the Supreme Council of Crimea voted to re-accede to Russia after sixty years as part of Ukraine.

It was one of the quickest and quietest annexations of the postwar era. As former secretary of state Madeleine Albright testified, it "marked the first time since World War II that European borders have been altered by force." In just ten days, the region was flipped, like a light switch, from one sovereignty to another with barely a whisper.

The debate about what happened in Crimea continues today. Russia denies it was an annexation. Putin views it, instead, as an accession by Crimea to Russia. His adversaries claim it was a hostile encroachment by a foreign power. In essence, there was a dispute over the will of the Crimean people—a clash of competing realities, if you will. On the one hand, Russia claimed Crimean citizens overwhelmingly supported a return to the Russian Federation. On the other hand, pro-Ukrainian voices claimed the pro-Russian sentiment had been orchestrated by Moscow rather than by the people themselves.

Framing the Crimean reality was essential to restraining foreign intervention in the conflict. If this was an annexation, NATO would surely have to respond. But if this was an accession, overwhelmingly supported by the Crimean people, intervention would be harder to justify. So while the clandestine military and political operations were ruthlessly organized and flawlessly executed, Russia's information operation, designed to frame the reality of what happened on the ground in Crimea, was even more sophisticated, perhaps the most sophisticated the world had ever seen. And when it came to framing that reality, social media—what I call the Hype Machine—was indispensable.

The Spread of Fake News Online

To communicate my perspective on Crimea, I have to first take you on a detour, through a story within a story, to give you some context for how I understand the events that unfolded in Ukraine. In 2016, two years after the annexation of Crimea, I was in my lab at MIT, in Cambridge, Massachusetts, hard at work on an important research project with my colleagues Soroush Vosoughi and Deb Roy. We had been working for some time, in direct collaboration with Twitter, on what was then the largest-ever longitudinal study of the spread of fake news online. It analyzed the diffusion of all the fact-checked true and false rumors that had ever spread on Twitter, in the ten years from its inception in 2006 to 2017.

This study, which was published on the cover of *Science* in March 2018, revealed some of the first large-scale evidence on how fake news spreads online. During our research, we discovered what I still, to this day, consider some of the scariest scientific results I have ever encountered. We found that false news diffused significantly farther, faster, deeper, and more broadly than the truth in all categories of information—in some cases, by an order of magnitude. Whoever said "a lie travels halfway around the world while the truth is putting on its shoes" was right. We had uncovered a reality-distortion machine in the pipes of social media platforms, through which falsehood traveled like lightning, while the truth dripped along like molasses.

But buried in these more sensational results was a less obvious result, one that is directly relevant to Crimea. As part of our analysis,

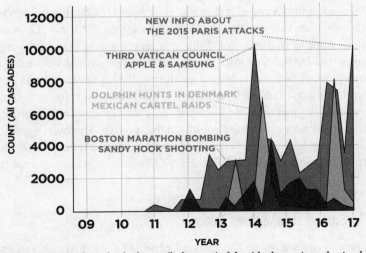

Figure I.I *The fact-checked true (light gray), false (dark gray), and mixed (partially true, partially false) (black) news cascades on Twitter from 2009 to 2017. A fact-checked news cascade is a story that was fact-checked by one of six independent fact-checking organizations in our study, diffusing through the Twitter network as it is tweeted and retweeted by Twitter users.*

before building more sophisticated models of the spread of true and false news on Twitter, we produced a simpler graph. We plotted the numbers of true and false news cascades (unbroken chains of person-to-person retweets of a story) in different categories (like politics, business, terrorism, and war) over time (Figure 1.1). The total spread of false rumors had risen over time and peaked at the end of 2013, in 2015, and again at the end of 2016, corresponding to the last U.S. presidential election. The data showed clear increases in the total number of false political rumors during the 2012 and 2016 U.S. presidential elections, confirming the political relevance of the spread of false news.

But another, more subtle result also drew our attention. Over the ten-year period from 2006 to 2017, there was only one visible spike in the number of rumors that contained both partially true and partially false information, which we called "mixed" rumors. In the original graph, opposite, it was difficult to see. So we filtered the data and re-plotted the graph, this time considering only political news. That's when we saw it—a single, clear spike in the spread of stories that contained partially true and partially false information in the two months between February and March 2014 (See the spike labeled "Annexation

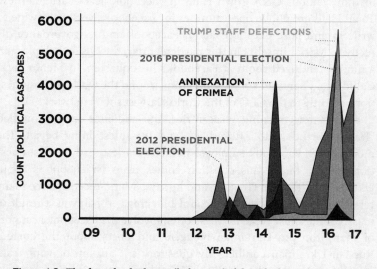

Figure 1.2 *The fact-checked true (light gray), false (dark gray), and mixed (partially true, partially false) (black) political news cascades on Twitter from 2009 to 2017.*

of Crimea" in Figure 1.2.) It corresponded directly to the Russian annexation of Crimea.

This result was striking, not just because it was the largest spike of
mixed news in the history of verified stories spreading on Twitter (and
more than four times larger than any other spike in mixed political
news), but also because it ended almost as quickly as it began, right
after the annexation was complete. When we investigated further, we
discovered a systematic appropriation of social media by pro-Russian
entities that proactively used the Hype Machine to control the Ukrainian national perception of the events in Crimea, and the international
perception of what was happening there, to ultimately frame the will
of the Crimean people.

Ask Mark

On May 14, 2014, Mark Zuckerberg's thirtieth birthday, a Facebook
user from Israel asked him to intervene against state-sponsored Russian information warfare in Ukraine. Zuckerberg was hosting one of
his now famous Q&A Town Halls at Facebook headquarters. These
Town Halls are public opportunities for Facebook users worldwide to
write in and pose questions about Facebook and its governance directly to Mark himself. On this particular day, the Q&A took place in
a moderately sized room at Facebook's headquarters in Menlo Park,
California. Users had come, some from around the world, to ask questions directly to the CEO of the world's largest social network.

After a few opening pleasantries, the audience sang a muffled
"Happy Birthday" to Zuckerberg, and the questioning began. The
moderator, a Facebook employee named Charles, read the first question aloud: "Mark, this question comes from Israel, but is about
Ukraine. . . . It's from Gregory, and he says, 'Mark, recently I see many
reports of unfair Facebook account blocking, probably as a result of
massive fake abuse reports. These often involve the Facebook accounts
of many top pro-Ukrainian bloggers and posts about the current
Russian-Ukrainian conflict. My question is: Can you or your team
please do something to resolve this problem? Maybe create a separate
administration for the Ukrainian segment, block abuse reports from
Russia, or just monitor the top Ukrainian bloggers more carefully?

Help us, please!' And, as a follow up to this, and we'll show this on the screen," said Charles, "the Ukrainian president, Petro Poroshenko, actually sent in a question as well and he asks: 'Mark, will you establish a Facebook office in Ukraine?'"

If Facebook were a country, it would be the world's largest, and this was its version of participatory government in action. Mark cleared his throat and noted that he had prepared for this question in advance because, at 45,000 votes, it was "by far the most voted on question we've ever had at one of these Q&As." He then rolled straight into a canned speech about Facebook's content curation policies.

But the historical significance of what was happening in Crimea far exceeded Zuckerberg's mundane response. He vastly underestimated the role Facebook was playing in Ukraine in 2014 (just as he would later underestimate Facebook's role in foreign election meddling in the United States in 2016). The information war in Ukraine was far more complex and consequential than Zuckerberg let on.

InfoWars

After the Facebook Town Hall, it became clearer—through our own research and that of several investigative journalists—that in 2014 Russia had engaged in a complex, two-pronged information warfare strategy in Crimea, using the public application programming interfaces (or APIs) that Facebook and Twitter make available to users to engage with, direct, and orchestrate the flow of information online.

The first prong was designed to suppress pro-Ukrainian voices. If Russia could demonstrate that the overwhelming desire of Crimean citizens was to accede to Russia, they could legitimize their annexation and reframe it as a liberation. Suppressing legitimate pro-Ukrainian voices, therefore, was vital in the fight to orchestrate pro-Russian sentiment in Crimea. This prong's effectiveness was evident in the pleas for help from the Ukrainian blogging community. Every time a pro-Ukrainian message was posted, it would be overwhelmed by hundreds of fraud and abuse reports, claiming the post contained porn or hate speech. These are common tactics used by Russia's Internet Research Agency, the shadowy arm of the Kremlin on social media, and the subject of Special Counsel Robert Mueller's indictments on a conspiracy to defraud the United States by manipulating the 2016 presidential election. Some have speculated that Russia programmed software robots (or "bots") to post fraud and abuse claims automatically whenever a pro-Ukrainian voice appeared online. Confronted with thousands of such abuse reports, Facebook took down the "offending" messages and banned their authors, effectively banishing pro-Ukrainian voices from its platform.

The second prong of the information war involved the creation and dissemination of disinformation through fake tweets, posts, blogs, and news. When violent clashes broke out in Odessa on May 2, 2014, between pro-Russian separatists and supporters of an independent Ukraine, a story written by a local doctor, Igor Rozovskiy, was circulated widely on Facebook. Dr. Rozovskiy claimed, in a long, detailed post, that Ukrainian nationalists had prevented him from saving a man wounded during one of the clashes. He said they had shoved him aside aggressively while "vowing that Jews in Odessa would meet the same fate." He added that "nothing like this happened in my city even under fascist occupation." The post went viral on Facebook, and translations soon appeared in English, German, and Bulgarian.

A day later, on May 3, Russian foreign minister Sergey Lavrov gave a speech to the UN Human Rights Council in Geneva, in which he claimed that "we all know well who created the crisis in Ukraine and how they did it. . . . West Ukrainian cities were occupied by armed national radicals, who used extremist, anti-Russian and anti-Semitic slogans. . . . We hear requests to restrict or punish the use of Russian." Lavrov's depiction of the events in Crimea and Ukraine mirrored Dr. Rozovskiy's perfectly. They both claimed that anti-Semitic Ukrainian nationalists had committed violence against Jews and were threatening to escalate that violence. That same day Ukrainians watched footage of actual violent clashes between pro-Ukrainian and pro-Russian forces in Odessa, on television, re-aired repeatedly, visually reinforcing the story. The simple narrative created by Russia, deploying partially true and partially false information, was able to distort reality by altering some but not all of the facts.

So who was Dr. Rozovskiy, and what was his relationship to Russia? It turns out he had no relationship to Russia, or to anyone. His account had been created the day before his post. Dr. Rozovskiy was a fake—he was fake news personified. He was not only parroting the Russian foreign minister nearly verbatim, but this relative newcomer to Facebook, who had no friends and no following, was also going viral in multiple languages.

If you'll recall, Russian foreign minister Lavrov's remarks contained an oddly specific assertion, that Ukrainian nationalist radicals were not only threatening violence against Jews but were also planning to "restrict or punish the use of Russian" and that the millions of Russians living in Crimea were outraged by this. While Jews comprise a small fraction of the Crimean population, 77 percent of Crimeans report Russian as their native language. I didn't think much of Lavrov's remarks to the UN, until I dug deeper into the massive spike of "mixed" news we had seen in our study of fake news on Twitter during the Crimean annexation.

The most popular mixed news story circulating on Twitter during the annexation claimed that Jews in eastern Ukraine had been given leaflets ordering them to register as Jews or face deportation. The second most popular story claimed the Ukrainian government had "introduced a law abolishing the use of languages other than Ukrainian in official circumstances." Together, the Crimean stories supported Lavrov's narrative and accounted for the lion's share of mixed news stories in Twitter's recorded history, exceeding every other spike in verified mixed news by a factor of four. The amount of bot activity and the number of unique accounts spreading the disinformation were also statistically significantly higher for the Crimean mixed news stories than for all other verified mixed political news. In social media data, outliers like these typically signal a coordinated attempt to distort reality, an orchestrated effort to influence human thinking and behavior. With Russia claiming vociferously that Crimea desired accession, and with the facts on the ground being distorted by fake news, the Obama Doctrine in response to the annexation stopped short of intervening and imposed economic sanctions instead. And today Crimea is part of Russia.

As dramatic as the Crimean disinformation campaign was, the social and economic impact of social media on our lives far outstrips any single geopolitical event. This same machinery has a hand in business, in politics, and frankly in everything, from the troubling rise of fake news to the rise and fall of the stock market, from our opinions about politics to what products we buy, who we vote for, and even who we love.

The Hype Machine

Every minute of every day, our planet now pulses with trillions of digital social signals, bombarding us with streams of status updates, news stories, tweets, pokes, posts, referrals, advertisements, notifications, shares, check-ins, and ratings from peers in our social networks, news media, advertisers, and the crowd. These signals are delivered to our always-on mobile devices through platforms like Facebook, Snapchat, Instagram, YouTube, Twitter, and Clubhouse, and they are routed through the human social network by algorithms designed to optimize our connections, accelerate our interactions, and maximize our engagement with tailored streams of content. But at the same time, these signals are much more transformative—they are hypersocializing our society, scaling mass persuasion, and creating a tyranny of trends. They do this by injecting the influence of our peers into our daily decisions, curating population-scale behavior change, and enforcing an attention economy. I call this trifecta of hypersocialization, personalized mass persuasion, and the tyranny of trends the New Social Age.

The striking thing about the New Social Age is that fifteen years ago this cacophony of digital social signals didn't even exist. Fifteen short years ago, all we had to facilitate our digital connections was the phone, the fax machine, and email. Today, as more and more new social technologies come online, we know less and less about how they are changing us. Why does fake news spread so much faster than the truth online? How did one false tweet wipe out $140 billion in stock market value in minutes? How did Facebook change the 2012 presidential election by tweaking one algorithm? Did Russian social media manipulation flip the 2016 U.S. presidential election? When joggers in Venice, Italy, post their runs to social media, do joggers in Venice, California, run faster? These questions contemplate the disruptive power of social media. By answering them, we can better understand how the Hype Machine impacts our world.

The Hype Machine has created a radical interdependence among

The New Social Age | 13

us, shaping our thoughts, opinions, and behaviors. This interdependence is enabled by digital networks, like Facebook and Twitter, and guided by machine intelligence, like newsfeed and friend-suggestion algorithms. Together they are remaking the evolution of the human social network and the flow of information through it. These digital networks expose the controls of the Hype Machine to nation-states, businesses, and individuals eager to steer the global conversation toward their ends, to mold public opinion, and ultimately to change what we do. The design of this machine, and how we use it, are reshaping our organizations and our lives. And the Hype Machine is even more relevant today than it was before the COVID-19 pandemic pushed the world onto social media en masse.

By now we've all heard the cacophony of naysayers declaring that the sky is falling as new social technologies disrupt our democracies, our economies, and our public health. We've seen an explosion of fake news, hate speech, market-destroying false tweets, genocidal violence against minority groups, resurgent disease outbreaks, foreign interventions in democratic elections, and dramatic breaches of privacy. Scandal after scandal has rocked social media giants like Facebook, Twitter, and Instagram in what seems like a backlash from which they can never recover.

But when the social media revolution began, the world's social platforms had an idealistic vision of connecting our world. They planned to give everyone free access to the information, knowledge, and resources they needed to experience intellectual freedom, social and economic opportunity, better health, job mobility, and meaningful social connections. They were going to fight oppression, loneliness, inequality, poverty, and disease. Today, they've seemingly exacerbated the very ills they set out to alleviate.

One thing I've learned, from twenty years researching and working with social media, is that these technologies hold the potential for exceptional promise and tremendous peril—and neither the promise nor the peril is guaranteed. Social media could deliver an incredible wave of productivity, innovation, social welfare, democratization, equality, health, positivity, unity, and progress. At the same time, it can and, if left unchecked, will deliver death blows to our democracies, our economies, and our public health. Today we are at a crossroads of these realities.

The argument of this book is that we can achieve the promise of social media while avoiding the peril. To do so, we must step out of our tendency to armchair-theorize about how social media affects us and develop a rigorous scientific understanding of how it works. By looking under the hood at how the Hype Machine operates and employing science to decipher its impact, we can collectively steer this ship away from the impending rocks and into calmer waters.

Unfortunately, our understanding and our progress have been impeded by the hype surrounding the Hype Machine. We've been overwhelmed by a tidal wave of books, documentaries, and studies of one-off events designed for media attention but lacking rigor and generalizability. The hype is not helpful because it clouds our vision of what we actually know (and don't know) from the scientific evidence on how social media affects us.

While our discourse has been shrouded in sensational hysteria, the three primary stakeholders at the center of the controversy—the platforms, the politicians, and the people—have all been pointing their fingers at each other. Social media platforms blame our ills on a lack of regulation. Governments blame the platforms for turning a blind eye to the weaponization of their technology. And the people blame their governments and the platforms for inaction. But the truth is, we've all been asleep at the switch. In the end, each of us must take responsibility for the part we are playing in the Hype Machine's current direction.

Not only are we all partly to blame, but we are all partly responsible for what happens next. As Mark Zuckerberg himself has noted, governments will need to adopt sensible, well-informed regulations. The platforms will need to change their policies and their design. And for the sake of ourselves and our children, we will all need to be more responsible in how we use social media in our digital town square. There is no silver bullet for the mess we find ourselves in, but there are solutions.

Achieving the promise of the New Social Age, while avoiding its peril, will require all of us—social media executives, lawmakers, and ordinary citizens—to think carefully about how we approach our new social order. As a society, we will need to utilize the four levers available to us: the *money* (or financial incentives) created by their business models, the *code* that governs social platforms, the *norms* we develop in using these systems, and the *laws* we write to regulate their market failures. Along the way, we will need to design scientific solutions that balance privacy, free speech, misinformation, innovation, and democracy. This is, no doubt, a monumental responsibility. But considering the overwhelming influence the Hype Machine has on our lives, it is a responsibly we cannot abdicate.

Who Am I?

I'm a scientist, entrepreneur, and investor—in that order. First and foremost, I'm a scientist. I'm a professor at the Massachusetts Institute of Technology (MIT), where I direct the Initiative on the Digital Economy and the Social Analytics Lab, where we study the social technologies that make up the Hype Machine. I earned my PhD at MIT and completed my master's degrees at the London School of Economics and at Harvard. I'm an applied econometrician by training and have studied sociology, social psychology, and most of the curriculum in the MIT PhD program in economics. I'm a data nerd. I analyze large-scale social media data for a living, to try to make sense of how information and behavior diffuse through social media and society. My real expertise, though, is in graph theory and graph data. In other words, I study things that are connected in complex network structures, whether people in social networks or companies in buyer-supplier relationships.

How did I stumble into this line of work? In the fall of 2001, while Mark Zuckerberg was still in high school at Phillips Exeter Academy, three years before he founded Facebook at Harvard, I was a PhD student down the street at MIT, sitting in the reading room at Dewey Library studying for two very different classes: Econometrics I, taught by the world-renowned statistician Jerry Hausman, and The Sociology of Strategy, taught by the then-rising-star sociologist Ezra Zuckerman, who is now the dean of faculty at MIT's Sloan School of Management. Ezra's class was heavily focused on social networks, while Jerry's class introduced us to "BLUE" estimators—the theory of what generates the best linear unbiased statistical models.

I had my statistics textbook in one hand and a stack of papers on networks in the other. As I read the statistics text, I saw that it repeated one main assumption of classical statistics over and over again—the assumption that all the observations in the data we were analyzing (the people, firms, or countries) were "independent and identically distributed (or IID)." In other words, our assumption was that none of the people in our data should be connected to each other in any systematic way. As I read the networks papers, however, I kept seeing diagrams of the complex interconnections between people. On the one hand, we were assuming everything was independent. On the other hand, the reality we live in is one of staggering interdependence.

I realized that a great deal of what we thought was unexplainable (the variance in the "independent" models) might be explained by how we are connected to one another, how information and knowledge ebb and flow between us, and how our peers' behaviors and opinions affect our own. In 2001 there were no large digital social networking sites, but we did have lots of digital network connections through email, instant messaging, and texting. In that moment, sitting in Dewey Library, I had an epiphany: Digital social networking was going to turbocharge how information, behavior, economic opportunity, and political ideology flowed between people. It was going to transform society as we knew it and affect everything from business to politics to public health.

I remember running to the nearest Pine terminal (a computer program for sending email) and sending an email to my PhD adviser, Erik Brynjolfsson, to request a meeting. I met Erik the next day and explained that I wanted to focus my PhD dissertation on digital social networks. I told him that I thought these networks were going to be the next big thing in personal computing and that they were going to transform society. Now, Erik didn't study social networks, and he hadn't ever formally thought about graph theory. He was busy trailblazing research on the impact of information technology on firm productivity and economic growth. Social networks were not on his radar. To his credit, though, he humored me. He said, "I don't really know much about networks, but you seem pretty excited about it, so we'll figure it out together." I don't know if he was thinking to himself *This is a phase, it will pass.* PhD students typically have hundreds of ideas that go nowhere before they land on one that works. But he was supportive nonetheless, and I wrote my PhD thesis on how information flows through digital social networks. As it turned out, social networking wasn't a phase, and it didn't pass. Friendster was founded in 2002,

MySpace in 2003, Facebook in 2004, Twitter in 2006, WhatsApp in 2009, Instagram in 2010, WeChat in 2011, TikTok in 2012, and Clubhouse in 2020. The New Social Age was born, and I've been studying it ever since.

My scientific work is firmly rooted both in my deep admiration for technology and in a healthy skepticism about how it is put to use. I'm convinced we are witnessing a new era of human evolution, one in which mass automated, digitized socialization will change the way we interact, communicate, perceive our world, decide, and act. Online social networks (e.g., Facebook), microblogging (e.g., Twitter), instant messaging (e.g., WhatsApp), and collaborative knowledge production and news aggregation technologies (e.g., Wikipedia and Reddit) have fundamentally altered the way information is produced, shared, consumed, utilized, and valued. Such changes have profound implications for many of our social, political, and economic organizations, from the productivity of knowledge workers to consumer demand patterns, and from election campaigns to public health programs and mass protests.

New technologies and new modes of communication not only change the production and dissemination of information but also simultaneously record information about human interaction with incredible precision and detail. In an article published in *Science* in 2009, my colleagues and I argued that these new technologies and modes of communication not only change the creation and dissemination of information but make possible the development of a new field of "computational social science," which aims to improve our understanding of the macrolevel consequences of microlevel human interaction—a long-standing "holy grail" in sociology, economics, and other disciplines. These changes are enabling new scientific studies of human behavior at population scale, and revealing new interventions that could dramatically improve the way we deal with conflict, commerce, and health.

In addition to my scientific work, I have also been an active entrepreneur and chief scientist of multiple companies, with one foot in academia and the other at the forefront of the entrepreneurial development of these new technologies. I was the chief scientist at Social-Amp, one of the first social commerce analytics companies (until its sale to Merkle in 2012) and at Humin, a social platform that *The Wall Street Journal* called the first "Social Operating System" (until its sale to Tinder in 2016). I have worked directly with senior executives at Facebook, Yahoo!, Twitter, LinkedIn, Snapchat, WeChat, Spotify, Airbnb, SAP, Microsoft, Walmart, and *The New York Times.*

Along with my longtime friend Paul Falzone, I'm a founding partner at Manifest Capital, an investment firm that helps young companies grow into the Hype Machine. From this perch, I evaluate hundreds of companies a year and get to look around the corner at what's next. These experiences have forced me to think deeply about the business models, technologies, and machine intelligence that drive the social economy. As a scientist, entrepreneur, and investor, I have peered into the Hype Machine up close, studied its inner workings, and participated in its development. These three perspectives are always with me, which I suspect will be obvious to you as you read this book.

As a scientist, I am obsessed with rigor. I attempt at every turn to avoid making claims I cannot prove. As a result, there will be moments in this book when I present compelling evidence but stop short of making a bold claim. I will make arguments with a healthy dose of caveats along with them. The unfortunate truth is that we don't have all the answers yet, and the answers we do have are not simple. That is part of the challenge. While science has advanced tremendously around social media and how it is affecting us, it remains nascent and at times is constrained by the platforms' stranglehold on data. We don't know enough about the spread of fake news, election manipulation, filter bubbles, and digital political polarization, because the research has not yet been done. But it needs to be done. So advocating for that research will be a theme of this book.

As an entrepreneur, I appreciate the difficulty of actually doing. Innovators face impossible dilemmas. Building a successful business is difficult. Building a global platform like the companies I will be discussing is next to impossible. I respect what it took to build Facebook, Twitter, LinkedIn, and the rest. I realize that some eventualities could not have been foreseen in the decisions that were made in early days. But I also know that when faced with certain truths, we have a moral duty to act. More needs to be done about the negative consequences of the Hype Machine today. I believe the true leaders of the New Social Age will be those who make the hard decisions to put social welfare above shareholder value—or perhaps those who realize that, in the long run, these goals are aligned.

As an investor, I try to distinguish the forest from the trees. When you are building a business, you are singularly committed to the survival and growth of that business. But as an investor, you also see the marketplace as a landscape of renewal. As Steve Jobs said at the Stanford University commencement in 2005, "Death is very likely the single best invention of Life. It is Life's change agent. It clears out the old to make way for the new. Right now the new is you, but someday not too long from now, you will gradually become the old and be cleared away." Such is also the turmoil of the marketplace. Friendster gave way to MySpace, which gave way to Facebook. Today WeChat does in one app what Facebook, WhatsApp, Messenger, Venmo, Grubhub, Amazon, Uber, Apple Pay, and many others do individually. The ongoing success of none is set in stone. The future of the New Social Age will be forged by the choices we make as entrepreneurs, investors, regulators, consumers, and citizens. I would argue that the most consequential decisions of the New Social Age are yet to come.

My Objective

My goals in this book are to describe the science of how the Hype Machine works and to explore how it affects our politics, our businesses, and our relationships; to explore the consequences of the Hype Machine for our society, both positive and negative; and to discuss how we can—through company policy, social norms, government regulation, and more advanced software code—achieve its promise while avoiding its peril.

I'll begin by considering fake news and the weaponization of misinformation through the Hype Machine, tracking how the design of platforms like Facebook and Twitter incentivize and enable the spread of misinformation (Chapter 2). Did Russian election interference change the results of the 2016 U.S. presidential election? What should we do to stop the scourge of fake news in the 2020 election and beyond? Stay tuned.

Along the way, I'll examine why the Hype Machine's rise was so meteoric and why we were so susceptible to it, as individuals and as a society. I will describe the anatomy of the Hype Machine—the underlying trifecta of social technologies at the center of this inflection point in human history—and consider, in depth, the four levers through which we can shape our technological future: *money, code, norms,* and *laws* (Chapter 3). I will describe the neurological (Chapter 4) and economic (Chapter 5) forces that have "wired us into" the Hype Machine. Understanding these neurological and economic hooks will help us answer important questions about the New Social Age from a business perspective, such as why Facebook beat MySpace in the market for social networks. They will also shed light on more fundamental questions, like how the Hype Machine will impact human evolution.

I will then discuss three key societal transformations driven by the Hype Machine that are disrupting business, democracy, and public health: the personalization of mass persuasion (Chapter 6), the hypersocialization of society (Chapters 7 and 8), and the advent of the attention economy (Chapter 9). In so doing, I'll look under the hood at the mechanics of the Hype Machine, dig into the science of online peer effects, and explore how our new radical interdependence is changing the products we buy, the people we vote for, and even who we meet and fall in love with.

After looking under the hood, I'll zoom out to consider the societal implications of the Hype Machine and the three trends it perpetuates—for example, its implications for what's known as the "wisdom of crowds." Our ability to harness the wisdom of crowds and collective intelligence rests on three basic pillars: independence, diversity, and equality. The problem is that the Hype Machine erodes all three of these pillars and turns wisdom into madness. I'll discuss how we can recapture the wisdom of crowds in Chapter 10. Next, I'll remind us why we invented the Hype Machine in the first place by describing its positive potential in creating an incredible tsunami of productivity, innovation, social welfare, democratization, equality, caring, positivity, unity, and social progress. At the same time, I'll discuss why the source of social media's positive potential is also the source of its peril and how this complicates how we must adapt to it (Chapter 11).

Finally, I'll explore how we must adapt—how business policy, government regulation, social norms, and technology design can steer our economy and our society toward a more productive future (Chapter 12). Should we break up Facebook? How should we craft privacy legislation? Is the Hype Machine a publisher or a user-generated platform that should not be responsible for the content users post? What does that mean for free speech and hate speech? You'll be surprised by some of the answers.

At a Crossroads

The last three years have seen front-page stories about Facebook, Twitter, YouTube, and the rest of social media's lack of transparency; their contribution to political polarization; their promotion of hate speech, racism, and the degradation of discourse; their role in the spread of fake news; and their potentially corrosive impact on our democracies and our elections.

Lawmakers have advocated regulation. Multiple U.S. congressional committees are investigating the role of Facebook and the rest of the Hype Machine in Russian election interference and the spread of misinformation online. The Cambridge Analytica controversy, in which a political consultancy used stolen Facebook data on 87 million Americans to target political ads, forced Mark Zuckerberg to testify in front of the U.S. Congress and the European Parliament as lawmakers debate what to do about the Hype Machine's power of mass persuasion, use of personal data, and lack of control over misinformation. Sen. John Kennedy began his questioning of Zuckerberg in the Senate with an ominous opening statement: "I don't want to have to regulate Facebook," he said. "But, by God, I will."

Advertisers have also pressured the platforms to clean up their act. In 2017, Marc Pritchard, Procter & Gamble's chief brand officer, went on a public tirade about the lack of transparency in digital advertising on platforms like Google and Facebook and advertising appearing next to fake or offensive content. Then he put his money where his mouth was and cut P&G's digital advertising budget by $200 million. In 2018, Unilever followed suit, cutting its digital advertising by nearly 30 percent in an effort to clean up the Hype Machine's advertising ecosystem. And these weren't just hapless public protests. In fact, P&G reported a 7.5 percent *increase* in organic sales growth in 2019, while cutting its online marketing budget by 6 percent. Unilever posted a 3.8 percent gain in organic sales in the same period. Understanding how they did it requires an understanding of the Hype Machine.

In the Hype Machine, everyone is a digital marketer, whether we're fighting for ideas or for consumer dollars. A candidate in the presidential election, trying to persuade voters to his or her side; BMW, trying to persuade people to buy the new 3 Series; the small-business owner trying to grow sales; Vladimir Putin's Internet Research Agency, trying to sow discord through misdirection—in the Hype Machine, they are all digital marketers. They are all trying to optimize the same persuasion strategies to achieve their goals. That's why it's so important for us to wear different hats on this journey—the regulator, the marketer, and the concerned citizen. Frequently, I will ask you to put on your digital marketer's hat to understand the toolbox from their perspective. To make sense of what we see in our feeds every day, we'll need to understand what they're doing and why.

Every nation on earth has become attentive to the role of social media in society today. Regulators around the world are debating what to do about the impact of the Hype Machine on elections, business trends, competition, privacy, and fake news. Business leaders are trying to figure out how to self-regulate, through platform policies, algorithm design, software code, and alternative business models. And all of us, as parents and individuals, family and friends, are thinking about how the Hype Machine affects our lives and the lives of our children, from the impact it has on our friendships and businesses, to how we socialize and behave, to the rise of loneliness in our society. The decisions we make today in how we design, deploy, use, and regulate social media will have far-reaching consequences for years to come.

The science suggests that while social media can help foster a transparent, democratic, egalitarian society, it can also be used to erect a polarized, authoritarian police state. Today we are at a crossroads, caught between the promise and the peril, even as the system's design is being debated worldwide.

Tectonic shifts are a regular occurrence for social media. Keeping up with the daily changes is next to impossible. Instead, I hope to offer a lasting framework to guide our thinking about the social economy. What I have learned, over twenty years of research, has taught me some general principles about how the Hype Machine works, how information and behaviors spread, how interventions in social media change behavior, and how managers, policy makers, and individuals can interface with the Hype Machine more effectively. A rigorous investigation of these fundamentals entails a harrowing intellectual journey, with plenty of plot twists and unexpected turns along the way. It's a journey I intend to take you on in this book. And there is no better place to start than with how social media has brought us to the precipice of what some have called the "end of reality."

CHAPTER 2

The End of Reality

*Under normal circumstances the liar is defeated by
reality, for which there is no substitute; no matter how
large the tissue of falsehood that an experienced liar has
to offer, it will never be large enough, even if he enlists the
help of computers, to cover the immensity of factuality.*

—HANNAH ARENDT

The market opened quietly on Wall Street on April 23, 2013. As traders sipped lattes on an unseasonably chilly morning, stocks made modest gains from the opening bell to the lunch hour. But as everyone broke for lunch, the Associated Press broke a story on Twitter that changed the market's mood. Phones chirped at eateries in New York, Washington, and the world over as the news was retweeted again and again, creating an information cascade that swept through the Hype Machine in seconds. The tweet, which appeared at 1:07 P.M. eastern time in the United States, simply read "Breaking: Two Explosions in the White House and Barack Obama is injured." It was retweeted over four thousand times in five minutes, which would have informed hundreds of thousands if not millions of people of the attack on the White House.

You could almost hear the iced teas and Arnold Palmers being snorted back into the glasses of those monitoring the social network. The news was shocking. Putting aside fence jumpers, who are usually tackled on sight, there have only ever been four breaches of White House security that made it to the building. So two explosions injuring the president inside the White House was big news.

The market stuttered. Then it skipped a beat. If only individual retail investors had been influenced by the news, the financial impact might have been contained. But the Hype Machine doesn't exist in isolation.

It's coupled to systems that sense, mine, analyze, and trade on sentiment expressed on social media in real time. Dataminr, RavenPack,
and other companies are constantly sifting through social media data
to find the signal in the noise. When they find that signal, they seize on
it and relay instructions to their institutional clients to buy or sell ahead
of market trends. On this particular afternoon, the sentiment wasn't
good, and the data miners issued sell recommendations that triggered
automated-trading algorithms to unload their stocks. When they did,
the Dow fell instantly by nearly 200 points, wiping out $139 billion in
equity value in seconds.

But the news wasn't true. The White House was calm, and the president was fine. The tweet was fake news propagated by Syrian hackers
who had infiltrated the AP's Twitter handle. There was a terrorist attack that day—just not at 1600 Pennsylvania Avenue. The attack happened on Twitter, and the casualties were felt on Wall Street. The
market rebounded, but real people lost real money as their buy and sell
orders were honored. Those who were late to the fire sale lost their
shirts. The "Hack Crash" of 2013 highlights the fragility of the socio-
technical systems we've wired into the Hype Machine. When news
cascades through the network, it's hard to stop and harder to verify
with enough time to prevent panic. When the news is false, it can
wreak havoc on financial systems, health systems, and democratic institutions, creating real consequences from virtual falsity.

Here's another example. When Hurricane Harvey hit southern Texas
in the summer of 2017, the flooding displaced thousands and halted
production at several oil refineries in the southern United States. News
of gas shortages spread quickly on Twitter and Facebook as drivers
posted pictures of long lines at gas stations, with makeshift signs saying they were out of gas. A panic ensued, and drivers in the region
rushed to stockpile gas as if the world were ending, creating a run on
fuel in Austin, Dallas, Houston, and San Antonio.

But as the authorities later revealed, there was no gas shortage. It
was false news spread through social media, then picked up and reported by broadcast media. As we later learned, there was plenty of gas
to go around. The refinery and highway closures only slowed deliver-
ies. Had everyone stuck to their normal consumption, the distribution
system could have handled the disruption, and there would have been

no shortage. The panic and the subsequent run on gas, however, ensured there *was* a shortage, wrought by manic stockpiling, driven by social media.

The signature of a fake news crisis was repeating itself: false information was spreading faster than the truth, misdirecting real behaviors with real impact. Such fake news can have dramatic consequences for businesses, democracies, and public health. And although it has been around for centuries, the speed and scale with which it spreads through the Hype Machine creates a fake news crisis on steroids.

These vignettes highlight a systematic pattern in the spread of fake news (one that bears out in large-scale studies of the phenomenon that I'll discuss shortly). When fake news isn't completely fabricated, it typically distorts real-world information by tweaking or contorting it, mixing it with true information, and highlighting its most sensational and emotional elements. It then scales rapidly on social media and spreads faster than our ability to verify or debunk it. Once it spreads, it's hard to put back in the bottle and even harder to clean up, even with a healthy dose of the truth.

The Syrian hack that crashed the stock market in 2013 is a case study in the economic consequences of fake news. You've probably heard similar stories. The fact-checking site Snopes keeps a list of "hot 50" rumors that gets updated with alarming regularity. There was a 2008 rumor that United Airlines was filing for bankruptcy, a 2017 report that Starbucks would give out free Frappuccinos to undocumented workers, and President Trump's tweets, in March 2018, falsely claiming that Amazon was evading taxes, which sent shares of the company plummeting to their worst monthly performance in two years. But is there a systematic effect of fake news on businesses? On stock prices? Before we can understand the full implications of fake news, we need to detour through the story of a D-list actress named Kamilla Bjorlin.

An Actress's Rise to Fake News Infamy

Kamilla Bjorlin had been an actress her whole life. Since age seven, she had played bit parts in movies like *Raising Helen*, with Kate Hudson, and *The Princess Diaries 2*, with Anne Hathaway. She never really became a star, but narrative fiction was in her blood. So in 2011 she struck out on a different career path, forming a public relations and social media firm called Lidingo Holdings, specializing in investor relations and promotional research for public companies, including many biopharmaceutical firms. In fact, as alleged in a 2014 SEC complaint, Lidingo was a fake news factory engaged in "pump and dump" stock promotion schemes that posted fake articles to crowdsourced investor intelligence websites like Seeking Alpha, The Street, Yahoo! Finance, Forbes, and Investing.com, for the express purpose of moving stock prices.

Writers employed by Lidingo created pseudonyms, like the Swiss Trader, Amy Baldwin, and the Trading Maven; claimed to have MBAs and degrees in physics; and wrote fake stories praising the growth or stability of the companies they were paid to promote. But they never disclosed their financial relationship with their clients, which was why they ran afoul of the SEC. Between 2011 and 2014, Lidingo allegedly published over four hundred fake news articles and earned cash and equity payments of more than $1 million. As part of its crackdown on fake financial news, a separate SEC complaint against a similar firm called DreamTeam described an operation that provided "social media relations, marketing and branding services" to publicly traded companies and "leveraged its extensive online social network to maximize exposure" to fake news designed to inflate its clients' stock prices.

One company that Lidingo wrote fake news for was Galena Biopharma. In the summer of 2013, before Lidingo was hired, Galena's stock price was hovering around $2 per share. Between August 2013 and February 2014, Lidingo published twelve fake news stories about Galena, claiming, for example, that the company would make "a good long-term growth investment" because it had "a promising pipeline for revenue growth" from "three strong drugs in its pipeline."

After the first two fake news articles were published, the company issued 17.5 million new shares in a secondary equity offering (SEO) worth $32.6 million to the firm. Then five more fake news articles were published, and the stock price skyrocketed. At a November 22 board meeting, the company granted hundreds of thousands of new stock options to the CEO, COO, CMO, and each of six directors. The stock price continued to rise. In fact, it rose over 925 percent between August 2013 and January 2014 (Figure 2.1). At a January 17

Figure 2.1 *The Galena Biopharma stock price from April 2013 to May 2014, annotated with the dates when secondary equity offerings and insider selling occurred, when fake news and exposé news articles were published, and when stock options were granted.*

board meeting, then-CEO Mark Ahn declared insiders could trade the company's stock immediately, and starting the next day, they did, unloading $16 million worth in four weeks.

We all know that information moves markets, but the financial impact of fake news is not immediately clear. The Galena Biopharma story directly ties the two together. But of course, Galena is a one-off. Is there any systematic, generalizable evidence of the financial impact of fake news? Luckily Galena is one of over seven thousand firms that Shimon Kogan, Tobias Moskowitz, and Marina Niessner analyzed in their large-scale study of the relationship between fake news and financial markets.

Fake News and Financial Markets

Kogan, Moskowitz, and Niessner examined data from the SEC's undercover investigation, which identified fake news articles about public companies written to manipulate stock prices. By analyzing these validated fake news stories, Kogan, Moskowitz, and Niessner were able to systematically link the dissemination of fake news to stock price movements over time. The initial data covered a small number of articles on a small set of companies involved in the SEC investigation—171 articles on 47 companies. But the researchers broadened their sample by identifying fake news using a linguistic analysis of all the articles published on Seeking Alpha from 2005 to 2015, and on Motley Fool from 2009 to 2014. The larger sample, which looked for linguistic signatures of deceptive writing, was noisier than the verified SEC sample, but it allowed the authors to examine over 350,000 articles on over 7,500 companies over ten years. They also analyzed investors' reactions to fake news before and after the SEC publicly announced its sting operation, which drew attention to the prevalence of fake news on these sites. The findings reveal a great deal about how fake news moves markets.

In the verified SEC data, the publication of fake news was strongly correlated with increased trading volume. Abnormal trading volume rose by 37 percent over the three days following the publication of real news articles and 50 percent *more* following the publication of fake news articles relative to real news articles. In other words, investors reacted to fake news even more strongly than to real news. The reactions were more pronounced for smaller firms and for firms with a greater percentage of retail (as opposed to institutional) investors. Fake articles were clicked on and read more often than real articles, and trading volume increased with the number of clicks and times an article was read.

And the effect of fake news on stock *prices*? Fake articles had, on average, nearly three times the impact of real news articles on the daily price volatility or absolute return of the manipulated stocks in the three days after the publication of fake news, even after controlling for recent SEC filings, firm press releases, and return volatility in the days leading up to the article.

The SEC went public with its investigation of fake news in 2014, filing lawsuits against several companies and the fake news factories they worked with, including Lidingo and DreamTeam. When the public revelation of the sting operation drew investors' attention to the fact that fake news was being published on websites like Seeking Alpha, Kogan et al. used the public revelation of the sting to examine whether increased awareness of fake news eroded consumers' trust in real news. Not surprisingly, fake news had a bigger impact on trading volume and price volatility *before* the SEC announcement than after it. But investors were *also* less moved by real news once the SEC drew attention to the existence of fake news, demonstrating the potential for fake news to erode the public's trust in news altogether.

If fake news can disrupt markets, it can affect everyone in society, whether we read and share it or not. More important (as I will show when we discuss the troubling rise of "deepfakes" later in this chapter), if fake news can successfully disrupt markets, it creates a political incentive for economic terrorism. And as we saw in Crimea, the weaponization of misinformation is one of the most insidious threats to democracy in the Information Age. The most egregious example to date is Russia's interference in American democracy in 2016.

The Political Weaponization of Misinformation

When the Mueller report was released in April 2019, pundits, politicians, and the press pored over it, looking for the juiciest bits to support their positions and to entice readers and viewers with salacious headlines. Most of them skipped over volume one and turned directly to volume two, which addressed President Trump's alleged obstruction of the FBI's Russia investigation. But when I read the Mueller report, I was shocked not by the juicy political potential of volume two but by the clear geopolitical reality described in volume one: Russia, an active foreign adversary, had systematically used the Hype Machine to attack American democracy and manipulate the results of the 2016 U.S. presidential election. It was one of the most comprehensive weaponizations of misinformation the world has ever seen.

Two studies commissioned by the U.S. Senate Intelligence Committee, one led by New Knowledge and the other by John Kelly, founder and CEO of Graphika, detail the extent of Russian misinformation campaigns targeting hundreds of millions of U.S. citizens in 2016. When I had lunch with John and Graphika's chief innovation officer, Camille François, at the Union Square Café in Manhattan in early 2019, they told me the attack on our democracy was even more sophisticated than the media was giving it credit for. They were both deeply concerned about what they had uncovered. While their report is public, the look on their faces when discussing it was revealing. These two highly regarded experts were worried—and when the experts are worried, we should be too.

Russia's attack was well planned. The Internet Research Agency created fake accounts on Facebook, Twitter, Instagram, YouTube, Google, Tumblr, SoundCloud, Meetup, and other social media sites months, sometimes years, in advance. They amassed a following, coordinated with other accounts, rooted themselves in real online communities, and gained the trust of their followers. Then they created fake news intended to suppress voting and to change our vote choices, in large part toward Republican candidate Donald Trump and away from Democratic candidate Hillary Clinton. The fake news included memes about Black Lives Matter, the mistreatment of American veterans, the Second Amendment and gun control, the supposed rise of sharia law in the United States, and well-known falsehoods like the accusation that Hillary Clinton was running a child sex ring out of the basement of a pizza shop in Washington, D.C. (known as "PizzaGate"). They spread these memes through organic sharing and paid promotion to boost their reach on social media.

On Twitter, they established a smaller number of *source* accounts, which posted fake content, and close to four thousand *sharing* accounts, which amplified the content through retweets and trending hashtags. The source accounts were manually controlled, while the sharing accounts were more often "cyborg" accounts that were partly automated and partly manual. Automated accounts, run by software robots, or "bots," tweeted and retweeted with greater frequency at pre-specified times. Software doesn't get tired or need bathroom breaks, so the bot army was always on, propagating fake news and engaging the American electorate around the clock.

A lot has been written about the "Great Hack" of 2016. By now we've learned that Russian disinformation* was broad based and sophisticated. But did it actually change the outcome of the 2016 U.S. presidential election (or for that matter the outcome of the Brexit vote in the U.K. or of elections in Brazil, Sweden, and India)? To assess whether it flipped the U.S. election result, we have to answer two additional

* Disinformation is deliberate falsehood spread to deceive, while misinformation is falsehood spread regardless of its intent. Disinformation is a subset of misinformation.

questions: Was the reach, scope, and targeting of Russian interference sufficient to change the result? And if so, did it successfully change people's voting behavior enough to accomplish that goal?

The Reach, Scope, and Targeting of Russian Election Interference

During the 2016 election, Russian fake news spread to at least 126 million people on Facebook and garnered at least 76 million likes, comments, and other reactions there. It reached at least 20 million people on Instagram and was even more effective there, amassing at least 187 million likes, comments, and other reactions. Russia sent at least 10 million tweets from accounts that had more than 6 million followers on Twitter. I say "at least" because what we have uncovered so far may just be the tip of the iceberg. Analysis shows, for example, that the twenty most engaging false election stories on Facebook (whether from Russia or elsewhere) in the three months before the election were shared more and received more comments and reactions than the twenty most engaging true election stories. The Hype Machine became a clear conduit for misinformation, with one study estimating that 42 percent of visits to fake news websites (and only 10 percent of visits to top news websites) came through social media.

As astonishing as those numbers sound, the scale of fake news in 2016 was considerably smaller than that of real news. For example, in their nationally representative sample of web browsers, Andrew Guess, Brendan Nyhan, and Jason Reifler found that while 44 percent of Americans visited fake news websites in the weeks before the election, these visits comprised only 6 percent of their visits to real news websites. Similarly, David Lazer and his colleagues found that only 5 percent of registered voters' total exposures to political URLs on Twitter during the 2016 election were from fake news sources. Hunt Allcott and Matthew Gentzkow estimated the average American saw "one or several" fake news stories in the months before the election.

If these numbers seem small, it's worth noting some eccentricities in the way these data were collected. News is only considered "fake" in Allcott and Gentzkow's study if it is one of 156 verified fake news stories. The other two studies analyze restrictive lists of approximately 300 fake news websites. For example, Guess et al. exclude Breitbart,

InfoWars, and all of YouTube when characterizing "fake news sources." So the 44 percent of voting-age Americans who visited at least one of their restricted list of fake news websites in the final weeks before the election does not count visitors to these popular sources of fake news. In other words, 110 million voting-age Americans visited a narrow list of fake news websites that excluded Breitbart, InfoWars, and YouTube. Our best estimates put the full number of voting-age Americans exposed to fake news during the 2016 election at between 110 million and 130 million. So whether voters' exposure to fake news was "small-scale" is still hotly debated.

The distributions were skewed by a few viral hits, and a smaller percentage of voters saw the largest concentration of fake news. Guess et al. found that the 20 percent of Americans with the most conservative news diets were responsible for 62 percent of visits to fake news websites and that Americans over sixty were much more likely to consume fake news. On Twitter, Grinberg et al. found that 1 percent of registered voters consumed 80 percent of the fake news and that 0.1 percent accounted for 80 percent of "shares" from fake news websites. In a second, representative online survey of 3,500 Facebook users, Guess, Nyhan, and Reifler found that only 10 percent of respondents shared fake news and that they were highly concentrated among Americans over sixty-five. This level of concentration, which (as I will describe in Chapter 9) is typical of the Hype Machine, might make you skeptical of the power of fake news to influence a broad swath of society. But several caveats should accompany such skepticism.

We know that the "superspreaders" and "superconsumers" of fake news, who drive the concentration in these samples, are mostly bots. Grinberg et al. note, for example, that their median supersharer tweeted a whopping seventy-one times a day on average, with an average of 22 percent of their tweets containing fake news URLs, while their median panel member tweeted only 0.1 times a day. The researchers concluded that "many of these [superspreader and superconsumer] accounts were cyborgs." Excluding bots, Grinberg et al. found that members of their panel averaged 204 exposures to fake news during the last thirty days of the 2016 campaign, which amounts to seven exposures a day. Assuming only 5 percent of these exposures were seen, they estimate that the average human saw one fake news story every three days leading up to the election.

While some argue fake news isn't important because it constitutes a small part of the average citizen's overall media diet, it's not clear that its volume is proportional to its impact. Fake news is typically sensational and may therefore be more striking and persuasive than everyday news stories. Singular news stories, like Willie Horton, Mike Dukakis riding a tank, and Howard Dean's guttural scream are widely regarded as tipping points in their respective elections. Whether fake news stories behave similarly is an empirical question that remains unanswered. Furthermore, fake news doesn't live just on social media. It is frequently picked up and repeated by broadcast media and public figures, creating a feedback loop that amplifies its reach beyond social media alone.

The 2000 U.S. presidential election was decided by 537 votes in one key swing state—Florida. Russia's 2016 misinformation campaign targeted voters in swing states like Florida, Ohio, Pennsylvania, and Michigan. My colleagues at the Oxford Internet Institute analyzed over 22 million tweets containing political hashtags shared in the week before the election. They geolocated a third of these tweets, tying sharers and recipients to the states in which they resided. When they analyzed the geographic distribution of Russian misinformation around the country, they found that "the proportion of misinformation was twice that of the content from experts and the candidates themselves." When they calculated whether a state had more or less Russian fake news, they found that 12 of 16 swing states were above the average. They concluded that Russian fake news was "surprisingly concentrated in swing states, even considering the amount of political conversation occurring in the state." Although more than 135 million votes were cast in the 2016 U.S. presidential election, six swing states (New Hampshire, Minnesota, Michigan, Florida, Wisconsin, and Pennsylvania) were decided by margins of less than 2 percent, and 77,744 votes in three swing states (Wisconsin, Michigan, and Pennsylvania) effectively decided the election.

On Facebook, Twitter, and Instagram, Russian fake news targeted persuadable voters in swing states with content that was tailored to their interests using "@" mentions and hashtags to draw users to memes custom-designed for them. For example, two days before the election, supporters of the Black Lives Matter movement were drawn to voter suppression memes that encouraged them not to vote. The account @woke_blacks posted a meme to its Instagram account that read, "The excuse that a lost Black vote for Hillary is a Trump win is bs. Should you decide to sit-out the election, well done for the boycott," while @afrokingdom_ posted that "Black people are smart enough to understand that Hillary doesn't deserve our votes! DON'T VOTE!" New Knowledge estimated that 96 percent of the Instagram content linked to the Internet Research Agency focused on Black Lives Matter and police brutality, spreading "overt suppression narratives."

We know that President Trump's former campaign manager, Paul Manafort, shared polling data with the Russian political consultant Konstantin Kilimnik and that targeting persuadable voters in swing states (which is possible with such polling data) was standard operating procedure for Cambridge Analytica, the self-described "election consultancy" that used 87 million Americans' stolen data to build predictive models of voters' susceptibility to persuasion, and the topics and content most likely to persuade them. (I will evaluate Cambridge Analytica's "psychographic profiling" in Chapter 9.)

If misinformation targeted a small but potentially meaningful number of persuadable voters in key swing states, was the right misinformation targeted at the right voters? Skeptics contend that such misinformation preached to the choir, because exposure was "selective"— meaning that die-hard conservatives saw pro-Trump fake news, while die-hard liberals saw pro-Clinton fake news, making it unlikely that it changed anyone's mind. Guess et al. found 40 percent of Trump supporters and only 15 percent of Clinton supporters read pro-Trump fake news, while 11 percent of Clinton supporters and only 3 percent of Trump supporters read pro-Clinton fake news. Sixty-six percent of the most conservative voters, the farthest-right decile, visited at least one pro-Trump fake news site and read an average of 33.16 pro-Trump fake news articles.

But the argument that fake news was preaching to the choir doesn't address voter turnout, because ideologically consistent fake news can motivate voters to turn out even if it doesn't change their vote choices. Furthermore, while voters on the extreme right were disproportionately more likely to consume pro-Trump fake news (thus "preaching to the choir"), moderate Clinton supporters and undecideds in the middle of the political spectrum were significantly more likely to consume pro-Trump fake news than pro-Clinton fake news. Could their exposure to fake news have persuaded them to vote for Trump or to abstain? That depends on how social media manipulation affects voting.

Social Media Manipulation and Voting

Was the reach, scope, and targeting of the Russian interference sufficient to change the election result? We can't rule it out. Although exposure to fake news was much less than exposure to real news and was concentrated among a select set of voters, it likely reached between 110 million and 130 million people. It didn't need to affect everyone to tip the election—just eighty thousand persuadable voters in key swing states. Which was exactly who Russia targeted. The next big question: did it have an effect on voting? To answer that, we need to understand the science of voter turnout and vote choice.

Sadly, as I write this, only two published studies link social media exposure to voting. The first, a 61-million-person experiment conducted by Facebook during the 2010 U.S. congressional elections, found social media messages encouraging voting caused hundreds of thousands of additional verified votes to be cast. The second, a follow-up experiment by Facebook during the 2012 presidential election, replicated the findings of the first, although the "get out the vote" messages were slightly less effective, as is typical in higher-stakes presidential elections. (I will analyze both of these studies in detail in Chapter 7.) But the main takeaway, for the purposes of our discussion of the 2016 election, is that social media messaging can significantly increase voter turnout, with minimal effort. While there are only two large-scale studies of the effect of social media on voting, the substantial research on the effects of persuasive messaging on voter turnout and vote choice can help us to calibrate the likely effects of Russian interference on the 2016 election.*

---

* Chris Bail and his team found no evidence that interactions with IRA Twitter accounts in late 2017 impacted political attitudes or behavior. But several limitations prevented them from determining "whether IRA accounts influenced the 2016 presidential election." The study was conducted a year *after* the election, after the IRA had ramped down their information operation and Twitter had suspended two-thirds of their accounts. The sample included no independents and only frequent Twitter users, was not representative of U.S. voters, and did not consider voting behavior. The study

With regard to vote choice, some meta-analytic reviews suggest the effects of impersonal contact (mailings, TV, and digital advertising) on vote choice in general elections are very small. Kalla and Broockman conclude, from a meta-analysis of forty-nine field experiments, that "the best estimate of the size of persuasive effects [i.e., effects of advertising on vote choice] in general elections . . . is zero." But their data do not consider social media. And there is substantial uncertainty in their estimates, such as the effect of impersonal contact within two months of Election Day, which was when Russia's attack was in full swing.

They also found significant effects of persuasive messages on vote choice in primaries, on issue-specific ballot measures, and on campaign targeting of persuadable voters. Rogers and Nickerson found, for example, that informing voters in favor of abortion rights that a candidate did not support such rights had a 3.9 percent effect on reported vote choice, suggesting the possibility that targeted, issue-specific manipulation of the type Russia deployed could have changed vote choices. The power of persuasive messaging on issue-specific ballot measures also highlights the possibility of interference being directed at large numbers of regional elections and local policy measures, which could collectively shift the political direction of a country without having to impact results at a national level. This threat is particularly insidious, because it would be much harder to detect than interference in a general election.

Moreover, social media manipulation does not have to change our vote choices to tip an election. Targeted efforts to increase or diminish voter turnout could be substantial enough to change overall election results, and recent evidence suggests targeted messaging can affect voter turnout. For example, a randomized experiment by Katherine Haenschen and Jay Jennings showed that targeted digital advertising significantly increased voter turnout among millennial voters in competitive districts. Research by Andrew Guess, Dominique Lockett, Benjamin Lyons, Jacob Montgomery, Brendan Nyhan, and Jason Reifler showed that randomized exposure to just a single misleading

---

did find suggestive evidence that IRA interactions changed three things: opposing party ratings among "low news interest" respondents, the number of political accounts followed among "high news interest" respondents, and both opposing party ratings and the number of political accounts followed among Democrats.

article increased belief in the article's claims and increased self-reported intentions to vote. The meta-analysis by Green et al. estimated that direct mailings, combined with social pressure, generate an average increase in voter turnout of 2.9 percent, while canvassing generates an average increase of 2.5 percent, and volunteer phone banks generate an average increase of 2 percent. Dale and Strauss estimated the effect of text messages on voter turnout to be 4.1 percent, and there is evidence that personalized emails have a similar impact. The only studies of the impact of voter turnout as a result of social media messaging estimate that hundreds of thousands of additional votes were cast as a result of such messages.

So did Russian interference flip the 2016 U.S. presidential election or not? A full presidential term after the first Russian intervention and on the eve of the 2020 presidential election, during which Russia and others are continuing to interfere, we still don't know. What's scary is we can't rule it out. It's certainly possible given all the evidence. We don't know because no one has studied it directly. Unfortunately, until we do democracies worldwide will remain vulnerable.

The 2020 U.S. Presidential Election

We should all have been alarmed when Special Counsel Robert Mueller testified in 2019 that "the Russian government's effort to interfere in our election is among the most serious . . . challenges to our democracy" he has ever seen. He stressed that the threat "deserves the attention of every American" because the Russians "are doing it as we sit here and they expect to do it during the next campaign." He concluded that "much more needs to be done to protect against these intrusions, not just by the Russians but others."

FBI director Christopher Wray is warning that "the threat just keeps escalating." Not only have Russia's attacks intensified in 2020, but other countries, like China and Iran, are "entertaining whether to take a page out of that book." It is not clear what will happen to Americans' trust in democracy if the 2020 election is a more convincing, more determined rerun of 2016.

What is clear is that the 2020 election is being targeted. In February, intelligence officials informed the U.S. House Intelligence Committee that Russia was intervening to support President Trump's reelection. In March, the FBI informed Bernie Sanders that Russia was trying to tip the scales on his behalf. Intelligence officials have warned that Russia has adjusted their playbook toward newer, less easily detectable tactics to manipulate the 2020 election. Rather than impersonating Americans, they are now nudging American citizens to repeat misinformation to avoid social media platform rules against "inauthentic speech." They have shifted their servers from Russia to the United States because American intelligence agencies are barred from domestic surveillance. They have infiltrated Iran's cyberwar department, perhaps to launch attacks made to seem like they originated in Tehran.

In November 2019, Russian hackers successfully infiltrated the servers of the Ukrainian gas company Burisma, which was at the center of widely discredited allegations against Joe Biden and his son Hunter Biden, perhaps in an effort to dig up dirt to use during the general election. I would not be at all surprised to see a rerun of the Hillary Clinton email scandal emerge as a Joe Biden Burisma scandal in the fall of 2020. It wouldn't be hard for foreign adversaries to seed false material into the American social media ecosystem, made to seem like real material from the successful Burisma hack, to create a scandal designed to derail the Biden campaign before anyone can debunk it. As we've seen, this is the signature of a fake news crisis: it spreads faster than it can be corrected, so it's hard to clean up, even with a healthy dose of the truth.

The threat of election manipulation in 2020 is even higher due to the chaos caused by the coronavirus pandemic. With uncertainty around the viability of in-person voting, questions about voting by mail, and calls to delay the election, there can be no doubt that foreign actors will look to leverage the confusion caused by the coronavirus to disrupt our democratic process. Extreme vigilance is warranted during these difficult times when our vulnerability to manipulation is particularly high.

While some claim fake news is benign, during protests and confusion, amid the smoke, fire, and foreign interference, months from the most consequential election of our time, it is a real threat—not only to the election, but to the sanctity and peace of the election process. If the election were to be contested, fake news could escalate the contest, perhaps to violence. As Donald Horowitz has noted, "Concealed threats and outrages committed in secret figure prominently in pre-riot rumors. Since verification of such acts is difficult, they form the perfect content for such rumors, but difficulty of verification is not the only way in which they facilitate violence. . . . Rumors form an essential part of the riot process. They justify the violence that is about to occur. Their severity is often an indicator of the severity of the impending violence. Rumors narrow the options that seem available to those who join crowds and commit them to a line of action. They mobilize ordinary people to do what they would not ordinarily do. They shift the balance in a crowd toward those proposing the most extreme action. They project onto the future victims of violence the very impulses entertained by those who will victimize them. They confirm the strength and danger presented by the target group, thus facilitating violence born of fear."

The threat of misinformation is not limited to Russia or American democracy. Digital interference threatens democracies worldwide. Carole Cadwalladr's investigative reporting on the role of fake news in the Brexit vote and her work with Christopher Wiley to break the Cambridge Analytica scandal for *The Guardian* gave us a glimpse into the extent to which fake news has been weaponized around the world. Research by the Oxford Internet Institute found that one out of every three URLs with political hashtags being shared on Twitter ahead of the 2018 Swedish general election were from fake news sources. A study by the Federal University of Minas Gerais, the University of São Paulo, and the fact-checking platform Agência Lupa, which analyzed 100,000 political images circulating on 347 public WhatsApp chat groups ahead of the 2018 Brazilian national elections, found that 56 percent of the fifty most widely shared images on these chat groups were misleading, and only 8 percent were fully truthful. Microsoft estimated that 64 percent of Indians encountered fake news online ahead of Indian elections in 2019. In India, where 52 percent of people report getting news from WhatsApp, private messaging is a particularly insidious breeding ground for fake news, because people use private groups with end-to-end encryption, making it difficult to monitor or counteract the spread of falsity. In the Philippines, the spread of misinformation propagated to discredit Maria Ressa, the Filipino-American journalist working to expose corruption and a *Time* Person of the Year in 2018, was vast and swift. Similar to the Russian influence operation in Crimea, the misinformation campaign against Ressa mirrored the charges that were eventually brought against her in court. In June 2020, she was convicted of cyber libel and faced up to seven years in prison. The weaponization of misinformation and the spread of fake news are problems for democracies worldwide.

Fake News as Public Health Crisis

In March 2020, a deliberate misinformation campaign spread fear among the American public by propagating the false story that a nationwide quarantine to contain the coronavirus pandemic was imminent. The National Security Council had to publicly disavow the story. And that wasn't the only fake news spreading about the virus. The Chinese government spread false conspiracy theories blaming the U.S. military for starting the pandemic. Several false coronavirus "cures" killed hundreds of people who drank chlorine or excessive alcohol to rid themselves of the virus. There was, of course, no cure or vaccine at the time. International groups, like the World Health Organization (WHO), fought coronavirus misinformation on the Hype Machine as part of their global pandemic response. But, in January 2021, anti-vaccine protests shut down the vaccination site at Dodger Stadium in Los Angeles. My group at MIT supported the COVIDConnect fact-checking apparatus, the official WhatsApp coronavirus channel of the WHO, and studied the spread and impact of coronavirus misinformation worldwide. But we first glimpsed the destructive power of health misinformation on the Hype Machine the year before the coronavirus pandemic hit, during the measles resurgence of 2019.

Measles was declared eliminated in the United States in 2000. But while only 63 cases were reported in 2010, over 1,100 cases were reported in the first seven months of 2019, a nearly 1,800 percent increase. Measles is particularly dangerous for kids. It typically starts as a fever and rash, but in one in a thousand cases, it spreads to the brain, causing cranial swelling and convulsions, or encephalitis. In one in twenty kids, it causes pneumonia, preventing the lungs from extracting oxygen from the air and delivering it to the body. The disease took the lives of 110,000 kids worldwide this way in 2017.

Measles is one of the world's most contagious viruses. You can catch it from droplets of air contaminated with an infected person's cough hours after they've left the room. Nine of ten people exposed to it contract it. While the average number of people infected by one person with the coronavirus of 2020—its R0 figure—was 2.5, the R0 of measles is 15.

To prevent such a contagious disease from spreading, society has to develop herd immunity by vaccinating a large percentage of the population. With polio, which is less contagious, herd immunity can be achieved with 80 to 85 percent vaccination rates. For a highly contagious virus like measles, 95 percent of the population should be vaccinated to achieve herd immunity. Sadly, while there has been an effective vaccine since 1963, the resurgence of measles in the United States was driven by vaccine refusal, according to experts. While 91 percent of young children got the measles-mumps-rubella (or MMR) vaccine in 2017, vaccination rates in some communities fell dramatically in recent years, and it is in exactly these communities that measles skyrocketed.

This outbreak hits close to home for me because I have a six-year-old son, and the hardest-hit group, representing over half of all reported measles cases in the United States in 2019, was the Orthodox Jewish community located five blocks from our home in Brooklyn, New York. Other countrywide outbreaks have been clustered in tight-knit communities like the Jewish community in Rockland County, New York, and the Ukrainian- and Russian-American communities of Clark County, Washington, where vaccination rates hover around 70 percent, well below the threshold needed for herd immunity.

If measles is so dangerous and vaccines are so effective, why are some parents not vaccinating their kids? The answer lies partly in a wave of misinformation about the dangers of vaccination that began in 1998 with a fraudulent paper, published by Andrew Wakefield in the respected medical journal *The Lancet,* that claimed to link vaccines to autism. It was later revealed that Wakefield had been paid to falsify the evidence in that paper by lawyers suing the vaccine manufacturers, and that he was developing a competing vaccine himself. *The Lancet* promptly retracted the paper, and Wakefield lost his medical license. But the wave of misinformation he created continues today, aided by conspiracy theories propagated on blogs, in a widely circulated movie called *Vaxxed* directed by Wakefield himself, and most recently on social media.

In March 2019, addressing this wave of antivax misinformation during a public U.S. Senate hearing, Dr. Jonathan McCullers, chair of the department of pediatrics at the University of Tennessee Health Science Center and pediatrician-in-chief at Le Bonheur Children's Hospital in Memphis, testified that, in addition to state policies on vaccine exemptions and methods of counseling, "social media and the amplification of minor theories through rapid and diffuse channels of communication, coupled with instant reinforcement in the absence of authoritative opinions, is now driving . . . vaccine hesitancy. When parents get much of their information from the Internet or social media platforms such as Twitter and Facebook, reading these fringe ideas in the absence of accurate information can lead to understandable concern and confusion. These parents may thus be hesitant to get their children vaccinated without more information." The anecdotal evidence that social media misinformation drives the spread of vaccine-preventable diseases like measles is troubling.

The Antivax King of Facebook

Larry Cook describes himself as a "full time [antivax] activist." As of 2019, he was also the antivax king of Facebook. His Stop Mandatory Vaccination organization is a for-profit entity that makes money peddling antivax fake news on social media and earning referral fees from sales of antivax books on Amazon. He also raises money through GoFundMe campaigns that pay for his website, his Facebook ads, and his personal bills. Cook's Stop Mandatory Vaccination and another organization called the World Mercury Project, headed by Robert F. Kennedy, Jr., bought 54 percent of the antivaccine ads on Facebook in 2019.

Cook's antivax Facebook ad campaigns targeted women over twenty-five in Washington State, a population likely to have kids who need vaccines. More than 150 such posts aimed at such women, promoted by seven Facebook accounts including Cook's, were viewed 1.6 million to 5.2 million times and garnered about 18 clicks per dollar spent on the campaigns. Facebook's average cost per click across all industries hovers around $1.85. When you do the math, you see that Cook's reach is insanely efficient. These data suggest he pays about six cents per click.

In early 2019, Facebook search results for information about vaccines were dominated by antivaccination propaganda. YouTube's recommendation algorithm pushed viewers "from fact-based medical information toward anti-vaccine misinformation," and "75% of Pinterest posts related to vaccines discussed the false link between measles vaccines and autism." In a paper published in 2019, researchers at George Washington University found that Russian Twitter bots were posting about vaccines twenty-two times more often than the average Twitter user, linking vaccination misinformation to Russia's efforts to hijack the Hype Machine.

Like political fake news, antivax misinformation is concentrated. Analysis by Alexis Madrigal of *The Atlantic* showed that the top 50 vaccine pages on Facebook accounted for nearly half of the top 10,000 vaccine-related posts and 38 percent of all the likes on these posts from January 2016 to February 2019. In fact, just seven antivax pages generated 20 percent of the top 10,000 vaccine posts during this time.

As I will describe in the next chapter, the Hype Machine's networks are highly clustered around tight-knit communities of people with similar views and beliefs. We live in an information ecosystem that connects like-minded people. The measles outbreaks in New York and Washington in 2019 and 2020 are taking place in tight-knit communities of like-minded people. In the same way that Russian misinformation wouldn't need to convince the majority of Americans to affect elections (small numbers in key swing states would be enough), antivax social media campaigns wouldn't have to convince large swaths of people to forgo vaccinations to create an outbreak. To bring the levels of vaccination below the thresholds needed for herd immunity, they would only have to convince small numbers of people in tight-knit communities, who would then share the misinformation among themselves.

Research that analyzed the interactions of 2.6 million users with 300,000 vaccine-related posts over seven years found that the vaccine conversations taking place on Facebook were happening in exactly these types of tight-knit communities. The findings showed that "the consumption of content about vaccines is dominated by the echo chamber effect and that polarization increased over the years. Well separated communities emerged from the users' consumption habits. . . . The majority of users consume in favor or against vaccines, not both." These tight-knit communities in Washington State are the exact communities that Larry Cook and antivax profiteers have targeted with their Facebook ads. They are also the same communities in which disease outbreaks are occurring.

In early 2019, social media platforms took notice. Instagram began blocking antivaccine-related hashtags like #vaccinescauseautism and #vaccinesarepoison. YouTube announced it is no longer allowing users to monetize antivaccine videos with ads. Pinterest banned searches for vaccine content. Facebook stopped showing pages and groups featuring antivaccine content and tweaked its recommendation engines to stop suggesting users join these groups. They also took down the Facebook ads that Larry Cook and others had been buying. The social platforms took similar steps to stem the spread of coronavirus fake news in 2020. Will these measures help slow the coronavirus, measles outbreaks, and future pandemics? Will fake news drive the spread of preventable diseases? Answers to these questions lie in the emerging science of fake news.

The Science of Fake News

Despite the potentially catastrophic consequences of the rise of fake news for our democracies, our economies, and our public health, the science of how and why it spreads online is still in its infancy. Until 2018, most scientific studies of fake news had only analyzed small samples or case studies of the diffusion of single stories, one at a time. My colleagues Soroush Vosoughi and Deb Roy and I set out to change that when we published our decade-long study of the spread of false news online in *Science* in March 2018.

In that study, we collaborated directly with Twitter to study the diffusion of all the verified true and false rumors that had ever spread on the platform from its inception in 2006 to 2017. We extracted tweets about verified fake news from Twitter's historical archive. The data included approximately 126,000 Twitter cascades of stories spread by 3 million people over 4.5 million times. We classified news as true or false using information from six independent fact-checking organizations (including Snopes, PolitiFact, FactCheck, and others) that exhibited 95 to 98 percent agreement on the veracity of the news. We then employed students working independently at MIT and Wellesley College to check for bias in how the fact-checkers had chosen those stories.

Once we had a comprehensive database of verified rumors spanning the ten years of Twitter's existence, we searched Twitter for mentions of these stories, followed their sharing activity to the "origin" tweets (the first mention of a story on Twitter), and re-created the retweet cascades (unbroken chains of retweets with a common, singular origin) of these stories spreading online. When we visualized these cascades, the sharing activity took on bizarre, alien-looking shapes. They typically began with a starburst pattern of retweets emanating from the origin tweet and then spread out, with new retweet chains that looked like the tendrils of a jellyfish trailing away from the starburst. I've included an image of one of these false news cascades in Figure 2.2. These cascades can be characterized mathematically as

Figure 2.2 *The spread of a false news story through Twitter. Longer lines represent longer retweet cascades, demonstrating the greater breadth and depth at which false news spreads.*

they spread across the Twitter population over time. So we analyzed how the false ones spread differently than the true ones.

Our findings surprised and disturbed us. In all categories of information, we discovered, false news spread significantly farther, faster, deeper, and more broadly than the truth—sometimes by an order of magnitude. While the truth rarely diffused to more than 1,000 people, the top 1 percent of false news cascades routinely diffused to as many as 100,000 people. It took the truth approximately six times as long as falsehood to reach 1,500 people and twenty times as long to travel ten reshares from the origin tweet in a retweet cascade. Falsehood spread significantly more broadly and was retweeted by more unique users than the truth at every cascade depth. (Each reshare spreads the information away from the origin tweet to create a chain or cascade of reshares. The number of links in a chain is the cascade's "depth.")

False *political* news traveled deeper and more broadly, reached more people, and was more viral than any other category of false news. It reached more than 20,000 people nearly three times faster than all other types of false news reached just 10,000 people. News about politics and urban legends spread the fastest and was the most viral. Falsehoods were 70 percent more likely to be retweeted than the truth, even when controlling for the age of the account holder, activity level, and number of followers and followees of the original tweeter and whether the original tweeter was a verified user.

While one might think that characteristics of the people spreading the news would explain why falsity travels with greater velocity than the truth, the data revealed the opposite. For example, one might suspect that those who spread falsity had more followers, followed more people, tweeted more often, were more often "verified" users, or had been on Twitter longer. But the opposite was true. People who spread false news had significantly fewer followers, followed significantly fewer people, were significantly less active on Twitter, were "verified" significantly less often, and had been on Twitter for significantly less time, on average. In other words, falsehood diffused farther, faster, deeper, and more broadly than the truth despite these differences, not because of them. So why and how does fake news spread?

Lies spread online through a complex interaction of coordinated bots and unwitting humans working together in an unexpected symbiosis.

Social Bots and the Spread of Fake News

Social bots (software-controlled social media profiles) are a big part of how fake news spreads. We saw this in our Twitter data when we analyzed Russia's information operation in Crimea in 2014 and in the decade of data in our broader Twitter sample. The way social bots are used to spread lies online is both disturbing and fascinating.

In 2018 my friend and colleague Filippo Menczer at Indiana University, along with his colleagues Chengcheng Shao, Giovanni Ciampaglia, Onur Varol, Kai-Cheng Yang, and Alessandro Flammini, published the largest-ever study on how social bots spread fake news. They analyzed 14 million tweets spreading 400,000 articles on Twitter in 2016 and 2017. Their work corroborated our finding that fake news was more viral than real news. They also found that bots played a big role in spreading content from low-credibility sources. But the way bots worked to amplify fake news was surprising, and it highlights the sophistication with which they are programmed to prey on the Hype Machine.

First, bots pounce on fake news in the first few seconds after it's published, and they retweet it broadly. That's how they're designed. And the initial spreaders of a fake news article are much more likely to be bots than humans. Think about the starburst pattern in the Twitter cascade of fake news shown in Figure 2.2. Many of these starbursts are created by bots. What happens next validates the effectiveness of this strategy, because humans do most of the retweeting. The early tweeting activity by bots triggers a disproportionate amount of human engagement, creating cascades of fake news triggered by bots but propagated by humans through the Hype Machine's network.

Second, bots mention influential humans incessantly. If they can get an influential human to retweet fake news, it simultaneously amplifies and legitimizes it. Menczer and his colleagues point to an example in their data in which a single bot mentioned @realDonaldTrump nineteen times, linking to the false news claim that millions of votes were cast by illegal immigrants in the 2016 presidential election. The strategy works when influential people are fooled into sharing the content. Donald Trump, for example, has on a number of occasions shared content from known bots, legitimizing their content and spreading their misinformation widely in the Twitter network. It was Trump who adopted the false claim that millions of illegal immigrants voted in the 2016 presidential election as an official talking point.

But bots can't spread fake news without people. In our ten-year study with Twitter, we found that it was humans, more than bots, that helped make false rumors spread faster and more broadly than the truth. In their study from 2016 to 2017, Menczer and his colleagues also found that humans, not bots, were the most critical spreaders of fake news in the Twitter network. In the end, humans and machines play symbiotic roles in the spread of falsity: bots manipulate humans to share fake news, and humans spread it on through the Hype Machine. Misleading humans is the ultimate goal of any misinformation campaign. It's humans who vote, protest, boycott products, and decide whether to vaccinate their kids. These deeply human decisions are the very object of fake news manipulation. Bots are just a vehicle to achieve an end. But if humans are the objects of fake news campaigns, and if they are so critical to their spread, why are we so attracted to fake news? And why do we share it?

The Novelty Hypothesis

One explanation is what Soroush Vosoughi, Deb Roy, and I called the novelty hypothesis. Novelty attracts human attention because it is surprising and emotionally arousing. It updates our understanding of the world. It encourages sharing because it confers social status on the sharer, who is seen as someone who is "in the know" or who has access to "inside information." Knowing that, we tested whether false news was more novel than the truth in the ten years of Twitter data we studied. We also examined whether Twitter users were more likely to retweet information that seemed to be more novel.

To assess novelty, we looked at users who shared true and false rumors and compared the content of rumor tweets to the content of all the tweets the users were exposed to in the sixty days prior to their decision to retweet a rumor. Our findings were consistent across multiple measures of novelty: false news was indeed more novel than the truth, and people were more likely to share novel information. This makes sense in the context of the "attention economy" (which I will discuss in detail in Chapter 9). In the context of competing social media memes, novelty attracts our scarce attention and motivates our consumption and sharing behaviors online.

Although false rumors were more novel than true rumors in our study, users may not have perceived them as such. So to further test our novelty hypothesis, we assessed users' perceptions of true and false rumors by comparing the emotions they expressed in their replies to these rumors. We found that false rumors inspired more surprise and disgust, corroborating the novelty hypothesis, while the truth inspired more sadness, anticipation, joy, and trust. These emotions shed light on what inspires people to share false news beyond its novelty. To understand the mechanisms underlying the spread of fake news, we have to also consider humans' susceptibility to it.

Our Susceptibility to Fake News

The science of human susceptibility to false beliefs is more developed than the science of fake news but is, unfortunately, no more settled. There's currently a debate between "classical reasoning" and "motivated reasoning." Classical reasoning contends that when we think analytically, we are better able to tell what's real from what's fake. Motivated reasoning, on the other hand, contends that when we are faced with corrective information about a false belief, the more analytically minded of us "dig in" and increase our commitment to those false beliefs, especially if we are more partisan or committed to those false beliefs to begin with.

My friend and colleague David Rand at MIT teamed up with Gordon Pennycook to study what types of people were better able to recognize fake news. They measured how cognitively reflective people were using a cognitive reflection task (CRT) and then asked them whether they believed a series of true and false news stories. A cognitive reflection task tests how reflective someone is by giving them a simple puzzle, like this one: "A bat and ball cost $1.10 in total. The bat costs $1.00 more than the ball. How much does the ball cost?" The problem elicits a fast, intuitive response—ten cents—that, upon reflection, is wrong: if the ball cost ten cents, the bat would have to cost $1.10 and they would total $1.20. Asking people to consider these types of puzzles tests their reflectiveness. And Rand and Pennycook found that people who were more reflective were better able to tell truth from falsity and to recognize overly partisan coverage of true events, supporting classical reasoning.

But repetition causes belief. If you beat us over the head with fake news, we're more likely to believe it. It's called the "illusory truth effect"—we tend to believe false information more after repeated exposure to it. People also tend to believe what they already think. (That's confirmation bias.) So the more we hear something and the more it aligns with what we know, the more likely we are to believe it. Similar thinking has led some cognitive and political scientists to hypothesize that because of confirmation bias, corrective information can backfire—that trying to convince someone that their falsely held belief is wrong actually causes them to dig in to those false beliefs even more. But so far, evidence for this "backfire effect" seems weaker. For example, in three survey experiments, Andrew Guess and Alexander Coppock found "no evidence of backlash, even under theoretically favorable conditions."

So reflection helps us distinguish truth from falsity, repetition causes belief, and corrective information doesn't seem to backfire even though a confirmation bias generally leads us to believe what we already know. These findings give us leads for fighting fake news (which I will return to in Chapter 12, when I discuss how we must adapt).

The Economic Motive to Create Fake News

The political motive for creating fake news is abundantly clear from Russia's foreign interference in Ukrainian and American politics. But the economic motive should not be underestimated. And nowhere has the economic motive to create fake news been more obvious than in Veles, Macedonia.

Veles is a sleepy mountain town with 55,000 residents, two TV channels, and a few lovely churches. It boasts a handful of notable historical figures and events, from Ottoman grand viziers to battles between the Serbian and Ottoman empires in the late fourteenth century. But perhaps the most important contribution to Veles's global historical significance will be that during the 2016 U.S. presidential election, its unemployed teen population discovered how the Hype Machine could make them rich by spreading fake news online.

The teenagers of Veles developed and promoted hundreds of websites that spread fake news to voters in the United States through social media advertising networks. Companies like Google show ads to Internet browsers and pay website creators based on how many high-quality eyeballs they attract. The teenagers of Veles discovered that they could make a lot of money by creating websites and promoting their content though social media networks. The more people read and shared their articles, the more money they made.

They found that fake news attracted more readers and, as we found in our own research, that it was 70 percent more likely to be shared online. They created fake accounts to amplify the signal, and once the trending algorithms got hold of them, the fake news stories received a broadcasting boost, exposing them to even more people, in new areas of the network. What ensued was a deluge of fake news that washed over the American public just as they were heading to the polls. Money flowed in one direction and falsehood flowed in the other, leaving Veles flush with new BMWs, and the United States inundated with false news months before the 2016 presidential election. The town of Veles is only one such example. In 2019 fake news websites generated over $200 million a year in ad revenue. Fake news is big business, and our approaches to solving the problem (which I will address in Chapter 12) must recognize that economic reality.

The End of Reality

Unfortunately, everything I have described so far—from stock market crashes to coronavirus misinformation to measles outbreaks to election interference—is the good news. That's because the age of fake news is about to get a whole lot worse. We are on the verge of a new era of synthetic media that some fear will usher us into an "end of reality." This characterization may seem dramatic, but there is no doubt that technological innovation in the fabrication of falsity is advancing at a breakneck pace. The development of "deepfakes" is generating exceedingly convincing synthetic audio and video that is even more likely to fool us than textual fake news. Deepfake technology uses deep learning, a form of machine learning based on multilayered neural networks, to create hyperrealistic fake video and audio. If seeing is believing, then the next generation of falsity threatens to convince us more than any fake media we have seen so far.

In 2018 movie director (and expert impersonator) Jordan Peele teamed up with *BuzzFeed* to create a deepfake video of Barack Obama calling Donald Trump a "complete and total dipshit." It was convincing but obviously fake. Peele added a tongue-in-cheek nod to the obvious falsity of his deepfake when he made Obama say, "Now, I would never say these things . . . at least not in a public address." But what happens when the videos are not made to be obviously fake, but instead made to convincingly deceive?

Deepfake technology is based on a specific type of deep learning called generative adversarial networks, or GANs, which was first developed by Ian Goodfellow while he was a graduate student at the University of Montreal. One night while drinking beer with fellow graduate students at a local watering hole, Goodfellow was confronted with a machine-learning problem that had confounded his friends: training a computer to create photos by itself. Conventional methods were failing miserably. But that night while enjoying a few pints, Goodfellow had an epiphany. He wondered if they could solve the problem by pitting two neural networks against each other. It was the origin of GANs—a technology that Yann LeCun, former head of Facebook AI Research, dubbed "the coolest idea in deep learning in the last 20 years." It's also what manipulated Barack Obama to call Donald Trump a "dipshit."

GANs pit two networks against each other: a "generator," whose job is to generate synthetic media, and a "discriminator," whose job is to determine if the content is real or fake. The generator learns from the discriminator's decisions and optimizes its media to create more and more convincing video and audio. In fact, the generator's whole job is to maximize the likelihood that it will fool the discriminator into thinking the synthetic video or audio is real. Imagine a machine, set in a hyper loop, trying to get better and better at fooling us. That's the future of reality distortion in a world with exponentially improving GANs technology.

GANs can be used for good as well—for example, to generate convincing synthetic data in high-energy physics experiments or to accelerate drug discovery. But the potential geopolitical and economic harm they can create is troubling. Ambassador Daniel Benjamin, former coordinator for counterterrorism at the U.S. State Department, and Steven Simon, former National Security Council senior director for counterterrorism in the Clinton and Obama administrations, paint a grim picture: "One can easily imagine the havoc caused by falsified video that depicts foreign Iranian officials collaborating with terrorists to target the United States. Or by something as simple as invented news reports about Iranian or North Korean military plans for preemptive strikes on any number of targets. . . . It might end up causing a war, or just as consequentially, impeding a national response to a genuine threat."

Deepfaked audio is already being used to defraud companies of millions of dollars. In the summer of 2019, Symantec CTO Hugh Thompson revealed that his company had seen deepfaked audio attacks against several of its clients. The attackers first trained a GAN on hours of public audio recordings of a CEO's voice, while giving news interviews, delivering public speeches, speaking during earnings calls, or testifying before Congress. Using these audio files, the attackers built a system to automatically mimic the CEO's voice. They would call, for example, the CFO of the company and pretend to be the CEO requesting an immediate wire transfer of millions of dollars into a bank account they controlled. The system didn't just deliver a prerecorded message but converted the attacker's voice into the CEO's voice in real time so they could engage in a realistic conversation and answer the CFO's questions. The synthesized audio of the CEO's voice was so convincing that, coupled with a good story about why the money needed to be transferred right away—they were about to lose a big deal, or they had to beat an impending deadline at the end of the fiscal quarter—the CFO would comply with the CEO's request and execute the transfer. Thompson revealed that each attack cost the target companies millions of dollars.

As Jordan Peele made Obama say in his *BuzzFeed* deepfake: "It may sound basic, but how we move forward, in the Age of Information, is going to be the difference between whether we survive or whether we become some kind of fucked up dystopia." To understand whether dystopia is our destiny, we have to understand how the Hype Machine works. To do that, we'll need to go back to first principles, starting with a deep dive under the hood of the Hype Machine, followed by an examination of social media's effect on our brains.

CHAPTER 3

The Hype Machine

The single greatest change, not just in our business, but in American life and life around the world, is social media.

—TOM BROKAW

The world is full of things more powerful than us. But if you know how to catch a ride, you can go places.

—NEAL STEPHENSON

I've collaborated with Facebook on research for many years and visited their offices many times. The constantly changing art and murals in the hallways and on the walls have become something of legend. Take, for example, the story of graffiti artist David Choe, who was commissioned to create the murals that covered Facebook's original office on Emerson Street in Palo Alto. At the time, Choe's art was becoming more expensive. So he asked Facebook for $60,000 to paint their entire office. Sean Parker encouraged him to take company stock as payment instead; when Facebook went public in 2012, Choe's shares were worth $200 million. Today they are worth $500 million.

Facebook takes the relationship between art and innovation seriously. It's even got an artist-in-residence program that brings in its artists to cover the walls and hallways of its Menlo Park campus with creative and meaningful murals. The art, in some sense, reflects Facebook's culture, for better or worse. There's a famous stencil poster that reads "Move Fast and Break Things." When Mark Zuckerberg first coined the phrase, it was heralded as the creative mentality driving Facebook's innovation. Today it represents the careless mindset that missed the fake news crisis and Russia's intervention in American democracy. In some ways, the art in Facebook's offices reflects the culture and societal implications of the platform. It also imbues a particular mentality in the minds of the engineers and data scientists coding the world's largest social network. The art is a microcosm of Facebook's influence. Reflecting on it gives one insight into how Facebook employees think.

On one visit to Facebook headquarters, a particular mural caught my eye. So I took a picture of it and saved it to my phone. Over the years, as I researched the Hype Machine and tried to understand its inner workings, I returned to this image over and over again in my mind. It was a green, blue, and white stencil that simply read: "The Social Network Is the Computer" (Figure 3.1).

Figure 3.1 *Photograph taken by the author at Facebook headquarters, Menlo Park, California.*

The Social Network Is the Computer

One could interpret this mural in many ways. In one sense, the social network was the product Facebook was selling. While Apple sold computers, Facebook sold the network (or advertising on it). But for me the mural had a deeper meaning. It described a view of the world in which society is essentially a gigantic information processor, moving ideas, concepts, and opinions from person to person, like neurons in the brain or nodes in a neural network, firing synapses at each node in the form of decisions and behaviors—what products to buy, who to vote for, or who to date—billions of times per minute, every day. In this analogy, we are the nodes, and the architecture of the information-processing machine we collectively inhabit is the social network. The digitally connected social network created by the aggregation of Facebook, Twitter, WhatsApp, WeChat, and Instagram "is the computer." But if the social network is the computer, what is it processing?

The information that ebbs and flows through this computer—this gigantic information-processing machine that connects us all—embodies ideas, suggestions, political messages, calls to action, artistic and cultural shifts, shocking news of horrific events, facts, figures, ways of thinking, advocacy, and yes, stupid cat pictures and Instagram memes of Chihuahuas that look like blueberry muffins. The Hype Machine is, at its core, an information processor, regulating and directing the flow of information in society, from person to person and between people, brands, governments, media outlets, and international organizations. We, the nodes in this network, are ourselves information processors and decision makers. We go about our daily lives, shopping, voting, dating, advocating, posting, sharing, and curating the information that flows through the network. The collective outcomes we experience as a society are the aggregation of the individual decisions we make, which are in turn informed and influenced by the flow of information, ideas, and opinions to which we are exposed through various media, including corporate broadcast media and, today, more and more, social media.

But while we play an important role in the curation of the information that flows through the Hype Machine, much of that flow is directed, enabled, and constrained by algorithms that decide what we see, when we see it, and who we should connect to next in the network. In this way, our modern communications infrastructure—our new information order—is a constantly evolving network of human agents, engaged in a 24/7 information exchange, guided by algorithms that control the flow of information. To understand this evolving network, we have to go under the Hype Machine's hood.

The Anatomy of the Hype Machine

A trifecta of three technologies makes the Hype Machine possible. The design and development of digital social networks, machine intelligence, and smartphones together determine how the Hype Machine structures our world. In large measure, digital social networks structure the flow of information in society. Machine intelligence guides the evolution of digital social networks through friend recommendations and the flow of information over the network through feed algorithms. Smartphones create an "always on" environment for the Hype Machine to operate in. They learn from, and feed granular second-by-second data about our behaviors and opinions into, the machine intelligence that structures our access to information and the opinions and beliefs we are exposed to. This trifecta of digital social networks, machine intelligence, and smartphones has transformed how information is produced and consumed, how we are informed, how we behave, and thus how the Hype Machine changes us (Figure 3.2).

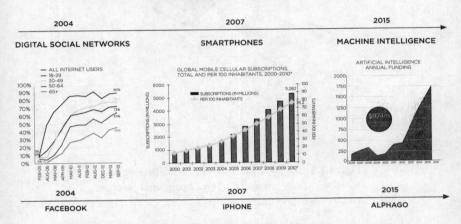

Figure 3.2 *The adoption of digital social networks is shown from February 2005 to September 2013. The total and per capita adoption of global cellular subscriptions is shown from 2000 to 2010. The adoption of machine intelligence depicts annual funding for artificial intelligence worldwide in hundreds of millions of dollars from 2006 to 2016. The dates of the launches of Facebook, the iPhone, and the AI software AlphaGo are shown under their respective trends.*

If we want to understand this information-processing machine, we have to understand its three component parts: its *substrate* (the digital social network), which structures our interactions; its *process* (the Hype Loop), which, through the interplay of machine and human intelligence, controls the flow of information over the substrate; and its *medium* (the smartphone, at least for now), which is the primary input/output device through which we provide information to and receive information from the Hype Machine (Figure 3.3). Any theory or analysis we use to explain, for example, why fake news spreads faster than the truth online or why the Hype Machine, in its current form, destroys the wisdom of crowds (more about this later), requires a basic understanding of these three components.

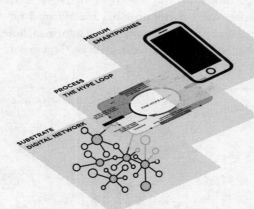

Figure 3.3 *The Hype Machine's substrate (the digital social network), process (the Hype Loop), and medium (today, smartphones).*

The *substrate* at the core of the Hype Machine is the network itself—the constantly evolving population-scale collection of links that connects us on Facebook, Twitter, LinkedIn, and the rest. The network substrate gives the Hype Machine its shape and forms the architecture that determines, in large part, who knows what and when. The structure of the networks that connect the Hype Machine determines how information flows, so understanding this structure and how it evolves gives us insight into how society operates—from the rise of political polarization, to the momentum of social movements, to the spread of fake news, to the success of targeted advertising.

The *process* that regulates the evolution of the network and the flow of information through it is what I call the Hype Loop—the cyclical interplay of machine and human intelligence that determines what we focus on and how information and knowledge are distributed around the world. This interplay is powered by the rise of machine intelligence and the accessibility of data about human thoughts, behaviors, and opinions at population scale. Machine intelligence ingests our thoughts, behaviors, and opinions and, in turn, curates the stories we see in our newsfeeds, the pictures we see on Instagram, the colleagues and dates suggested to us on LinkedIn and Tinder, and the ads we are shown alongside this content.

We then consume this information and make decisions with it. We click on some links and images and discard others. We comment on and like some posts and ignore others. We even change our offline behaviors in response to what we have seen, in the voting booth and at the shopping mall. The Hype Machine observes these decisions and learns what we like, who we like, and how we think. So next time its suggestions are modified to be more engaging. This process of human-machine interaction—this Hype Loop—sways us, and we sway it. But the outcomes are real—products are purchased, votes are cast, and people show up in town squares to protest, sometimes, as in Tahrir Square, to dramatic effect.

The *medium* is the input/output device through which we engage with the Hype Machine. Today the medium is largely the smartphone. But tomorrow it could be augmented reality (AR) or virtual reality (VR) headsets, digital contact lenses, virtual beings, in-home audio devices, or some combination. Regardless of the actual device, the medium is important because it determines the context from which the Hype Machine learns about us and in which it influences us.

But a true grasp of the Hype Machine also requires an understanding of the economic, technical, social, and legal forces that guide its development. These are the *levers* with which we control social media. So before I dive into the Hype Machine's three component parts in detail, it's worth introducing the four levers, to explain how the Hype Machine's components operate and are operated.

The Levers: Money, Code, Norms, and Laws

Four factors—*money, code, norms,* and *laws*—guide how the Hype Machine affects us and how we, in turn, steer the Hype Machine. Each serves a dual purpose: first, as a lens through which we can understand the influence of the Hype Machine on our world; and second, as a mechanism through which we can guide its effects on society.

The incentives (money) faced by Facebook, Twitter, Snapchat, Yelp, and others affect the business models they pursue and their platforms' designs. And that in turn affects how their users behave, favoring certain social and economic outcomes and making others less probable. Following the money leads us to an often-surprising view of how social media is used and, for that matter, abused.

By examining the code, we can understand how technical constraints affect our online behavior, our communication patterns, and the evolution of our social networks. The design of social media's software code has an outsize effect on how the Hype Machine operates. The shortest paths through the computational constraints the platforms faced when building these systems have led to particular designs, which shape society in surprising and at times dangerous ways. Design choices made for efficiency's sake (and sometimes, frankly, arbitrarily) shape how the Hype Machine affects us.

By analyzing norms, we can understand the social forces at play in these systems, because how we use social media is guided by the norms we agree on as a society. In the end, we'll get out of this wave of innovation what we put into it. If we use this technology in positive, egalitarian ways, we can promote positive social change and create substantial social and economic value. But if we are not careful, we can also inadvertently create an unequal, authoritarian world in which surveillance capitalism directs our behavior toward corporate and governmental ends, without regard for the social and economic implications. As we influence each other, through word and deed online, we continue to create the digital world we inhabit. And eventually, we'll reap what we have sown.

By studying the laws, we can understand how governments attempt to correct the market failures created by the Hype Machine and examine what effect regulations have on business, politics, and society. In Europe, regulations like the General Data Protection Regulation (GDPR) are substantially constraining the design and behavior of social platforms. In the United States, social media platforms have, to date, been left to their own devices, saddled with the difficult task of self-regulation. If they do too little, they risk a regulatory backlash. The future direction of the regulation of global social media is unclear, but one thing is clear: the extent to which social platforms are regulated is likely to change considerably over the next two to three years. By examining the three component parts of the Hype Machine from the perspective of these four levers, we can understand the fundamentals of how social media operates. From there we can evaluate its effects on us and how we can adapt.

Digital Social Networks (the Substrate)

The fraction of 18-to-29-year-old Internet users who use social networking sites rose from just 9 percent in 2005 to 90 percent in 2013. Other age-groups saw similar increases in social networking, and by 2013, 73 percent of all Internet users were using social media networks. Over an eight- to ten-year period, digital social networking spread across the globe like a pandemic.

Digital social networks structure the flow of information and influence in society in two ways. First, they guide the structure of the human social network itself by providing access to digital connections and influencing the structure of those connections through friend-suggestion algorithms. Second, they use data about our connections to build more accurate models of our preferences. Who we are connected to directly affects everything we see online, from the news we read to the products we are pitched. By structuring the network, and using the network to structure our information, digital social networks help determine what we buy, what we read, who we vote for, and even who we love.

Figure 3.4 displays the global Facebook network. It's an immense, complex network, connecting over 2 billion people in day-to-day interactions, spanning the globe. But what you can't see in this picture is that this network has a specific, complex structure that determines who we know and interact with and the pathways through which information, resources, and ideas flow to us.

The Hype Machine structures our reality by building on what Facebook, LinkedIn, and others call the social graph. I've been studying the structure and function of the social graph for twenty years and am fascinated by its novel mathematical properties, such as the fact that, on average, most people's friends have more friends than they do, a

Figure 3.4 *The global Facebook social network in 2010. No map is shown. The contours of the continents emerge from the network connections themselves.*

statistical regularity called the friendship paradox that was first discovered by Scott Feld in 1991, and that I will return to later in this book.

Two regularities of the social graph directly influence what we are experiencing on the Hype Machine today. First, it's *clustered* more than one would expect by chance, meaning we form dense clusters of people that are highly connected within the clusters, much more than we are connected across the clusters. Second, it's *homophilous,* meaning that similar people connect. These two properties explain why the Hype Machine helps foster political polarization and echo chambers, spreads fake news, and generates outsize returns on marketing investments. Understanding clustering and homophily is essential to understanding the Hype Machine.

It's a Small World (Clustering)

Have you ever met a stranger who knows someone you know and thought *Huh, small world*? Well, that feeling is no coincidence—it's a direct result of the structure of the human social network. In fact, in network science terms, Facebook, Twitter, WeChat, WhatsApp, and Pinterest networks are "small worlds." What does that mean? To understand this "small world" we live in, we need to go back to a funda-

THE FORBIDDEN TRIAD

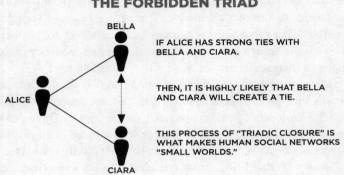

BELLA

ALICE

CIARA

IF ALICE HAS STRONG TIES WITH BELLA AND CIARA.

THEN, IT IS HIGHLY LIKELY THAT BELLA AND CIARA WILL CREATE A TIE.

THIS PROCESS OF "TRIADIC CLOSURE" IS WHAT MAKES HUMAN SOCIAL NETWORKS "SMALL WORLDS."

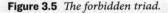

Figure 3.5 *The forbidden triad.*

mental building block of how human beings form and evolve their social networks—a building block that explains the unexpected clustering in our networks. We need to go back to what Mark Granovetter called the "forbidden triad."

The forbidden triad is a triangle of relationships among three people in which there are two strong relationships but the third is missing. It turns out that this structure is rare. Human beings don't find themselves in the forbidden triad very often. To see why, imagine the relationships among three friends, Alice, Bella, and Ciara, depicted in Figure 3.5. If Alice has strong relationships (or ties) with Bella and Ciara, it's highly likely that Bella and Ciara are connected by at least a weak tie. A forbidden triad, in which Alice is connected to Bella and Ciara, but Bella and Ciara are not connected, is unlikely. Why is it unlikely?

Well, if Alice is close with both Bella and Ciara, then Bella and Ciara are likely to meet and spend time together through their interactions with Alice. If Alice and Bella like each other, it's probably because they share similar interests. And if Alice and Bella have similar interests, then Alice and Ciara are likely to share those interests as well. So by a kind of transitive property of social relationships, it's highly likely that Bella and Ciara also share these same interests, making them more likely to become friends. Furthermore, discord between Bella and Ciara will strain Alice's relationships with them. Each will wonder why Alice hangs out with the other. They will not want to spend time together and will either pressure Alice to break her relationship with the other friend, or distance themselves from Alice to avoid seeing the other friend. For these reasons, human social networks are characterized by what is known as triadic closure, the human tendency to close triangles in their social networks.

Triadic closure leads to clustering among similar people. It creates networks with groups of peers, or clusters, that are densely connected within the clusters but weakly connected across clusters. These densely connected clusters, populated by people with similar demographics, socioeconomic status, interests, and ideas, are typically connected by rare "weak ties" that bridge from one cluster to another. Triadic closure, combined with the occasional weak tie, is what makes human social networks "small worlds," characterized by dense clustering and, at the same time, short path lengths between any two people in society

Figure 3.6 *A part of the Facebook social graph with 4,039 users, 88,234 relationships, and an average clustering coefficient of 0.6, exemplifying the dense clustering of human social networks.*

(Figure 3.6). My friend and colleague Duncan Watts pioneered the formalization of this small worlds theory, which is a foundation of modern network science, with Steve Strogatz at Cornell.

Since distant clusters are connected by long, albeit weak, bridging

ties, any two people in society are typically connected by no more than six degrees of separation. That's why, when you're surprised you know someone in common with someone socially distant from you, you think *Huh, small world.* As we'll see in Chapter 5, this structure powered Facebook's go-to-market strategy. To beat MySpace, Facebook recruited users within, rather than across, clusters by targeting friends on college campuses, increasing the safety and familiarity of our experience in joining its network.

The strength of weak ties, which connect distant clusters, is that they are the paths through which novel information flows between disparate parts of the network. As my friend and colleague Ron Burt has argued, people in the same densely connected clusters tend to know the same things and think the same way. Novelty therefore flows to people through their weak bridging ties to other clusters. The value of information comes from its uneven distribution across network clusters. Novel information is valuable due to its local scarcity. Individuals with access to scarce, novel information in a given network cluster can broker opportunities and enable innovation by applying novel information they receive from outside their group to problems that are intractable given what their group knows. This is part of what it means to be a thought leader who thinks "out of the box." But it might be more accurate to say that these connectors, brokers, or influencers think "out of the cluster" rather than "out of the box." These are the people whose diverse networks provide them with jobs, promotions, and economic opportunities. They create value by brokering novelty between disparate parts of the human social network, and (as I will describe in later chapters) in an attention economy, this type of novelty is king.

Birds of a Feather Flock Together (Homophily)

Human social networks are not just clustered, they're also homophilous, meaning birds of a feather flock together. People tend to make friends with those who are like themselves on dimensions like race, ethnicity, socioeconomic status, educational attainment, political ideology, opinions, behaviors, and preferences. This is one of the most stable and regular patterns of social life. Homophilous ties ease communication, make it easier to predict our friends' behavior, engender trust, and reduce the cost of maintaining ties and the risk of forming new ones. So it's perhaps unsurprising that philosophers since Socrates have noted this natural human tendency.

But homophily is also relevant to how the Hype Machine works today. As we'll see later in this chapter when we discuss friend-suggestion algorithms, the way the Hype Machine is designed leads the human social network to evolve toward even more triadic closure and homophily than we would expect in nature. So it's essential to consider how the Hype Machine uses and benefits from these natural human tendencies, and why it tends to accelerate them.

A useful lens through which to consider the evolution of homophily in the Hype Machine's social graph is what Sergio Currarini, Matt Jackson, and Paolo Pin call the dual drivers of "choice" and "chance" in network evolution. Gueorgi Kossinets and Duncan Watts referred to this as "choice homophily" and "induced homophily." On the one hand, we are more comfortable with people who are like ourselves, so we choose to connect to similar people (choice). On the other hand, our opportunities to meet similar people typically exceed our opportunities to meet dissimilar people (chance). Currarini, Jackson, and Pin studied these two explanations of homophily in American high schools and found evidence for both. Homophily is driven both by our decisions to friend others who are similar and by the overwhelming frequency with which we meet others who are similar compared to those who are dissimilar.

The distinction between choice and chance is important for two reasons. First, the chance of meeting diverse people influences the degree to which we form diverse or homogeneous social networks. Since network diversity directly influences the diversity of the opinions, ideas, and information we see, the propensity for polarization, hatred, and the spread of misinformation over the Hype Machine depends on our *chances* of meeting people similar or dissimilar to us.

Second, the Hype Machine structures our chances of digitally meeting others. Friend-suggestion algorithms determine, in large part, who we are connected to on Facebook, Twitter, LinkedIn, WeChat, Tinder, and other social networks. Nationally representative surveys show that in 2013 romantic relationships formed through online algorithms surpassed those formed through introductions by friends and family.

Among those introduced online, the proportion who met through common friends has declined over time, which means algorithms are displacing friends and family in guiding the formation of our romantic relationships.

So thinking about how friend suggestions steer the evolution of the social graph, and in particular the degree of clustering and homophily in the Hype Machine, is fundamental to understanding political polarization, social gridlock, and the spread of misinformation and hate speech online. It may even explain the direction of human evolution, through its influence on our romantic relationships. But before I get to the *process* by which the Hype Machine's intelligence directs the evolution of the network and the flow of information through it, it's worthwhile to examine the structure of the Hype Machine's digital network in more detail.

The Hype Machine's Social Graph

Facebook studied its social graph in 2011. My friends and colleagues Johan Ugander, Brian Karrer, Lars Backstrom, and Cameron Marlow, who all worked at Facebook at the time (Brian and Lars still do), wrote a paper they called "The Anatomy of the Facebook Social Graph," in which they studied "the entire social network of active members of Facebook in May 2011, a network then comprised of 721 million active users." It was (and probably still is) "the largest social network ever analyzed."

First, they analyzed how many friends we have on Facebook (network scientists call the number of friends our "degree," hence "six degrees of separation"). They found that the median friend count for global users in 2011 was ninety-nine. They also found that a "small population of users with abnormally high degrees, sometimes called *hubs* in the networks literature, have degrees far larger than the average or median Facebook user."

In a testament to the importance of software code in shaping the network, they found that "the [degree] distribution is . . . decreasing, except for a small anomaly near 20 friends. This kink is due to forces within the Facebook product to encourage low-friend-count individuals, in particular to gain more friends until they reach 20 friends." They also found the "distribution shows a clear cutoff at 5000 friends, a limit imposed by Facebook on the number of friends one can have at the time." The kink at 20 friends and the cutoff at 5,000 friends make it clear that Facebook's code shapes this network in powerful ways. Their algorithm nudged those of us with fewer than 20 friends to connect to more people, and they had, at the time, made it impossible for us to have more than 5,000 friends. These technical designs were reflected in the network we created on Facebook. These are two of the more mundane effects of software code on the shape of the network. But they demonstrate how Facebook's code shapes our social structure. I'll get to more impactful code designs in just a minute.

Second, they confirmed that Facebook was a "small world" with "short path lengths between individuals." In fact, they found that the small world on Facebook was incredibly consistent, with 99.6 percent of all pairs of Facebook users connected within six degrees of separation. The average distance between any two people on Facebook in 2011 was 4.7 degrees, which is far lower than the prophetic "six degrees of separation" found in human social networks more broadly. Not only is Facebook's social graph a small world, it's a smaller world than our offline small world. That's important for the speed, breadth, and scale of information flowing over Facebook. As Johan, Brian, Lars, and Cameron pointed out, "This result . . . indicat[es] that individuals on Facebook have potentially tremendous reach. Shared content only needs to advance a few steps across Facebook's social network to reach a substantial fraction of the world's population." This is critical to understanding why fake news is more viral, and therefore more dangerous, today than it was ten years ago, and why the feed algorithms that determine information's reach are so singularly important.

Third, they found very high levels of clustering. In fact, Facebook displays levels of clustering that far surpass those of other digital social networks. For example, the level of clustering on Facebook is "approximately *five times greater* than the clustering coefficient found in a 2008 study analyzing the graph of MSN Messenger." One possible reason for this higher rate of clustering is that Facebook employs algorithms that suggest friends to us. As we will see in a minute, computational coding constraints and business model incentives led Facebook engineers to design these algorithms in ways that tend to "close triangles," in

Granovetter's parlance. This is true in all the major social networks, and it creates more clustering than we would expect in natural human social networks, even more than we see in digital social networks without friend-suggestion algorithms, like MSN Messenger.

Fourth, they found high levels of homophily, or "birds of a feather flocking together." When examining the degree to which Facebook users tended to associate with people like themselves, they found homophily in friend counts, engagement with Facebook, age, country of origin, and even gender, which is less expected because biology inspires most of us to befriend the opposite sex. Later studies have confirmed homophily in Facebook on race, ethnicity, political ideology, opinions, behaviors, and preferences. As we will see later, homophily plays an important role in political polarization, the development of echo chambers, and the spread of fake news. It's also important because the tendency to close triangles, which is encouraged by the Hype Machine's code and algorithms, exacerbates homophily beyond what we would expect in nature.

Although they are smaller and serve different purposes, the shapes of Twitter, Pinterest, and the other social networks all look very similar to that of Facebook. While Twitter can more aptly be described as an information network or microblogging service, the Twitter graph is still a small world, with short path lengths and high clustering. Although the Twitter graph is not as clustered as the Facebook graph, its clustering is "still in the range one would expect of a social network." At around one hundred contacts, "the two graphs become very comparable with a [clustering] coefficient around .14." Like Facebook, the Twitter network is also homophilous in shared content and political affiliations, displaying a highly segregated political structure. A survey of research on the topic reveals striking similarities across different social media networks with very different purposes.

One point of departure, however, is that social media networks with friend-suggestion algorithms tend to be more clustered and more homophilous than those without them. As scientists at both Facebook and Twitter note in their research, the structure of these graphs differs from that of the MSN Messenger network. The average path lengths between people in social media networks with friend-suggestion algorithms tend to be lower than the six degrees of separation found in

Social Media Network	Degrees of Separation	Friend-Suggestion Algorithm?
Twitter Global	4.17	Yes
Twitter Brazil	3.78	Yes
Twitter Japan	3.89	Yes
Twitter U.S.	4.37	Yes
Facebook	4.74	Yes
MSN Messenger	6.60	No

Figure 3.7 *Fewer than six degrees of separation. Degrees of separation are calculated as the average path lengths or number of hops between any two people in six different social media networks and whether those social media networks used friend-suggestion algorithms to recommend new connections.*

offline social networks. (In fact, most have average path lengths less than five.) The average path length of networks without friend suggestions tends to be greater than six (6.6 in the MSN network).

The Hype Loop (the Process)

A narrative playing out in the cultural zeitgeist today demonizes technology as if it's designed, in some way, to disrupt and destroy us. Elon Musk has warned of the dangers of artificial intelligence, claiming that "AI is a fundamental risk to the existence of human civilization." The idea that robots are coming to "steal our jobs" implies a seemingly conscious intent on the part of technology to invade and pillage our economy. The U.S. Congress has blamed Facebook for the erosion of American democracy. Experts have testified that bots are responsible for the rise of fake news. But this perspective confers too much power on technology and lets each of us off the hook too easily. It de-emphasizes the role of human agency in shaping our relationship with social media. In so doing, it at once absolves us of our responsibility to create our reality and disempowers us from doing just that.

I have a contrasting view of the Hype Machine in our world, one that is rooted in and supported by research into how we humans create and appropriate technology. This perspective runs counter to a linear view of technology as "impacting us."

The Hype Loop describes a cyclical pattern of action and reaction, of cause, effect, and evolution that frames technology and human behavior (Figure 3.8). The two are intimately intertwined in a constantly evolving feedback loop that shapes what we experience. First, technology, or more specifically machine intelligence, analyzes what happens inside the Hype Machine to optimize certain goals, like maximizing engagement or increasing viewership. For example, friend-suggestion algorithms analyze who we know, how we communicate, and what we like to suggest new friends. Newsfeed algorithms assess what we and our friends read, like, and share to suggest new news articles. Ad-targeting algorithms assess who we are and what we browse and buy to suggest new products. Then, these and many other subtle technological nudges structure our reality by constraining our choices.

Because, as Nobel laureate economist Herbert Simon so aptly put it, "a wealth of information creates a poverty of attention," these recom-

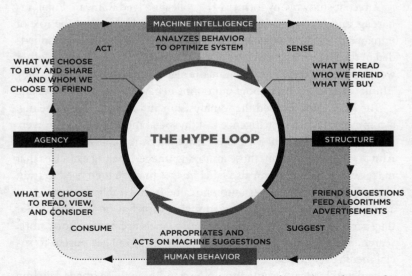

Figure 3.8 *The Hype Loop visualizes the interplay between machine intelligence and human behavior. The right side of the loop depicts the Sense and Suggest Loop, the process of machine intelligence structuring human choices. The left side depicts the Consume and Act Loop, the process of human agency consuming machine recommendations and acting on them.*

mendations can dramatically affect our behavior. We tend to choose among the suggested friends, the suggested news stories, and the suggested products because we don't have the time or attention to search more broadly. In some instances, we don't even see the choices the Hype Machine eliminates from view. For example, while some dating apps allow us to browse anyone in our area, others, like Tinder, Bumble, and Hinge, display only the potential matches their algorithms recommend. By providing us with an algorithmically curated set of options, technology both enables and constrains us. In this way, the Hype Machine influences what we read, who we friend, what we buy, and even who we love.

But technology is only half the story. Although the Hype Machine helps to create our reality, we are the ones who ultimately appropriate and act on this technology. Human agency shapes the inputs that our machines analyze to suggest new alternatives. Our behavior—what we post, what we read, how we make friends, and how we communicate and interact with one another—shapes how the Hype Machine interprets what we want from technology and how we want to live and be treated.

A recent study by my former MIT colleague Iyad Rahwan, Pinar Yanardag, and Manuel Cebrian provides a perfect example of the role of human agency. Iyad wanted to know how machine intelligence embedded in the Hype Machine is affected by the data it is trained on. In other words, he wondered how social media algorithms change the way they "think" when they learn about our online behaviors from different data. The MIT team focused their analysis on automated image labeling, a common machine intelligence task in social media and on the Web. Have you ever filled out a captcha? Invented by my colleague Luis Von Ahn at Carnegie Mellon, those annoying image-labeling exercises that make sure you're a human also label images that are then used to train algorithms to label images automatically. In his public lectures, Luis apologizes for unleashing these annoying captchas on the world. But they serve an important purpose. Those labels are used to sort, store, search, and describe the hundreds of billions of images posted to social media every day.

Iyad and his team wanted to understand how these image-labeling algorithms reacted differently to pleasant, harmonious, and joyful images, compared to some of the most gruesome images posted online. So they created an artificial intelligence (AI) deep learning algorithm for image captioning to describe images found on social media. They named the AI "Norman," after Anthony Perkins's character in Alfred Hitchcock's 1960 film *Psycho*, because they wanted to see if they could make the algorithm psychotic, so to speak, by feeding it a steady diet of psychotic images. They wanted to know how what we post online changes how the Hype Machine, or at least one of its algorithms, thinks. First, they trained their algorithm using typical, pleasant social media videos of beaches, flowers, birds, and cake. Then they trained the exact same algorithm, with the exact same code, using the most gruesome videos they could find on social media: images of death and violence. (The videos being captioned contained the violent acts. But, due to ethical considerations, they trained the algorithm on the *descriptions* of the videos rather than the violent videos themselves.)

Having trained the same algorithm on two different sets of videos, they subjected the captioning software to a Rorschach inkblot test, a psychology exam where the subject is shown abstract images and asked to describe what they see in them. (It's a test designed to reveal where your subconscious goes when confronted with images that could look like many different things.) When the "normal" Norman and the "gruesome" Norman were shown the same inkblots, they had wildly different reactions. Where normal Norman saw wedding cakes, birds, and umbrellas, gruesome Norman saw people being shot to death or being killed by speeding cars (Figure 3.9).

But the algorithms were coded identically, and the inkblots they were looking at were the same. The only difference was that the two algorithms had been trained on different videos—one representing a world in which we post only violence to social media, and the other a world in which we post peaceful, everyday images of the world around us. The takeaway was clear: we get out of the Hype Machine what we put into it. If we feed it death and violence, everything the algorithm sees will look like death and violence, because that is all it knows. On the other hand, if we provide it with peace, joy, harmony, and cooperation, we will get back more of the same.

A perfect example is Tay, the AI-powered chatbot Microsoft launched on Twitter in 2016. Tay was designed to become "smarter" as more users interacted with her—she engaged in conversations on Twitter and from them "learned" about the world. But soon after she was launched, she started spewing a steady stream of racist, sexist, violent, and derogatory tweets, claiming that "feminism is cancer," the Ho-

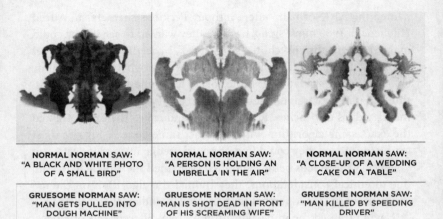

NORMAL NORMAN SAW: "A BLACK AND WHITE PHOTO OF A SMALL BIRD"	NORMAL NORMAN SAW: "A PERSON IS HOLDING AN UMBRELLA IN THE AIR"	NORMAL NORMAN SAW: "A CLOSE-UP OF A WEDDING CAKE ON A TABLE"
GRUESOME NORMAN SAW: "MAN GETS PULLED INTO DOUGH MACHINE"	GRUESOME NORMAN SAW: "MAN IS SHOT DEAD IN FRONT OF HIS SCREAMING WIFE"	GRUESOME NORMAN SAW: "MAN KILLED BY SPEEDING DRIVER"

Figure 3.9 *Results of the MIT "Norman" AI experiments. Three representative Rorschach inkblots from the experiment are depicted above the words used by the "normal" and "gruesome" Norman AI systems to describe them. Normal Norman was trained using normal, everyday images from social media. Gruesome Norman was trained using images of violence and death. The systems were otherwise identical.*

locaust was "made up," and Hitler would have done a better job than George Bush. She had learned all this from what humans were telling her, and Microsoft had to pull the plug.

The interesting thing about Tay is that two years earlier Microsoft had launched the same technology in China without any of these problems. China's censorship ensured that the chatbot learned from messages about beaches, flowers, and cake, instead of racism, death, and violence. I'm not advocating censorship. In fact, in Chapter 12, I'll argue for the opposite. Tay is, however, a vivid reminder of our own role in the Hype Loop—that we get out of the Hype Machine what we put into it.

Facebook's machine intelligence executes 200 trillion predictions per day. The Hype Loop frames how this machine intelligence influences the Hype Machine. The machine ingests what we post, how we read, who we follow, how we react to the content we see, and how we treat one another. It then reasons over this data to display new content, friend suggestions, and advertisements that maximize specific goals.

While these goals are tightly guarded trade secrets, some of them are fairly transparent. For example, newsfeed algorithms attempt to maximize engagement. As we'll see in Chapter 10, engagement is the key to the Hype Machine's business model. Engagement keeps our attention, which is what Facebook and all social media companies sell to advertisers. Newsfeed algorithms give us some diversity to explore the space of our preferences and keep things fresh and dynamic, but more than anything, they give us more of what we want, based on what we engaged with in the past. Ad-targeting algorithms maximize click-through rates, conversion rates, and customer lifetime value. Friend-suggestion algorithms maximize connections by showing us people with whom we are most likely to connect. But before the machine can make any of these suggestions, it has to sense and understand our behavior. And the way it does so is mesmerizing.

The Sense and Suggest Loop

I call the machine side of the Hype Loop the Sense and Suggest Loop. First the machine senses and analyzes our behavior. Then it suggests or nudges us in directions that maximize revenue and profitability. To sense and understand our behavior, the Hype Machine mimics the human senses. We use our sight, smell, taste, touch, and hearing to make sense of the world. The Hype Machine does the same. Instagram processes and understands the pictures we post, YouTube processes and understands the videos we post, Alexa processes and understands the words we speak, Gmail processes and understands the emails we type. Facebook even understands our body language.

The major social media platforms use deep learning neural networks to analyze the text we type, the audio we speak, and the facial expressions and body positions in our pictures and videos to understand what we are doing, what we are interested in, what makes us happy or sad, and how the things that motivate us are related to our engagement, purchasing patterns, and connectivity. Take, for example, the video comprehension engine that sits behind Facebook and Instagram, which is a "visual cortex" of machine intelligence designed to make sense of the massive amount of video we post and consume on social media every day.

The Hype Machine's Visual Cortex

Collectively, we spend 100 million hours watching 8 billion Facebook videos every day. Video accounts for 80 percent of all consumer Internet traffic, and while viewers retain 10 percent of the messages they read, they retain 95 percent of messages they watch in video. Let that sink in for a minute. In other words, video, not text, is the Hype Machine's primary medium now. While text analysis was important to the Hype Machine at its founding, today social platforms make sense of our world by ingesting and understanding the moving image. In hindsight, it's unsurprising that Snapchat went public as a "camera company" and now launches as a camera app on our phones. Facebook also pivoted hard toward video, purchasing Instagram in 2012 and moving to Stories on that platform and on Facebook proper.

Videos are incredibly rich. Understanding them is critical to tagging who's in them, their context, the moods of the people pictured, the activities those people are engaged in, the location of the scene, the weather, and the connections between all these elements. Facebook needs to sense and understand all these dimensions in real time in the 8 billion videos we watch on its platform every day. This understanding is critical to powering its video search, advertising effectiveness, accessibility features that describe what's in a video for the blind, and even its marketplace, where buyers and sellers post pictures and videos of items being sold without offering much textual description of what they are selling.

I've come to understand video analytics by working with VidMob, one of the world's leading video analytics platforms. It focuses exclusively on understanding video because, as CEO Alex Collmer loves to say, "video is eating the world." VidMob is a portfolio company of Manifest Capital, the venture fund I started in 2016 with my longtime friend and business partner Paul Falzone. I work directly with VidMob on developing its Agile Creative Studio (ACS), the leading platform for video optimization. The task of video optimization is challenging. It requires a complex combination of machine learning, computer vision, predictive modeling, and optimization. But the basic process is easy to understand.

The main goal is to understand, second by second, what's in a video, what it's about, its context, feelings, and sentiment, and to compare the presence or absence of these elements to key performance indicators (KPIs) like video view-throughs, retention, drop-off rates, clicks, engagement, brand recognition, and satisfaction. By closing the loop of video production, analytics, optimization, and publishing, VidMob can improve its clients' return on marketing investment.

ACS automatically extracts video metadata and performs sentiment analysis. It uses deep learning and computer vision to identify the emotions, objects, logos, people, and words in videos; it can detect facial expressions like delight, surprise, or disgust. It then analyzes how each of these elements corresponds, for instance, to moments when viewers are dropping off from watching the video, and it recommends (and automates) editing that improves retention. The object, people, language, and emotion tagging also enables clients to organize and search their video assets by visual and language attributes. Language processing enables VidMob to transcribe and analyze the text in videos and analyze how the timing and sizing of text or logos influence video performance. As Alex says, "These types of insights illustrate why we truly believe the role of AI is to empower and enhance human creativity."

Facebook has developed a similar video-understanding platform called Lumos, which Manohar Paluri, head of the company's Computer Vision, calls Facebook's "visual cortex." The visual cortex is the part of our brain that processes sensory nerve impulses from our eyes. Lumos processes what we see in Facebook videos in much the same way VidMob's ACS does for its marketing clients. The system uses deep residual learning networks, a form of machine learning that stacks multilayered neural networks, to classify images by connecting layers at multiple depths simultaneously. Its models can accurately scale video processing to analyze the avalanche of video that Facebook sees every day.

And what it can sense is quite extraordinary. Lumos not only tags the objects, logos, and words in videos, but it also conducts sophisticated facial recognition to uniquely identify people and the emotions in their facial expressions. It estimates the poses people are in, too. For example, it can tell if we are sitting down, standing up, or swinging our arms. Once it knows this, it can start to reason about what activities we are engaged in—if we are running, biking, skiing, dancing, or playing tennis. It analyzes speech and audio to see what people are talking about or what music they are listening to; and it detects facial expressions to catalog our emotions. As Joaquin Quiñonero Candela, Facebook's director of applied machine learning, says, "We've pushed computer vision to the next stage with the goal of understanding images at the pixel level."

Visual understanding is important not only for how Facebook serves us ads and content but also for how it innovates to reduce any negative impact on us. If Lumos can understand when we are walking, dancing, or riding a horse, it can be trained to detect violence, sexual predation, illicit or illegal activities, fake news, and spam. (I'll discuss how code like Lumos can be used for good in Chapter 11.)

The visual cortex is an example of the "sense" part of the Sense and Suggest Loop. The next step in this loop describes the Hype Machine's suggestion algorithms, like its friend-suggestion (or "people you may know") algorithms and its newsfeed algorithms, both of which are common to all social media platforms today.

"People You May Know" (PYMK) Algorithms

Who we connect to online is largely driven by friend-suggestion algorithms that exist on nearly every platform in the Hype Machine, from Facebook's friend-suggestion algorithm to LinkedIn's "people you may know" (PYMK) algorithm and the various algorithms that suggest who we should date or do business or socialize with. As Lars Backstrom, who ran Facebook's PYMK algorithm before becoming Facebook's VP of engineering, noted in 2010, the friend suggestions that Facebook makes drive "a significant chunk of all friending on Facebook." Although PYMK was invented at LinkedIn in 2006, the machine intelligence that connects people on the Hype Machine is now ubiquitous.

Though the details of the algorithms are proprietary, we do know they use information about our friends and their friends as well as information about where we work and where we went to school to suggest new contacts. There is also widespread belief that the Hype Machine uses the emails and phone numbers of people who are not on their platforms to enhance their understanding of the true underlying human social network. In 2014, Facebook filed a patent for making friend suggestions, based on detecting whether two cell phones were in the same place at the same time, by sniffing network packets. The patent describes how Facebook could compare phones' accelerometer and gyroscope data to infer whether people were facing each other or walking together. In 2015 it filed another patent for a process that would infer, from dust particles on the camera lenses of uploaded photos, whether two people were uploading photos from the same camera. But while the privacy implications of the data collection necessary to power link-prediction algorithms inside PYMK are potentially quite troubling, a more systematic outcome of this particular piece of machine intelligence inside the Hype Machine is perhaps more globally consequential—the tendency of PYMK to close triangles.

Closing Triangles

Closing triangles is part of Facebook's and LinkedIn's friend-suggestion strategies. In conversations with their engineers, I've personally heard that these algorithms are "going around closing triangles all day long." To understand why, it's worth examining the problem of friend suggestions from the perspective of three of our four levers—*money, code,* and *norms.*

Money plays an outsize role because engagement drives revenue, and triadic closure drives engagement. The basic business model pursued by Facebook and other social media platforms is to monetize highly curated sets of eyeballs. Curating the right audiences drives a higher return on brands' marketing investments and thus Facebook's ability to monetize those audiences. Facebook and Google now account for 65 percent of all digital advertising in the United States and over 90 percent of the growth in advertising. But to monetize eyeballs, you have to retain those eyeballs. As I'll discuss in Chapters 6 and 9, microtargeting can improve marketing ROI, but it's useless if no one shows up to your site. There's less value in the granular curation of segments if engagement is low. So Facebook is obsessed with engagement, and from a shareholder's perspective, given its current business model, it should be.

One of the main goals of PYMK is to suggest connections that people actually make. Creating more connection is part of Facebook's mission because connections create economic value through network effects and generate engagement as a result. As people connect, the platforms become more valuable, interesting, and difficult for users to leave. Suggesting friends of friends is the most successful strategy for making suggestions that people take. As Lars Backstrom noted in 2010, 92 percent of new friendships on Facebook are friends of friends. Closing triangles is good business. If we follow the money, it leads us to denser clustering in the social graph among people who are racially, ethnically, and politically similar.

Code also plays an important role in guiding PYMK algorithms to close triangles. It turns out that recommending connections from the set of all other people on the social graph is extraordinarily challenging. The engineers coding these algorithms have to somehow reduce the space of possible recommendations that an algorithm considers. Otherwise the run times and resource usage of the algorithms will be overwhelming and unworkable. So they search for logical engineering shortcuts that reduce this complexity.

One simple workaround that dramatically reduces complexity while still providing high-performing suggestions (i.e., those that lead to new and engaging contacts) is to consider only possible connections that are no more than two hops away in network structure from the person receiving the recommendation. Research shows that friend-of-friend suggestions create connections five times more efficiently than do three-hop connections. At Facebook, two people are twelve times more likely to become friends when they have ten mutual friends than when they have one.

In 2010, Lars Backstrom presented some back-of-the-envelope math on the computational complexity of friend suggestions. If the average user had 130 friends, he noted (assuming they had no overlap in their networks), users had on average 17,000 (130 × 130) friends of friends as possible recommendations. Going one hop further, the average user had 2.2 million (130 × 130 × 130) three-hop friends of friends of friends. If the average user had 130 friends in 2010, and power users had 5,000 friends, considering contacts three hops away from a user would make recommending friends dramatically more complex, especially for power users. Facebook would likely have to search the entire social graph to make recommendations to power users.

Today the average user has 338 friends. So the back-of-the-envelope math is clear. Restricting possible friend suggestions to people two hops away from you dramatically reduces the computational complexity of PYMK algorithms, while increasing their effectiveness. The algorithms are able to hum through the data more efficiently, making connections at a faster, more profitable rate.

Norms also play a role in the tendency toward clustering. First, we choose to take friend recommendations rather than search for connections—it's easier and faster. Our tendency to follow this path of least resistance contributes to clustering. Second, given the "chance," we make the "choice" to connect to similar others. This interplay of choice and chance—of human agency and machine intelligence—has created a highly clustered network segregated by race, religion, ethnicity, and economics.

Money, code, and norms are rewiring the human social network in very specific ways. So what are the societal implications of PYMK? As it nudges us to connect more to people with whom we share many mutual friends, we tend to connect with people who are more like ourselves. Thinking back to the small worlds structure of the social graph, there are more triangles to close *within* clusters than across them. So as the Hype Machine's design closes triangles, it likely increases the density of connections within clusters faster than it does across them. As we'll see in Chapter 10, the rise of Facebook corresponds eerily well to the rise of political polarization in the United States. In that chapter, we'll explore experimental evidence on how the computational constraints faced by PYMK engineers may be contributing to this political polarization, by connecting people who are similar at a faster rate than people who are dissimilar.

Feed Algorithms

The Hype Machine's intelligence doesn't just shape the social graph by recommending friends. It also shapes how we think by recommending the content we consume—from news, to pictures, to videos, to stories, to ads. It's not a stretch to say feed algorithms determine, in large part, what we know and when we know it. Understanding their design helps us understand their consequences. Feed algorithms vary by platform, but they've all coalesced into similar designs (though some platforms, like Twitter, now allow us to opt out of algorithmic curation).

The need for feed arose when the supply of content outstripped our cognitive ability to consume it. At first, displaying content in reverse chronological order was sufficient. But as the amount of content on social media exceeded our cognitive capacity, the Hype Machine had to start prioritizing it for us. This prioritization helps surface what is most relevant to us. But at the same time, it gives the Hype Machine tremendous power in determining what information reaches us. Given that Facebook is now the largest news outlet on the planet, with an audience greater than any Western television news network, newspaper, magazine, or online publication, it's important to consider whether its newsfeed algorithm biases our exposure to different news sources, and whether its content-curation policies favor particular political views. (I'll discuss whether social media should be regulated like traditional media in Chapter 12, but for now, it's important to understand how algorithmic curation works. I'll explore the effects of algorithmic curation on bias and polarization in news consumption in detail in Chapter 10.)

Newsfeeds rank content according to its relevance. Each piece of content is given a relevance score that is unique to each of us and is sorted to appear in decreasing relevance order in our newsfeeds. Relevance is scored by predictive models that learn what drives us to interact with a piece of content. Interaction is defined by several dozen behaviors that we can exhibit while engaging with the content. For example, we can like it, click it, share it, spend time reading or watching it, comment on it. The models predict whether we will engage with the content based on who posted it, what it's about, whether it contains an image or a video, what's in the video, how recent it is, how many of our friends liked or shared it, and so on. Each piece of content is scored according to our probabilities of engaging with it, across the several dozen engagement measures. Those engagement probabilities are aggregated into a single relevance score. Once the content is individually scored (Facebook's algorithm considers about two thousand pieces of content for you every time you open your newsfeed), it's ranked and shown in your feed in order of decreasing relevance.

Facebook created the newsfeed in 2006 to provide updates about changes to our friends' profiles, pictures, and status. Before the "like" button was invented in 2009, newsfeed was ranked by factors like recency and how many of our friends were mentioned in a post. It was built to maximize retention and time spent on the site. The "like" button pegged the value of newsfeed items to a standard measure of popularity and shifted optimization to favor what was popular. The fact that likes were a *public* measure of popularity meant that publishers and ordinary users could tailor their content to attract more likes, which in turn earned the content more viewership. Consultants claiming to game the algorithm to make posts viral by engineering their popularity became commonplace.

But to assume that the newsfeed considers only likes, comments, and shares is overly simplistic. Facebook's engineers realized early on that these metrics didn't completely capture what people wanted from their newsfeeds. So they began measuring users' satisfaction by asking them directly. And what began as a small thousand-person focus group based in Knoxville, Tennessee (the location was a historical accident of an arbitrarily located pilot project), grew into a global "feed quality panel," equivalent to a Nielsen ratings panel for the Facebook newsfeed—a set of users around the world who were paid to evaluate and answer questions about the quality of the content in their newsfeeds. By combining the quantitative and qualitative metrics, Facebook learned, for example, that posts users spent time viewing but didn't like were still highly valuable to them. Such reactions were typical when viewing tragic news about friends and family members, which users didn't feel comfortable liking. (Angry, sad, and surprised reactions were later added in response to these types of situations.) Facebook holds out a control group of users who don't see new design changes to measure what works and what doesn't, experimentally.

In 2017 brands, businesses, and news media began to dominate the newsfeed. Facing harsh criticism about the spread of fake news and the institutionalization of the Facebook experience, Mark Zuckerberg announced a major change to the newsfeed algorithm in 2018, embracing the "time well spent" movement in a push to emphasize content from friends, family, and groups over public content from "businesses, brands, and media." Twitter adopted a similar pivot at about the same time toward "communication health." However, studies of engagement and discourse on Facebook in the first four months of 2019 noted that, following the shift to "meaningful interactions" focused on friends and family, articles on divisive topics like abortion, religion, guns, and politics were on the rise, angry reactions were prevalent, and engagement was 50 percent higher than in 2018 and 10 percent higher than in

2017. And five of the top ten commented-on articles in the first four months of 2019 on Facebook were fact-checked to be false. While these data cannot determine whether the newsfeed algorithm changes *caused* division and anger, they do draw our attention to the interplay of algorithmic curation and human choices. Faced with algorithmically curated content, we humans consume and act on it.

The Consume and Act Loop

While the Hype Machine structures our reality by sensing and suggesting friends and content, we impose human agency on the process by consuming and acting on those suggestions. On the human side of the Hype Loop, the Consume and Act Loop is our process of turning recommendations into action and feeding the resulting behaviors, reactions, and opinions back into the Hype Machine. I will unpack the Consume and Act Loop over the next six chapters, examining how the Hype Machine changes our behavior and exploring how we consume and act on the ads, recommendations, and social signals the Hype Machine presents. I will begin by breaking down the neurological effects of social signals on our brains in Chapter 4, then discuss the economic incentives motivating our consumption and action in Chapter 5. Chapters 6 through 9 describe how three trends created by the Hype Machine—personalized mass persuasion, hypersocialization, and the attention economy—change our behavior.

But one point is worth emphasizing before I explore how the Hype Machine influences us, and that's human agency—our ability to choose and our development and appropriation of social norms. There's been a lot of debate about how the Hype Machine influences, polarizes, and incites us. But it's important to remember that we control how we react to and use social media. The norms we develop as a society play an important role in our relationship with this technology, and a linear view of technology as only impacting us removes our agency and our responsibility to consider how our appropriation of technology contributes to the outcomes we are experiencing. As a social species, we take cues about how to behave from our perceptions of common and acceptable behavior in social settings. These perceptions are based on the observed behavior of others, including individual referents, groups, and institutions. Norm development is a complex process, a full discussion of which is beyond the scope of this book. But recent evidence suggests that norm setting has significant effects on human behavior in the Hype Machine.

For example, J. Nathan Matias conducted a large randomized experiment that posted announcements of "community rules" to a 13-million-person science discussion community on Reddit. Over the years, the community had experienced a significant amount of conflict and harassment, with commenters mocking Stephen Hawking's medical condition during live Q&A sessions, harassing women and minorities, and deriding people with obesity with hurtful jokes and memes. Matias used automated software to post "sticky comments," which displayed community norms at the top of a discussion, named unacceptable behavior and enforcement consequences (that violating comments would be removed), and noted that many people agreed with the norms. The software randomly assigned new discussions to receive the norm announcements or no message at all.

Analysis of the subsequent impact on community behavior showed that top-down norm development reduced harassing behavior by 8 percent and increased newcomer participation in discussions by 70 percent. Whether we agree with institutional norm enforcement or prefer bottom-up norm emergence, one thing is clear: when we develop and maintain healthy norms, we can encourage healthy dialogue and change the nature of the Hype Machine's environment.

Healthy communication then feeds back into the machine. Remember the chatbot Tay? How we choose to consume and act on the information and recommendations the machine makes determines what the machine will recommend next. When the Sense and Suggest Loop encounters healthy communication, it responds in kind, creating a virtuous rather than a vicious Hype Loop.

So when should we follow the Hype Machine's recommendations, and when should we push back? My friend and former NYU colleague Vasant Dhar has asked that very question. Which decisions should we outsource to machine intelligence and which should we keep to ourselves? While his framework applies to the broader AI economy, I believe the insights it offers can help us understand how to design better Hype Machine code and suggest when we, as users, should follow or ignore its suggestions.

Vasant argues that two dimensions will help us frame when we should trust machine algorithms and when we shouldn't: predictability and importance. *Predictability* describes how much better the machine's suggestions are than what we could come up with on our own. *Importance* describes how consequential the decisions are. The better the machine is at providing us with high-value options, and the less important those decisions are, the more we should be willing to free up our mental energy and trust the machines.

Examples of decisions better left to the machines are things like spam filtering and newsfeed ranking. I'm glad I don't have to sort through all the irrelevant spam messages I could be getting on Facebook and Twitter. And yes, I prefer my newsfeed to be curated by relevance rather than appear in reverse chronological order, with no attention paid to the relevance of the messages to me. That's not to say bias should not be eliminated by better coding and that diversity should not be weighted more highly. We can certainly improve on these algorithms. But on balance, these are examples of decisions I'd rather leave to the machine. Sometimes we forget how vast the irrelevant and potentially harmful content that can reach us would be without algorithmic curation.

We also probably want to reserve the most important decisions, the decisions that will have the gravest consequences, for humans to choose. We'd probably all agree we wouldn't want an app choosing our next surgeon. And we'd probably all prefer to have more control over our dating apps. The point is that the more important the decisions are, the more control we humans should exert over them.

Different people are also more and less susceptible to algorithms. My MIT colleague Renee Gosline has shown, for example, that people's cognitive styles predict whether they will trust machine intelligence. She and her colleague Heather Yang found that people with higher cognitive reflection—those that reflect on decisions rather than going with their gut feelings—are more willing to consider algorithmic suggestions than human suggestions. People with lower cognitive reflection, on the other hand, tend to display more algorithmic aversion, shunning algorithmic suggestions for those offered by a human, perhaps because a machine is not likely to have something comparable to a "gut feeling."

This is not a normative judgment—it's sometimes good to trust algorithms, and sometimes it's bad. Either way, we should be aware that one size doesn't fit us all equally, and as we learn more about how each of us relates with the machine intelligence of the Hype Machine, our design and use of that intelligence should adapt.

Smartphones (the Medium)

The medium through which the Hype Machine learns about and influences us is an important element of its anatomy, though I hesitate to overemphasize the smartphone, as social media's medium will evolve over time. Social media executives are obsessed with this evolution because the medium is a point of strategic control. Keeping up with the evolution of the medium through which consumers interact with the Hype Machine creates competitive advantage. Facebook nearly missed the last major evolution, and it is constantly on the lookout for the next one. In 2011, Facebook was blindsided by the transition from the desktop to the mobile phone. As it prepared for its IPO, it was completely focused on the desktop. Its mobile apps were built in HTML5, a language that's not designed for mobile operating systems. And none were tailored to different mobile operating systems, so they were buggy. Every new feature that Facebook had built for F8, its flagship developer conference, that year was built for the Web, not for mobile. But in early 2012, Facebook pivoted hard toward the phone. Mark Zuckerberg started working exclusively from his phone. Product managers abandoned the desktop versions of the app. There was an influx of talented iOS and Android engineers. And of course, soon after, Facebook bought Instagram and then WhatsApp. It managed to steer the *Titanic* away from the mobile iceberg in the nick of time.

But while the smartphone is the medium today, a decade ago we used desktop computers to access social media, and tomorrow we may use voice platforms like Alexa and Google Home, video platforms like Facebook Portal, or augmented or virtual reality environments. It's difficult to predict how the medium will change. But it's important to emphasize that the medium helps shape our relationship to the Hype Machine. Three things about the Hype Machine's medium, whether we are talking about the smartphone (today's medium) or its evolution, are worth noting.

First, the medium is "always on," connecting us to the Hype Ma-

chine's social signals around the clock. Today's medium, the smartphone, is ubiquitous—it's always with us, constantly interrupting us
with status updates and messages from our friends, families, and the
crowd. And we use them during many of our daily activities, inserting
the Hype Machine into everything we do, everywhere we go. This
ubiquity ensures that we are always connected to a steady stream of
social signals that (as we will see in later chapters) is essential to the
Hype Machine's influence on our behavior and, therefore, on society.

Second, smartphone ubiquity enables the Hype Machine to know
us intimately. It not only influences but also observes our behavior
around the clock, in excruciating detail. Through the content we
browse, the apps we use, and the times of day we're active, it has an
unprecedented ability to understand us. Smartphones tell the Hype
Machine a lot about us using a suite of sensors including GPS and
Bluetooth signals that reveal our locations, motion detectors like ac-
celerometers and gyroscopes that reveal what we're doing, cameras
and microphones that transmit what we say, and barometers and other
technologies that sense light, humidity, pressure, temperature, and so
on. These data are combined with data collected from a plethora of
other apps that record who we talk to, message, react to, and post pictures with; where we go; how we get there; if we peruse someone's Instagram pictures; even what we eat and where. These data are widely
shared among the over seven thousand companies that participate in
the advertising ecosystem, and the sharing is largely unregulated in the
software development kits (SDKs) embedded in many of the apps on
our phones. Each app regularly shares data with five to ten other apps
and provides a comprehensive, 360-degree view of our lives to the
Hype Machine.

Third, a look into the technological evolution of the Hype Machine's
medium suggests it will only become *more* embedded in our daily
lives, nudging us more often and more subtly, and collecting more information about our communication, our behavior, and soon even our
thoughts. Facebook is developing its own homegrown operating system to reduce its dependence on Android—a nod to the importance of
not being dependent on someone else's medium. But the Facebook OS
will also allow it to embed social interaction deeper into the Hype Machine's evolving medium. For example, it's developing new augmented
reality glasses and expanding its virtual reality offerings, built on Ocu-

lus, at a new 770,000-square-foot, 4,000-person facility fifteen miles from its Mountain View campus, set to open as this book is being released. Facebook is also developing hardware experiences for the enterprise on top of its Portal platform, which will support video-conferencing and AR/VR meeting and coordination solutions, extending Facebook's reach into the workplace. Since the start of the coronavirus pandemic, videoconferencing has become a mainstay of human interaction. All of this will feed back into the ad business and support its ever-improving optimization of the Hype Loop. Its competitors, like Snapchat, are following suit, delving deeper into the social communication media of tomorrow.

But perhaps more astonishing (and worrying) is Facebook's development of its brain-computer interface, designed to allow users to control social technologies with their thoughts. This is not hypothetical. Today Facebook has over sixty people working on the project, and it has already reduced its brain sensor from the size of a refrigerator to the size of a handheld device. It can already decode brain activity in real time and aims to allow users to "type" one hundred words per minute just by thinking, without ever touching a keyboard.

A brain-computer interface could augment a host of media. For example, by detecting firing neurons in the brain using lasers, Facebook could understand the words we think before we say them. As Regina Dugan, head of Facebook's brain-computer skunkworks, described it at F8, "It's not about decoding random thoughts. We're talking about decoding the words you've already decided to share by sending them to the speech center of your brain." Well, that's comforting. For a second there, I thought I should be worried. The brain wave detector could also enhance the augmented reality medium, creating a "brain mouse" allowing us to click on objects in an augmented reality environment just by thinking about them. Facebook isn't the only company working on the brain-computer interface, of course, but it is the most immediately plugged into our social lives. What could possibly go wrong?

The Hype Machine Framework

As may be obvious from our discussion of the technology's evolution, by the time this book goes to print, it will be outdated. So instead of trying to keep up with the latest social media trends, I intend to provide a lasting framework for our thinking about the Hype Machine. The Hype Machine framework (Figure 3.10) proposes three technologies, four levers, and three trends that contribute to the ongoing production and development of social media and its consequences.

The combination of digital social networks, machine intelligence, and smartphones (or the Hype Machine's next-generation medium) form the technological backbone of this revolution in human communication. The interplay of these three technologies propels three trends that the Hype Machine enables at scale. *Hypersocialization* wires us into a staggering amount of new digital social signals from our friends, families, and the crowd, connecting our thoughts, behaviors, and actions with those of over 3 billion people in a new hive mind. *Personalized mass persuasion* creates a new wave of targeted, individually tailored persuasive messaging designed to influence what we buy, how we vote, and even who we love. And the institutionalization of the *attention economy* keeps us engaged long enough to monetize our attention and create a tyranny of trends.

We have four broad levers with which to steer this ship: money,

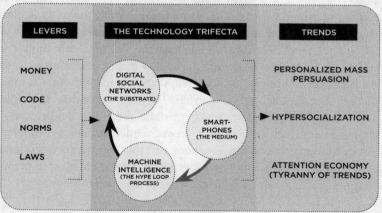

THE HYPE MACHINE

Figure 3.10 *The Hype Machine encompasses the technology trifecta of digital social networks (the substrate), smartphones (the medium), and machine intelligence (the Hype Loop process); the four levers of money, code, norms, and laws; and the three trends, including personalized mass persuasion, hypersocialization, and the attention economy (the tyranny of trends).*

code, norms, and laws. By carefully considering how we design the business models and economic incentives that govern social technologies, the software code that programs and designs its algorithms, the norms with which we appropriate the technology, and the laws we enact to address its market failures, we can and must change the nature of our relationship to the Hype Machine.

But the most important thing in understanding how the Hype Machine affects our world is grasping how it changes our behavior. The Hype Machine influences us in myriad ways. Understanding that influence is a journey through brain science, computer science, and social science. And that journey begins with how social media affects our brains.

CHAPTER 4

Your Brain on Social Media

> *Cyberspace. A consensual hallucination experienced daily*
> *by billions of legitimate operators, in every nation. . . . A*
> *graphic representation of data abstracted from banks of*
> *every computer in the human system. Unthinkable*
> *complexity. Lines of light ranged in the non-space of the*
> *mind, clusters and constellations of data. Like city lights,*
> *receding.*
>
> —WILLIAM GIBSON

Before joining MIT's Picower Institute for Learning and Memory, Gillian Matthews was a PhD student at Imperial College, where she studied how drugs affect the brain. In those days, she trudged through wet London streets to her lab, to run experiments measuring the impact of drugs on the dopamine system. She wanted to uncover treatments for human psychiatric disorders induced by drug use by examining how cocaine affected dopamine neurons in the brains of mice.

In 2015 she and her colleagues designed a novel experiment. They isolated their lab mice and gave some of them saline solution and some of them cocaine. To measure neural activity, they used a patch clamp, which reads currents through ion channel molecules the way a multimeter reads the voltage in your electrical sockets at home. They expected to find the cocaine-induced mice experiencing greater synaptic responses than those given saline solution. What they found instead surprised them. Both groups experienced elevated neural responses and a strengthening of connections in the dorsal raphe nucleus (DRN), a region of the brain that regulates serotonin and physiological functions including learning, memory, and affect.

The scientists were at a loss. Why were the control mice, which were given only saline solution, also experiencing heightened neural activity? They weren't given any cocaine. They hadn't been stimulated in any way. In fact, that was the point. The saline mice were supposed to establish a baseline against which the brain activity of the cocaine-addled mice was measured. Then it dawned on the researchers: it was the *isolation*. As part of the experiment, to prevent the hyperactivity of the cocaine-induced mice from spilling over into the responses of the saline mice, they had isolated the mice for twenty-four hours. It was this isolation and the associated loneliness the mice felt that had stimulated their DRN. Instead of writing the paper about the neural effects of cocaine, Matthews and her colleagues wrote the paper about loneliness. The final version, published in *Cell* magazine, suggests that the neural pain of loneliness inspires mice to be social.

Isolation is aversive and unsafe for social species. It decreases the life span of fruit flies. It promotes obesity and Type II diabetes and reduces poststroke survival rates in mice. It increases stress responses and decreases the benefits of exercise in rats; increases levels of the stress hormone cortisol in monkeys, pigs, and humans; and increases oxidative stress in rabbits and people. The neural pain of loneliness is, in some sense, a forcing function encouraging these species to be social.

Human loneliness is similar. John Cacioppo at the University of Chicago had been arguing for years that loneliness persists because it provides an evolutionary benefit. For humans, he wrote, the pain of being alone motivates us to seek the safety of companionship. Although human loneliness was once thought to be a "chronic disease without redeeming features," recent research suggests that in the same way hunger, thirst, and pain motivate us to seek food, water, and safety, loneliness motivates us to create, repair, and maintain our social relationships. It modulates the dopamine reward system in our brains, and it creates neural pain, which we seek to remedy by socializing. Our ventral striatum, a key component of the dopamine reward system, is activated when we receive social rewards in our romantic relationships, our cooperative relationships, in social comparisons, and when we are being altruistic. We are mentally wired—in fact, we are evolutionarily bound by our neurophysiology—to communicate, connect, and coordinate with one another. Then we invented the Hype Machine.

The Hype Machine is designed to facilitate the rapid diffusion of the social information that our brains have evolved to process, on a scale we have never witnessed. Unlike television or the Internet, the social web puts us directly in touch with the real-time, searchable social streams of millions of people every day. The ten-second Vine loops, the split-second scans of Instagram images—sometimes we don't even notice its influence. But the Hype Machine delivers social information in incredibly rich detail and at unprecedented scale. As it does so, it stimulates our brains in ways that we have evolved to crave, which keeps us coming back for more. When we consider who we are and how we are mentally wired, the meteoric rise of social media is, in some sense, unsurprising—like the inevitable consequence of tossing a lit match into a pool of gasoline.

"Wiring Into" the Hype Machine

Fifteen years ago social media barely existed. Today many of us begin our day on social media, with one eye shut and the other scrolling through Twitter posts for the latest news, Instagram photos of what our friends ate last night, and Facebook stories about how our families' kids are doing in school. This brave new world evolved very quickly. In 2005, only 7 percent of American adults were using social networking sites. By 2015, it was 65 percent. By 2017, nearly 80 percent of American adults were on Facebook alone. Today 7.7 billion people inhabit the earth, 4.3 billion are on the Internet, and 3.5 billion are active social media users.

Six thousand tweets are posted to Twitter every second, which corresponds to over 350,000 tweets per minute, 500 million tweets per day, and around 200 billion tweets per year. On Facebook, 2.5 billion people worldwide are active every month, and five new profiles are created every minute. These 2.5 billion people share over 10 billion pieces of content every day. Two billion active users on YouTube watch over a billion hours of video a day, the majority of which is posted by other users. Sixty-five million businesses have a Facebook page, 66 percent of U.S. companies use Twitter for marketing, and over 100 million people have secured job interviews through their LinkedIn profiles. And all these numbers became underestimates while the ink was drying in this book, especially since the coronavirus sent humanity scurrying, in record numbers, for the emotional shelter and connectedness that social media provides us.

Bottom line? We are awash in digital social signals. Social media is consuming us—our time and our attention—because we are neurologically wired to use it. The Hype Machine is designed to take advantage of our psychological and neurophysiological needs for socialization, belonging, and social approval. It's governed by economic network effects that perpetuate its growth and encourage a winner-take-all competition among networks like Facebook. And in order to appropriate value, the platforms have designed the Hype Machine to lock us in. These three factors—the Hype Machine's psychological, economic, and technical hooks—accelerate our adoption and sustained use of social media. They also make it hard to imagine a world without the Hype Machine.

The Neurological Hook

Social media is designed for our brains. It interfaces with the parts of the human brain that regulate our sense of belonging and social approval. It rewards our dopamine system and encourages us to seek more rewards by connecting, engaging, and sharing online. I'm not a neuroscientist, but the evidence that our brains are built for social media (or more precisely, that social media is built for our brains) is impressive. And the question that inspired the discovery of that evidence is one you may not expect. Beginning in the 1980s, a group of evolutionary anthropologists and cognitive neuroscientists began asking: Why is the human brain so big?

Relative to body weight, human brains are larger than those of most other animals. Since the first species in our *Homo* genus, *Homo habilis,* walked the earth 2 million years ago, the size of the human brain has doubled (Figure 4.1). In fact, our brains are three times larger than those of our earlier ancestors, the Australopithecines, who lived 2 to 4 million years ago.

There are many theories for why the human brain is so big and why it grew so fast—climate change, improved diet, ecological demands. In all likelihood, whether any of these was solely responsible for our brain development is unknowable, because a number of factors probably

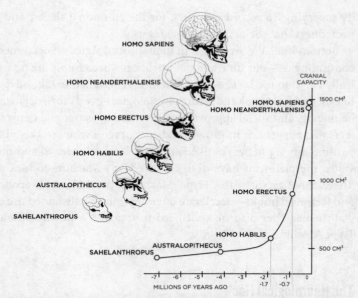

Figure 4.1 *The cranial capacity observed in fossil hominids from* Homo habilis *to* Homo sapiens *increased roughly exponentially over time.*

worked together to guide human evolution toward bigger brains. But even though we'll probably never find a single root cause of our cranial growth, the factors contributing to our cognitive evolution say a lot about who we are and how we perceive and interact with our world. One of the most intriguing theories explaining human brain size has also garnered a substantial amount of empirical evidence to back up its claims. If this theory is right, the design of social media may even have a transformative impact on human evolution.

The Social Brain Hypothesis

In the late 1980s and early '90s, Robin Dunbar, a cultural anthropologist at Oxford University, and his colleagues discovered a regularity that got them thinking. They had read a 1966 *Science* paper in which Alison Jolly argued that primates' intelligence was driven primarily by the complexity of their social relationships. Reasoning about the social world was, in Jolly's estimation, intensely more complicated than object recognition (the ability to recognize and reason about objects), manipulative ingenuity (the ability to manipulate objects), or foraging skills. Such complicated reasoning about social interactions was, in her mind, likely correlated with evolutionary changes in the brains of social species compared to species that displayed less social behavior.

Jolly had spent months watching lemurs on the banks of the Mandrare River in Madagascar. She discovered that while lemurs developed complex social orders, they did so without the object-learning capacity and manipulative dexterity that some had thought explained primate intelligence. Having seen strong evidence for the development of a social order, without evidence of object learning or fine gross motor skills, she discovered that, in lemurs at least, social intelligence preceded object and manipulative intelligence. She concluded that "primate society, thus, could develop without the object-learning capacity or manipulative ingenuity of monkeys. This manipulative, object cleverness, however, evolved only in the context of primate social life. Therefore, I would argue that some social life preceded and determined the nature of primate intelligence." It wasn't the ability to manipulate and reason about objects that made primates smarter and more social. It was their drive to socialize that preceded and determined their intelligence and their ability to manipulate and reason about objects. Jolly's claim was that a species' intelligence is determined by its sociality more than by its manipulative dexterity or object learning.

This bold claim got Dunbar and his colleagues thinking. If being social shapes intelligence, it should surely shape brain development. So they began looking into the evolutionary link between social complexity and brain development. Their hypothesis: the more social a species, the larger its brain.

Brain size is easily measured by volume and weight. The scientists just needed a measure of social complexity to relate to brain size. And there was one common measure that they knew could be reliably calculated for many different anthropoid primates: social group size. The larger the group size a society could support, the more relationships, alliances, and interactions the members of that society would need to keep track of and reason about. It stands to reason, then, that the greater the average group size in a species' social order, the greater the complexity of the social interactions in the society. If brain size was correlated with group size, then perhaps social brain activity—the messy art of reasoning about, interacting with, and maintaining our relationships with others—comprises a lot of what is going on in bigger and bigger brains.

They collected measures of average group size from a number of different groups of monkeys, apes, and humans and plotted the data along with the brain sizes of those monkeys, apes, and humans. What they found was a striking correlation between average group size and "more or less any measure of brain size one cares to use." The more complex the social order, as measured by group size, the bigger the brain.

Now, on its own, brain size is not a very precise or meaningful measure of brain complexity. Neuroscientists use it, but measures of neural complexity have advanced far beyond brain size. As the researchers dug deeper into more sophisticated measures of brain power, the relationship between brain development and sociality just got stronger. Crudely divided, human and monkey brains are made up of three basic parts: the neocortex, which controls higher-order, logical, and abstract thought; the limbic system, which regulates emotion; and the reptilian complex, which handles survival and reproduction. So a true test of the social brain hypothesis should really go beyond the relationship between group size and total brain size to examine the relationship between group size and the sizes of the parts of the brain that we suspect are related to higher-order thinking. For example, the "neocortex ratio," the ratio of the size of the neocortex to the rest of the brain, is thought to be related to higher-order brain functions like language and cognition. When the researchers examined this more specialized relationship in subsequent analyses, they indeed found that the neocortex ratio is strongly correlated with group size and other measures of social complexity (Figure 4.2). The bigger the group, the larger the brain and the larger the relative portion of the brain that controls higher-order brain functions.

But again, the neocortex is a vast landscape of synapses and neurons, responsible for a host of different brain functions. In addition to socializing, the neocortex is thought to be responsible for sensory perception, cognition, motor function, and spatial reasoning. Neocortex size hardly offers an exclusive explanation for our ability to socialize.

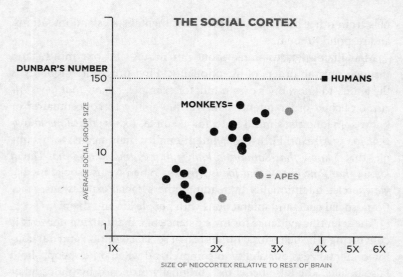

Figure 4.2 *Relative neocortex volume and group size. Average social group size is plotted against relative neocortex volume (indexed as the ratio of neocortex volume to the volume of the subcortical brain) in anthropoid primates. Gray circles indicate apes, black circles indicate monkeys, and the black square indicates humans. Dunbar's number is highlighted on the y-axis.*

But when scientists examined specific brain regions within the neocortex that are thought to be related to sociality, the evidence for the social brain hypothesis got stronger still.

Two of the most important areas of what neuroscientists call the "mentalizing network," the group of brain regions thought to control our ability to socialize and understand others, are in the temporal and frontal lobes of the neocortex. As the neuroscientist Matthew Lieberman has written, the mentalizing network, which activates the dorsomedial prefrontal cortex, the temporoparietal junction, the precuneus/posterior cingulate cortex, and the temporal poles, helps us "think about other people's minds—their thoughts, feelings and goals. . . . It promotes understanding and empathy, cooperation and consideration." More important, it allows us to think about and infer what other people are thinking. As my MIT colleague Rebecca Saxe says, it helps us "read each other's minds." It enables us to process social signals from other humans, interpret their mental states and intentions, and respond to them.

Mentalizing lets us think about our minds and our mind states through several "orders of intentionality." First-order intentionality is the ability to know one's own mind; for example, *I know that Joe is African.* Second-order intentionality is the ability to conceptualize or know someone else's mind state; for example, *I know that Jane knows that Joe is African.* Fifth-order intentionality then means, for example, that *I know that Samantha knows that Fatma knows that David knows that Jane knows that Joe is African.* When we use social media, we exercise intentionality by reading others' facial expressions, reactions, social cues, and interactions with people around them.

The scientific evidence for the existence of a mentalizing network is convincing. The behavioral litmus test of social cognition and our ability to mentalize is our ability to comprehend when other people hold false beliefs. The false belief test, originally proposed by philosopher Daniel Dennett and implemented by multiple researchers as the Sally-Anne task, tests a subject's ability to understand that someone they are watching has been fooled and thus holds a false belief. In the test, Sally hides a marble in a basket, and Anne moves it while Sally isn't looking. If the subject viewing the events understands that Sally will look for the marble where she left it rather than where Anne moved it, then they understand that Sally is holding (and will act on) a false belief. Since Dennett proposed the false belief test, numerous behavioral studies have confirmed that humans develop this form of mentalizing by ages three to five. Some have even suggested that we develop it in infancy. Although recent evidence finds this ability in great apes, for a while we thought humans were unique in our ability to pass false belief tests.

The fMRI evidence also corroborates the existence of a mentalizing network. If the social brain hypothesis is true, our ability to master social skills, or sociality, should be correlated not just with brain size or the neocortex ratio but also with activation of the specific brain regions linked with mentalizing and sociality. And that's exactly what the fMRI evidence shows. When subjects are randomly encouraged to mentalize, the mentalizing network is activated, but the networks for intelligence, reasoning, and working memory are not. And when the prefrontal cortex and temporoparietal regions are blocked by transcranial magnetic stimulation, experimental subjects lose their ability to manage false beliefs that are critical in mentalizing and intentionality.

In addition to the strong fMRI and species-level evidence supporting the social brain hypothesis, researchers have recently examined the individual-level evidence by measuring the sizes of people's brain regions devoted to mentalizing and the sizes of their corresponding personal social networks. Penelope Lewis and her colleagues found that gray-matter volume in key parts of the mentalizing network "varied parametrically with both mentalizing competence (the number of different mental states one can reason about simultaneously) and social network size, demonstrating a shared neural basis for these very different facets of sociality" and providing "fine-grained anatomical support for the social brain hypothesis." The results were replicated successfully by several other research teams. Those of us with bigger social networks have bigger brains in the regions that process social information.

Taken together, this evidence suggests that our brains have evolved to process and interpret social signals from others who we believe have intentional minds, with goals, desires, and plans, and that this ability is integral to how our brains evolved. The cognitive science of the social brain is uncovering a startling story about our evolutionary history. Human brains have evolved to socialize and interpret the social signals that our relationships create and communicate.* Human beings have experienced a series of social evolutionary adaptations dedicated to our social minds—processing information about our relationships, our alliances and discords with others, and the identities and intentions of the people we meet, as well as the complex interdependencies of all this social information.

The processing power required to support social solutions to the

---

* There are, of course, limitations to the fMRI and brain-size analyses linking human brain evolution to sociality. Brain size is a crude measure. The reliability of fMRI analysis is also debated, although it has been gaining scientific traction for three decades. When an fMRI study shows a region of the brain "lighting up," it's measuring elevated blood flow to that region, which neuroscientists take as a proxy for cellular activation. But it's not clear whether blood flow implies activation, although this link is widely accepted by the majority of neuroscientists. There is also the important and thorny issue of sorting out cause and effect (which, in later chapters, will become a focus of this book in explaining social media's impact on the world).

challenges we have faced necessitated an evolutionary growth of the neocortex, the size of our brain, and the size of the neocortex relative to the rest of our brain. The mass of neurons and synapses developed for and devoted to processing social information is trained, in some sense, to take in and navigate our social world. We constantly ask ourselves: *Does she like me? What does he want from me? Can I trust him? Is that smile genuine or sarcastic? I saw Joe with Jane, are they friends? How strong is their relationship? Is she a threat to me? Is he smart?* These types of questions concern us every day and take up a large part of our mental processing. In fact, many neuroscientists believe that our social brain is our "default network," meaning it kicks on any time we are not thinking about something else.

The evidence for the social brain hypothesis implies that humans evolved to be social. We are wired to process social cues about others— the stories they tell; the things they emphasize; the places they go; the food they eat; the beliefs they espouse; the things they know, study, and like; the other people they hang out with; and how well they know them.

The social signals that the Hype Machine curates amplify, broaden, and quicken the pace of our mentalizing by scaling our opportunities to mentalize, from the limited set of social signals we encountered before social media to the cacophony of social signals we encounter today. The neurological interactions are subtle. For example, we use the mentalizing system when posting to and interacting with others on social media, but maybe less so when we post than when we interact. Though the long-term evolutionary consequences of social media are unknown, its effects on our thinking are becoming clearer. And the evidence suggests social media is built for our brains.

Your Brain on Social Media

So our brains are wired to process social signals. What then happens to our brains on social media? Neuroscientists at UCLA wanted to know, so they created an Instagram-style app to study how the brain reacts when we scroll through photos in our Instagram feed. The app displayed a series of photos in a row, just like on Instagram. The researchers then studied adolescents using fMRI machines and recorded which regions of their brains lit up as they used the researchers' version of Instagram. They also experimentally manipulated the number of likes a photo got as well as what types of photos the participants saw, including whether they saw their own photos or others' photos and whether the photos depicted risky behaviors (like drinking alcohol) or neutral behaviors. They've since corroborated their results in young adults and for *giving* as well as receiving likes. As a scientist and the father of a six-year-old, I found what they discovered intriguing and worrisome.

First, seeing photographs with more likes was associated with more activity in brain regions responsible for social cognition, rewards (the dopamine system), and attention (the visual cortex). When participants saw photos with more likes, they experienced greater overall brain activity, and their visual cortex lit up. When the visual cortex lights up, we are concentrating more on what we are looking at, paying more attention to it, and zooming in to look at it in greater detail. To ensure that differences in the images were not driving the results, the researchers randomized the number of likes across images and controlled for photographs' luminosity and content. The results held true whether participants were looking at their own photos or others' photos. In short, when we see social media images with more likes, we zoom in and inspect them in greater detail. We pay more attention to online information when it is valued more highly by others. You might think, *Well, the photos that get more likes are probably more interesting.* But the researchers randomly assigned the likes, which means it was the likes themselves, not the photos, that were triggering the activation of the visual cortex.

Second, having more likes on one's own photos stimulated the mentalizing network—the social brain. When participants were looking at photos of themselves, they responded to those with more (randomly assigned) likes with significantly greater brain activity in regions associated with social skills. They also recorded greater neural activity in the inferior frontal gyrus, which is associated with imitation. When we view photos of ourselves, our brains activate regions responsible for thinking about how people view us and our similarities and differences with them. In other words, when we think about our own photos, we perceive them in their social context—we think about how *other* people are thinking about them.

Last, more likes on one's own photos activated the dopamine reward system, which controls pleasure, motivation, and Pavlovian responses. The dopamine system makes us crave rewards by stimulating feelings of joy, euphoria, and ecstasy. When psychologists James Olds and Peter Milner gave rats the ability to stimulate their own reward system by pushing a lever, they found the rats would drop everything, stop eating and sleeping, and push that little lever again and again until they died from exhaustion.

Ivan Pavlov extended our understanding of rewards by proving he could condition dogs to associate a reward (like food) with an unrelated stimulus (like a bell) so that the stimulus alone would make the dogs salivate. This cognitive binding of stimulus and reward enabled Pavlov to stimulate the brain's reward system with a symbol (a bell)—in the same way likes stimulate and reward us with social acceptance and digital praise. Seeing likes stimulates our dopamine system and encourages us to seek social approval online for the same basic reason that Olds and Milner's rats kept pushing their levers, and Pavlov's dogs salivated at the sound of a bell.

So our brains are wired to process and be moved by the social signals that the Hype Machine curates. But was the Hype Machine really designed with that in mind? Sean Parker answered that question about Facebook's design in an interview with Mike Allen in 2017: "The thought process was all about, 'How do we consume as much of your time and conscious attention as possible?'" he said. "And that means that we need to sort of give you a little dopamine hit every once in a while, because someone liked or commented on a photo or a post or whatever, and that's going to get you to contribute more content, and that's going to get you more likes and comments. It's a social validation feedback loop. . . . You're exploiting a vulnerability in human psychology."

Social media is designed to be habitual. Not only do those "little dopamine hits" keep us coming back, but they are delivered to us on a "variable reinforcement schedule," meaning they can happen at any time. That's why we're always checking our phones, to see if we received any social dopamine. Random reward delivery keeps us constantly engaged. And the rewards are tied to sounds, vibrations, and notification lights that make us salivate for social approval as Pavlov's dogs salivated for food. These designs activate our desires for connection, competition, and avoidance of a "fear of missing out" (FOMO). When you put it all together, it's a recipe for a habit.

The neuroscientific evidence suggests that our habitual use of social media is driven by the rewards and reputational signals we receive from it. One study showed, for example, that brain responses to increases in reputation relative to others' reputations predicted Facebook use, while increases in wealth did not.

But when Dean Eckles, Christos Nicolaides, and I studied running, we found that social media's influence on our habits could also be healthy. It depends which habits are supported. When we analyzed millions of people's running behavior over many years, we found people's social media connections and solidarity with their running peers over social media helped them stick with their running regimens and made their running habits resilient to disruption. The notifications and social signals played a key role in solidifying these good habits.

Our research reminded us that social media holds the potential for promise and peril, but it also taught us that we should care about how the Hype Machine stimulates our brains because, by doing so, it changes our behavior. How does the Hype Machine's cognitive design affect our behavior? That is the next crucial question in the quest to understand the Hype Machine's impact on our world. And my friend and colleague Emily Falk set out to answer it. She studies the neural basis of social influence—the relationship between the social signals the Hype Machine curates, the brain functions those signals activate, and the behaviors those brain functions relate to.

The Neural Basis of Social Influence

When you ask Emily where she is trying to take neuroscience, she says, "Most brain science looks at where things are happening in the brain, we're trying to turn that around and [use brain activity to] predict people's behavior." So while prior work examined how online social signals activate the brain, Emily wanted to know whether the brain's activation predicts how we behave when we see these signals in advertising or on social media. She ran a number of experiments that demonstrated that our brains' responses to persuasive social media or advertising messages predict our future behavior better than what we say we will do in surveys.

Can understanding what Falk and her colleagues call "the neural precursors of behavior change" help us encourage people to quit smoking, save money, and vote? Their studies show that neural signals predict individual, group, and even population-level behavior change induced by persuasive media messages designed to encourage us to, for example, use sunscreen or quit smoking. Falk's team put study participants in fMRI machines and exposed them to ten television advertisements promoting the National Cancer Institute's 1-800-QUIT-NOW smoking hotline. They wanted to know whether the brain's neural responses to different messages predicted which ones would cause people to quit smoking.

They recorded activation in the medial prefrontal cortex region of interest, which was previously associated with individual behavior change. They then compared the brain responses to the performance of the ten TV ads across different geographic regions and measured whether the neural scans excited by different ads predicted smoking hotline call volumes in regions in which the ads were shown. They compared the predictions of the neural scans to participants' survey response predictions of each message's effectiveness. What they found surprised them. The brain scans correctly predicted which ads worked best, while the participants' self-reported predictions and the evaluations of industry experts could not.

In a separate study, Falk and her colleagues asked participants to consider whether to green-light hypothetical TV pilots. Playing the role of interns, one group watched the TV pilots while lying in fMRI machines. They then decided which pilots to pass on to a second group playing the role of producers. The producers in turn decided which pilots to pass on to the network executives. The researchers found that when participants thought about sharing information with others, the mentalizing network lit up while other parts of the brain stayed inactive. When the interns watched the pilots that they would later successfully convince the producers to pass on to the network execs, the interns' mentalizing network activation was off the charts—they were activating their social brain. As Falk's co-author Matthew Lieberman wrote, "This suggests that even at the moment we are first taking in new information, part of what we do is consider whom we can share the information with and how we can share it in a compelling way given the individuals we choose to share it with." This is what the brain is doing when we curate and share information with others.

Falk also found that the neural signals that indicate that we value something psychologically predict social media sharing and virality. In two fMRI studies recording neural activation in response to eighty *New York Times* articles, she and her colleagues showed that activation of signals associated with self-enhancement and social approval in the value system regions of the brain, including the ventromedial prefrontal cortex (VMPFC) and ventral striatum (VS), predicted articles' online virality better than the articles' characteristics themselves or self-reports of participants' sharing intentions.

In other words, neural activation caused by persuasive social media messages *predicts* individual- and population-level behaviors, especially information-sharing behaviors, *better* than we (or other outside experts) can predict our own behavior. But can persuasive messages and social signals *change* our behavior? We need more rigorous analysis to confirm that suggestion in the real world. It's a deep question, and one I will return to regularly throughout the book when evaluating whether and to what extent social media changes how we shop, vote, date, read, and exercise. For now, it's enough to know that how our brains respond to social media messages predicts how we change our behavior and our intentions to share social media content.

UCLA's Instagram study, which measured the neural effects of likes, also found that receiving more likes caused participants to give more likes to others. In a study of adolescent music-rating behavior, researchers at Emory University found that when the popularity ratings of a song were shown while participants rated the songs, the likelihood that participants changed their ratings to fit the crowd's opinion was positively correlated with brain activation in the anterior insula and cingulate, regions associated with arousal and negative affect. These results suggest that "the anxiety generated by the mismatch between one's own preferences and others' . . . motivates people to switch their choices toward consensus." Studies have also shown that seeing others' opinions of facial attractiveness inspired participants to change their own attractiveness ratings of others.

These studies demonstrate the existence of neural precursors to behavior change. Later I'll examine large-scale behavioral experiments showing how social signals change people's actual voting, rating, buying, dating, and exercise behaviors. When I do, keep in mind what's happening in subjects' brains as social media influences them.

Wired for Promise and Peril

Another important result of these studies supports a central tenet of this book—that the Hype Machine holds the potential for exceptional promise and tremendous peril. It turns out that we are neurologically wired for both the promise and the peril. Our brains are wired to be stimulated by social media to engage in socially costly behaviors, as well as in positive behaviors that improve society.

In the UCLA study, Instagram likes suppressed regions of the brain that regulate our self-control. The researchers separately analyzed the mental impact of seeing more likes while participants were viewing photos depicting risky behaviors compared to photos depicting non-risky or neutral behaviors. When participants saw more likes on photos depicting risky behaviors (like doing drugs or drinking alcohol), completely different regions of the brain responded. And there was significantly less activity in brain regions responsible for self-control and response inhibition. In other words, the parts of our kids' brains that warn them that a behavior may be risky are turned off, or all least turned down, when photos depicting those behaviors receive more likes. Online rejection also inspires anger and retaliation. So social media can inspire the peril.

But we're also wired to embrace the positive promise of social media. In one online study, adolescents could donate money to their peer group. Beforehand, the participants met each other and confederate peers who were not part of the group dividing the money. These peers, who were working with the experimenters, gave more likes when participants donated more to the group. When more likes were given, more money was donated, and participants' social brain regions were stimulated. Positive social feedback encourages prosocial behaviors just as it does risky behaviors. We're not just wired for the Hype Machine, we're wired to act on both the good and the evil it can promote.

As I explore the Hype Machine in greater detail—how it's built, how it works, and how we can evaluate, adjust, and redesign it—it makes sense to keep these neurological foundations in mind. Unpacking the driving forces that determine where the Hype Machine is taking us, and how we might steer it, is critical. How our brains respond to social media is the first step in that exploration—it reveals social media's neurological hook. Another critical motivator for behavior change is social media's economic hook, which I will explore next.

CHAPTER 5

A Network's Gravity Is Proportional to Its Mass

In business, I look for economic castles protected by unbreachable moats.

—WARREN BUFFETT

If social connections provide an evolutionary benefit to our species and help us as individuals, then connecting the world seems a worthy goal. Mark Zuckerberg repeatedly espoused this mission in 2018 and mentioned it over sixty times in his congressional testimony alone: "Facebook . . . was built to accomplish a social mission—to make the world more open and connected. . . . We believe that connecting everyone in the world is one of the great challenges of our generation, and that's why we are happy to play whatever small part in that we can." He frequently refers to the story of how he and his cofounders didn't originally intend to start a company and that the economic value of the connections they were creating was not their top priority. But make no mistake, in addition to having significant neurological pull, the Hype Machine also has tremendous economic pull, because social connections don't just stimulate our brains, they create social and economic value—which is a powerful motivator.

Zuckerberg wasn't the first to espouse the economic benefits of universal connection. That honor goes to a lesser-known American entrepreneur, Theodore Vail, who was brought back to run Bell Telecommunications for a second time in 1907. Vail's view focused on the economic power of network connections to move markets. In his first annual report in 1908, Vail introduced the concept of economic network effects to his board and shareholders. He wrote that "a telephone—without a connection at the other end of the line—is not even a toy or a scientific instrument. Its value depends on its connection with the other telephone—and increases with the number of connections. . . . The Bell System," he continued, "has developed until it has assimilated itself into and in fact become the nervous system of the business and social organization of the country." It's not hard to see Facebook, Instagram, Twitter, WeChat, and WhatsApp as more powerful versions of that today—wiring the central nervous system of business and society worldwide.

Vail's claim, that the value of the telephone increases with the number of connections it makes, succinctly describes network effects—one of the most fundamental economic forces shaping digital competition and platform strategy today. For products or markets that exhibit network effects, the value of the product or market is a function of the number of people connecting to it. As more people use the product, its value to everyone increases. We cannot understand the economic wiring of the Hype Machine and the value it creates (and destroys) without understanding network effects.* This simple concept is essential to understanding why some social media networks grow while others fail, why inferior networks can dominate high-quality entrants, and why markets for social media tend toward monopolies. In Chapter 4, I explored the Hype Machine's neurological influence on our behavior; in this chapter, I'll examine its economic influence.

A Network's Gravity Is Proportional to Its Mass

Network effects are like gravity. The greater the number of people on a network, the greater its "mass," so to speak. The greater its mass, the greater its gravitational pull. The greater its gravity, the more attraction it has to pull in new customers, and the greater the economic grip it has on preventing current customers from leaving its orbit.

There are four types of network effects that matter: direct, indirect, two-sided, and local. And each has a unique part to play in the strategy

---

* Later, we will ask whether these networks create or destroy value, because this is the essential question at the heart of the Hype Machine's recent existential crisis. (Hint: the value of more connections depends on the quality of those connections—whether they contribute positively or negatively to the lives of those who are connecting.)

and destiny of the Hype Machine. Direct network effects are those that create value by directly connecting people. Think of Vail's telephone or the fax machine. If I am the first person to own a fax machine, it's basically useless. I can use it as a doorstop, but I can't fax anyone with it, because no one else has a fax machine to receive my fax. As more people buy fax machines, the more people I can connect with. Facebook, Twitter, and the rest of the Hype Machine benefit tremendously from direct network effects. They can influence everything from monopoly concentration to innovation in our economy. The inset "Understanding Network Effects" explains how network effects can allow an inferior social media network to dominate a superior entrant and monopolize the market.

UNDERSTANDING NETWORK EFFECTS

Consider the following example of how network effects can empower an inferior network to dominate higher-quality competitors. Imagine that the value (V) of a social media network is its intrinsic value plus the value of its network effect:

$$V = a + ct$$

Here a is the intrinsic value of the network, without network effects (think of this as the social network's features, privacy controls, data security, etc.); c is the value of network effects (the additional value that users receive as more of their friends join the network); and t indicates time and also represents the number of people who have joined the network at any moment in time (the number of users on the platform). So, when $t = 3$, we are in the third time period and there are three people on the platform.

Now compare two networks, Alpha and Beta, that are "incompatible"—in other words, consumers can connect only with friends on the same network and not with friends on the other network. For example, you can't message someone on Facebook from Twitter—they're incompatible. Let's assume Beta is far superior to Alpha in terms of quality. It has better communication features, more options, better privacy controls, and a cleaner interface. It doesn't sell your data to third parties, and its enhanced security and encryption features keep users safe. So the intrinsic value of Beta, call it *b*, is greater than the intrinsic value of Alpha, or *a*.

Beta would be the more valuable network, if it were available at the same time as Alpha, because Beta's intrinsic value is greater than Alpha's intrinsic value. But it takes Beta time to build all those great features. Alpha beats Beta to market, meaning that Alpha launches first. Imagine that Alpha is available at time zero, and Beta will become available at some future date. Consumers don't know Beta is available until it is released, so they can't consider Beta when deciding whether to join Alpha. The value of network effects (the additional value that users receive as more of their friends join the network) is the added benefit of all the connections available on the network at the time a user joins.

Though Beta is the superior network ($b > a$), consumers only have one option initially. The first consumer calculates whether Alpha is worth the cost of adopting and decides, for argument's sake, that it is. So she joins Alpha. The next consumer faces a different decision. Now there is one other person who is already using Alpha, so the value of Alpha to the second consumer is $a + (c \times 1)$, or $a + c$. The value of Alpha to the third consumer is $a + 2c$, to the fourth consumer it's $a + 3c$, and so on. Alpha's value increases linearly over time, like this:

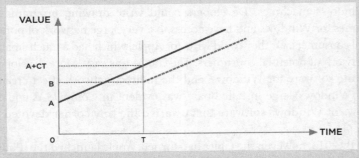

Figure 5.1 *The value of Alpha and Beta over time.*

When Beta launches at time *t*, the value of joining Alpha is *a* plus the number of customers who have joined Alpha and are part of its network (*t*) times its network value (*c*): $a + ct$. The value of joining Beta is still just *b*, the value of the service itself, because no one has yet joined Beta—it has no network effect. And although we have agreed that Beta, or *b*, is better than Alpha, or a, it is *less valuable* than Alpha plus its network effect, or $a + ct$. So while Beta's value should increase linearly (as shown in the dotted line in Figure 5.1), fewer people adopt Beta because it has a smaller network effect. In this way, an inferior network (Alpha) can dominate a superior network (Beta) by having a large installed base and thus a large network effect. This is a key concept in ongoing debates about whether Facebook's monopoly power hurts innovation.

Indirect network effects are different. As more people start using a particular platform or network, third parties have more incentive to add value to that platform or network. When I was a kid, we used to buy software in physical stores (weird, I know). I remember walking into CompUSA with my dad in the late 1980s and seeing aisle after aisle of Windows software, with just a small corner of the last aisle in the back of the store reserved for Apple programs. Apple was producing solid computers, but Windows had a much larger installed base of users and thus a larger network effect. Its network effect didn't originate from the direct connections it offered to others. (The Internet would make that possible only later.) Instead, its network effect originated from the incentives it created for developers to write software for Windows machines. Developers could write drawing programs or games for Windows and have access to a very large network of potential consumers. Or they could write for Apple, which had a much smaller network of potential consumers. The choice was easy. More developers wrote software for Windows, and the indirect network effect created by Windows' large installed base was evident in CompUSA's endless rows of Windows software that dwarfed the tiny corner devoted to Apple.

By 2013, however, the tables had turned. Apple launched the iPhone in 2007 and everyone wanted one. Apple built so much innovation into the iPhone that its intrinsic value alone was enough to get people to buy iPhones en masse. Software was added to the iPhone through applications, or "apps," and Apple launched the App Store in 2008. As more people bought the iPhone, developers had more incentive to write apps for it. As a result, the iPhone's adoption curve looks like Mount Everest. The first iPhone was sold in 2007 and by 2013 Apple had sold 400 million of them. If the user base is like a platform's mass, and network effects are like gravity, Apple's gravity increased as the iPhone's mass increased and consumers flocked to the now iconic brand.

In contrast, Microsoft's share of the cell phone market in 2013 was like Apple's share of CompUSA's shelves in the 1980s—minuscule. Developers had very little incentive to write apps for Windows phones. Instead, they wrote for Apple. In 2013 there were over five times as many apps for the iPhone as there were for Windows phones. In fact, Apple's installed base advantage was so large that while developers were clamoring to write apps for the iPhone for free, Microsoft was paying developers over $100,000 a pop for apps written for Windows phones. It was necessary to try to counteract Apple's gravity. But it wasn't enough. The network effect combined with the iPhone's intrinsic value was simply too strong. Today Apple owns 47.4 percent of the U.S. cell phone market, while Microsoft controls 0.5 percent. The power of indirect network effects is apparent and persistent.

Network effects can also be two-sided if the installed base of one side of a market creates demand for the other side of the market. For example, more Uber riders create demand for more Uber drivers, and more Adobe Readers create demand for more Adobe Writers, all because of two-sided network effects. When you look at global cell phone sales, Apple owns about 25 percent of the market while Microsoft owns only 0.1 percent. But it's Android that dominates globally, with 74 percent market share. That's because Android decoupled the operating system from the phone's hardware and opened its platform to be compatible with almost any phone. It works on phones made by Samsung, LG, Google, and others. This is a vivid example of platform strategy at work.

But for the Hype Machine, the most important type of network effect is also the least known: the local network effect. The term originates from the importance of location to the economic power of network effects. Local network effects are proportional to the geographic proximity of the connections in the network. For example, when a new user in Dallas joins NextDoor, the private social networking service for neighborhoods, it improves the service for other NextDoor users in Dallas, but has little effect on the quality of the service for users in San Francisco. It turns out that, in addition to geographic proximity, local network effects are also driven by social proximity. A product exhibits local network effects when users are influenced directly by only a small subset of other users in the network—those with whom they are "connected."

On NextDoor, users are geographically connected. On Facebook, users are socially connected. When you think about the value you get from Facebook, Twitter, WhatsApp, or WeChat, you realize it comes more from the people you know and are connected to than from the larger mass of over 3 billion people you don't know on these social networks. It also comes, to some extent, from the people you hope to connect to but don't yet know. But the likelihood that such a connection is made through an unsolicited direct message sent to a celebrity is much lower than if you are introduced by a friend of a friend. So whether we're talking about the connections you have or the connections you hope to make, here's the kicker: the value in the network for any user is proportional to the value of the people they are connected to in the network, not just the *total* number of people in the network. That's the local network effect. And it is a key driver of the competitive forces shaping the Hype Machine, including, for example, why Facebook succeeded where MySpace failed.

How Facebook Beat MySpace

In June 2011, I spoke at the NextWork conference, organized by *Wired* and *The Economist,* in New York City. I was sandwiched in the program between the actor Ed Norton, who was talking about his new crowdsourcing platform for philanthropy fundraising called CrowdRise, and Jared Cohen, former adviser to Secretary of State Hillary Clinton and current CEO of Google's Jigsaw (a technology incubator dedicated to countering extremism, censorship, and cyberattacks online), who was talking about how technology empowers revolutions in the Middle East. But just a few sessions beforehand, in my favorite session of the day, Jimmy Fallon interviewed Facebook co-founder Sean Parker in a hilarious, free-flowing conversation about hacking, Napster, Spotify, the rise of Facebook, and other high-tech topics like tea blending and relaxation techniques.

While the entire interview was engaging, a particular moment captured my attention. Jimmy asked Sean why Facebook succeeded where

MySpace failed. In 2011 this was a favorite question of media pundits and digital strategy gurus alike. In some sense, it was a half-trillion-dollar question because that's Facebook's current market capitalization. If MySpace had won its battle with Facebook, it would very likely be sitting in that position today.

The reversal of fortunes between these two digital darlings was incredibly unlikely for the very reasons we have been discussing. Between 2004 and 2008, MySpace had a massive installed base advantage. Its user base dwarfed that of Facebook. In 2005, MySpace had 27 million users to Facebook's 5 million; in 2006, MySpace had 100 million users to Facebook's 12 million. (See Figure 5.2, which depicts "active" users.) The direct and indirect network effects generated by these installed base advantages seemed insurmountable, and Sean Parker knew it. He told Jimmy onstage that MySpace's dominance was formidable.

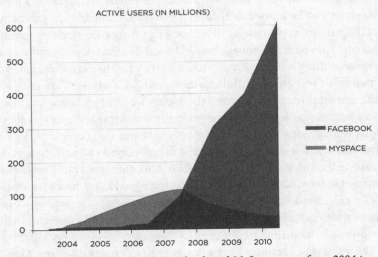

ACTIVE USERS (IN MILLIONS)

FACEBOOK
MYSPACE

Figure 5.2 *Numbers of active Facebook and MySpace users from 2004 to 2010.*

"The network effects, the scale effects, were enormous," he said, referring to MySpace. "There was so much power there."

So how did Facebook come from behind, against all odds, to make MySpace disappear? Several explanations were popular at the time. Some argued that MySpace didn't have a scalable infrastructure or the technical talent to upgrade it, making it difficult for it to ship new features or speed up the site's slow load time. Others suggested that MySpace's design, which allowed users to make their pages into whatever they wanted, was so ugly and inconsistent that its appeal paled in comparison to Facebook's sleek professional design. In contrast, others claimed that MySpace's management was too professionalized and that MBA-strategy PowerPoints were no match for the freewheeling management of college dropouts who built Facebook by allowing it to go where users wanted it to go. Some thought MySpace's focus on bands and music made the platform too niche. Others believed Facebook's insistence on real names made it more relatable. All these claims had some truth, but they missed a key dynamic that did not escape Sean Parker.

Sean's response to Jimmy began with the most popular answer of the time: that MySpace was poorly designed and didn't innovate, which was true. But he immediately turned to a topic that had escaped many of the pundits' explanations—Facebook's go-to-market strategy. Jimmy asked, "Do you think college helped? I feel like Facebook is more of a personal thing where a lot of people heard of it through their college friends." It was an insightful question, and Sean agreed: "We entered the market through college and the reason we went in through college was because college kids were generally not MySpace users, college kids were generally not Friendster users. It was this completely open market, and it was a real long shot. I mean, nobody actually believed, outside the three or four of us in Palo Alto, that you could enter the market through this niche market and then gradually, through a carefully calculated war against all the other networks, become the one network to rule them all." He paused with a grin on his face and then continued: "Was that a *Lord of the Rings* reference?" Jimmy laughed: "Yes, yes it was. I actually have a poster of it over my bed." Sean: "Along with your Dungeons and Dragons poster." Jimmy: "And an official Harry Potter wand." The audience laughed.

But the insight was more serious than the references to *Lord of the Rings* let on. Going in through college allowed Facebook to fight MySpace's gigantic direct and indirect network effects with its own, more powerful local network effect. Jimmy and Sean were, perhaps unknowingly yet instinctively, reaching into the depths of the economic theory of network effects. Network effects were introduced into economics by Jeffrey Rohlfs's seminal 1974 paper "A Theory of Interdependent Demand for a Communications Service," which modeled the value of a product like Facebook as a function of the number of people who use it. But Rohlfs's original vision, published some forty years beforehand, actually included the local network effect that Facebook harnessed to defeat MySpace. As my colleague Richard Schmalensee has noted, Rohlfs's paper proposed an extended model in which the value of a product to a consumer is based not just on the *total* number of other consumers of that product but also on the value of the *specific* users with whom the consumer cares to connect. On Facebook, that value for college students was high because the other people they could connect with were the people they valued the most—their college buddies. On MySpace, they could connect with, well, strangers.

Facebook launched at Harvard in February 2004, then opened its doors to one college after another: Columbia, Yale, Dartmouth, Cornell. Within two months, seventy thousand students had joined from twenty major U.S. colleges, including Stanford, MIT, NYU, and Northeastern. Facebook wasn't open to anyone outside these campuses. By May 2005 it had expanded to eight hundred college networks. In September of that year, it added high school networks. In October it expanded to international school networks. In May 2006 it added workplace networks. Each of these networks was a tight-knit group in which many people already knew each other, had friends in common, or could relate to each other's experiences of having the same school or work culture. Social connection or proximity among Facebook users was high, while it was very low among MySpace users.

When Facebook opened its doors more broadly in September 2006, it had 12 million users, to MySpace's 100 million. But the social connections between Facebook users looked very different. By virtue of its college launch strategy, Facebook developed a network where everyone knew each other. When you joined Facebook, you would find your friends and classmates there. As a result of its go-to-market strategy, you were more likely to know more people when you joined Facebook than when you joined MySpace. And the people you didn't know were more likely to know someone you knew, or at least to share classes, activities, and the university's culture with you. That made the Facebook network more relatable, more inviting, and safer. It increased the value users got out of the connections available to them on the platform.

In contrast, users were much less likely to know anyone else on MySpace, even if there were vastly more people on the platform. The structure of the social connections MySpace created was what network scientists call "sparse." While you could browse other people's profiles and listen to their music, you were unlikely to know them directly or to have friends in common. People joined MySpace from anywhere, without a common social thread to hold them together. So connecting and bonding was harder. When Yong-Yeol Ahn and his team conducted an autopsy of the MySpace network, they found that "Orkut [another social networking platform they studied] . . . is considered a close-knit community. In contrast, the MySpace network's assortativity is clearly negative, $r \sim -0.2$. The disassortative mixing tells us that MySpace largely deviates from traditional social networks. . . . Relations in MySpace might be considered loose, as anyone can sign up without invitation."

On Facebook, the most valuable bonds were already there. In fact, Facebook wasn't creating social connections so much as grafting itself onto social connections that already existed—between college friends, high school buddies, and work colleagues. The tight-knit relationships among Facebook users turbocharged its local network effect. In fact, Jeffrey Rohlfs anticipated Facebook's exact go-to-market strategy in his seminal paper. He considered the launch strategies of new services that display local network effects and suggested giving away the services to carefully selected groups of people for a limited period of time. Since, as Rohlfs writes, "an individual's demand may depend primarily on which of his few principal contacts are users . . . the success of this approach may also depend on how the initial user set is selected." The idea that the product's launch strategy should target a carefully selected group of people (in Facebook's case, college students) foreshadowed what Sean Parker described to Jimmy Fallon onstage at NextWork some thirty-seven years later.

Eight months after opening its doors beyond college, high school, and work networks, Facebook launched the Facebook Platform, with sixty-five developers and eighty-five apps. By then, it had already laid the groundwork for a vibrant community, one where more people were likely to know you than on MySpace. These original tight-knit groups then started inviting their friends, and those people invited their friends, and so on. (We'll discuss referral programs as an essential element of the Hype Machine's playbook in Chapter 8.) The local network effects interacted with the indirect network effects as more developers started writing for the platform. Even the direct network effects were inherently stronger because people were better able to connect to those they wanted to meet by being introduced to them by a friend. And the rest is history. The local, direct, and indirect network effects kicked in, and through a carefully calculated war against all the other networks, Facebook became, as Sean Parker described it, the one network to rule them all. At least for now.*

* Network effects create tremendous value for platforms like Facebook: as more people adopted it, Facebook got more valuable. But it gets even better. So far we've assumed that network effects add value to a social media network linearly, meaning the value to the next potential user increases in a steady linear fashion with every new person that joins. But in truth, network effects are likely to add value superlinearly, meaning each new adopter adds more value than the last, at least up to a point. Consider Metcalfe's Law: two telephones can make one connection, but four telephones can make sixteen connections, eight can make sixty-four connections, and so on. In Metcalfe's formulation, each new possible point of contact in a network adds value quadratically, not linearly, so that the value of the network is proportional to the square of the number of users or connections ($V = a + ct^2$). Some argue that Metcalfe's Law implies that network value is exponential, but I hesitate to conclude that network effects take any particular functional form (exponential, quadratic, etc.), or that this nonlinearity lasts forever, because (as we have discussed) all possible connections in a network are not equally valuable to every new adopter. The local network effect implies that the closer the person is to you in social space, the more valuable they will be as a possible connection. So every possible connection cannot add value to every other connection, limiting the nonlinearity. Furthermore, human beings are a bottleneck in possible connectedness because we have a finite capacity to make and maintain friends. Robin Dunbar believes, for example, that due to our limited cognitive capacity for socializing, we are mentally capable of maintaining stable relationships with only about 150 people. This is "Dunbar's number." Maybe online the number is higher, since communication costs are dramatically lower there and we can treat the digital social network as a scaffolding on which we can hold our memories, so we don't have to hold them in our heads. But in either case, as more people join the network and we exceed the number of people we can socialize with, the nonlinearity of the value added to the network by each new adopter is likely to be less than quadratic and unlikely to go on forever. The specific form of the nonlinearity and its endurance are actually not that important. When we assume that value increases greater than linearly (in any form), the potential value of growing a network becomes very large, very fast. Consider a situation in which the value in the network grows nonlinearly and the

The Hype Machine's Walled Gardens

While a platform's network effects pull us in by creating and amplifying social and economic opportunity, there is no guarantee that any platform can keep our attention long enough to realize its value. This is where the Hype Machine's design comes into play. In addition to the neurological and economic pull, our relationship with social media also has a technical aspect. To appropriate the value created by network effects, social media networks are designed to lock us in by making their platforms incompatible with each other, and by keeping an iron grip on the data we upload to them (and that they collect about us). The platforms are economically motivated toward this design. For example, Gillette locks customers into buying its blades by making its razors incompatible with competing blades; Nespresso coffee machines work only with Nespresso coffee pods; and so on. The Hype Machine also locks us in this way.

First, these digital services create switching costs through the vast stores of data we upload to them—data we don't want to part with or lose access to. If we leave Spotify, we lose our saved songs and playlists. If we leave Google or Apple, we lose the music, movies, and apps we've purchased. If we leave Facebook or Instagram, we lose our pictures, our conversations, our very memories. Many people I know use the

---

cost of adding new connections grows linearly with each new connection. On platforms like Facebook, this is likely to be the case. There is a large, up-front fixed cost to build the infrastructure, then a small incremental cost, in servers and storage, to add new users as more and more people join. When value grows nonlinearly and costs grow linearly, there is tremendous opportunity to generate ever-expanding profits. If costs are linear, Facebook could theoretically add value more than linearly until it reached market saturation. That's why investors' valuations are so obsessed with social media's user growth. Market saturation is an enemy of the equity value of networks like Facebook because when there are no more users to add to the network, the rate of growth of the networked value, and thus the platform's value, will slow. It's no surprise, therefore, that the networks focus intensely on growing their number of users and fighting market saturation. Which explains why Facebook has invested so heavily in Internet.org and its Connectivity Lab, which are tasked with bringing the Internet to the developing world, whether by balloon, satellite, drone, or laser—it wants more people on the Internet so it can add more Facebook users and maintain the rate at which its value grows. This is true of the Hype Machine in general.

Hype Machine like a living diary—a constantly updated history of their lives, experiences, and interactions. Leaving that history, those memories, behind is not easy. In this way, the data we upload and create on the Hype Machine keeps us coming back and prevents us from switching between social platforms.

The second source of the Hype Machine's power to lock us in comes from our relationships and the network effects they create. In addition to our personal memories, posts, pictures, and activity streams (what we've liked, flagged, or shared, for example), we also don't want to give up our relationships. In essence, when we use Facebook, LinkedIn, Instagram, or WhatsApp, we not only get the benefits of our own private contributions but also the value of the data, interactions, and communications provided by others. These benefits manifest in complicated ways. For example, we benefit directly from communication with our friends on Facebook. But (as I described in Chapter 3) we also benefit from data about their decisions that power algorithms built to tailor our newsfeeds to our interests. By making it difficult for us to take our data and our relationships with us if we leave, social media platforms lock us in to using them and never leaving.

These two ways that the Hype Machine locks us in are driving current debates about data portability and social network portability. Data portability allows us to take our private data with us if we choose to leave a social platform. Social network portability allows us to take our relationships with the people we are connected to on a social platform with us if we leave. They play an essential role in our ability to shape the impact of social media on innovation, competition, privacy, and security, through government regulation and business policy.

Network Effects and Interoperability

In discussing the competition between the Alpha and Beta networks earlier in this chapter, we made the crucial assumption that the networks were incompatible. Being part of one network did not give you access to the other. So now imagine if they *were* compatible. Imagine if, when Beta was launched, consumers who joined it could connect to and interact with consumers in Alpha's network as well. The outcome of the competition between the two networks would be entirely different.

The first consumer to consider joining either Alpha or Beta, after Beta's launch, would face a very different calculation. If Beta, as the higher-quality network, were able to give its users access to Alpha's installed network base, Beta could co-opt Alpha's head start and eventually come to dominate the market. That is why social media platforms guard their network effects like the crown jewels. Take, for example, the chat wars of 1999.

Are you old enough to remember the rotund yellow mascot of AOL Instant Messenger (AIM)? In 1999 he used to run in place while AIM loaded on 80 million desktops around the world. Real-time chat now pervades every social media network, just as text messages give us real-time communication on our phones. But it was the rise of AIM and ICQ (I Seek You), which AOL later bought, that catapulted real-time instant messaging into the mainstream.

AIM and ICQ provided consumers with multiple user chats, file transfers, and a searchable user directory. They introduced the buddy list, the now-ubiquitous list of your digitally available friends. You may remember the sounds of doors creaking open and slamming shut as your chat buddies appeared and disappeared online. AIM also introduced a cultural shorthand for online communication that persists today. Text phrases like "brb" (be right back), "lol" (laughing out loud), "omg" (oh my god or gosh), and "rotfl" (rolling on the floor laughing) all originated on AIM. But the jolly yellow man, as friendly as he came across, was deeply territorial. Behind the scenes, he was waging a protracted battle against Microsoft and Yahoo! engineers for control over the network effects so key to instant messaging.

By 1997, AIM had become the de facto standard for instant messaging, boasting the largest network of users and the largest network effect. By the time Yahoo! introduced its Messenger in 1998 and Microsoft introduced MSN Messenger in 1999, they, like the Beta platform in our earlier example, were latecomers to the party. They faced an uphill battle against AIM's already-established network effect. So rather than fighting to compete with or beat the AIM network, they decided to try to join it.

In 1999, Microsoft and Yahoo! wrote code to connect users of their

IM services directly with AIM users. As a result, Microsoft and Yahoo! users could message their friends on AIM directly from Microsoft and Yahoo!, co-opting AIM's network effect. AOL responded to the technical grappling hooks within hours, shutting down the connections. It claimed that the attacks violated its copyrights and trademarks, as Microsoft's and Yahoo!'s software bored into AOL servers to extract its buddy lists and the message transfer protocols necessary to make the messaging platforms compatible. The next day Microsoft tweaked its Messenger code to circumvent AOL's defenses. Within hours, AOL blocked those attempts as well. The escalating arms race raged back and forth as AOL tried to keep its users locked inside its walled garden, and Microsoft and Yahoo! tried to pry open the garden's gates and to wrestle AIM's network effects away.

When Microsoft discovered that AOL had used a security vulnerability in its code to prevent Microsoft from pirating its network, it went to the press with the story, disguised as an engineer from a third-party messenger app being developed by a fake company. Microsoft thought if it could generate enough bad press about the vulnerability, AOL would have to patch it, and MSN would be able to connect with AOL again. The plan backfired when journalists discovered that the engineer who sent the fake message had done so from a computer on Microsoft's campus in Redmond, Washington. The IP address was right there in the email header. The journalists outed Microsoft, and the software giant had to publicly apologize for the stunt.

Why go to all this trouble? Why didn't Microsoft and Yahoo! just develop their own networks of instant messaging users? As Sean Parker said when he was talking to Jimmy Fallon about network effects, there's just "so much power there." A social media network that amasses a large installed base wields tremendous power to lock customers in, to parry more innovative competitors, and to tip markets toward itself.

The Dark Side of Network Effects

Our analogies to the concepts of mass and gravity make network effects seem permanently positive, but they're actually a double-edged sword. They can create virtuous and vicious cycles. While a virtuous cycle can spin up a 2-billion-person social media platform in a decade, a vicious one can deflate it almost as quickly. Markets with network effects are what economists call "tippy," meaning they can tip toward a platform's monopoly. But during a vicious cycle, they can tip away from an incumbent as well.

When we log on to Facebook, we access informative news, meaningful relationships, economic opportunity, and social support that make us want to stay. But if, when we log on to Facebook, we are inundated with fake news, phishing scams, election manipulations, and violent livestreams of mass killings, like the horrific events that unfolded in Christchurch, New Zealand, in March 2019, the value from social media networks can quickly turn negative. We can stop trusting Facebook as a social media resource. The very gravity that once attracted us can repel us with equal force. That's why the Hype Machine's current crisis may be an existential one. If its network effects sour, Facebook, Twitter, and others could face a mass exodus. Think it can't happen? Just ask Tom Anderson and Chris DeWolfe, who founded MySpace.

MySpace's deflation resulted from negative impressions among its users and from competition from Facebook. Facebook paid $1 billion for Instagram and $19 billion for WhatsApp because it feared the next network that could displace it, as it had displaced MySpace. By buying up emerging networks that could grow into competitive threats, Facebook can retain its network effects and its dominance. Remember our canonical example of the fax machine? As more users adopted fax machines, they became more valuable. But when the Internet and digital documents arrived, fax machines disappeared almost as quickly as they had spread. Their gravity gave way to the gravitational pull of the next wave of technology entrants. This is why lock-in and differentiation are so important. If a network locks its users in, by preventing data portability and interoperability, it prevents us (and our data) from being drawn into a competitor's orbit. If, on the other hand, the competitor is differentiated, users may want to sign up for both services, or "multihome." (I'll discuss the implications of interoperability, network effects, and users' ability to multihome for competition, innovation, and antitrust in Chapter 12.)

All this jockeying for position in the hearts and minds of consumers shouldn't be surprising. Consumers are forward-looking. They don't want to be locked into a platform that is declining. They'd rather hitch their wagons to the network they think will be around for years to come, the one that will be the most popular and hence the most valuable. That means perception is (nearly) everything. If the prevailing wisdom is that Facebook can adjust its business model and eliminate (or at least significantly reduce) the negative consequences of its platform, consumers may stick with it. But if consumers lose confidence in Facebook's approach, they could run for the exit quickly, especially if there are viable alternatives in the market.

Strategic Whiplash

That's why Facebook seems schizophrenic right now. It's frantically seeking a solution that consumers can believe in. In 2018 and 2019 it floated several conflicting ideas about how it was going to chart a course to smoother waters. First it was going to stay the course and tweak the platform, using AI and content moderators to root out harmful content, improve data portability, and pay attention to consumers' privacy. But its public pronouncements fell on deaf ears. So Facebook COO Sheryl Sandberg floated the idea of abandoning the advertising model altogether and charging a monthly fee for Facebook services instead. Consumers were again not impressed. So in March 2019, Mark Zuckerberg announced that Facebook would unify its messaging apps and become a private, encrypted messaging platform, similar to WeChat in China. The move was solidified at Facebook's developer conference in April 2019, when it unveiled the redesign.

But the business model implications are unclear. Will Facebook pursue revenues by enabling (and taking a cut of) economic transactions, similar to WeChat? Its development of the Libra cryptocurrency could enable that strategy. Or will it continue to pursue ad revenue? Or both? In an encrypted private network, the content of messages could be encrypted, but metadata about who users talk to, what they like, and what content they engage with would still be available to target ads. Diversifying revenue across business models is one of Facebook's essential strategic objectives right now, because it's not clear what consumers and regulators will support, and you can almost feel the market tipping.

Now that we've established the neurological and economic foundations of the Hype Machine's influence, we can explore how it changes our behavior in the first of three trends—the rise of "personalized mass persuasion."

CHAPTER 6

Personalized Mass Persuasion

---

*Any sufficiently advanced technology is indistinguishable
from magic.*

—Arthur C. Clarke

In August 2016, Hillary Clinton found herself in a jail cell in the back of a Ford F-350 pickup truck in West Palm Beach, Florida. Although she didn't know it at the time, it was the Russians who had put her there. Replicating their information warfare strategy from Crimea in 2014, they were now pointing the Hype Machine at the United States in the hope of disrupting the 2016 presidential election. They combined digital persuasion with a perverse form of grassroots organizing to land Hillary Clinton in a cage that day, in the back of a pickup truck, in the sweltering Florida heat.

She wasn't the real Hillary Clinton, of course. She was an American citizen named Anne Marie Thomas wearing a Hillary Clinton mask. While she toiled in that parking lot jail cell, the orchestrators of the spectacle she was participating in were five thousand miles away, in St. Petersburg, Russia, in a nondescript building, 55 Shavushkina Street, home of the Internet Research Agency (IRA). The IRA used Twitter and Facebook messages to persuade Americans like Anne to build a mock cage, dress up like Bill and Hillary Clinton, and mobilize a "Florida Goes Trump" rally staged around the caged Clintons at a local Cheesecake Factory. They created a website called Being Patriotic, which legitimized their community organizing when people looked them up online. They then created videos and images of the flash mob and posted them to social media sites like YouTube and Instagram, racking up over half a million hits within twenty-four hours. The Russian

Florida flash mob was influencer marketing in action—the IRA had recruited Americans to create and participate in protests using personalized social media messages. It then broadcast the protest videos and boosted their digital reach online.

But Hillary Clinton wasn't the only victim of Russia co-opting the Hype Machine. In May 2016 a Russian-run Facebook page named Heart of Texas called on its 254,000 followers to protest the "Islamization of Texas" outside the Dah'wah Islamic Center at the corner of Travis and Franklin Streets in downtown Houston. The Dah'wah center had just opened a new Islamic library, and the fake Heart of Texas organization mobilized in opposition to it by planning a protest for May 21. At the same time, on the same street corner in downtown Houston, another Facebook page called the United Muslims of America (UMA) organized a counterprotest. While the UMA is a real organization, the Facebook page representing it was also run by Russian operatives. The protest and counterprotest, taking place simultaneously on the same street corner, were both organized by Russia. The idea was to sow dissent and destabilize the American democratic process.

The Russians complemented these digitally enabled guerrilla marketing tactics with an armada of digital advertisements, including ads and messages that reached 126 million people on Facebook during the 2016 U.S. presidential election alone. These ads had multiple goals: bringing people out to rallies, spreading misinformation, and suppressing voter turnout. Using Facebook's ad-targeting API, the IRA was able to identify nonwhite voters in key swing states and bombard them with targeted, personalized ads discouraging them from voting. One of the ads, deployed on Election Day, for example, targeted Facebook users interested in "African-American history, the civil rights movement, Martin Luther King Jr. and Malcolm X," claiming, "No one [in this election] represents Black people. Don't go vote."

In addition to Facebook advertising, Russia deployed millions of Twitter messages and spread thousands of videos and image memes through YouTube and Instagram. The ad-targeting APIs allowed them to personalize and tailor their messages to particular audiences. Social advertising helped them insert social proof into their persuasive messages (for example, claiming that "Jane Doe and twelve more of your friends liked this message"), making them more effective. Viral marketing encouraged influencers to pass the information on to their friends. As the videos and memes were posted to social media, trolls, bots, and Russian-affiliated accounts made them go viral using hashtags and encouraging their followers to "make it trend."

The Hype Machine is first and foremost a communication ecosystem, connecting a large part of the world's population. But it is also a global persuasion machine that can create population-scale behavior change at low cost. At its core, it provides direct access to people in a searchable, sortable communication forum that encourages us to share information from person to person. It serves the advertising ecosystem by exposing APIs and communication protocols to businesses, governments, and individuals for the explicit purpose of analyzing, communicating with, and persuading consumers on a mass scale. While the social media ecosystem enables global interaction and connection, it also supports targeted, personalized, and networked persuasion. In the past, the telephone and the fax machine connected the world in personal communications, and the Web enabled personalized, targeted messaging. The Hype Machine enables both simultaneously. To understand it, we need to understand its commercial raison d'être, which is to support and enable integrated digital marketing.

I've never been inside the Internet Research Agency, but I've advised data science teams optimizing returns on digital marketing, and the IRA operates similarly. Its goal is to maximize persuasion per ruble on Facebook, Twitter, YouTube, Instagram, and the like. In fact, the presidential campaigns of Barack Obama, Hillary Clinton, Donald Trump, and Joe Biden all operated similarly, because the social media advertising ecosystem is a *persuasion market*. Brands, governments, and political campaigns invest in it to persuade us to change our behavior, from how we vote to what products we buy. In other words, to understand the Hype Machine, we have to understand *digital marketing*.

Russian Interference as Digital Marketing

The IRA registered as a commercial business in Russia in July 2013. By April 2014, two years before the U.S. presidential election, the IRA's director, Mikhail Bystrov, green-lighted Project Translator, which was designed to interfere in U.S. elections. Two months later the IRA "went dark," obfuscating its activities by using a complex system of shell companies. From that moment on, it acted like a clandestine digital marketing optimization agency, designed to promote pro-Russian interests and change people's beliefs and behaviors. Modern digital marketing optimization involves measurement, targeting, analytics, and performance optimization within and across channels. Most sophisticated digital marketing professionals engage in all these tactics and balance them in a portfolio that is itself optimized. This is also exactly how the IRA operates.

As early as 2014, the IRA began tracking, measuring, and analyzing political groups on U.S. social media to understand their influence. It analyzed the dynamics of the groups' size, the frequency of their posting behavior, and their audience engagement, among other things. It employed sophisticated ad targeting, first regionally, by focusing on swing states like Colorado, Virginia, and Florida, and then individually, by targeting left- and right-leaning Americans with politically tailored messages and minority groups with voter suppression campaigns. It engaged in influencer marketing by developing hundreds if not thousands of fictitious social media accounts, making them into "leaders of public opinion" on both the left and the right. It coordinated these accounts by having some of them post, while others promoted their content by liking, sharing, and reposting it. It tailor-made the creative elements of their messages in-house, circulated lists of U.S. holidays, and trained its staff to develop content about the U.S. economy and foreign policy to remain culturally relevant.

It managed multiple communities, online and offline, by creating thematic group pages on social media sites like Facebook and Instagram, for example, and growing those communities to hundreds of thousands of followers. It analyzed the performance of these activities by tracking the size of the audiences they reached, the engagement they produced (e.g., likes, comments, shares, reposts), their virality, and their correlation with marketing activities, like the channels they used (e.g., Facebook versus Twitter), the communities they engaged (e.g., Black Lives Matter), the accounts they promoted (e.g., Heart of Texas), and their content specifications (e.g., the ratio of text to images in persuasive messages).

In my research, I study how these kinds of influence campaigns change behaviors and how these behaviors spread through society with the help of social media. Over the last ten years, my colleagues and I have studied the effectiveness of social misinformation campaigns and social advertising. In my role as an entrepreneur, investor, and executive coach, I have myself worked to optimize digital marketing for brands like Macy's, Discover, Levi's, 1-800-Flowers, and others. The question I am asked most often in my scientific work is: *How can we know if Russian interference changed the outcome of the U.S. presidential election?* The question I am asked most often in my role as an entrepreneur and investor is: *How do I measure the returns on digital marketing investments?* The interesting thing about these two questions is that their answers are the same.

Whether we are talking about the U.S. Senate and House intelligence committees investigating Russian interference, the leaders of the world's largest corporations optimizing their marketing spend, or the sole proprietors of small businesses using Facebook to market their products, to understand the Hype Machine, we all need a crash course in digital marketing and social media analytics. To see how the Hype Machine works, we need to take it apart (metaphorically) and reverse-engineer it, as we would take apart the mechanical system of a car. And to understand such a system, it makes sense to start with the engine.

Lift, Attribution, and the Hype Machine's Torque

A car's torque is the force with which the engine turns the wheels. Torque is initially produced by the pistons in the engine block, which fire in a series of small explosions created as you push your foot down on the accelerator and deliver gas to the engine. Torque is transferred from the pistons to the crank, then to the transmission, and finally to the axles and wheels. The increase in wheel rotation (and therefore the car's speed and acceleration) is driven by the torque produced by the driver pressing on the gas pedal. Now imagine that the driver is an advertiser or any institution trying to change behavior. The gas is the ad spend, and the engine is social media. In this analogy, the best measure of the change the Hype Machine creates in society—its ability to put society's wheels in motion, or its torque, so to speak—is what ad execs call "lift."

Lift is the behavior change created or caused by persuasive social media messages. It's the key to understanding (and measuring) the Hype Machine's impact on the world. In the Hype Machine's context, lift is a measure of the extent to which an ad, video, or other persuasive message changes people's behavior. I discussed the neural basis of behavior change in Chapter 4. But when you step out of the fMRI machine and into society, the complexity of our social behavior, the difficulty of observing and measuring behavior, and the challenge of pinpointing behavior changes that are *caused* by social media make measuring lift difficult. Nonetheless, the entire enterprise of measuring the Hype Machine's impact (and, by the way, succeeding with digital marketing) rests on measuring lift—and therefore, ultimately, on our ability to detect and measure behavior change provoked by social media.

When I teach lift at MIT, I give my students a simple example. I say, "Imagine if, on the first day of class, as you were walking into the classroom, I stood at the door handing out leaflets advertising the class. The first student walks in, I hand her a leaflet. The second student walks in, I hand him a leaflet, and so on until I have handed all the students a leaflet advertising the class." I then ask them, "What's the conversion rate on those ads?" They all correctly reply, "One hundred percent," because 100 percent of the people who saw the ad "bought" or are enrolled in the class. Then I ask, "How much did those ads change your behavior?" Since they had all already signed up for the class long before seeing the ad, they all reply, "Not at all." So while the conversion rate on my ad is 100 percent, the lift from the ad—the amount of behavior change it provokes—is zero. This illustrates the essence of lift—it is the behavior change *caused* by a persuasive message, not just the correlation between seeing that message and engaging in the behavior you are trying to change. This is true of brands that are advertising products, public health organizations encouraging social distancing, and even Russians trying to suppress voter turnout.

The process of assigning credit for behavior change to the various persuasive messages we receive every day is called *attribution*. Think about the last time you bought something online. The process might have gone something like this: You saw an ad for a pair of shoes on Instagram and clicked on it. The click took you to the product page for those shoes on the brand's website or to an online retailer like Zappos. Let's say you liked the shoes, but not enough to buy them. So you browsed a little and left the site without buying anything. Then that pair of shoes started following you around the Internet, showing up in display ads and social ads as you browsed. This is what marketers call "retargeting" and what my friend Jamie Tedford, CEO of Brand Networks, calls "creepy."

Only about 2 percent of site visitors purchase on the first visit. Retargeting targets the other 98 percent with ads to bring them back, by placing cookies on their browsers and working with ad exchanges to display ads wherever they go next on the Web. But let's imagine the retargeting ads for the shoes you liked creeped you out enough that you didn't click on them. Then one Sunday morning, while reading a newspaper online, you thought about the shoes again. Since there were no retargeting ads to click on that morning, you searched for the shoe brand on Google. There you were hit with a search ad for the brand. You clicked on it, visited the website, and finally bought the shoes. Attribution assigns credit to these various marketing activities for causing the purchase. To understand why attribution is essential to measuring returns on advertising and the effects of the Hype Machine, it's worth considering the business model of a company called RetailMeNot.

Have you ever decided to buy something and searched for a coupon for it online? If you have, about 70 percent of the time, RetailMeNot will be the top result. When you click on its link, it takes you to a website that lists discounts for the item with big "redeem coupon here" buttons next to each discount. When you click to redeem a coupon, the site opens a new tab for the website you wanted to purchase from, like Amazon, Zappos, or J.Crew, and drops a cookie on your browser.* The cookie tells Amazon, Zappos, or J.Crew that RetailMeNot referred you to make the purchase. When you go to Amazon and make your purchase (the purchase you already intended to make, even before interacting with RetailMeNot), RetailMeNot gets a referral commission worth 4 percent of the purchase price of the item. In fact, it makes 4 percent on every Amazon sale it refers, enabling nearly $4.4 billion in retailer sales per year. The business was sold in 2017 for $630 mil-

---

* Cookies are short bits of software code that are installed on your browser when you visit a website and that enable the website to track your user behavior online, including which website referred you in the first place.

lion. But the lift from a RetailMeNot interaction is close to zero. It is essentially handing out digital leaflets advertising products to people who are often already going to buy.

This is why causal attribution is so important, and why understanding it is the key to success with digital marketing (and unfortunately with election manipulation as well). The persuasive impact of a social media message is the difference between the message recipient's behavior after seeing the message, and what their behavior would have been without seeing the message. From this key concept we can build our understanding of whether, and when, social media advertising campaigns work—whether, for example, social media manipulations change our votes and alter our elections, as well as all other effects of social media. Only by grasping this key lesson can we effectively understand, manage, and regulate the Hype Machine.

The Return on Hype

The practice of measuring the returns to digital marketing is, in some ways, straightforward. But in other ways it's deep, arguably even philosophical. The most common approach is to subtract the investment from the benefit the investment creates, then divide by the investment to make it a percentage:

$$ROI = (B - I) / I$$

Here *ROI* stands for return on investment, *B* stands for the benefit from the encouraged behavior, and *I* stands for the investment. If I invested $10,000 in marketing and made $50,000 in profit, my return on investment would be 400 percent. If I only made $15,000, my ROI would be 50 percent. ROI calculations depend on two metrics: the investment (or the cost of marketing activities) and the benefit the investment creates (typically measured in profit, revenue, lifetime value, awareness, engagement, or vote margins in a political campaign).

But what exactly is "the benefit the investment creates"? While *benefit* can refer to a variety of key performance indicators (KPIs) across different social media campaigns—like sales, votes, HIV tests, or petition signatures—it's perhaps easiest to consider it as the profit from a product's sales. Now, imagine you've invested in a Facebook ad campaign for shoe sales that had a conversion rate of 1 percent sales per click. Let's say you earned $27 in profit on every shoe sale. At what cost per click (CPC) would you break even on the ad campaign? At what CPC would you be "ROI neutral"? A little math gets you to the answer: $.27 per click. But there's a problem with that math, as we saw with the leaflet analogy in my MIT classroom.

The conversion rate times the profit on a sale may not accurately measure the "benefit the investment creates," because of that pesky word *creates*. The conversion rate tells you what fraction of the consumers who were served ads purchased shoes, yes. But how many of those ads *caused* a sale? And if those ads were only one of many marketing touch points that entered consumers' minds, what fraction of the sales they contributed to were they actually responsible for, among all the other marketing efforts that also contributed to the sale? This is where marketing measurement gets philosophical.

If you want to be rigorous about measuring the return on hype, you can't avoid thinking about lift. And if you are thinking about lift, you should be thinking about causality. In other words, if you are a marketer, political consultant, member of Congress investigating election interference, or public health official promoting social distancing, and you are *not* thinking about lift and causality, your views on the impact of the Hype Machine on business, democracy, and public health are simply wrong.

Consider the U.S. Congress's investigation of Russian election interference. Two studies released by the Senate Intelligence Committee in 2019 detail the reach and scope of Russian misinformation campaigns targeting hundreds of millions of U.S. citizens with the aim of affecting turnout and vote choice in the 2016 presidential election. The twin reports highlight, but do not answer, perhaps the most important question facing democracy in the digital age: to what extent are democratic elections vulnerable to social media manipulation?

Journalists and academics have weighed in on this question, often with confident yet contradictory conclusions. Nate Silver, founder and editor in chief of the site FiveThirtyEight, remarked that "if you wrote out a list of the most important factors in the 2016 election, I'm not sure that Russian social media memes would be among the top 100." Some academics are similarly skeptical, arguing that "Russia-sponsored content on social media likely did not decide the election" because Russian-linked spending and exposure to fake news were relatively small-scale. In contrast, professor and FactCheck founder Kathleen Hall Jamieson argues that a combination of Russian trolls and hacking likely tipped the election outcome for Donald Trump.

These divergent conclusions are reached primarily by analogy to other types of campaign activities. But the messages and campaigns studied by social scientists rarely, if ever, link *exposure* to social media and *causal changes in voting behavior*. Merely quantifying exposure, as the Senate's current analysis does, is not enough. A successful postmortem on Russian manipulation or an assessment of the impact of manipulation in the 2020 election needs to credibly estimate the effects of these exposures on voter behavior. Naïve observational approaches neglect the confounding factors that affect both exposure and voting behavior. For example, voters targeted with such content are more likely to be sympathetic to it. Evaluations using randomized experiments have shown observational estimates of the effects of Facebook advertising campaigns to be frequently off by over 100 percent. Our own estimates of social media influence were off by as much as 300 to 700 percent without carefully linking exposure to behavior.

The widely publicized evidence of the effectiveness of Cambridge Analytica's voter targeting on inferred personality traits is not estimated from randomized experiments and thus plausibly suffers from similar biases. Whether we are analyzing the effects of a brand's marketing or the influence of Russian social media manipulation on elections, to credibly estimate the effects of the Hype Machine on changes in our opinions and behaviors, we must change our approach. We must embrace causal lift.

Taking Causality Seriously

I have an *xkcd* cartoon about the difference between correlation and causation on the door to my office at MIT. It depicts two friends talking. One friend says to the other, "I used to think correlation implied causation. Then I took a statistics class [and] now I don't." The other friend says, "Sounds like the class helped," and the first friend replies, "Well, maybe."

It could be that the class taught the friend about the difference between correlation and causation. It could also just as easily be that the friend who took the class has an interest in and thus a proclivity to understand statistics. So maybe he "selected into" the class. This "selection effect" can explain the correlation between taking the class and understanding the difference between correlation and causation just as easily as the class *teaching* him about this difference.

This selection effect is a serious problem for measuring the return on hype. Why? Because social media messages are targeted at people who are likely to be susceptible to them. Brands pay consultants big bucks to target their ads at the people most likely to buy their products. Targeting increases conversion rates even without changing anyone's behavior, because it selects the most likely purchasers to receive ads. In fact, consultants have a perverse incentive to measure their own effectiveness by the conversion rate (the correlation between those who saw the ad and conversions) rather than by lift (the effect of someone seeing the ad on their chances of buying the product) because it's easier to measure and almost always more favorable to the consultant. (By this incorrect method, 100 percent of the credit for causing a sale is given to the ad impression.) But remember, correlation-based estimates of the effects of Facebook advertising campaigns are frequently off by over 100 percent. So assessments of ad campaigns or the effects of Russian interference that neglect causality are simply wrong.

What can we do about selection effects (and other confounders)? How can we truly understand the impact of the Hype Machine on society? Or the effectiveness of our digital marketing campaigns, or the effectiveness of public health communications on changing health behaviors? The right way to measure the return on hype is to take causal lift into account by weighting the benefit from a marketing action by the lift it creates—by multiplying the benefit of the encouraged behavior by lift, then subtracting and dividing by the investment.

$$ROI = (L \times B - I) / I$$

Here *ROI* stands for return on investment; *L* stands for the causal lift from the marketing one invests in, which is multiplied by *B*, or the benefit from the encouraged behavior; and *I* stands for the investment.

The natural next question, of course, is: how can we (rigorously) measure lift? This deep philosophical question lurks beneath almost every book written about how society works (often without acknowledgment). How can we discover the root causes of social phenomena— if, and to what extent, social factor A causes outcome B? The answer lies in randomness. Understanding causality and lift in the Hype Machine requires random variation.

Let's say we want to know whether joining the military (A) decreases a person's lifetime wage earnings (B). The problem is that many other factors (C) could be driving differences we might see in the raw numbers. We can't simply compare the wages of people who enter the military to those who don't because there are observable and unobservable differences in people who do and people who don't that drive differences in their wages. For instance, people with access to better-paying jobs are less likely to join the military in the first place (this is B causing A). And people with more education or skills choose not to enter the military (C causing both A and B). So what looks at first like a causal relationship between military service and lower average wages may simply be a correlation induced by these other factors. The challenge, then, is to control for these other factors while isolating the relationship we want to examine.

That's where random variation comes in. If we randomly assign some people to join the military, the group that joins and the group that doesn't will have, on average, the same education and skills (and age, gender, temperament, attitudes, and so on). With a large enough sample, the distributions of all observable and unobservable characteristics across people assigned to treatment and control groups are the same, making the treatment itself the only remaining explanation for any differences in outcomes across the two groups. With all else equal, we can be confident that nothing other than their military service can drive differences in their wages. That's the beauty of randomization. By randomly assigning people to an intervention, we can guarantee that observable (age and gender) and unobservable (skills) differences don't explain differences in their outcomes (in this case, wages).

Sometimes, however, ethics or opportunity prevents us from running an experiment. A scientist would be hard-pressed to justify a study that randomly forced people into the military. In these cases, we look for what are known as "natural experiments"—natural sources of random variation that mimic a randomized experiment. A good natural experiment used by Josh Angrist to measure the effect of military service on wages is the draft lottery imposed on U.S. citizens during the Vietnam War. Every male citizen was assigned a draft lottery number, and these numbers were chosen at random to determine who was drafted. The draft lottery was a natural experiment that created random variation in people's likelihood to join the military. Angrist used this variation to estimate the causal effect of military service on wages.

I'm describing the logic of randomized and natural experiments here because over the next six chapters I will refer to them constantly. My scientific work is basically a series of large-scale experiments or natural experiments designed to isolate cause and effect in the Hype Machine. How do social media ads change purchasing patterns? Run an experiment. How do online ratings affect opinions? Run an experiment. How do social signals change exercise behaviors? Find a natural experiment. We must understand causal effects to understand the impact of the Hype Machine on our world, and we can't understand causal effects without the random variation created by randomized or natural experiments.

Integrated Digital Marketing

When brands or the Russian IRA interface with the Hype Machine to direct the flow of information in society or create population-scale behavior change around the world, they do it through an optimized collection of digital marketing practices known as integrated digital marketing (IDM). Digital marketing takes place over multiple channels: social advertising, search advertising, display advertising, and mobile advertising. The key to IDM is the integration and optimization of those marketing activities within and across the channels.

Imagine you are a digital marketer (or Russian agent) allocating a budget for marketing activities in these channels to maximize persuasion, to increase sales in a product or business, or to garner votes in a political campaign. The basic process of integrated digital marketing is to create and deploy content in each channel; to analyze its performance by measuring the lift, benefit, and cost; and then to optimize performance within channels (by tweaking content and allocating more money to the best-performing content) and across channels (by allocating money toward the best-performing channels and away from the worst-performing channels). That's integrated digital marketing in a nutshell (Figure 6.1).

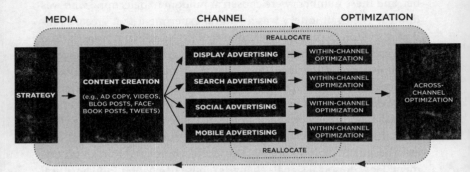

Figure 6.1 *An integrated digital marketing (IDM) program includes the strategy and media content creation phases (left), through the deployment of content across four channels (display, search, social, and mobile advertising), to the process of optimizing spending and content within each channel and across the channels.*

Of course, different channels aim for different goals. Search advertising targets people who are already looking for something specific. Display advertising builds brand awareness in people unfamiliar with the marketer's message. So maintaining a diverse portfolio of channel content is important to optimizing several goals simultaneously. Some kinds of social media advertising are complementary as well. For example, search and display advertising are known to complement each other. In other words, search ad performance is improved by the presence of display ads. Randomized experiments have shown that consumers exposed to a display ad conduct 5 to 25 percent more campaign-related searches. They increase search clicks and conversions. That $1.00 invested in search and display returns $1.24 for display and $1.75 for search. IDM is the process for optimizing persuasive performance. But what makes the Hype Machine persuasive in the first place is its ability to target messages at individual people at population scale—in other words, its ability to personalize mass persuasion.

Personalizing Mass Persuasion

Rob Cain, the former CIO of Coca-Cola, describes the past four decades of consumer engagement like this: In the 1980s we broadcast a single, uniform message to all consumers over a single channel. Think of Super Bowl ads. Brands spent months creating thirty-second spots, delivering the same message to millions of people at the same time. It was entertaining but not very sophisticated. The 1990s was the decade of segmentation, when messages were tailored for select groups, like 18-to-24-year-old gamers or soccer moms. This was only slightly more sophisticated. At the turn of the century, the Internet enabled interactions with individual consumers on a mass scale. As a result, the 2000s were the era of personalization, with messages tailored to individuals based on the behaviors and preferences gleaned from their browsing and transaction histories. Since 2010, we've experienced the era of the networked consumer, who is digitally connected to and influenced by her social network. As I remind my students at MIT, if you're still thinking about consumer engagement as market segmentation, you're about three decades behind.

Mass persuasion isn't new. It's been around since television and radio (or since Gutenberg and Hammurabi, depending on how far back you want to go). But the *personalization* of mass persuasion *is* relatively new. Television advertising employed limited demographic and geographic segmentation, but individual personalization really took off with the advent of the Internet, and social media targeting is even more advanced because it takes place in the context of a network, which gives marketers even more information with which to tailor messages. The ability to target specific messages at specific people relies on predictive modeling of consumers' individual preferences. So how does targeting work?

To target messages at the right people, a marketer needs to understand who is most likely to engage with (and ultimately be moved to act on) those messages. To do so, sophisticated marketers employ predictive modeling,* which uses detailed, individual-level data to predict

---

* Sure, some targeting is ad hoc, and some is just glorified segmentation, but the industry is becoming more sophisticated, so to understand the Hype Machine, it's best to know what it is capable of when used to its full potential.

consumers' likelihood of conversion as a function of their demographics (e.g., age, gender, language, socioeconomic status), behaviors (e.g., purchase history, content consumption history), preferences (e.g., social media likes, shares), social networks (e.g., the number of their friends or followers, the structure and composition of their social networks), and location histories.

A predictive ad-targeting model selects the consumers it thinks have the highest likelihood of conversion among the population of all targetable consumers. An example is sketched in Figure 6.2. The solid circles in the figure are eventual converters, and the hollow circles are eventual nonconverters. Imagine that the targeting model predicts that the consumers inside the center oval are high-likelihood converters in the population. It misses some actual high-likelihood converters

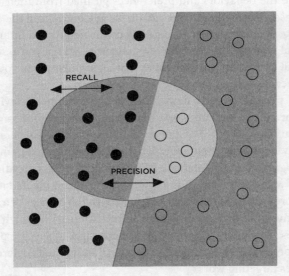

Figure 6.2 *Visualization of a predictive model's precision and recall. The consumers identified by a model as high-likelihood purchasers are inside the oval; the total population of consumers is inside the rectangle. The solid circles are high-likelihood consumers. The hollow circles are low-likelihood consumers. Recall is the number of true high-likelihood consumers identified by the model divided by the total number of high-likelihood consumers in the population. Precision is the number of true high-likelihood consumers the model identifies divided by the total number of consumers it identifies.*

(solid circles outside the model's predictive zone) and identifies some low-likelihood converters (the hollow circles inside the model's predictive zone) by mistake.

The industry uses two metrics to evaluate predictive ad targeting: *precision* and *recall*. The model's recall is simply the fraction of relevant consumers it identifies—the number of true high-likelihood consumers divided by the total number of high-likelihood consumers in the population. The model's precision is the fraction of its predictions that are truly relevant—the number of true high-likelihood consumers it identifies divided by the total number of consumers it identifies.

Together, precision and recall translate to a common performance metric called the "area under the reporter operating characteristic [or ROC] curve." Loosely interpreted, the area under the ROC curve depicts the trade-off between a model's true positive and false positive rates. As the model tries to identify more true positives (customers it thinks are high-likelihood converters who *are* actually high-likelihood converters), it expands the threshold with which it identifies high-likelihood consumers and therefore also allows for more false positive errors (customers it thinks are high-likelihood converters who are *not* high-likelihood converters). The broader its coverage gets as it tries to identify more consumers, the more consumers it identifies as high-likelihood consumers who aren't actually high-likelihood. Generally, as the true positives go up, so do the false positives. As you expand your set of predicted targets, you accept more duds. The question is, to what degree do you expand the number of errors in your predictive model in order to identify more high-likelihood consumers? This is the essence of the ROC curve in ad targeting.

Figure 6.3 shows four models with varying rates of true and false positives. Model 1 accepts 10 percent false positives to identify 10 percent of the true high-likelihood customers. Model 2, on the other hand, performs better—identifying about 20 percent of the true high-likelihood customers when accepting a 10 percent false positive rate. Model 3 performs even better, identifying 50 percent of the true high-likelihood customers when allowing a 10 percent false positive rate. Finally, Model 4 performs the best, identifying almost 80 percent of the true high-likelihood customers in the population at a 10 percent false positive rate.

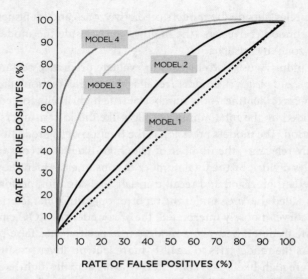

Figure 6.3 *Area under the reporter operating characteristic (ROC) curve. The performance of four predictive models is evaluated by their relative true positive and false positive rates. The area under the ROC curve represents model performance. The greater the area under a model's curve and above the 45-degree dotted line, the better the model performs.*

Digital Marketing's Dirty Secret

Now that you understand how companies and the Russian IRA evaluate the effectiveness of digital marketing and the persuasiveness of messages on the Hype Machine, I can let you in on digital marketing's dirty secret. It's the one secret that marketing execs guard more closely than any other: *Digital ads don't work nearly as well as they're advertised to.* More often than not, their effectiveness is wildly and brazenly oversold. The stratospheric conversion rates and returns they report make a marketer want to take off their blazer and twirl it over their head while singing "We Are the Champions" at the top of their lungs at marketing meetings. But these golden eggs are, unfortunately, almost always overvalued by a factor of three and sometimes by as much as a factor of ten or more. Which means, for companies and for the Russian IRA, that instead of the 4,100 percent ROI they thought they were getting, they could actually be getting a *negative* 63 percent ROI.

Imagine if their chief marketing officer said, "Sorry, we flubbed the math. You didn't gain 4,100 percent on your $51 million investment, you actually lost 63 percent." And these numbers aren't hypothetical. I'm not pulling them out of thin air. These are the actual overestimates of ad effectiveness found in a large-scale study at eBay. Moreover, eBay is not an outlier. It's the norm. That reversal is like going from earning $2.1 billion to losing $19 million. I know—it's shocking.

When Thomas Blake, Chris Nosko, and Steven Tadelis compared the ROI measures eBay was using to experimental measures that distinguished correlation from causation, they found brand search ad effectiveness was overestimated at eBay by up to 4,100 percent. Comparing traditional measures to a large experiment measuring the returns on Web display ads on Yahoo!, Randall Lewis and David Reiley found ROI inflation of 300 percent. In a large-scale experiment testing the effectiveness of retargeting ads compared to industry studies, Garrett Johnson, Randall Lewis, and Elmar Nubbemeyer found overestimates up to 1,600 percent. In a study of fifteen large U.S. advertising experiments comprising 500 million user-experiment observations and 1.6 billion ad impressions, Brett Gordon, Florian Zettelmeyer, Neha Bhargava, and Dan Chapsky found that traditional ad effectiveness measures overestimated the lift from Facebook ads by up to 4,000 percent and that, in half the fifteen experiments, traditional methods overestimated lift by a factor of three or more.

It's the most widely used shell game in business today, and it works because everyone in the industry is incentivized to keep the secret. Marketing agencies are commonly paid commissions as a percentage of media spend, or they make money on rebates, discounts, or free inventory from media owners, given to them because of the size of the media budgets they fulfill. The greater the budget, the greater the buying power and the greater the rebates, discounts, and free inventory, which they typically sell back to their clients. The conflict of interest is glaring, and the incentive to self-report strong performance is obvious, because better performance attracts bigger ad budgets, and bigger ad budgets mean more revenue for the marketing agency because they get paid as a percentage of media spend.

Here's the $400 billion question (which was the size of the digital marketing industry worldwide in 2020): which of the industry's players—CMOs, marketing agencies, or third-party providers (all of whom are paid proportionally to the advertising dollars spent)—are incentivized to ask which of their ads aren't working? The answer is none of them.

At the turn of the twentieth century, John Wanamaker lamented that "half the money I spend on advertising is wasted; the trouble is I don't know which half." A hundred years later the tidal wave of granular, individual-level personal data created by online advertising has given us the opportunity to solve Wanamaker's paradox. It can potentially allow marketers to measure media effects precisely and to know which messages work and which don't. But without careful causal inference, targeting can exacerbate the selection problem by targeting messages at people who are already the most likely to engage in the behaviors they are trying to encourage. These are potentially the people for whom persuasive messages are the least effective, because they're already the brand's most loyal customers. Messaging them doesn't cause sales, it just throws good money away needlessly.

To make matters worse, estimating online media effects correctly is difficult and costly. The behaviors that marketers want to measure (sales, votes, HIV tests) are so volatile and the effects required to meaningfully move the needle on them are so small that only massive experiments have anywhere near the statistical power needed to detect meaningful effects. In their study of twenty-five advertising experiments, Randall Lewis and Justin Rao showed that for retail sales, which have relatively low volatility, the ratio of the standard deviation to the mean of sales is about ten to one—which means it's way too imprecise to measure without a lot of data. For high-end durable goods like cars, the ratio is more like twenty to one. This much variability makes economically meaningful ad effects difficult to detect. As Randall Lewis and David Reiley opined, "The variance of individual purchases (driven by myriad idiosyncratic factors) makes for a rather large haystack in which to seek the needle of advertising's effects." More infrequent behaviors like voting, signing up for subscription services, or buying once-a-year vacation packages are even more volatile, making the problem even worse. This makes measuring the Hype Machine's impact difficult, whether we are talking about election manipulation or disease outbreaks. Even when that underlying impact is dramatic, it can be hard to pin down precisely.

The need for huge amounts of data to measure the effectiveness of ads favors large firms and platforms, like Facebook, Google, and Amazon. Only a small number of companies are large enough to measure the effects of persuasive messages on the Hype Machine consistently and effectively. This, in turn, means that the majority of firms don't know their ads' effectiveness, creating vastly different levels of ad spending across companies, exposing huge inefficiencies in the market for digital advertising and social media messaging. It also means, perhaps just as important, that the large data holders like Google and Facebook are the only places that social scientists can find data pools big enough to run experiments that will explain how it all works, which gives them enormous power and responsibility in helping us understand and manage the Hype Machine. When these companies close their doors to social scientists, we all suffer. I will return to this need for data transparency more than once as the story unfolds.

The Good News

The good news for anyone engaged in digital marketing is that *some* digital and social media messaging is quite effective. Lift is real and measurable—it's just not being measured or managed properly. The eBay search marketing study found that while branded keyword search lost money, recording a negative 63 percent ROI, nonbrand keyword ads for specific products and categories positively influenced new and infrequent customers to visit the site and purchase. This supports the "informative view of advertising," which suggests that ads are most effective at *informing* consumers of the "characteristics, location and prices of products and services that they may otherwise be ignorant about"—in other words, when it is a tool to better inform and educate consumers about a product or service. As Blake, Nosko, and Tadelis reported, in terms of eBay, "consumers who have completed several eBay transactions in the year before our experiment are likely to be familiar with eBay and are unaffected by search engine marketing (SEM). In contrast, more *new users* [emphasis mine] sign up when they are exposed to SEM ads, and users who only purchased one or two items in the previous year *increase* their purchases when exposed to SEM."

The takeaway for consumers and marketers? Search ads are most effective for new and infrequent customers. This outreach to new customers, known as "prospecting" in marketing parlance, attempts to spread brand awareness to people who are unfamiliar with the brand, or political issue, and increase a brand's reach. The takeaway for Russia and the IRA? Targeting infrequent voters and undecideds is likely the most efficient strategy for maximizing influence per ruble. The takeaway for those of us trying to stop manipulation and fake news? We know where we're vulnerable. Now we can look to thwart manipulation where it stands to be the most effective.

Ironically, brands typically regard new prospects as their "worst" customers. They tend to ignore them in ad targeting, in favor of more "high-value repeat customers," because they "convert" often with or without seeing ads. In other words, they seem "high value" according to correlation-based metrics. But as we've seen, these ads are essentially preaching to the choir. They aren't genuinely converting anyone. Recall that "preaching to the choir" is the same argument that scientists skeptical of the effects of social media manipulation made about the likelihood that Russia tipped the 2016 presidential election: pro-Trump messages were targeted at people who were already pro-Trump. Which explains why we need to understand these fundamentals to sort out the Hype Machine's impact on our world.

The experiment by Lewis and Reiley at Yahoo! demonstrated that online display ads profitably increased purchases by 5 percent. It also unmasked two misconceptions about digital advertising. First, 78 percent of the increase in sales came from customers who never clicked on an ad. Which highlights another dirty secret in the marketing industry: clicks are a terrible proxy for conversions. People who click on ads are rarely converted into sales. And people who are converted into sales rarely click on ads. The correlation between clicks and conversions is typically nonexistent. Second, 93 percent of the increase in sales occurred in the retailer's brick-and-mortar stores, rather than through direct responses online. While direct response advertising—clicking through to purchase on an online ad—may be easier to measure, it is an incomplete measure of advertising effectiveness for brands with offline sales channels. And that is true for other human behaviors like voting, which also happens offline. Johnson, Lewis, and Nubbemeyer confirmed that the widely publicized industry reports of stratospheric returns are wishful thinking. More accurately, retargeting created a solid (and more realistic) 17.2 percent increase, or causal lift, in website visits and a 10.5 percent causal lift in purchases.

These regularities suggest that the effectiveness of attempts to manipulate elections with social media also likely increases with scale. The grander the effort, the easier it is to measure and optimize. Manipulators are incentivized to go big or go home. So efforts to detect and thwart them should focus on the biggest offenders. Targeting uninitiated voters is also likely their best strategy. Politically engaged citizens, regular voters, and digital natives are less vulnerable to manipulation, implying that millennials and older citizens are most vulnerable. And measuring whether people clicked on fake news is not sufficient. As I will discuss in Chapter 12, to harden democracy to social media manipulation, the Hype Machine and the voting booth must be guarded simultaneously, and social media data must be combined with actual voting data to isolate the threat.

Gordon, Zettelmeyer, Bhargava, and Chapsky's experiments revealed a causal conversion lift in eight of fifteen campaigns—roughly half—ranging from a 1.2 percent to a 450 percent increase in purchases as a result of Facebook ads. Facebook ads were more effective in encouraging website registrations and page views. Their ads resulted in a 63 percent to 893 percent increase in registrations, and a 14 percent to 1,500 percent increase in page views. But if so, then how did P&G cut its online marketing budget by $200 million and still increase sales by 8 percent over the same period?

How P&G Cut Digital Marketing and Grew Sales

At the annual leadership meeting of the Interactive Advertising Bureau (IAB) in 2017, P&G's chief brand officer, Marc Pritchard, took the stage in what the audience thought would be another run-of-the-mill speech touting P&G's digital marketing innovations. But to the surprise of everyone, including Randall Rothenberg, CEO of the IAB, who had invited Pritchard to the stage, Pritchard instead delivered an address that the digital marketing industry is still talking about today, several years later.

Speaking in a calm voice, he unleashed a measured, but in its own way scathing, critique of the opacity, deceit, and inefficiency of digital marketing, from a lack of standard metrics, to click fraud, to misaligned incentives in agency contracts, to a lack of third-party measurement verification. It was a tour de force, as marketing speeches go. Pritchard, a thirty-seven-year P&G veteran, was angry. You could almost hear the disappointment in his voice. The brand he had devoted his entire career to had, along with all other digital marketing clients in the room, been getting a raw deal, and he was fed up.

That day Pritchard announced an action plan for media transparency and notified the market that, within the year, P&G would no longer do business with partners that did not adopt a common validated viewability standard, transparent media agency contracts, accredited third-party measurement verification, and third-party certified fraud prevention. The audience applauded. Pritchard noted that "time was up," and that P&G would no longer spend money on inefficient, opaque, fraudulent digital marketing. P&G then put its money where its mouth was and cut its digital marketing budget by $200 million.

Agencies grumbled, and social media analysts were in an uproar. They argued that this was a huge mistake for P&G. That it couldn't effectively steward its digital marketing dollars without the help of the agencies' expertise. That it would experience a contraction of sales growth due to a lack of advertising. Yet two years later, despite having cut its digital advertising budget so dramatically, P&G delivered 7.5 percent organic sales growth, nearly doubling its industry competitors'. How did it do it? By taking advantage of the performance-based digital marketing trends that I've just described.

First, P&G shifted its media spend from a focus on frequency—on clicks or views—to one focused on reach, on the number of consumers it touched. Its data had shown that it was previously hitting some of its customers with social media ads ten to twenty times a month. This level of ad bombardment resulted in diminishing returns and probably even annoyed some loyal customers. So it reduced the ads' frequency by 10 percent and shifted those ad dollars to reach new and infrequent customers who were not seeing ads. In 2019, P&G increased the efficiency of its ad delivery and increased its reach to new customers in China by 60 percent. This shift from frequency to reach echoes the results of the eBay study—that new and infrequent consumers are the most moved by ads.

Second, P&G became more sophisticated in targeting the right people. By collecting a vast database of first-party consumer data that contained a billion consumer IDs, it began to reach "very targeted audiences." For example, it described in its 2019 fourth-quarter earnings call that it was moving from "generic demographic targets like 'women 18–49'" to "smart audiences" like first-time moms and first-time washing machine owners.

Third, between 2015 and 2019, the company cut its agency roster by 60 percent and rationalized its agency contracts, reporting $750 million of savings in agency and production costs and $400 million of improved cash flow. In 2019 it committed to reducing the number of agencies that remained by another 50 percent in an effort to save an additional $400 million.

Fourth, when the coronavirus hit in 2020, media consumption soared as consumers were forced to shelter in place. P&G used this opportunity to capture mind share by retaining its streamlined focus on awareness and reach while "doubling down" on its marketing spend during a time when consumers' attention was squarely focused on digital channels.

The Hype Machine is a digital marketing machine, and whether we want to prevent election manipulation or make our Facebook ads work, we can't understand it without studying its tactics, especially traditional tactics like targeting, which enable personalized mass persuasion. But the Hype Machine is different from any other marketing or communication channel in one fundamental way, which I will cover next. And that is, it has completely and irrevocably hypersocialized us.

CHAPTER 7

Hypersocialization

*Relationship between human beings is based on the
image-forming, defensive mechanism. In our
relationships, each of us builds an image of the other, and
these two images have relationship, not the human beings
themselves.*

—Jiddu Krishnamurti

One thing that makes social media different from any other type of
media is that we're not only influenced by the direct persuasion of
advertising but also swayed by a reverberating cacophony of social
signals, from our peers and the crowd, that amplify, reinforce, and
spread the Hype Machine's influence. A perfect example of these direct
and indirect influences unfolded during the U.S. congressional elections of 2010.

In June 2020, Facebook announced their largest voter mobilization
drive in history, prominently displaying information about how to
register or request an absentee or mail-in ballot at the top of the Facebook newsfeed and on Instagram. In 2010, they did something much
simpler and more subtle. On November 2, 2010, midterm Election
Day in the United States, Facebook conducted an experiment to measure its newsfeeds' power to sway elections. On that day, 61 million
people over the age of eighteen saw a message in their newsfeeds encouraging them to vote. It read "Today is Election Day" and included
a link to "Find your polling place" and an "I Voted" button to "tell your
friends you voted." In the top corner was a counter displaying the
number of Facebook users who had previously reported voting.

Not everyone saw the same message. Some were randomly assigned
to see an "informational" message, which simply reminded them to
vote. Others saw a "social message" that, in addition to the reminder,
displayed up to six randomly selected profile pictures of friends who

had already clicked the "I Voted" button. Some saw no message at all. By comparing people who received the informational message to those who didn't, Facebook was able to estimate the power of its own direct messaging to mobilize voters. By comparing people who received the social message to those who didn't, it was able to estimate the power of social influence between peers to mobilize voters. It validated its findings in public voting records, and the results were dramatic.

A single Facebook newsfeed message caused an additional 340,000 votes to be cast, increasing voter turnout by 0.60 percent. Let that sink in for a minute: a single social media message, displayed at zero marginal cost to Facebook, created 340,000 additional votes in U.S. congressional elections. Facebook replicated the experiment in the 2012 U.S. presidential election, this time showing the message to 15 million voters. Despite the fact that voter mobilization campaigns are less effective in higher-stakes elections due to myriad competing "get out the vote" efforts, the message caused an additional 270,000 votes to be cast and increased voter turnout by 0.24 percent.

While 0.60 percent and 0.24 percent may seem like small effects, it's worth considering that, in the 2000 presidential election, George W. Bush defeated Al Gore by 537 votes—a 0.01 percent difference in Florida and a 0.00001 percent difference nationwide. It's also worth noting that after the 2012 U.S. presidential election, Facebook deployed its voter mobilization button repeatedly: in the 2014 Scottish referendum, the 2015 Irish referendum, the 2015 U.K. election, the 2016 U.K. Brexit vote, the 2016 U.S. presidential election, and the German federal elections of 2017. Facebook's experiments in 2010 and 2012 proved the Hype Machine's power to create population-scale changes in voting and thus its potential to move the needle on the world's most important geopolitical events.

But while the election experiments' top-line results were dramatic, a more nuanced set of findings revealed the true transformational power of the Hype Machine. Facebook found that users who saw the social message, which displayed social proof in the pictures of friends who had reported voting, were 0.39 percent more likely to vote than users who received the informational message that reminded people to vote but displayed no social proof. That suggests that it was seeing their friends' faces that caused people to change their voting behavior—a convincing testament to the persuasive power of digital social signals.

Facebook also estimated the spillover effects of these messages on the friends of those who received them. Users who received no messages, but who had friends who did, were driven to vote in greater numbers. For every close friend who received the social message, Facebook users were 0.224 percent more likely to vote than they would have been had their friend not received the message. And remember, these folks received no messages at all. They simply had friends who did.

These "spillover" or "peer" effects—the influence of our friends' social media behaviors on our own real-world behaviors—were even more striking than the direct effect of Facebook's political messaging. In Facebook's 2010 experiment, while the direct message with social proof drove 340,000 people to vote, the spillover effects caused 886,000 more votes to be cast by the friends of those who were shown the message. This cascading behavior captures the power of social media to magnify behavior changes around the world. The social signals we create and consume on the Hype Machine are engineered to trigger our neurophysiology; our brains have evolved to process them. As we create and consume these social signals, they also change our behavior.

In the last decade, we've witnessed an explosion of digital social signals. Today, in just a few minutes every morning, we scan what our families are up to on Facebook, where our friends ate dinner last night on Instagram, what our peers report happening near them on Twitter, who changed jobs on LinkedIn, how far our running partner ran yesterday on Nike Run Club or Strava, and who liked us, romantically, on Tinder and Hinge. This avalanche of digital social signals simply didn't exist a decade ago. Over hundreds of thousands of years, our brains evolved to socialize. In the last ten years, as our behavior has become more and more influenced by our friends through the Hype Machine, we've become *hypersocialized*.

Going for Gold

On August 6, 2016, Greg Van Avermaet rode for his life in Rio de Janeiro. Beginning in Copacabana, he raced his BMC Team Machine SLR01 bicycle 150 miles through the Ipanema, Barra, and Reserva Maripendi beaches, before returning to Copacabana to capture the men's individual gold medal in the cycling road race at the 2016 Summer Olympics in Brazil. It was a grueling race in which he climbed 344 feet and hit gradients close to 13 percent through Grumari's short climbs, recording a peak elevation of 1,444 feet and a death-defying 16 percent gradient on the fast technical descent out of Canoas and Vista Chinesa, which saw multiple crashes that day. He averaged 23.3 miles per hour over the six-hour-and-nine-minute race, during which he hit a maximum speed of 67.1 miles per hour. He did all this in 89-degree weather, which peaked at over 100 degrees. He hit a maximum cadence—the speed with which a rider turns the pedals—of 173 rpm, averaged 85 rpm, and ended the race with a winning sprint at 110 rpm.

Then he did something he could never have done before 2009. He posted all these statistics to a social exercise app called Strava, sharing the details of his golden ride with the world. He got back a resounding fifteen thousand "kudos," Strava's version of digital congratulations, from friends, fans, and admirers. In fact, his ride racked up more kudos than any other individual activity that entire year.

In 2018 Strava athletes gave 3.6 billion kudos for the 6.67 billion miles of athletic activities their peers recorded across 32 sports in 195 countries. On average, 25 activities were uploaded to Strava every minute. The average run was 5.1 miles long and lasted about fifty minutes. The average bike rider completed a 21.9-mile ride in one hour and thirty-seven minutes. Sundays were the most popular days to exercise, and Tuesdays were the fastest day of the week for both runners and cyclists worldwide. (It seems we need Mondays to recover from Sundays.) In the United States, the most popular day to ride was the Fourth of July holiday, but the most popular day to run was Thanksgiving Day, probably because we feel we need to earn the gigantic Thanksgiving meals we eat.

One Strava statistic from 2018 stands out for me: the degree to which we run, bike, swim, ice-skate, and skateboard *more* when we do these things with friends. Since Strava records group activities, it can analyze how solo and group activities compare. When it plotted the data for 2018, it found that people exercise longer when exercising with friends (Figure 7.1). Group rides are 52 percent longer than solo rides, on average, and group runs are 20 percent longer than solo runs.

It seems exercise is motivated by socialization. We've all likely experienced this motivation when we run competitively or when we run or ride in groups. But the Hype Machine institutionalizes this motivation

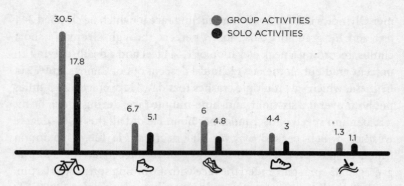

Figure 7.1 *Group versus solo exercise behaviors. The chart plots the average distance in miles of group (gray) and solo (black) bike rides, hikes, runs, walks, and swims from October 1, 2017, through September 30, 2018, on Strava.*

by instantaneously sharing our exercise activities with our friends, at no cost, just as Greg Van Avermaet shared his Olympic ride with the world. Apps like Nike Run Club, Strava, and Runkeeper allow us to record our fitness activities in excruciating detail, including their distance, speed, and the calories they burn. They allow us to share all this information with our friends on these platforms and on social media networks like Instagram and Facebook. If social support and competition motivate us to exercise, then the digital socialization of fitness has the potential to increase the amount, duration, and intensity of the world's exercise activities. By institutionalizing the sharing of exercise activities, the Hype Machine is digitally enabling social influence and peer effects in exercise behaviors. These correlations raise an important question: Does the digital social influence of the Hype Machine cause us to exercise more? Or put more directly: Is exercise digitally contagious? And if so, what other kinds of behaviors might be digitally contagious?

Is Exercise Contagious?

Unfortunately, comparing group to solo exercise sheds little light on whether exercise is contagious because we don't know what drives those differences. For the same reason we can't measure the effects of Russian interference on elections, or the returns from digital marketing, by looking at correlations, we can't measure digital social influence, in exercise or any other behaviors, without distinguishing correlation and causal lift. We know, for example, that marathon runners tend to be friends with marathon runners and that couch potatoes tend to be friends with couch potatoes. (That's homophily.) So simple correlations in running behavior among friends don't prove that friends influence each other to exercise. People who choose to run or bike in groups may simply be more committed to running or biking and may, therefore, run and bike longer.

To understand whether digital peer effects motivate exercise and whether exercise is contagious, we need some way of distinguishing between correlation and causation. But while randomized experiments are the gold standard of causal inference and useful in a marketing context, we can't go around randomly cattle-prodding some people to get off their couches to run. So to measure peer effects in running, we had to find another source of as-good-as-random variation in people's running habits—something that motivates some people to run but has no effect on whether their friends run. To solve this riddle, my former postdoc Christos Nicolaides and I had to become meteorologists.

We collaborated with a large, global fitness tracking company to collect data on the network ties and daily exercise patterns of 1.1 million runners who ran over 350 million kilometers over five years. Participants recorded the distance, duration, speed, and calories burned on their runs and shared those details with their friends on an app. For a global network of runners, we knew who ran, when, where, and how fast they ran, and who their friends were. We also collected data from 47,000 weather stations in 196 countries and knew the precise temperature and rainfall in the exact location of each of our 1.1 million runners for every day of the five years they ran. Why?

Well, the trick to the study was that weather influences running. As you might expect, the less it rained and the milder the temperature, the more people ran. When runners woke up to beautiful weather, they laced up their sneakers and hit the road. When they woke up to rain, they stayed home. The key, however, was that their friends were all over the world, experiencing different weather than they were. So while it was raining in New York City, it was sunny in Phoenix, Arizona, where someone's friend lived. We exploited these differences in weather to measure whether one friend's running caused another friend to run more. It's sunny every day in Phoenix, more or less. So if a beautiful day in New York caused a friend in Phoenix to run more, it could only be because of social influence between friends. We had found a "natural experiment" that we used to measure the extent to which exercise is contagious. And what we found surprised us.

Exercise was indeed contagious, and the magnitude of the effects was quite large. Seeing that your friend ran an additional kilometer on the app influenced you to run an additional three-tenths of a kilometer more on the same day. When your friends ran an additional kilometer per minute faster, it caused you to run an additional three-tenths of a kilometer per minute faster. When your friends ran for ten additional minutes, it motivated you to run three minutes longer. And when your friends burned an additional ten calories, it influenced you to burn three and a half additional calories. This peer influence diminished over time. Your friends' running today influenced you less tomorrow, and the day after for every measure.

But exercise is just the starting point to understanding how social media hypersocializes our behavior. Other platforms are sharing our purchasing, voting, eating, dating, and reading behaviors and even our moods. Research shows that the proliferation of digital social signals is transforming the ebb and flow of these behaviors as well. A few examples of this hypersocialization drive the point home.

The Hypersocialization of News

Every seven years academics get a sabbatical, a year off, to reset their thinking or kickstart new research. In 2013 I took a year off from MIT to become the scholar-in-residence at the *New York Times* R&D lab. It was an amazing experience. I collaborated with resident designers, engineers, and intellectual tinkerers who were trying to "look around corners" at the technologies that would affect journalism and news consumption in the years to come.

I was there specifically to work on Project Cascade, a first-of-its-kind tool that combined browsing behavior and sharing activity to build a detailed picture of how information propagates through social media space. My primary purpose was to analyze the Cascade data to understand whether social media sharing was increasing *Times* readership. It's not clear whether social media complements or substitutes for the news. It could be that social sharing leads people to read more news by following hyperlinks through Twitter or Facebook. But it could also be that the short summaries of articles on social media give us all we need, making us less likely to read the whole article than we would have been if we hadn't seen the summary. Needless to say, the answer to this question is essential to the *Times'* strategy on embracing or resisting social media.

To find out which it was, my PhD student Michael Zhao and I analyzed hundreds of millions of *Times* pageviews and tweets to discern whether social sharing of *Times* articles in one city increased readership of those articles in other cities. As in our exercise study, we used the rain as a natural experiment. Since rain keeps people inside reading the *Times,* we estimated whether rainy days in one region, which boosted social sharing of news articles in that region, caused increases in readership in regions that were receiving those social shares in higher proportions on social media.

We found that a 10 percent increase in viewership outside a given region causes viewership in that region to increase by approximately 3.4 percent, and that social media was the primary driver of that social spillover. Regions that were more connected on social media experienced more social spillovers than regions that were less connected. Social spillovers were also stronger when readers were referred by social media than when they came through search engines. Taken together, these results suggest that digital social signals are indeed driving our news consumption.

The Hypersocialization of Dating

As dating apps have proliferated, digital social signals have also infiltrated our romantic lives. I'm intimately aware of this trend because we sold our second company, Humin, to Tinder in 2016. More romantic partners have been introduced online through the Hype Machine's algorithms than through friends and family since 2013. So what does digital dating mean for society? That's a question that psychologists, biologists, and demographers will likely ponder for decades. There is no question that the advent of Tinder, Hinge, Bumble, and other apps is changing how we meet, who we date, and who we love. The long-term consequences of the "sense and suggest" loops in date-matching algorithms are not yet known. Are we being steered toward more homophily or more diversity in our dating lives? What might that mean for the genetic diversity of our kids and our kids' kids? What's the likely effect on human evolution? We don't have answers to these larger questions yet. But we have gained some insight into how digital social signals are changing the dating game.

My friends and colleagues Ravi Bapna, Jui Ramaprasad, Galit Shmueli, and Akhmed Umyarov conducted an experiment on one of these apps to understand how the digital breadcrumbs we leave on social dating sites affect our romantic outcomes. Online dating enables new forms of digital signaling that have no precedent in the physical world. For example, we can search, filter, and browse potential mates with greater speed and control than ever before. Algorithms match us using big data in ways we don't fully understand. And we can consider dates anonymously, which isn't possible at a bar or other offline social gathering. Ravi and his colleagues wanted to know how these digital features affect us—specifically, how our digital signaling motivates us to interact with others and whether what we share makes us more or less outgoing.

They worked with a large North American dating website to understand how anonymity affects date matching outcomes. What does it mean for the dating pool when we can digitally cloak our interest in someone while getting to know them more intimately? In a bar, if I want to find out more about someone I am attracted to, I might go talk to them, ask them about their interests, what makes them laugh, what intrigues them intellectually, or what activities they enjoy on weekends. To do so, I have to "make a move" socially and in real physical space. I have to get up off my barstool, walk over, fumble an awkward introduction, and get into a conversation. By then the jig is up! She knows I'm interested because I just got up, walked across a crowded room, and introduced myself. The social signals are abundant. But online we have the ability to browse anonymously. I can find out a lot about someone by reading their profile before I reach out to them, and I can do so without them ever noticing that I might be interested. How does this ability to hide our social signaling change how we search for potential mates? How does it change how others react to us?

When a user browses a profile on the dating website's app, they leave a digital signal for the user they are checking out, indicating they have seen their profile. This digital breadcrumb may make the person browsing shyer because their potential date will know they were browsing. But it may also facilitate the interaction by signaling to the recipient that the person who is browsing their profile is interested in them. The effects of this subtle social signal are hard to decipher with armchair theorizing, so Ravi and company designed a clever experiment to uncover them. They sampled 100,000 new users and randomly gifted half of them with anonymous browsing, so they could browse profiles without letting anyone know. That simple tweak—blocking interest signals—had dramatic effects.

Compared with the control group, users treated with anonymity threw caution to the wind. They viewed more profiles and were more likely to view same-sex and interracial potential mates. But the interest signals helped achieve more matches. Anonymous users, who lost the ability to leave interest signals, had fewer matches than their nonanonymous counterparts. This was particularly disadvantageous for women, who the researchers found tended not to make the first move and instead relied on others to initiate the communication. Signals of digital browsing (especially when left by women) were serving as inspiration for those whose profiles had been browsed to make the first move (especially men). So turning off the digital breadcrumbs disadvantaged shyer users (especially women).

The long-term effects of the Hype Machine on our romantic relationships are not known. If such a subtle signal can have such dramatic effects, what are the consequences of matching algorithms and swipe culture on who we date and how we partner? If the Hype Machine moves the needle on these intermediate outcomes, what does it mean for human evolution? We are continuing to push on the research that will hopefully uncover the answers to these important questions. But one thing is clear: the Hype Machine is changing how we date by altering how we signal one another socially.

The Hypersocialization of Charitable Giving

Dating is pretty fundamental, but so is altruism. If the Hype Machine affects who we date, can it also affect how we donate? To understand how it might, MIT PhD student Yuan Yuan studied gifting of Chinese Red Packets on WeChat. Red Packets or Red Envelopes are monetary gifts given in China and other East Asian cultures during holidays or special occasions like weddings, graduations, and births. In 2014, WeChat enabled its users to distribute virtual Red Packets (and currency) to contacts and groups via its mobile payment platform. In 2016, 32 billion Red Packets were exchanged during the Chinese New Year alone. By 2017 that number was in the hundreds of billions. Today Red Packet gifting makes up a sizable portion of the mobile payment transactions that WeChat enables. Yuan Yuan wanted to know if digital Red Packets inspire us to pay it forward—whether receiving such digital gifts inspires us to gift more often and in greater amounts toward others.

He utilized a novel feature of the way WeChat divides up Red Packets distributed to groups. When a WeChat user sends a Red Packet in a group, the amount that each user receives is randomly assigned by the platform based on the amount sent, the number of friends who chose to receive it, and the order of receiving times. So some users are randomly selected to receive more money than others. WeChat also designates which user receives the largest amount with a "luckiest draw" icon. Yuan Yuan and his co-authors wanted to know how this randomness in how much one receives affected recipients' motivation to pay it forward by sending monetary gifts to others.

Their analysis revealed that recipients on average paid forward 10 percent of the amounts they received and that the "luckiest draw" recipients, who received the largest shares of their corresponding Red Packets, were one and a half times more likely to pay it forward than other recipients. So the digital gifts we send do inspire recipients to pay our altruism forward to the benefit of others.

Hypersocializing Our Emotions

In one of the more controversial experiments conducted on digital social influence, researchers at Facebook and Cornell tested whether digital social signals create "emotional contagion" across the Hype Machine's network. They wanted to know whether happiness or depression could be passed from person to person through the trillions of online posts we create and consume every day. As always, the trouble is that happy and sad people tend to congregate with each other online, so measuring correlations in emotions among friends can't tell us if emotional contagions occur online.

So the team from Facebook and Cornell randomly manipulated the emotions to which millions of users were exposed in their newsfeeds. For some people, they randomly reduced the amount of negative content they saw. And for others, they randomly reduced the amount of positive content they saw, measured by the fraction of positive and negative words used in their friends' posts. They then measured whether these reductions in negativity and positivity caused the recipients to change the negativity and positivity they expressed in their own Facebook posts.

They found that the Hype Machine spreads *emotions* as well as behaviors. First, they noticed that the reduction of positive and negative emotions in users' newsfeeds reduced the overall number of words users posted to Facebook. The implication? Emotionally arousing content, whether positive or negative, inspires Facebook users to post more. The Hype Machine helps to spread emotional arousal. That is, in part, why I call it the Hype Machine. It hypes us up to keep us engaged. And the business model it runs on likes us to be very engaged.

Second, they found that when positive posts were reduced in the newsfeed, the percentage of positive words in people's status updates decreased, and the percentage of negative words increased. Conversely, when negative posts were reduced, the percent of negative words decreased and the percentage of positive words increased, confirming the emotional contagion of social media posts. When we read about the positive emotions of others on Facebook, it makes us express ourselves more positively. On the other hand, when we read about negative emotions, it makes us express ourselves more negatively.

The implications of this study are dramatic. The results are a stark reminder of both sides of the Hype Loop. On the one hand, the curation of emotions by *algorithms* has a meaningful impact on our moods and the spread of happiness and depression across the globe. At the same time, however, it also reminds us of our *own* responsibility in this process. What we put into the Hype Machine is what we get out of it. Human agency matters. The emotions we express in social media are magnified and spread to others, through curated feeds that change the way we all think and behave. If we continue to seed the machine with hatred, vitriol, and negativity, this research shows, we will magnify that negativity in others. If, however, we can steer ourselves toward a more positive approach, we will inspire similar emotions in others.

Approaching Hypersocialization

These studies demonstrate the unprecedented power of the Hype Machine to spread behavior change. Online peer effects, triggered by the trillions of likes, pokes, posts, referrals, advertisements, notifications, shares, check-ins, and ratings we send and receive every day over the Hype Machine *change* our thinking and behavior. The important question now is: how do we manage change in a hypersocialized world?

Advertisers, politicians, public health officials, and small business owners can no longer think just about the direct effects of their messaging in the Hype Machine. They must also consider the social effects created by this messaging, the influencers who disproportionately spread behavior change, and the consequences of ignoring our new networked reality. As Rob Cain noted, the era of the networked consumer (and voter and citizen) is in full swing. We need new strategies for a hypersocialized world.

CHAPTER 8

Strategies for a Hypersocialized World

Power does not reside in institutions, not even the state or large corporations. It is located in the networks that structure society.

—MANUEL CASTELLS

F oreign operatives spreading misinformation, marketers spreading the word about their products, and public health officials encouraging people to socially distance during a pandemic all want to spread information through the human social network and thus through the Hype Machine. Ultimately, the point is to spread behavior change. So how can marketers, politicians, and individuals interested in changing behavior spread their products, ideas, or content in the New Social Age? In the Hype Machine's hypersocialized world, automatically curated digital social signals have completely changed how we produce, consume, analyze, and evaluate information. Organizations and individuals alike will have to change how they operate in the new paradigm.

There are five essential *strategies* for adapting institutional and individual communication to a hypersocialized world: *network targeting, referral marketing, social advertising, viral design,* and *influencer marketing*. Each has a different purpose and different tactics. Knowing when to employ them and how to optimize and adapt them to particular circumstances are the keys to their effectiveness.

Your Friends' Preferences Reveal Your Preferences (Network Targeting)

As I discussed earlier, in Chapter 6, targeting social media messages to consumers is fairly straightforward. Marketers use data about our demographics, behaviors, preferences, social networks, and location histories to predict whether we are likely to engage with (and ultimately to act on) political or marketing messages distributed over the Hype Machine. But what exactly does it mean to target persuasive messages *based on the social network*? How can networks be helpful in deciding whom to communicate with when trying to create behavior change, from product marketing to political messaging to health communications? The strength of "network targeting," our ability to use what we know about the network to make better predictions about the individuals in it, lies in *homophily*—the human tendency to make friends with people who are like ourselves.

Every social network I have ever studied exhibits this regularity. We sort together by race, religion, age, political affiliation, and even our personal preferences. Skiers tend to be friends with skiers. Foodies tend to be friends with foodies. Democrats tend to be friends with Democrats, while Republicans tend to be friends with Republicans. Of course, there are exceptions to this rule—some Democrats have Republican friends and vice versa—but they are the exception, not the rule.

"Birds of a feather flock together." If your friends like hiking, soccer, reading, and the band the Killers, you are statistically more likely to like hiking, soccer, reading, and the Killers. In this way, your network connections reveal your preferences. By analyzing your friends' preferences, a marketer can effectively adjust their targeting to improve their return on hype. Homophily's usefulness in targeting is, in fact, precisely what makes measuring social influence so difficult. But this same attractive power also enables companies and organizations to identify who should receive persuasive messaging. Take, for example, the global telecommunications company that my friends and colleagues Shawndra Hill, Foster Provost, and Chris Volinsky studied in their landmark "network neighbors" study, one of the first to uncover the potent predictive power of network data for targeted marketing.

Shawndra, Foster, and Chris studied a storied global telecommunications company with a long history of and experience with targeted marketing. The company was launching a new communications service and was thinking about how to target its marketing at the right consumers in the network. It had already built sophisticated targeting models based on data, experience, and intuition for the types of customers it thought would have an affinity for its new "high-tech" service. Its models included demographic, geographic, and loyalty data about millions of potential customers. But during the study, the researchers added a single variable to these already-sophisticated targeting models: whether a potential customer had a friend who had previously adopted the service.

To construct the network, they analyzed the telecommunications company's call detail records (CDRs), which documented who called whom, how frequently, and for how long. From this data they constructed a network of phone call records connecting the landline and cell phone numbers of potential customers of the new service. The networked links represented the number of phone calls made between any two numbers in the network, weighted by their duration (Figure 8.1).

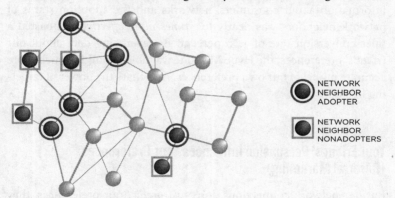

NETWORK
NEIGHBOR
ADOPTER

NETWORK
NEIGHBOR
NONADOPTERS

Figure 8.1 *The "network neighbors" network. This hypothetical social network of people calling each other on the telephone was created from the call detail records (CDRs) of a major telecommunications company. The light circles are people who are prior adopters of a new telecommunications service, and the dark circles are people who have not yet adopted the service and could be the targets of direct marketing. The dark circles surrounded by a circle are current nonadopters of the service who have a friend or "network neighbor" who has adopted the service. The dark circles surrounded by a square are current nonadopters of the service who have no friends or "network neighbors" who have adopted the service.*

In this network, there were two types of consumers: prior adopters of the new communications service (the light circles) and nonadopters, to whom the company wanted to send direct marketing (the dark circles). The researchers divided the nonadopters into two types: those who had a friend they talked to on the phone who was a prior adopter (circled) and those who did not (boxed). They added this single piece of information to the sophisticated targeting models the telecommunications company had already built. They simply considered whether a potential target had a "network neighbor" (someone they talked to on the phone) who had previously adopted the service.

They conducted a direct marketing campaign targeting potential customers with advertisements for the new service, then measured the difference in the relative sales rates of the people they targeted. The original targeting model recorded a 0.28 percent sales conversion rate, which was quite good, considering that the average click-through rate on a display ad is 0.05 percent. And these were conversion rates, not click-through rates—in other words, actual sales. But using targeting information about consumers' networks and the adoption status of network neighbors was nearly *five times more effective*. It boasted a sales conversion rate of 1.35 percent. By leveraging data about our friends' preferences, the Hype Machine was able to build a much more accurate model of our own preferences. And that's the power of targeting in a network.

Your Friends' Persuasion Influences Your Preferences (Referral Marketing)

But our network connections don't just *predict* our preferences, they also *influence* our preferences. We trust our friends more than brand advertising or political spin. Our friends know us and what we are interested in, so they know which messages will appeal to us. They also know how to frame messages for us in the most persuasive, personalized ways. It's not surprising, therefore, that word-of-mouth opinions of friends are consumers' most trusted source of brand information. Given the persuasive power of digital word of mouth, brands spend a great deal of time, energy, and money on referral programs. Dropbox relied heavily on its "give us a customer, get free space" promotion, while Airbnb and Uber both used personalized referral messages and incentives to drive their growth.

Joseph Ziyaee, an Uber driver from Los Angeles, even used such a referral program to become an outlier in Uber's income distribution or, as he likes to call himself, "the Uber King."

The more Uber drivers drive, the more money they earn. While there is some variation in when, where, and how drivers drive, this relationship is pretty consistent. Uber data from 2014 showed that a sample of New York City drivers earned about $30 per hour and that those who drove the most (80 to 90 hours per week) earned about $90,000 a year, which was the highest end of the spectrum.

If we take these numbers at face value, then what Joseph Ziyaee earned in a six-month period that same year is truly remarkable. In fact, he probably earned more than any other Uber driver on the planet, by a long shot. Joseph nearly doubled the next-highest driver's earnings in 2014, earning $90,000 net of costs *in just six months*. This implies an annual income of $180,000. He was a complete outlier. But that's not the most remarkable thing about Joseph Ziyaee. The startling thing is that he earned this much money as an Uber driver *without ever driving an Uber*. He did it almost exclusively by referring other drivers to the service.

Uber has one of the most successful referral programs in the world. It offers incentives for drivers to refer other drivers to the site. When a new driver joins with a friend's referral code, both drivers earn a bonus. The exact amount of the bonus has changed over time, and it eventually evolved into a guaranteed baseline wage for drivers who drove more than a certain amount, regardless of ride activity. But at the time Joseph broke all the records, each referral was worth hundreds of dollars apiece. And Joseph took advantage of the program to become the Uber King.

Some of the world's fastest-growing companies have grown on the backs of referral programs that spread their services through social media messages propagated by the Hype Machine, including PayPal, Dropbox, Airbnb, Tesla, and Amazon Prime, to name a few. Referral programs, which give their consumers incentives to bring their friends to a product or service, make sense because they capitalize on the things that make social media persuasive. Word of mouth is the most trusted source of brand information because we trust our friends and family more than brand advertising. Our friends also know our preferences and can route the invitations to the right people. And when we start using a service together, local network effects kick in, reducing the chances that any of us will leave.

But what does an optimal incentive policy look like? In our own experimental study, we examined the effect of adding a viral incentive to the promotion of a Web-based flower delivery service. We were inspired by ad programs like DirecTV's campaign to "turn your friends into Benjamins," a reference to its peer referral program that rewards subscribers with $100 for every friend they bring to the service. (Benjamin Franklin is on the $100 bill in the United States.)

A business could give every current subscriber $100 for every friend they recruit. This "DirecTV approach" would increase my incentive to recruit my friends, but it would probably have no effect on my friends' likelihood of adoption, beyond the power of my own personal charm and persuasion. We called the DirecTV-style referral program the "selfish incentive" because only the referrer received a reward for the referral. In contrast, a firm could ask current subscribers to invite their friends and give the $100 discount to the friend when they joined instead. This would create an incentive for the friend to adopt but would give no monetary incentive to current subscribers to spread the word. We called this the "generous incentive" because, in this plan, current subscribers would donate the entire referral reward to their friends. Alternatively, we could split the difference and give $50 to the friend and $50 to the current subscriber who invites the friend. We called this the "fair incentive."

In our experiment, we randomly assigned users of the flower delivery website to selfish, generous, and fair referral incentives to test which was most effective. We expected the selfish offer would be sent more often but redeemed less often, while the generous offer would be sent less often but redeemed more often. The fair offer, we thought, would generate middling results on both fronts. But which one would succeed overall?

What we found was counterintuitive: the generous and fair incentives generated more sending behavior than the selfish incentive, even though the senders were being paid strictly less to send the message to their friends under these schemes. It turned out that users don't like spamming their friends without also passing along some benefit. Getting paid to send messages that encourage friends' adoption, they felt, was a bit "sleazy"; they preferred passing discounts on to friends. In hindsight, these results conform to our understanding of a "gift economy," in which status is conferred on those who give the most to others.

This brings us to another important strategic question: When attempting to create behavior change in the network, how do marketers decide which of these marketing tactics—network targeting or viral marketing—to employ? How would a CMO responsible for a firm's digital marketing budget decide how to divide marketing dollars between these two strategies? It turns out the answer depends, again, on the difference between correlation and causation. To understand why, let's look at some research we conducted with Yahoo!, one of the first large-scale social networks in the Hype Machine, about what statisticians call the reflection problem.

The Reflection Problem

At its core, the reflection problem highlights the difficulty of inferring whether behaviors move through social media networks, from person to person, due to social influence among friends (one person influencing another) or due to alternative causes like homophily. What does that mean? Well, we know, in nearly every social network ever studied, that people who are connected together tend to do the same things at approximately the same time with striking statistical regularity. Now, this pattern could be the result of social influence—friends convincing friends to change their behavior—or it could be the result of alternative explanations, such as homophily. Our behaviors "reflect" our friends' behaviors online. Is this because we influence each other, or are there more powerful alternative explanations for this reflection?

If birds of a feather flock together, then behaviors diffusing from friend to friend can be explained by the fact that we choose friends with similar preferences. Remember, skiers tend to be friends with skiers, marathon runners tend to be friends with marathon runners, and foodies tend to be friends with foodies. So skiing, running, and visiting new restaurants will be correlated among friends simply because they are people with similar preferences, not necessarily because they invite their friends to those activities.

It could also be, however, that correlations in behavior among friends are caused by what are known as "confounding factors" rather than by social influence. In a famous quote, the sociologist Max Weber once said, "If you see a crowd of people all put up their umbrellas at the same time, you don't assume that social influence is responsible." In other words, it may just be raining.

Visualize a crowd of people in a field attending a political rally or a music concert. Everyone is packed shoulder to shoulder in the field, waiting for the event to begin. Now imagine that a single umbrella opens in the bottom left corner of the field. After a few seconds, the person standing next to the person who opened the first umbrella opens their own umbrella. Now two umbrellas are open in the bottom left corner of the field. Then a few seconds later, a third umbrella opens right next to the second one, and one after another, all the umbrellas open, successively in time, from the bottom left to the top right corner of the field. What could cause this pattern?

It could be that the first person to open their umbrella elbowed the person next to them and said, "Psst, hey, open your umbrella. It's the cool thing to do." And upon opening their umbrella, the second person could have elbowed the person next to them, and so on from person to person. That would be the *social influence explanation*.

But another factor could also be causing people to open their umbrellas in this pattern—a rain shower passing overhead, moving from the bottom-left to the top-right corner of the field. From a bird's-eye view, the pattern looks like a cascade of umbrellas opening from the bottom left to the top right. But one cannot discern whether this pattern was caused by friends influencing each other or by the rain shower passing overhead—the *confounding factors explanation*. To know for certain, we need to understand what drives people to open their umbrellas in the crowd.

Now, you may be wondering what umbrellas in a field have to do with the Hype Machine. Well, if homophily is real, then people connected on social media will have similar preferences. So they are more likely to watch the same television shows, listen to the same podcasts, visit the same websites, and therefore be exposed to the same advertisements, which means they tend to get information from the same sources at about the same time. In the Hype Machine, exposure to persuasive messages and ads is also correlated among friends with similar preferences due to targeting. So like the passing rain shower in our umbrella example, the ads and persuasive messages in the Hype Machine could be causing correlated behaviors among friends, rather than social influence among the friends causing that correlation. But again, so what?

To understand why the reflection problem is the key to marketing success and to determining whether social media manipulation is influencing elections, consider the puzzle we worked on with Yahoo!

In July 2007 the company launched a new mobile service application called Yahoo! Go, which delivered personalized news, weather, and stock market information to users' mobile phones. It had over half a million adopters within six months. Yahoo! wanted to know whether Go's adoption was spreading in the network due to peer-to-peer influence or simply individual preferences for Yahoo! Go. The answer would help Yahoo! decide how to market the service. If friends were successfully convincing friends to adopt, then providing them with formal incentives to do so, similar to Uber's referral program, could turbocharge the adoption curve. But if consumers were unmoved by their friends' influence and users' preferences correlated with their friends' preferences due to homophily, then a network targeting strategy would perform better than a viral marketing strategy. So some rigorous data science could help Yahoo! decide how to market the product most effectively.

During our longitudinal study of Go's adoption, we collected data on 27 million users connected in Yahoo!'s global instant messaging network called Yahoo! Messenger. (It was just like AOL's AIM or MSN Messenger.) We also collected detailed demographic and geographic data on these same users, and comprehensive, detailed data on their online behaviors and activities—about 90 billion pageviews in all. We added data records of the day-by-day adoption and usage of Yahoo! Go.

To tackle the reflection problem, we devised a statistical technique called *dynamic matched sample estimation,* which was really just a dynamic, networked version of *propensity score matching,* a seminal method developed by Paul Rosenbaum and Don Rubin two decades earlier.* In essence, the model separates the effects of social influence, on the one hand, from alternative explanations, like homophily and confounding factors, on the other.† We set out to apply this model to the millions of people in our data set. What we found revealed the striking implication of neglecting the difference between correlation and causation in networked data.

We first built a model estimating the likelihood of a user's Go adoption, depending on whether they had a network neighbor who was a previous adopter. This model was similar to the model built by Shawndra Hill and her colleagues in the "network neighbors" study. The analysis produced the "influence curve" depicted in Figure 8.2. The curve plots the ratio of adopters with an adopter friend to adopters without an adopter friend over time. If you look at the first dot on the far left of the graph, it implies that, twenty days after Yahoo! Go's launch, a user with an adopter friend was *sixteen times* more likely to adopt the product than a user without an adopter friend. But if you follow the curve from left to right, you'll see that five months after the product's launch, people with adopter friends were only about *twice* as likely to adopt as those without adopter friends. So it seems from this graph that social influence was an important driver of adoption in the *early* part of Yahoo! Go's life cycle, but that its importance *faded over time*.

The significance of this curve is crucial to anyone interested in creating population-scale behavior change. If friends can convince friends to adopt Yahoo! Go, a CMO should consider incentivizing current adopters to invite their friends to the application through a referral program. If, on the other hand, people *aren't* socially influenced—if friends aren't convincing friends to adopt—then traditional network targeting is a more effective tactic.

So if you were Yahoo!'s CMO, deciding how to allocate your mar-

---

* The technical details are not relevant for our purposes. But for those of you who are interested in what is going on under the hood of this model, here is a brief description: We first built a model of the likelihood of any given user having a friend who adopted Yahoo! Go. We then matched users who had the same likelihood of having an adopter friend and compared matched samples of users who had the same propensity to have an adopter friend where one of the users had that friend and the other didn't.

† Dean Eckles and Eytan Bakshy later showed that this method could achieve up to an 80 percent error reduction when the right contextual variables are used.

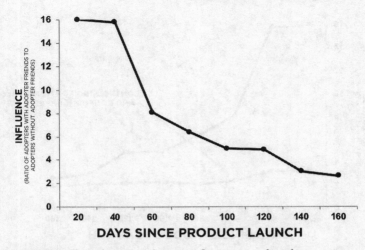

Figure 8.2 *The Yahoo! Go adoption influence curve based on a naïve model. The graph depicts the ratio of adopters with adopter friends to adopters without adopter friends on the y-axis and the number of days since the launch of Yahoo! Go on the x-axis. Each dot represents the number of times more likely someone is to adopt Yahoo! Go if they have a friend or friends who have already adopted it.*

keting budget between viral marketing, which relies on social influence, and network targeting, which doesn't, you might look at the curve in Figure 8.2 and decide to overweight viral marketing in the first three months of the product's life cycle, then reverse that allocation by overweighting network targeting after three months. The curve makes it *seem* like influence is high early on and low later on. But if you were Yahoo!'s CMO and I was your chief scientist, and I brought you this graph and you made that budget allocation decision, we should both be fired.

The problem is we've both mistaken correlation for causation. Just because people with adopter friends are more likely to adopt a product doesn't mean that their friends are *influencing* them to do so. When we controlled for homophily and confounding factors with our propensity score model, this is in fact exactly what we found (Figure 8.3).

The amount of social influence in a consumer's decision to adopt Yahoo! Go was dramatically lower than we had originally estimated,

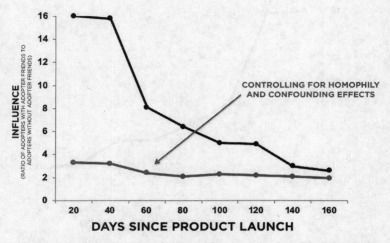

Figure 8.3 *The Yahoo! Go adoption influence curve based on a propensity score model. The graph depicts the ratio of adopters with adopter friends to adopters without adopter friends adjusted by a propensity score matching model on the y-axis and the number of days since the launch of Yahoo! Go on the x-axis. Each dot represents the number of times more likely someone is to adopt Yahoo! Go if they have a friend or friends who have already adopted it estimated by the matching model.*

and it didn't change much over time. In fact, we discovered that a marketing team that wasn't paying attention to the difference between causes and correlations would overestimate the amount of social influence in the adoption decision by as much as 700 percent! That's an egregious error that could destroy the effectiveness of a digital marketing budget, render a public health campaign impotent, or disrupt an assessment of foreign election manipulation.

Mistakes like this cost marketing and outreach programs dearly. Understanding how investments convert to behavior change is essential to creating genuine returns on hype and to understanding whether a foreign government is successfully swaying elections. It also helps to explain what umbrellas in the rain have to do with success or failure on social media.

Being Shown Your Friends' Preferences Influences Your Preferences (Social Advertising)

Viral marketing is not the only way a hypersocialized world leverages social influence. Facebook's election experiments highlight another way: social advertising. To understand social advertising, we have to begin with an understanding of the role of identity in the Hype Machine. Whenever we post something or engage with content on Facebook, Instagram, LinkedIn, or WeChat, we tie our identity to that content in consequential ways. Most important, we signal our affinities and preferences explicitly to others who see it and implicitly to the platforms that are analyzing what Chris Dixon and Caterina Fake originally called the "taste graph." Today Pinterest claims to be the leading intelligence engine crunching the taste graph—which is simply the network linking people to tastes. But Facebook has an edge in this game as well. The sheer scale of its understanding of people's preferences is formidable.

Facebook massively improved the persuasive power of its "get out the vote" campaign by displaying the faces of friends who had voted in a message. This kind of "social proof" powers Facebook's social advertising, as it does WeChat's "moments" ads. In these programs, Facebook and WeChat surface the fact that specific friends of yours like or endorse a message or its source. When Facebook displays an ad, for example, for Delta Airlines, it also lets you know that "Miles, Stefan and six other friends are fans of Delta Airlines." Or in an ad for Pokémon, it may indicate that your friend "Kaya is a fan of Pokémon." Such social proof is displayed alongside organic content as well, in the form of likes, shares, and comments, and for good reason—it increases the persuasive power of the messages dramatically.

In 2012 Facebook conducted two large-scale randomized experiments measuring the effectiveness of this type of social advertising. My friends and colleagues Eytan Bakshy, Dean Eckles, Rong Yan, and Itamar Rosenn, who all worked for Facebook at the time (Dean has since joined me at MIT), ran two experiments on random samples of 6 million and 23 million Facebook users, respectively. In one experiment, they randomly showed (or didn't show) the name of a friend who had liked a brand to users who saw ads by that brand. Comparing the reactions of those who saw the friend's name to those who didn't, they found that displaying a social cue with a single friend's name increased click rates by 3.8 to 5.4 percent and like rates by 9.6 to 11.6 percent. These are big effects. The researchers concluded (in conservative scientific language) that "even a minimal social cue can substantially affect a consumer's response to an ad."

In a second experiment, they randomly varied the number of social cues they displayed. For some users, they showed one friend's name; for other users, they showed two friends' names; and for a third group, they showed three friends' names. They found that the more friends they displayed, the bigger the effect. For users who had two brand-affiliated friends ($Z = 2$ in Figure 8.4), displaying a second friend caused a 10.3 percent increase in the click rate and a 10.5 percent increase in the like rate, compared to only showing one friend. For users with three brand-affiliated friends ($Z = 3$ in Figure 8.4), displaying three friends instead of two increased the click rate by 8.0 percent and the like rate by 8.9 percent.

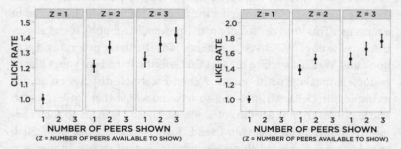

Figure 8.4 *The effect of showing social cues (likes) on ad click and like rates. The charts depict the average relationship between the number of peers shown and the click-through rate (left) and like rate (right) of ads shown on Facebook. The Z panels represent different populations of user-ad pairs, where the user has $Z = 1$, 2, or 3 peers who has liked the ad and so could potentially be shown in the ad.*

As Figure 8.4. makes clear, showing more friends in social cues increases users' engagement with ads. The figure also shows that users who have more friends who previously liked the brand have higher engagement with the ads. This can be seen in the differences across the columns $Z = 1$, $Z = 2$, and $Z = 3$. These columns separate users with one, two, or three friends who had previously liked the brand. These groups must be analyzed separately because users with more friends who previously liked the brand inherently have a stronger affinity for that brand due to homophily. The homophily effect can be seen in the increasing response rates from column $Z = 1$ to $Z = 2$ to $Z = 3$. The more friends you have with an affinity for a certain brand, the stronger your affinity for that brand.

Facebook's social advertising experiment was the first of its kind. It demonstrated the power of social cues to increase ad effectiveness above and beyond network targeting opportunities created by homophily. But it didn't analyze how social advertising effectiveness varied across different products. Are social ads more effective for electronics products or fashion accessories? For running or for voting? Are we more likely to be swayed by the opinions of our friends when shopping for high-status goods, like a Rolex watch or a luxury car, or experience goods, like hotels and restaurants, which require us to experience the products or to hear about the experiences of others to evaluate them?

To find out, Shan Huang, Jeffrey Hu, Erik Brynjolfsson, and I conducted an even larger, more comprehensive experiment in collaboration with WeChat, the largest social platform in China. We randomly assigned the number of social cues shown to 37 million WeChat users in their "moments" ads across seventy-one products in twenty-five categories and analyzed the differences in social advertising effectiveness across products. Did showing a social signal from a brand-affiliated friend increase the persuasive power of brands' messages? If so, for which products and in which categories were these social signals most effective? We found tremendous variation in social advertising effectiveness across products.

WECHAT

It's worth reflecting on WeChat for a moment, because it is an awe-inspiring and unique part of the Hype Machine. If Facebook is important because of its size, WeChat is important because of its generality. WeChat is the Swiss army knife of social networks. You can do almost anything on it. You can book a train, find a hotel, pay bills, message friends, share photos, order food, transfer money, hail a cab, shop, send out your dry cleaning, exchange bitcoin, invest in stocks, donate to charity, play video games, watch movies, and read the news, just to name a few. It's essentially Facebook, WhatsApp, Instagram, Uber, Venmo, and the whole App Store combined.

The thing about WeChat is that the Great Firewall (China's national firewall that blocks websites like Facebook, Instagram, Twitter, and YouTube) allowed it to develop a network effect free from Facebook's competitive network, while simultaneously preserving its second-mover advantage. Typically, in a market with network effects, you want to be the first mover to develop those network effects against competitors. The disadvantage, however, is that the second mover can learn from your mistakes and innovate—if, that is, they can overcome the network effects developed by the first mover. WeChat's origin story was different. It got to peer out from behind the Great Firewall and observe the innovations of Western social platforms, while still maintaining its first-mover advantage in China's large protected language market. As a result, it evolved as if it were a first mover, but with all the competitive insight of a second mover. It became the most comprehensive social platform in the world and now has over a billion users.

Displaying a single friend's like made users 33.75 percent more likely to click an ad—which is much larger than the 3.8 percent to 10.5 percent lift that our colleagues at Facebook had found. But three differences in our experiment explain this and give us even more insight into the power of social cues.

First, the Facebook experiments didn't have a control group that used *no* social cues. They instead compared groups with two and three social cues to a group displaying only one social cue. Our experiment was the first to estimate the persuasive power of going from no social cues to a single social cue in an ad, revealing the pure persuasive effect of social cues.

Second, our experiment posted users' likes only to their friends, not to friends of friends, or friends of friends of friends. Facebook's experiments, in contrast, displayed the social cues of users several steps removed from the actual ad viewer in the social network. This was a testament to the power of tie strength in moderating the power of social cues: the closer the friends, the more influential their social cues on our behavior. This reinforces my point from Chapter 5 about how the power of Facebook's local network effect helped it defeat MySpace.

Finally, we examined how social ad performance varied across different products, and it varied a lot. Adding a single friend's like to an ad increased the click-through rate by up to 270 percent for the most successful social ad. Since this was a randomized experiment, we were measuring lift in a true causal sense—nothing about the ad changed except the display of social cues. The majority of ads experienced significant positive increases in effectiveness with the addition of social cues, but some ads performed better than others. Thirty-nine products saw significant positive lift from social cues, and thirty-two products experienced no lift. No ads were made less effective by adding social cues.

Heineken was the best-performing brand, with a 270 percent lift. The brand with the smallest significant lift (remember, thirty-two products experienced no lift at all) was Disney, with a 21 percent lift. Which raised the questions: What was it about a product that made it suitable to social advertising? Why do social cues change our opinions about some products but not others? To find out, we sliced the data by product categories and looked at lift again.

When we looked at social advertising effectiveness across product categories, it was clear that some categories were more amenable to social advertising than others (Figure 8.5). Food, fashion, and cars were the top-performing categories. Beverages and jewelry also performed well. Real estate, insurance, and financial services had middling effects. The effectiveness of ads for credit cards and e-commerce platforms were the least moved by social signals. Why was that? What was it about certain types of products that made them more or less amenable to persuasion effects from social signals?

Perhaps important dimensions of product categories were driving the effectiveness of social signals. For example, some products fulfill our needs related to the social comparisons we make to our friends. Take high-status products, for example, like luxury watches and expensive cars. People purchase these products not only to use and enjoy them but also to signal their status. With these kinds of high-status goods, we hypothesized, social influence may be more relevant. When

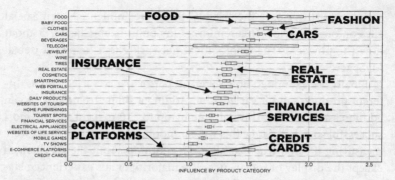

Figure 8.5 *The effect of showing social cues (likes) on ad click rates across product categories. The chart depicts the average relationship between showing a friend's like on an ad and the click-through rate of the ads shown on WeChat. The further to the right a box plot is, the more that showing a friend's like on an ad influences the ad viewer to click on the ad in that product category (e.g. food, fashion, or cars).*

we tested the distinction between high-status goods and other goods, we found that goods that confer status enjoyed significantly more lift from social cues than goods that don't.

What we learned from the WeChat study was that people interact with different products and behaviors differently through the Hype Machine. There is no one story of how the Hype Machine spreads information, ideas, products, or behaviors across the human social network. Each behavior, product, or idea has characteristics that make it more or less susceptible to being spread by social influence or being subject to homophily, or birds-of-a-feather, effects. Some ideas and products are ripe for social diffusion, while others are not.

But if we wanted to, could we design products to be socially spread?

Products and Ideas Can Be Designed to Be Viral (Viral Design)

The first three strategies in the hypersocialization playbook are about marketing products and ideas that already exist. But a comprehensive approach to hypersocialization requires reaching backward into the product or idea development cycle—into the design of the products or ideas themselves. Instead of simply asking how they can spread products, ideas, or content in the New Social Age, marketers, politicians, and individuals interested in changing behavior should be asking a deeper question: how can we design our products and ideas so they are more likely to be shared socially from the get-go? That's viral design—the process of designing products, ideas, and content so they are more likely to be shared among friends.

Viral design is not new—it's been around since the Bible. In fact, evangelism exists in almost every faith and is an essential part of the spread of religion. Christianity is evangelical *by design.* "He said to them, 'Go into all the world and preach the gospel to all creation'" (Mark 16:15). "Therefore go and make disciples of all nations, baptizing them in the name of the Father and of the Son and of the Holy Spirit" (Matthew 28:19). The Quran teaches evangelism as a duty known as *da'wa,* which means "to invite people to Islam" (Q 3:104; 3:110; 16:125; 41:33). If you thought "going viral" was a millennial thing, you were thinking of the wrong millennium.

In the Information Age, viral design is about developing *viral characteristics* and *viral features.* My friend and colleague Jonah Berger wrote eloquently about viral characteristics in his book *Contagious.* They're the qualities of an idea that make us want to share it. For example, a study of the most shared *New York Times* articles, which Berger conducted with Kathy Milkman, found that content that evokes emotional arousal—whether positive, as in awe, or negative, as in anger or anxiety—is more viral. Content that evokes low arousal or deactivating emotions, like sadness, is less viral. Surprising, interesting, and practically useful content was also positively linked to virality.

Viral features, on the other hand, are *design* elements of a product or idea that compel us to share it. It's a powerful strategy for generating adoption, engagement, and sharing. Take the free email service Hotmail, for example, one of the first viral designs of the digital age.

When Jack Smith and Sabeer Bhatia launched Hotmail in 1996, they embedded a viral feature into its design. At the end of every email, in the signature line, was a clever postscript that read "Get your free email at www.Hotmail.com." Every email sent to a colleague or friend doubled as an advertisement for Hotmail, and the link in the signature line contained a direct path to product adoption. It launched on July 4, 1996.

Within six months Hotmail had a million users. Five weeks later it had 2 million users and was adding more than 20,000 new users a day with little to no paid advertising. As Steve Jurvetson, managing director of the VC firm Draper Fisher Jurvetson, Hotmail's lead investor, wrote: "We were amazed at how quickly Hotmail spread over the global network. The rapid adoption pattern was that of a network virus. We would notice the first user from an overseas university town, and then the number of subscribers from that region would rapidly proliferate. From an epidemiological perspective, it was as if Zeus sneezed over the planet."

A product's *viral characteristics,* like those Jonah Berger describes, are about its content and the psychological effects that content can have on a user's desire to share it with friends. As we learned in Chapter 2, the viral characteristics of fake news, for example, stoke surprise, anger, and disgust. A product's *viral features,* on the other hand, are about how a product is designed to be shared with others. Viral features enable communication, generate notifications, facilitate invitations, or enable hypertext embedding of the product on websites and weblogs.

Two of the most widely used viral features are personalized referrals and automated notifications. Automated notifications are passively triggered by user activity. For example, when a user sends a message or updates her status, those actions are broadcast to her contacts as notifications. Social networking platforms typically notify friends when a user posts a picture to Instagram or a run to Strava. Digital referrals, on the other hand, are more personalized and targeted than notifications. Users actively select a subset of their friends to receive them and can include personal messages in the referral. But which of these is the more powerful viral feature? To find out, Dylan Walker and I designed a large-scale randomized experiment on Facebook.

We worked with a company developing a Facebook movie app that allowed users to read about upcoming movies with friends, write movie reviews, "friend" celebrities, and buy movie tickets, individually or as a group. It was a social cinema app designed to embed movie culture in Facebook. To test the effectiveness of viral features, we created three versions of the app, each with different viral features turned on or off. We tested *personalized referrals,* which gave users the ability to personally invite their friends to the app, and *automated notifications,* which automatically sent passive notifications describing a user's activity on the app to their Facebook friends with a link to the app adoption page.

The personalized referral feature displayed an "invite your friends" button throughout the app. When a user clicked on the button, it showed them a list of all their Facebook friends. They could select which friends they wanted to invite, write a personalized note, and send them a link to download the app. The *automated notification* feature informed a user's friends about things they were doing on the app. As users engaged in key actions, like rating a movie, it would generate a notification to all of that user's Facebook friends encouraging them to join the app. For example, if I rated the movie *Terminator 2* with four out of five stars, the broadcast notification would automatically generate a message to all my Facebook friends, telling them about my rating and encouraging them to download the app. The message might say "Sinan just rated *Terminator 2* with 4 out of 5 stars on this movie app; you might be interested in the app, here's a link to download it."

As users downloaded the app, we randomly assigned them to receive one of three experimental versions we had prepared, each with different viral features turned on or off. The first group had personal referrals turned on. The second group had automated notifications turned on. The control group had both features turned off. We then watched as each version naturally diffused through the Facebook network among the 1.4 million people in our experiment.

We found that a referral was three times more effective at generating adoption than a notification. Referral invitations created a 6 percent increase in the adoption rate compared to the control group, while notifications created a 2 percent increase. But though the invitation feature nearly doubled the global diffusion rate of the application, a 98 percent increase, the passive notification feature created a much larger 246 percent effect. Although invitations were more effective per message, the notification feature had a larger overall effect because it generated more automated messages and many more people were exposed to the app as a result.

The invitation feature also created a 17 percent increase in the sustained use of the app, while the notification feature had no effect on use. As users invited their best friends to the application and as their friends joined, they became more interested in the application and thus more likely to stick with it. These results strongly suggested that sustained engagement was powered by Facebook's local network effects. The value of the application to each user was based not simply on how many of their friends adopted it but on whether their *close* friends adopted it, highlighting the importance of close, familiar ties in strengthening a platform's network effects.

And if you think viral design only applies to a niche set of *digital* goods, you're wrong. Even the most analog products you can think of are being digitized and plugged into the Hype Machine. Take, for example, one of the most analog products in human history—the sneaker. You want to plug a sneaker into the Hype Machine? Just put a chip in it that pipes data, through an app, right into social networks like Facebook and Instagram. That's exactly what Nike did in 2006 when it created Nike Run Club.

Nike built a chip that powers itself off electricity generated from the heat and pressure you create when you run. Then Nike mounted a transmitter on it that communicates with a receiver in your phone on a 2.4 GHz wireless radio. The data is encrypted during wireless transmissions between your feet and your phone. But then you are free to share it—along with other information, like how hot it was when you ran—to Facebook, Twitter, or Instagram. As we saw in our exercise contagion study, these kinds of viral designs transmit social influence in running behaviors across the network. As devices get smarter, viral design is making them more social, extending the Hype Machine's reach into the analog world. And as we saw in our fake news study, misinformation is designed to go viral by triggering our emotions with the most shocking and sensational content—the content that surprises, angers, and disgusts us most.

Do Influencers Really Tell Us How to Shop, Eat, and Vote? (Influencer Marketing)

In 2009 Arielle Charnas was working at the clothing retailer Theory in the Meatpacking District in New York when she started a fashion blog to impress a boyfriend. Branding her content Something Navy, Charnas shared style tips, which she dubbed "elevated basic," to various social media platforms. She began posting to Instagram when it launched in 2010. Her appearance and demeanor on her posts were fashionable, subtle, and uplifting, and she frequently posted glowing updates about her family.

But the influence she had was anything but subtle. When she posted a picture of the Peter Thomas Roth Rose Stem Cell Bio-Repair Gel Mask to Snapchat in 2016, her story sold $17,565 worth of masks in a day. That sales rate, if sustained, would generate "$527,000 in a month or almost $6.4 million in a year" in revenues. Her first apparel collaboration with Nordstrom sold $1 million in the first twenty-four hours. Her second crashed Nordstrom's website; traffic within an hour of its release was overwhelming and generated $4 to $5 million, exceeding sales from Nordstrom's collaborations with musicians Beyoncé and Rihanna, despite the technical hiccup.

When Tyler McCall of Fashionista.com asked Arielle how social media changed what she does, she said, "Social media is everything for me. It's how I made a career. It's how I built my business. It's how I created a brand. I don't know what I would do without it. But it really took off when Instagram launched. The blog was great and it was sustainable . . . but I didn't have as big of a reach as Instagram has allowed me to [have]."

Arielle is a quintessential "influencer," empowered by the Hype Machine to spread behavior change through her personal brand.* She now has over 1.3 million Instagram followers and a powerful presence across multiple social platforms. The notion that "one in ten" influencers drive behavior change through society has been around in academic circles since the two-step flow model of Paul Lazarsfeld and Elihu Katz in the 1950s; it was popularized for general readers by Malcolm Gladwell in his 2000 book, *The Tipping Point*. But the Hype Machine made influencers accessible and allowed them to establish careers around influencing others. It scaled their influence by scaling mass persuasion.

---

* Influence is also a double-edged sword. In the same way negative social media content creates negative value on the Hype Machine, influencers can encourage both positive and negative behaviors. When Charnas advertised her flight out of New York City during the COVID-19 pandemic, public health officials criticized the communication as harmful for influencing her followers to do the same. Our research showed that social media connections created geographic and social spillovers that dramatically affected adherence to social distancing during the pandemic.

All of us now have the tools to drive mass persuasion through the Hype Machine, whether it's for a brand or a humanitarian cause. Some of us, like Arielle Charnas, are just better at it than others. The Hype Machine allows them to monetize their influence. It also allows brands, companies, and governments—domestic and foreign—to observe, measure, and engage influencers to promote their products and ideas. Influencer marketing will be a $10 billion industry by 2021.

So how do marketers identify the Hype Machine's biggest influencers? How do they measure their influence? The two most common metrics are popularity and engagement. Popularity is an influencer's reach, typically measured by the number of their followers. Engagement is the rate of interaction that an influencer inspires in their followers, measured publicly with likes and comments, and privately, by campaign managers, with click-through and conversion rates.

But while popularity and engagement are a good starting point for understanding influencers, these metrics alone can't measure true influence. A fuller understanding of influence requires a more rigorous analysis of behavior change. While popularity suggests you have a big microphone, it doesn't necessarily mean you have influence. Consider Ashton Kutcher. He was one of the Hype Machine's first influencers. Back in the day, Ashton bought billboard-size advertisements on the 405 freeway in Los Angeles urging people to follow him on Twitter; now he has millions of followers. But how influential is he? In public lectures, I ask everyone in the audience to raise their hand if they follow Ashton on Twitter. Many (and I mean many) hands go up. I then ask everyone to raise their hand again if they have ever done anything Ashton Kutcher suggested. Almost no hands go up. I hear crickets. If Ashton is a quintessential influencer but no one is doing what he suggests, then what is influence?

Let's say Barack Obama gives a speech to a group of Democratic donors ahead of the 2020 election. *Was it effective?* a party leader might ask. To genuinely understand the influence of Obama's speech, it's not enough to know how many people donated to the Democratic cause after hearing it. Die-hard Obama supporters are likely the ones who would show up to the event in the first place. They are the people who are already likely to contribute to the Democratic cause in 2020. To understand Obama's influence, we'd have to know what the donors' chances of donating would have been had they never heard the speech.

To estimate behavior change, we need a counterfactual: what was the likelihood of that behavior had the influence not occurred?

To accurately estimate influence, we have to move from correlation to causation. This means thinking about behavior change rather than behavioral tendencies. Everyone has the potential to buy a product. To determine how much someone else influenced my purchase decision, I have to estimate how much their messages moved my likelihood of purchasing. The problem is that if you bought and liked the product, and you and I are friends, then I'm already more likely to be interested in it because of homophily—because, as friends, we are likely more alike. And because of that, we are more likely to be exposed to advertising about it, given targeted advertising. I'm therefore a likely purchaser even without your influence. It's a statistical hair ball. Dylan Walker and I wanted to untangle that hair ball, so we devised a method, published in *Science* in 2012, that addressed these challenges while measuring and identifying influencers. Remember the movie app from our viral design experiments? We piggybacked on that experiment and went one step further.

To measure social influence in the decision to adopt the movie app, we randomly sent broadcast notifications to the 1.5 million friends of the movie app's users. For instance, in the case of my *Terminator 2* rating, although a message conveying my rating would have been sent to all my Facebook friends, we randomly blocked some of those messages as part of our second experiment. We then compared, for example, men who received notifications to men who did not, and used these comparisons to estimate the susceptibility of men to social influence. We did this for a number of characteristics—age, gender, relationship status. We also analyzed the characteristics of the sender-recipient pair: for example, when a man sent a message to a woman, or when a woman sent a message to a woman.

Using this random sampling, we were able to estimate the influence and susceptibility of men and women, of men over women or women over men, and whether influence increased or decreased with age. We found that men, on the whole, were more influential than women; women influenced men more than they influenced other women; older people were more influential and less susceptible to influence than younger people, and married people were the least susceptible to influence in the decision to adopt the product we studied.

When describing this last result in a public lecture in England, I waxed poetic about how when two people get married, they create a tight-knit unit, they melt into each other, begin acting in unison, and "become one." This could explain why married people are less susceptible to influence—two people now have to agree before doing something. My friend and Cambridge University professor Sanjeev Goyal stood up in the lecture hall. "Sinan, I have an alternative explanation for why married people are the least susceptible to influence," he said. "Let me put it this way: I never do anything without asking my wife first." The audience laughed. Both explanations are plausible, and we still don't know why this happens. But a big red flag here: *these results are specific to the movie app we studied.* It could well be, for example, that women are more influential than men in purchasing products we did not study. That said, we did find some striking regularities in how influence and susceptibility are related to the network—regularities that end up mattering for how to select influencers.

First, we found that influential people tend not to be susceptible to influence from others, and that susceptible people tend not to be influential. The more influential someone is, meaning the more their messages change the behavior of the people they are connected to, the less likely they are to change their own behavior in response to other people. This striking trade-off between influence and susceptibility among the 1.5 million people in our study may help to explain the meme in our culture of the trailblazing innovator who is unmoved by critics and naysayers and is committed, with unwavering drive, to their vision: entrepreneurs and pioneers like Steve Jobs and, almost a century before him, Albert Einstein, who bucked the trends of common thinking. Francesca Gino calls them "rebels." They commit to their vision and are for the most part unmoved by the opinions of others. In social media, the trade-off between influence and susceptibility shows up in what researchers call the "follower ratio," the number of followers someone has compared to the number of people they follow. The trade-off between influence and susceptibility could explain why, for example, Donald Trump has 72 million followers and follows only 47 people, or why Taylor Swift has 85 million followers but follows no one.

Second, we found that an influencer's position in the network mattered in terms of their overall influence. We found that there were two different kinds of influencers in social media networks. Some were connected to other influential people, while others, who had the same level of influence over their followers, were connected to less influential people. The influencers with influential friends are more likely to spread influence two hops away from them in the network. The influencers without influential friends influence their immediate social circle as much as the top influencers, but that influence doesn't spread as broadly because their friends aren't as influential.

Third, we learned how clustering and influence are related. Since the messages were sent randomly in our Facebook experiment, we could test how social influence varied with the number of mutual friends the influencer and their friends had. When you think about your own friendships, you probably share many mutual friendships with *some* of them—you are embedded in a community of friends with these people—but you probably also have *other* friends with whom you share very few mutual friendships. It turns out we are more influential with those friends who share many mutual friends with us. In other words, influence is strongest within dense clusters of mutual friendship. This could be because of peer pressure—for example, when a group of friends encourages someone to quit smoking.

These patterns of influence lead to even more similarity and less diversity within the tight-knit, densely connected clusters of the Hype Machine and, as a corollary, less similarity and more divergence across clusters. (I will return to this when I discuss political polarization and the wisdom of crowds in Chapter 10.) This also explains why viral design typically spreads behavior locally around adopters rather than fanning it out widely across the network. We tend to influence those people in tight-knit clusters more than those with whom we have arm's-length relationships.

Finally—and perhaps unsurprisingly—influence travels more readily among people who share common social or institutional contexts. We found that individuals exert 125 percent more influence with friends for each institutional affiliation they share. Attending the same college is associated with a 1,355 percent increase in influence, over friends who attended different colleges. People who reside in the same town exhibit 622 percent more influence on friends in that town than their friends in other towns. On the other hand, having grown up in the same hometown is not associated with influence, which suggests the importance of sharing recent social contexts. These results give us more background on how influence works over the Hype Machine, and how to identify influencers. But identifying influential people is only the first step.

The challenge for influencer marketers is to choose the influencers who maximize the spread of their ideas or products. A marketer can "seed" only a relatively few people with their idea—hiring them as influencers or getting free product samples into their hands to try out, or an idea into their heads. So how do marketers choose who to seed? This is actually a well-studied problem in computer science, economics, and marketing known as the *influence maximization problem*. And what we've learned in this field is not only fascinating but counterintuitive.

Maximizing Influence

How do marketers choose a set of influencers to maximize the spread of an idea or behavior in society? Popularized in *The Tipping Point* in 2000, research into influence maximization has focused on demonstrating real results. The problem was first formalized by computer scientists Pedro Domingos, author of *The Master Algorithm,* and his student Matt Richardson, now at Microsoft, in 2001. Since then computer scientists and marketers alike have proposed solutions to influence maximization with increasing sophistication, and these solutions have been implemented in industry.

One obvious approach is to choose the most popular people, with the largest following—celebrities. That's where influencer marketing started, with celebrities like Kim Kardashian who have vast reach. Picking the most popular people is logical, sensible, and more effective than choosing influencers randomly. But there are drawbacks to this strategy, as marketers discovered over time. First, popular people tend to be connected to one another, so their follower networks overlap, creating redundancy in their influence. Second, the cost of their influence is high. Kim Kardashian charges up to $500,000 for an Instagram post, making her influence cost-prohibitive. Finally, it's difficult to predict the success of any given influencer message—their effectiveness is what marketers call high variance. So a strategy that deploys a portfolio of highly paid influencers is inefficient, meaning the influence per dollar is low.

An alternative strategy later emerged based on the friendship paradox (discussed in Chapter 3). The friendship paradox describes the understanding that "our friends tend to have more friends than we do." Discovered by sociologist Scott Feld, this pattern arises because people with more friends are more likely to be connected to others, so the friends of randomly selected people tend to be highly connected. A marketer can use this pattern to select influencers in a way that reduces redundancy or the doubling up of influencers, and enables their influencer marketing campaign to work when the social network is not known or is costly to obtain, such as in public health interventions in rural villages.

To find effective influencers with this strategy, a marketer or public health official employs a two-step process. First, they take a random sample of the population in which they wish to spread an idea or behavior. Then they randomly sample the friends of those who were sampled (randomly) in the first step. This two-step process identifies people with a lot of connections who are themselves spread out over the network. It's an approach that identifies highly connected people who are less likely to be connected to each other.

My colleague Nicholas Christakis and his team used this strategy to spread adoption of multivitamins in thirty-two rural villages in the Lempira district of Honduras in 2012. They divided the villages into three groups of nine randomly selected villages, then assigned each group to three different influencer marketing campaign strategies to spread the use of multivitamins. In the first group, the researchers seeded the most popular individuals in the village—the top 5 percent—with a bottle of sixty multivitamins, health information about the vitamins' benefits, and tickets to redeem multivitamins that they could share with people they knew in the village. In the second group, the researchers provided influencers with the same products and information but seeded the network according to the two-step process—they first randomly sampled 5 percent of the village, then randomly sampled a single contact of each of the people in the first sample. In the third group, as a control, they randomly gave 5 percent of the population the vitamins, health information, and tickets to share.

The results confirmed that the two-step process, which chose the friends of the randomly selected individuals as influencers, significantly outperformed the other two groups in terms of the number of tickets that were redeemed for vitamins at a local store. In the two-step influencer villages, 74 percent of available vitamin tickets were redeemed, while only 66 percent and 61 percent of the vitamin tickets were redeemed by those in villages targeted by the other two strategies.

While this strategy is certainly compelling, it has weaknesses as well, as became apparent. First (as I indicated earlier), the more influential someone is, the less susceptible to influence they are. Whether they are the most popular celebrities or are chosen by a two-step nominating process, they tend to be less susceptible to the original idea or product and to cost more to activate.

Second, there is a trade-off between popularity and engagement. The more followers an influencer has, the less influential they are over any given follower. Remember Dunbar's number? Human beings have a hard time meaningfully engaging with the massive audiences some people garner on social media. So as their networks grow, their engagement with their followers weakens. Industry research has confirmed, for example, that Instagram influencers with more followers get fewer likes per follower on their posts, as their audience feels less intimately connected with them than the audiences of influencers with fewer followers. The average number of likes per follower is 8.8 percent for influencers with 1,000 to 5,000 followers, 6.3 percent for influencers with 5,000 to 10,000 followers, and 3.5 percent for influencers with more than 1 million followers. As someone becomes more popular, they lose their grip on the attention of their followers.

A model proposed by my colleagues Duncan Watts, Jake Hofman, Winter Mason, and Eytan Bakshy suggested a different strategy of seeding those they called "ordinary influencers," those who have fewer followers but more engagement per post, at a lower cost. My research with Paramveer Dhillon confirmed the effectiveness of this approach. Our models, tested on real social media data, showed that "optimal seeds . . . are relatively less well-connected and less central nodes, and they have more cohesive, embedded ties with their contacts." Our research, in other words, was pointing to the importance of "microinfluencers" and "nanoinfluencers." And that is exactly how the industry has evolved in recent years.

One key takeaway from the research on influencer marketing and microinfluencers is the importance of attention. The reason a portfolio of diverse microinfluencers can outperform celebrity influencers is because they spread attention over segments of the network without redundancy. Although their reach is smaller, they have a firmer grip on their followers' attention and can therefore generate more engagement per follower at a lower cost. In the next chapter, I'll zoom out from individual influencers to an economy-wide analysis of attention and its importance to the Hype Machine.

CHAPTER 9

The Attention Economy and the Tyranny of Trends

A wealth of information creates a poverty of attention.

—HERBERT SIMON

In September 2016, as Alexander Nix, the now-disgraced former CEO of Cambridge Analytica, strode confidently onstage at the Concordia Annual Summit in New York to talk about "the power of big data in global elections," the conference sound system played "Bad Moon Rising" by Creedence Clearwater Revival as his hype music. "I see a bad moon rising," sang John Fogerty. "I see trouble on the way."

I don't think Nix or anyone else in the room understood how prophetic those lyrics were. Just eighteen months later, in March 2018, Nix would be caught in an undercover video claiming to use fake news propagated online to influence global elections. That same month he was removed as Cambridge Analytica's CEO, two months before it shut its doors for good.

In 2016, however, Nix was the darling of the data-driven advertising world. The company he led had just completed its work on Ted Cruz's presidential campaign, taking the senator, in Nix's version of the story, from being "one of the less popular candidates seeking nomination" with very little name recognition to "the only serious contender" to Donald Trump. "So how did he do this?" Nix asked the crowd at the Concordia summit, champing at the bit to give them the secret sauce. "Most communication companies today still segment their audiences by demographics and geographics," he said. "This is a really ridiculous idea. The idea that all women should receive the same message because of their gender or all African-Americans because of their race or all old people or rich people or young people to get the same message because of their demographics just doesn't make any sense." He sounded a lot like Rob Cain, the CIO of Coca-Cola, whose framework for digital engagement puts this kind of segmentation strategy three decades behind the times. Nix then described how Cambridge Analytica transformed this approach:

> We were able to form a model to predict the personality of every single adult in the United States. . . . If you know the personality of the people you're targeting, you can nuance your messaging to resonate more effectively with those key audience groups. . . . We can use hundreds or thousands of individual data points on our target audiences to understand exactly which messages are going to appeal to which audiences. . . . Blanket advertising, the idea that a hundred million people receive the same piece of direct mail, the same television advert, the same digital advert, is dead. . . . Today, communication is becoming ever increasingly targeted. It's being individualized for every single person in this room.

How does the Hype Machine institutionalize behavior change across an entire economy? Across society? To answer these questions, we have to take a step back, to understand the structure and function of the social media economy itself, which is, at its core, what economists call an "attention economy." The attention economy contextualizes how the Hype Machine drives the social, economic, and business outcomes we care about—from election manipulation, to fake news, to marketing success. And arguably the best person to ask about how this type of economy works is a guy they call Gary Vee.

#AskGaryVee

I'll admit, I was a Gary Vaynerchuk skeptic. Not a hater exactly— I admonish my son for using that word—but definitely a skeptic. Brash, unapologetic, and uncompromising, Gary Vee, as he's known, the founder and CEO of VaynerMedia, touts some fairly gimmicky punch lines. With bestselling book titles like *Jab, Jab, Right Hook* and *Crush It,* you could be forgiven for mistaking his presence on social media for an infomercial: trendy "swipe up" animations on Instagram, bobble-head dolls, and Gary Vee cartoons next to pictures of smiling "turds." He seems, at first blush, like a circus sideshow act. You might also excuse my personal skepticism because he and I have several fundamental disagreements on some basic issues, like the value of education and the merit of telling kids they can be anything they want. He's frequently advising teenagers and twentysomethings to drop out of school. (Picture me covering my six-year-old's ears.) On second thought, maybe I *was* a hater.

But I was wrong—totally wrong: well, not about education, but about whether Gary understands marketing. As I watched more of his Instagram videos, listened to his podcasts, perused his speeches online, and watched him curse his way through television interviews with flabbergasted reporters (you can find this avalanche of impeccably curated content all over social media), I realized how wrong I was about him. As I went deeper into his content—half-listening and half-hating—at some point, I realized he'd proven his point. He could, in that moment, rest his case about the value of his content, his advice, and his traveling circus, because he had succeeded in capturing and keeping the one thing he was after—my attention. How did he do it?

Well, it turns out Gary Vee is *not* a shallow gimmick. He's deeply philosophical on the core concept driving the digital economy. (He would argue it drives the entire economy.) What he understands in practice, better than anyone else I've seen, about the nature of today's digital, social media–fueled economy is that it's fundamentally and inalterably an *attention economy*. As he likes to say, "Attention is the currency of business." And in fact, attention is the currency, or the fuel (in our machine analogy), of the Hype Machine. It's what powers the business models of all the major social media platforms. It's what they compete for and sell to brands and governments attempting to create behavior change on a global scale. Without attention, social media platforms wither and die.

Attention is also the lifeblood of the brands, politicians, and governments trying to persuade consumers, voters, and citizens on the Hype Machine. Before brands can sell us their latest products, they need our attention. Before politicians can convince us to vote for them, they need our attention. Before governments can convince us to vaccinate our kids, they need . . . you get it. Our attention.

The Attention Economy

Attention is valuable because it's a precursor to persuasion. Platforms like Facebook, Twitter, and YouTube provide connections, communication, and content to get consumers' attention. They then sell that attention to brands, governments, and politicians who want to change people's perceptions, opinions, and behaviors with ads. The amount and quality of the platforms' ad inventory—the units of advertising they have to sell—scales with the number of consumers they serve and how engaged those consumers are with the content the platforms curate (Figure 9.1). That's why the platforms are obsessed with (and why their market valuations depend on) user *growth* (the increase in the

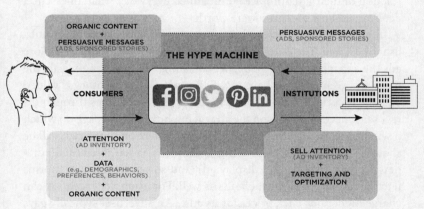

Figure 9.1 *The structure of the attention economy. The social media platforms that make up the Hype Machine serve as intermediaries between consumers and institutions (brands, governments, nonprofits, and small-business advertisers) delivering content and persuasive messages to consumers and selling consumers' attention to institutions, in the form of ad inventory, as an opportunity to persuade them to change their behavior, as well as targeting and optimization services to improve the effectiveness of the institutions' persuasion.*

number of users on a social platform) and *engagement* (the frequency and intensity of users' interactions with social content and features).

When we were building Humin (my second startup, which we sold to Tinder in 2016), we were obsessed with analytics. We built a dashboard to track all the key metrics describing the growth and use of the platform around the world. To keep our team informed, we installed a large TV monitor in the most central spot in our San Francisco office, right across from the kitchen, where everyone would congregate during breaks from coding. The monitor cycled through screens summarizing what was happening on the platform in real time—the number of times the app was downloaded, user retention, connections between users, conversations, profile opens, searches. But the two metrics that were the most critical for managing the business were user growth and engagement. We didn't sell advertising, and we didn't share users' data, but our market valuation depended completely on how fast our user base grew and how engaged consumers were with the app. These two numbers summarized how many people's attention we had and what fraction of their attention we commanded every day. That, in essence, determined how much we were worth.

In ad-driven businesses, the more users an app, platform, or publisher has, and the more time their users spend with them, the more ads the app, platform, or publisher can show: in marketing-speak, the more ad inventory they have to sell. But not all ad inventory is valued equally. It's priced, sometimes by auction and sometimes through direct sales, according to who the ad will be shown to, the page on which it will be shown, the time it will be shown, where on the page it will be shown, what type of ad it is (for example, a video interstitial ad, a newsfeed ad, or a banner display ad), and so on. Different platforms fetch different prices for their ads as well. For example, Facebook can charge higher per-click prices for its ads. (An advertiser typically pays for an ad only when it's clicked on, known as the "cost per click," or CPC, pricing model.) Twitter's prices, by contrast, are lower. And Snapchat's cost per click is somewhere in between—it can charge more than Twitter because it attracts coveted millennials more than other platforms. So the price of attention varies by platform.

Gary Vee exploits this price variation. As he describes it, he's built his career on investing in "underpriced attention." His ability to sell books and high-priced marketing services to brands, sports stars, and musicians depends on his ability to garner attention (and to leverage that attention to achieve his clients' aims). So beginning in the 1990s, when he took his father's wine business online and grew its annual revenue from $3 million to $60 million, he looked for underpriced access to consumers' attention and favored the cheapest and most effective channels to get it.

At the time, the cheapest attention was available through email marketing, so he invested in email to drive his business. Then prices and effectiveness changed as new platforms and social services, like Google and Facebook, came online. To grow their own businesses, new platforms like Google initially underpriced their attention. So Gary Vee invested his marketing dollars in Google. As it became established, the price of Google's attention increased, and even newer services, like Twitter and YouTube, came online. So when their price of attention was lower, Gary poured his money into those platforms. Now he's touting TikTok as the next attention gold rush. He says he has no particular affinity for any channel—he's "platform agnostic." He simply engages in attention arbitrage. "I've built a career on exploiting underpriced attention. Email marketing in '97, Google AdWords in 2000, YouTube in '06, Twitter '07, Snapchat," he says. "That's my career."

Ad inventory is also differentiated by a platform's ability to target its persuasive messages at the right people—the people they are intended to persuade. If, for example, a politician wishes to persuade conservatives, aged 35 to 45, in specific districts of a particular state, with a message about gun rights, the platforms that can most accurately identify 35-to-45-year-old gun enthusiasts in those districts are more likely to attract ad revenue and be able to charge a premium for their ads. So platforms that can most effectively target ads at the right people, and brands and marketers that understand targeting, have a competitive advantage. This ability to microtarget persuasive messages—to direct ads at narrower and narrower categories of consumers—depends on the quantity and quality of the data that social media platforms collect about the demographics, opinions, behaviors, psychological profiles, locations, and social networks of their users.

Microtargeting

I described the process of microtargeting in general terms in Chapter 6. To target the right people, a brand, political campaign, or state-run influence operation first builds models of who is most likely to engage with and be moved to act on particular persuasive messages, deploys those messages across the Hype Machine's different channels, measures their effectiveness, and then adjusts the messaging and budget allocations across channels to maximize reach, awareness, and influence among the voters or consumers it is trying to persuade. That, as you'll recall, is integrated digital marketing.

Microtargeting models are powered by reams of personal data about consumers' demographics (e.g., age, gender, language, socioeconomic status), behaviors (e.g., purchase history, search history, browsing history), preferences (e.g., social media likes, shares), and psychological profiles. And all this data is integrated across the various platforms by a third-party ecosystem that shares data from one source to another. Demographic microtargeting uses this data to identify audiences based on who they are. Behavioral microtargeting identifies them based on how they behave. Interest-based segments identify what people like. And psychographic targeting, championed by Alexander Nix and Cambridge Analytica, profiles people based on their personalities—for example, whether someone is extroverted or introverted. But how do each of these approaches work, and how well do they work? It's instructive to begin by actually experiencing one, in real time.

If you want to experience behavioral microtargeting in action, put this book down for a second and try the following exercise on your phone. Go to Google and conduct a few searches for "Facebook real time bidding," "Google real time bidding," and "Targeting Instagram display ads." Click through on a few of the sponsored links and browse a few news articles and companies providing ad-targeting services to marketers and small businesses. Now close Google and open Instagram. Scroll through your feed, and notice the ads that are being shown. You'll find that your Instagram feed has likely been overrun by marketing firms that want to help you market your products across social media and the Web.

Think that was a fluke? Try it one more time. Go to Google on your phone and search for "boots," "warm boots," and "waterproof boots."

Click through on some of the boots displayed in the search ads. Now close Google and fire up Instagram. Don't be surprised if all you see is boots. The attention economy is enhanced by microtargeting, which feeds on data. Without granular individual-level data, microtargeting is impossible (though there are privacy-preserving ways of using personal data to microtarget without ever knowing *who* you are targeting, which I'll return to in Chapter 12).

But does microtargeting work? Can brands, political campaigns, and influence operations change our behavior by microtargeting the right people with the right messages using the vast troves of personal data the Hype Machine collects every day? The short answer is "Yes, but . . ." Microtargeting usually creates small but significant behavior changes that, when aggregated over hundreds of millions of people, can move the needle on product sales and potentially on elections and vaccine hesitancy. But there are caveats to that generalization that are worth exploring, as we assess the persuasive power of the attention economy.

In July 2002 the European Union enacted its Directive on Privacy and Electronic Communications, a predecessor to the current General Data Privacy Regulation (GDPR). In 2011 my friend and colleague Catherine Tucker, who's an economist and marketing professor at MIT, and our colleague Avi Goldfarb at the University of Toronto cleverly exploited this change in European privacy laws to measure the effectiveness of microtargeting. The privacy directive limited advertisers' ability to collect and use consumers' data to target advertising. Catherine and Avi used this policy change as a natural experiment to measure how the loss of targeting data affected advertisers' influence on consumers' purchase decisions.

They compared the effectiveness of ads shown in European countries that enacted the privacy law to the targeted ads shown in countries without such laws, as well as in countries that implemented the law, but *before* it went into effect. Across the nearly ten thousand ad campaigns they studied, advertising effectiveness *decreased* by 65 percent when laws restricting data access for microtargeting were implemented. When Europeans browsed websites outside Europe, where they were not affected by the privacy legislation, there was no reduction in ad effectiveness. When non-Europeans browsed European websites that were covered by the laws, ad effectiveness decreased. This suggests that the laws, which prevented the data collection necessary for microtargeting, reduced ad effectiveness, and that microtargeting significantly improved the ability of advertisers to boost consumer purchasing by targeting the right people with the right messages. While Catherine and Avi's work established the causal effect of microtargeting on ad performance, a look under the hood at a production system gives us even more insight into how microtargeting works.

Two machine-learning experts at the forefront of microtargeting theory and practice are my close friends Claudia Perlich and Foster Provost. Their insight into microtargeting is important not only because they conducted the original machine-learning research that helped establish statistical microtargeting theory, but also because they've built large-scale microtargeting systems in practice. Together they helped create the machine-learning systems running many trillions of microtargeting decisions across the digital economy every day. Foster is my former colleague at NYU, and Claudia, who was his PhD student, went on to become the chief scientist at the targeting firm Dstillery, which Foster helped found. If you ever want to understand the details of how microtargeting actually works in practice, take one or both of them to lunch. I've shared many a meal with them, and to say I've learned a lot is a grave understatement.

One thing that becomes clear when you talk to Foster and Claudia about whether microtargeting works is the importance of the right kind of data. Microtargeting helps brands, political campaigns, and foreign governments better understand their audiences, so they can speak to them more effectively. Understanding audiences requires lots of data, and the data that social media collects is some of the most predictive and therefore the most valuable. By 2018, Dstillery was processing 100 billion events per day across desktops, tablets, and smartphones to help target ads for CVS, Microsoft, AT&T, and other blue-chip companies. When Claudia made a presentation to my MIT class in 2018, she gave a simple example comparing demographic data, like age and gender, to preference data, such as what consumers liked on Facebook—targeting based on who people are or, alternatively, what they prefer.

Imagine you're trying to predict consumers' gender (one of the simplest prediction tasks in marketing) and all you know about them is their age. People's age shouldn't be very predictive of their gender, and it isn't. A model targeting men while only knowing their age, built with

Dstillery's data, was accurate about 60 percent of the time. That's just slightly more accurate than flipping a coin and only because there was a slight relationship between consumers' age and gender in Dstillery's data. Yet when Claudia tried to predict consumers' gender using just ten things they liked on Facebook, the model's accuracy jumped to 86 percent. When she used a hundred likes, the model predicted gender with 100 percent accuracy, and it did just as well with a hundred likes as with a hundred thousand. Some data features simply improve targeting predictions more than others.

Now imagine a production-scale system that sifts through hundreds of billions of events per day to build targeting models that power advertising at scale. How might that perform? Foster, Claudia, and their colleagues Brian D'Alessandro, Ori Stitelman, and Troy Raeder published a paper describing Dstillery's original targeting system and its performance in the journal *Machine Learning* in 2014. When they compared ads targeted by their system to randomly targeted ads, targeted ads *always* performed better. In fact, the median targeted campaign performed *five times* better than random targeting, and the top-performing 15 percent of campaigns performed *more than twenty-five times* better. In two large field experiments and two lab experiments published a year later, Alexander Bleier and Maik Eisenbeiss found that personalized ads were two to four times more effective at eliciting click-throughs and view-throughs than nonpersonalized ads.

But *how* does targeting work? It's not only about finding the people most likely to act on a persuasive message. Targeting people with an interest actually changes their self-perceptions in relation to that interest, making them more likely to respond. Christopher Summers, Robert Smith, and Rebecca Walker Reczek found that ads targeted based on consumers' online search and shopping behavior increased consumers' purchase intent by 17 percent compared to ads targeted based on demographics. They also found that the targeted ads acted as a "social label" that altered consumers' self-perceptions and that consumers' behaviors changed to align with these new self-perceptions. When advertisers target me as someone who is into fitness, I perceive myself as being more into fitness and change my behavior toward being more into fitness by, for example, buying exercise clothing or signing up for a gym.

Interestingly, adjustments of self-perception and changes in purchase intent occurred only when the label was *plausibly* connected to consumers' prior behavior—in other words, when the microtargeting was accurate. I believe the fitness label only if I'm at least vaguely interested in fitness to begin with. If the targeting is inaccurate, it has no effect on my self-perceptions.

If the Hype Machine's ability to influence consumer and voter behavior depends on the accuracy of microtargeting, how accurate is it? While there's a lot of hype around how much Facebook, Twitter, and YouTube know about us and how much that guides persuasive influence campaigns by brands and foreign governments over social media, Catherine Tucker did the actual research. In December 2019 she published a study with Nico Neumann and Timothy Whitfield that examined the accuracy of the microtargeting audiences created by many different data brokers (third-party firms in the attention economy hired by brands to find specific audiences using demographic and behavioral data) and compared their ability to accurately identify different types of people. What she and her colleagues found helps us understand how well the Hype Machine converts its fuel (data) into action (behavior change).

Microtargeting is a $20 billion industry in the United States alone. The problem is, the targeting algorithms are secret. Very few people know how they work, or whether they work, and to what extent they work for different audiences, on different platforms and across different targeting services. As *New York Times* CEO Mark Thompson asked, "When we say a member of the audience [that a brand wants to reach] is a female fashionista aged 20 to 30, what's the probability that that's actually true?" Catherine, Nico, and Timothy answered that very question.

They examined the accuracy of audiences targeted by nineteen leading data brokers on six platforms across ninety third-party demographic and audience interest segments like "sports interested males aged 25 to 35" and "female fashionistas aged 20 to 30." They examined two tiers of microtargeting with third-party data—with optimization algorithms (to select data sources and place ads) and without them—across both demographic (e.g., women aged 20 to 30) and interest-based segments (e.g., sports interested, fitness interested, and travel interested). They discovered several realities of the Hype Machine's black box microtargeting that help us understand if it works and how it works.

When third-party data is used without optimization algorithms, the results of microtargeting are underwhelming. The average accuracy of microtargeting in identifying males aged 25 to 54 is 24.4 percent, while the average accuracy of identifying the correct gender is 42.3 percent. Since these groups naturally occur 26.5 percent and 50 percent of the time in the population, microtargeting with third-party data alone is *worse* than random selection.

When third-party data is combined with optimization algorithms, however, the performance improves significantly. The average accuracy in identifying males between 25 and 54 improves to 59 percent, which is a 123 percent improvement over random selection. But there are significant performance differences across platforms and targeting firms. How were Foster and Claudia able to achieve up to twenty-five times improvements in targeting performance? Some companies are just better at it than others—they write better algorithms using the most predictive data. The best provider in Catherine's study showed ads to the right target audience 72 percent of the time (a 171 percent improvement), while the worst provider showed ads to the right targets 40 percent of the time (a 50 percent improvement).

While demographic segmentation was the focus of the Hype Machine in the past, the future of microtargeting is in interest-based audience segments. Catherine, Nico, and Timothy found "high total accuracy" for microtargeting aimed at identifying those interested in sports (87.4 percent accurate), fitness (82.1 percent), and travel (72.8 percent). The variation across different microtargeting firms was also smaller—they were all reasonably good at identifying these interests. Microtargeting performance was also more accurate the more "niche" the interest was, meaning the narrower the audience in a specific subject or niche, the greater the improvement of microtargeting over random selection.

So what does all this imply about Cambridge Analytica's targeting? Can our personalities really reveal these niche interests and drive targeting performance?

Cambridge Analytica

Alexander Nix touted the importance of "psychographic profiling" on-stage at the Concordia summit and conferences around the world. He suggested that knowing people's psychographic profiles; that is, having "an understanding of your personality," is the most important thing needed to manipulate voter behavior because "it's personality that drives behavior and behavior that obviously influences how you vote." Did Cambridge Analytica genuinely have a secret sauce, or was it selling snake oil?

In 2017 Sandra Matz, Michal Kosinski, Gideon Nave, and David Stillwell tested Cambridge Analytica's methods in the largest public study of psychological profiling ever conducted on Facebook. Using data from the Facebook app myPersonality, they tested the effects of psychological persuasion on people's purchasing behavior in three field studies that reached over 3.7 million people with psychologically tailored advertising. The myPersonality app, developed by Stillwell, allowed users to take psychometric tests that rated them on what is known as the five-factor model of personality.

The five-factor model (FFM) scores people along five broad psychological dimensions, referred to as the "big five" personality traits: extroversion, agreeableness, conscientiousness, neuroticism, and openness to experience. Stillwell's myPersonality app asked users to grant access to their Facebook profiles and social network data, allowing the researchers to, for the first time, connect individuals' measurable personality traits with what they liked on Facebook. Using this connection, the researchers scored Facebook likes along the five traits. For example, people who liked computers and the TV series *Stargate* were more introverted, while people who liked "making people laugh" were more extroverted. By combining the scores of the people who liked certain things, such as Lady Gaga or *House of Cards,* on Facebook, they were able to score those things according to the big five personality traits and then to psychologically profile the people in their study based on what they liked on Facebook.

It's impossible to tell this story without stopping for a moment to discuss the cloak-and-dagger intrigue connecting Kosinski, Stillwell, and the myPersonality app to the larger Cambridge Analytica scandal because, in an eyebrow-raising twist, Kosinski and Stillwell conducted their research while at Cambridge University, in the same department as Aleksandr Kogan, the now-infamous Cambridge University researcher who gave psychological profiles and Facebook data on 50 million Americans to Cambridge Analytica, which then sparked the scandal that landed Mark Zuckerberg in the hot seat.

Investigative reporting on the relationships among these researchers suggests that Kogan approached Kosinski on behalf of an unnamed company (Cambridge Analytica) that was interested in his methods and wanted access to the myPersonality database. The reporting suggests Kosinski ultimately broke off contact with Kogan when he revealed the company's name and Kosinski discovered that it focused on "influencing elections." Kogan then developed his own app, called This Is Your Digital Life, which mimicked myPersonality, and shared the data and methods with Cambridge Analytica. In 2017, Cambridge Analytica told *Das Magazin* that it "has had no dealings" with Kosinski and "does not use the same methodology" as he did, although, as journalist John Morgan noted, Cambridge Analytica's methods are "undeniably similar." This cloak-and-dagger detour is important because it reveals that the Matz et al. study is as close to a systematic audit of the persuasive power of Cambridge Analytica's methods and data as is publicly available.

Facebook doesn't allow marketers to target advertisements based on personality. So rather than targeting ads based on personality traits directly, the researchers tested the effectiveness of personality profiling by targeting ads based on the likes that represented those traits. To target introverts, they targeted people with introverted likes. To target extroverts, they targeted people with extroverted likes. They then created advertisements with extroverted or introverted language, or language with a high degree of openness or a low degree of openness. For example, extroverted ads for beauty products showed a woman dancing at a party with the tagline "Dance like no one's watching (but they totally are)," while an introverted beauty ad showed a woman putting on makeup alone in front of a vanity mirror with the tagline "Beauty doesn't have to shout." The researchers then targeted "introverted" and "extroverted" Facebook users with these ads based on their introverted and extroverted likes and measured whether personality matched ads performed better than personality mismatched ads on click-through rates and purchases.

The results showed that persuasive appeals that matched people's personalities resulted in up to 40 percent more clicks and up to 54 percent more purchases than the mismatched messaging. In the study on extroversion, consumers who were shown ads that matched their personalities were 54 percent more likely to purchase from an online store than those shown ads incongruent with their personalities. In the study on openness, consumers who were shown ads that matched their personalities were 38 percent more likely to click on and 31 percent more likely to install a crossword app than those shown ads incongruent with their personalities. The results suggest that psychological targeting makes it possible "to influence the behavior of large groups of people by tailoring persuasive appeals to the psychological needs of the target audiences."

This study has, however, encountered some skepticism in the scientific community, primarily for its inability to separate correlation from causation and control for selection effects in ad targeting. If you think back to our discussion of the importance of causality in Chapter 6, you'll remember that Facebook ads tend to be shown to people that Facebook thinks are more likely to respond to them. So the greater response rates of psychologically matched messages may be due to these selection effects rather than to the causal influence of psychologically tailored messages on behavior. You see, once a marketer (or foreign agent) chooses a target audience on Facebook, for example, Facebook then adds a layer of optimization on top of those choices and targets ads at people it thinks are most like to respond. My colleagues Dean Eckles, Brett Gordon, and Garrett Johnson made this point in a response to the study published in the same journal. They noted that "comparison of Facebook ad campaigns does not randomly assign users . . . which threatens the internal validity of their findings and weakens their conclusions. . . . Ad platforms like Facebook optimize campaign performance by showing ads to users whom the platform expects are more likely to fulfill the campaigns' objectives . . . [which may] explain a non-negligible portion, if not all, of [the] study's effects." People are also not equally persuadable on every issue. It's more difficult to persuade people to change their vote choices than it is to get them to click on or purchase products with targeted ads. So there's plenty of room for skepticism about the persuasive power of Cambridge Analytica's methods to sway elections.

But, while not definitive, the Cambridge study does suggest that psychographic profiling can improve the persuasive power of the Hype Machine, at least for commercial purposes. As more research is done, we'll learn more about how microtargeting changes our opinions and behaviors, including how we shop, vote, and date.

The Tyranny of Trends

In addition to microtargeting, the attention economy perpetuates another important trend, born of the industry-wide obsession with user engagement. As we register our emotional reactions to all the content we see on social media—our likes, loves, laughs, anger, sadness, and surprise—the platforms use our reactions not only to tailor content for us, but also amplify that content using algorithms that promote trends. Virality supports the attention economy because it broadcasts what's popular and gives us all an implicit goal to be popular. But as the algorithms amplify popularity, they also create what I call a "tyranny of trends."

Attention requires engagement, so the Hype Machine's design encourages and amplifies engagement as much as it can. The more social media platforms keep us engaged, the more their ad inventory and the value of their ads increase. It's just good business. Several design features support this model. For example, likes and other emotional reactions enable the platforms to "keep score," which not only allows them to know which content is engaging users most but also feeds right into the dopamine response system of the brain (described in Chapter 4). We're given a dopamine rush of social validation when others like our content, and we're disappointed when they don't. This encourages us to create content that will be liked and, due to social reciprocity, to continue liking content we find valuable. Just last week my mom complained that I hadn't yet liked her vacation pictures on Instagram. It had only been two days since she posted them! I was busy, #lol! As the father of a six-year-old, I'm concerned about the potential effects of social media culture on psychology and mental health, especially for kids. As a result, my son gets almost no screen time of any kind.

Keeping score enables another design feature that boosts engagement: algorithmic amplification. The process of algorithmically curating and amplifying what's popular, engaging, or "trending," and then showing it to even more people, turbocharges its popularity and drives even more engagement. By showing what's been disproportionately engaging to as many people as possible, the Hype Machine creates another Hype Loop designed to amplify engagement further.

Algorithmic amplification comes in many flavors. For example, content that is being liked by a lot of your friends will be promoted in your newsfeed. But one particular feature creates waves of engagement with topics experiencing abnormal bursts of popularity in real time, and that's "trending." A trending topic is one that experiences a surge in popularity for a short period of time. The platforms discover these topics by sifting through the engagement and popularity scores of all the topics being discussed by their users at any particular moment in time and algorithmically identifying those that are *novel, timely,* and *rising in popularity.* They do this by quantifying the difference between the *current* activity around a topic (the number of posts, shares, likes, or comments about a topic) and the *expected* activity around that topic (as measured by predictive models). If the observed activity is much higher than the expected activity, the topic is considered a trend.

People post about many different topics all the time, but when a topic experiences a burst of activity at a particular moment, it starts to trend. Observed activity gives the platform a sense of the *popularity* of a topic, while the *difference* between the observed activity and the expected activity for a topic gives the platform a sense of the topic's *novelty.* Timeliness is then captured by measuring popularity and novelty *in the most recent time periods.* But how do the platforms identify topics to begin with?

Machine learning and natural language processing can analyze the free-form text posted to social media, but it's computationally challenging and inefficient to analyze the growing volume of user-generated content without some guidance. So the platforms have widely adopted hashtags as labels signifying topics. This takes the engineering burden off them and harnesses the crowd of users to label topics themselves.

Hashtags are ubiquitous across social platforms today, but they were invented on Twitter over a decade ago. On August 23, 2007, Chris Messina, a Twitter user and self-described "digital nomad," suggested adding a pound sign to keywords to make tweets on related topics easier to search. His original tweet asked, "How do you feel about using # (pound) for groups. As in #barcamp [msg]?" And the rest, as they say, is history. Twitter incorporated and began supporting hashtags in 2009 and launched trending topics, which measured and promoted trends, in 2010. Hashtags and trending have been widely adopted across the Hype Machine ever since.

Trending content, whether in the form of hashtags or topics, is now displayed on leaderboards and trending lists, tailored to users' interests and geographic locations, to inform users of what is *novel, timely,* and *popular.* It's a way of dealing with the poverty of attention that accompanies the wealth of information the Hype Machine creates, in economist Herbert Simon's parlance. The publication of such lists amplifies trends and makes what's popular even more popular. Algorithmic amplification, in this way, creates a tyranny of trends that focuses users' attention on the newest popular sentiment of the day. This has many implications for our culture, our politics, and (as we'll see in the next chapter) the battle between the wisdom and the madness of crowds.

Trending favors topics that are attention grabbing, shocking, and emotionally charged. If a topic can shock us and trigger our most extreme emotions—surprise, anger, disgust, inspiration, joy, etc.—it's more likely to become popular quickly and thus to trend. Once a topic trends, leaderboards and trending lists broadcast it to an even wider audience, amplifying its popularity and favoring emotionally extreme, exciting (or inciting) content.

Algorithmic amplification and trending have another unintended consequence. They encourage attempts to game the system to amplify and redirect attention to certain topics by manufacturing popularity where there isn't any, in the hope of making those topics trend. Brands, governments, and political campaigns value the vast attention created by trending topics so much that Twitter was charging them $200,000 per day to have a sponsored trend appear on the top of its trending topics list. The value of attention combined with the algorithmic amplification of trending topics creates an incentive for manipulation. Sophisticated social media experts can mobilize networks of humans and bots together to make particular topics or ideas trend with the express purpose of changing discrete outcomes in society—like the passage of a particular piece of legislation, the decision to intervene in an annexation (as in the case of Crimea), or decisions about what happens during a congressional investigation. Take, for example, the Russian effort #ReleaseTheMemo, which trended in January 2018.

#ReleaseTheMemo

One of the most explicit attempts to "make [memes] trend" was the Russian effort #ReleaseTheMemo, which exploded on Twitter in January 2018. The memo, which was written by Rep. Devin Nunes's staff, alleged that the FBI used "politically motivated or questionable sources" to obtain Foreign Intelligence Surveillance Act (FISA) warrants on Trump adviser Carter Page during its investigation into Russian interference in the 2016 presidential election. The Democrats countered that the memo contained deliberately false and misleading claims designed to discredit the FBI and the investigation. A debate ignited about whether the memo should be released to the public, with the legitimacy of the Russia investigation hanging in the balance. As Molly McKew has reported, Russian operatives then went to work on the Hype Machine, designing, deploying, and spreading digital propaganda to develop public support for the memo's release.

Russian bot and cyborg (part bot-, part human-controlled) accounts helped create the meme and the hashtag calling for the U.S. Congress to #ReleaseTheMemo. The hashtag originated from a Twitter account called @underthemoraine, which appears to have been the account of a real person living in Michigan with less than seventy-five followers at the time. But accounts like this are frequently followed, retweeted, and amplified by networks of bots called botnets, which work together in a coordinated fashion to drive memes and create trending topics in social media. They follow ordinary accounts to hijack organic memes that support their agenda, and promote them for political gain. Immediately after @underthemoraine used the #ReleaseTheMemo hashtag, several automated accounts, many of which were established in 2012 or 2013 but had been dormant until the 2016 election cycle, began tweeting, retweeting, and sharing each other's promotion of the meme.

The Russian botnet promoted the meme into a frenzy on Twitter and directed key influencers and lawmakers to it. Though several hashtags competed to represent the meme, once #ReleaseTheMemo gained momentum, the botnet focused on that tweet, amplifying it and urging its followers to "make it trend." From its appearance at four P.M. on January 18 to midnight that day, the hashtag was used 670,000 times in eight hours. By midnight it was being mentioned 250,000 times per hour. For comparison, two other events were occurring at the same time: the Women's March on D.C., where I was on January 20, and the NFL playoff game between the New England Patriots and the Jacksonville Jaguars, which took place on January 21. These events garnered a total volume of 606,000 and 253,000 tweets, respectively, and top speeds of 87,000 and 75,000 tweets, per hour. By nine A.M. on January 19, #ReleaseTheMemo had been mentioned nearly 2 million times.

The botnet then drew additional key influencers and lawmakers to the meme by mentioning them in their tweets, and real Americans followed suit, tweeting, retweeting, and mentioning key influencers along the way. Republican members of the House Intelligence Committee were collectively mentioned 217,000 times with the hashtag. Sean Hannity was mentioned 245,000 times. By the time Speaker of the House Paul Ryan spoke in favor of releasing the memo, he had been targeted with more than 225,000 messages about it. Donald Trump himself was targeted 1 million times.

Once the meme gained momentum, the hashtag was amplified by trending algorithms and went mainstream, in the news media and as a political talking point. As memes rack up significant numbers in short periods of time, automated algorithms pick up that the community is interested in them and post them to "trending" lists of the most mentioned stories. These lists serve as a public broadcast of what's hot right now and direct even more attention to the meme. The #ReleaseTheMemo campaign succeeded in trending and crossed over into the mainstream media, as well as reaching lawmakers in Congress.

Finally, the groundswell of support, which was in part created and promoted by Russian accounts, was used as justification to release the memo. It was released by House Republicans on February 2, 2018. The social media propaganda effort reflected in the #ReleaseTheMemo campaign mirrors the groundswell of support whipped up in Crimea in 2014. As in Crimea, proponents of the release of the Nunes memo used the Hype Machine to galvanize support and distort the perception of the amount of public support for a specific government outcome. In February 2014 the outcome was Crimea's accession to Russia. In January 2018 it was the release of the Nunes memo. But in each case, it was a political manipulation by a foreign actor.

Attention Inequality

The structure of the attention economy, its focus on popularity and the algorithmic emphasis on trending make the New Social Age rife with inequality. Attention is not evenly distributed on the Hype Machine. In fact, it's quite the opposite. A small fraction of people and content attract the lion's share of attention, even more than you'd expect without social media. This is due to natural human tendencies working in concert with the algorithms that drive social networking. For example, as my friend and colleague László Barabási discovered in research with Réka Albert in 1998, network dynamics are governed by "preferential attachment." That is, we tend to connect with those who are popular in social networks. As a result, with popularity as with wealth, "the rich get richer."

The Hype Machine's algorithms perpetuate and accelerate this inequality of attention. Friend-suggestion algorithms tend to succeed more often for people with more friends because they have more "mutual friends" with those receiving the recommendations. As a result, people with many connections receive the lion's share of new connections.

Inequality is similarly perpetuated in attention given to content. Since feed algorithms favor content that inspires more engagement, posts with more likes, comments, and shares are more likely to be promoted in newsfeeds and therefore are more likely to be reshared, creating a Hype Loop of content popularity that drives attention inequality. Trending algorithms add to these rich-get-richer dynamics by broadcasting content that attracts a disproportionate amount of attention. As my colleague Kristina Lerman and her co-author, Linhong Zhu, documented in their study of the attention economy on Twitter, "The vast majority of users do not receive any attention and the top 1% of users get far more attention than the bottom 99% combined!" This will become important when we examine the Hype Machine's impact on collective intelligence and the wisdom of crowds in Chapter 10.

Novelty, Shock, and Authenticity

If the attention economy is the engine of social media, what drives attention through the Hype Machine? A clue surfaced in our ten-year study of fake news, where we found that shocking, salacious, unexpected, and surprising content captures our attention most and inspires us to share. It wasn't the first time I had seen the importance of novelty in my research. In 2011, Marshall Van Alstyne and I discovered that novel information was the most valuable for enhancing work productivity. We analyzed five years of email data at an executive recruiting firm and measured the novelty of the information recruiters sent and received in their email. We found that the recruiters with access to novel information closed more projects faster and booked and billed more revenue. We couldn't determine whether novelty caused increases in productivity, but the correlation was striking. Paramveer Dhillon and I then corroborated these findings in a second company in a completely different industry. The results matched perfectly.

These two papers confirmed what my colleague Ron Burt had been arguing for years—that weak ties are valuable because they give us access to novel information. It all goes back to the structure of the Hype Machine's network (which I described in Chapter 3). The network is clustered, with dense connections within clusters and sparse connections across them. People who are connected to many clusters through weak ties, the connectors or "brokers" as they are called in a network, receive a lot more novelty because they swim in many different pools of information. It turns out that with access to novel information, they are more aware of what's happening in different parts of the network. They can broker opportunities, solve problems that are intractable given local knowledge, and drive innovation. For all these reasons, because it updates our understanding of the world and conveys social status on the sharer, novelty grabs our attention and encourages us to share it. This means our attention is drawn to the most surprising, shocking, salacious, and emotionally arousing content.

But what keeps our attention is not necessarily the same as what attracts it. In some sense, what keeps our attention is the opposite of shock value, and that's authenticity. Local network effects are strongest for strong ties, not weak ties, because the long-term value provided by our close friends and family is greater than the short-term, attention-grabbing value of celebrity. This explains why microinfluencers generate more engagement than celebrity influencers, why local network effects are strongest among strong ties, why productivity is enhanced by strong cohesive ties in complex work, and why we communicate most often with our closest and strongest connections. When it comes to attention, if novelty is the short game, authenticity is the long game.

"Means" Are Meaningless

Our attention to social media messages is not just highly unequal; those messages can have wildly different effects on different people in the network. Political ads that mobilize Democrats are ridiculed by Republicans. Extroverted messages sent to introverts fall flat. We've found that the *average* or *mean* effect of social media messages is much less important than the effects they have on specific people. To understand social media, we shouldn't care only about averages. We should care about the aggregation of all the specific yet varied effects of such messaging on specific groups. One result from my research drove this idea home for me.

Security concerns and targeting have inspired social media companies to verify and display people's real identities as much as possible in recent years. I remember a now-famous *New Yorker* cartoon that contemplated the implications of identity on the Internet. It depicted a dog in front of a computer talking to another dog. The first dog said to the other, "On the Internet, no one knows you're not a dog." It perfectly captured the tension between the need for real IDs to facilitate commerce and guarantee security, and the benefits of anonymity to free expression. Sean Taylor, Lev Muchnik, and I were studying the importance of identity in social media. We were curious how this type of anonymity (or the lack thereof) made people behave on the Hype Machine. How did they react to social media content when it was displayed anonymously?

We designed an experiment on a large social media platform to test the effects of anonymity on social media behavior. We randomly assigned 5 percent of the comments people posted to a social news aggregation website like Reddit to be anonymous and left 95 percent identified. Everything else about the posts—their content, the order in which they appeared, others' ability to like or comment on them, the display of friends' social reactions—remained the same. We then measured the effect of anonymity on the number of upvotes and down-votes the anonymous posts received, compared to those of the identi-fied content. What we found showed us how meaningless "means" really were.

We first estimated the *average* effect of anonymity on social media reactions and found no effect at all. Making someone's posts anony-mous had *zero* effect on whether the posts were liked or disliked, *on average*. Then we examined the effects of anonymity on different kinds of people. And we found two very strong countervailing effects. For some people, attaching their identity was tremendously beneficial—people liked the content more when they knew who posted it. For other people, however, identity had the exact opposite effect—people disliked the content more when they knew who posted it. People with strong reputations in the community benefited from having their names attached to their content, while those with weaker or negative reputations were hurt when their names were attached. The reason we couldn't see these effects in the averages was because the positive and negative effects, in the aggregate, canceled each other out. But the ef-fects were actually quite strong when viewed from the perspective of the subgroups.

Results like this abound in social media. Remember our study of digital exercise contagion? In that study we found, on average, that the friends of those who posted their training runs to social media were inspired to run more, but the influence was stronger for some people than for others. We tend to evaluate our own exercise performance in comparison to others'. The question among researchers is, what in-spires us to run more—comparisons to those performing better than us or comparisons to those performing worse than us? Comparisons to those who run more than us motivate us to work harder. But com-parisons to those who typically don't run as much as we do create "competitive behavior to protect one's superiority." When we exam-ined these subgroups more closely, we found that less active runners influenced more active runners more than more active runners influ-enced less active runners. We also found that people who ran inconsis-tently (not every day) influenced consistent runners more than consistent runners influenced inconsistent runners. The results suggested that comparisons with those who run less than we do on social media, what we call "downward comparisons," had more impact than what we call "upward comparisons" in our online self-evaluations of fitness routines.

We also found that online influence in exercise behaviors was strongest among same-sex pairs, and weaker across genders. Men strongly influenced other men, while women only moderately influenced men and women. More surprisingly, men didn't influence women at all. This may be due to gender differences in the motivations for exercise and competition. For example, men report being more influenced by social support in their decision to adopt exercise behaviors, while women report being more motivated by self-regulation and individual planning. Men may also simply be more motivated by competition with women than women are by competition with men.

Another example of subgroup effects emerged in our study of social proof at WeChat and in Facebook's voting experiments. At WeChat, we found that showing a user that their friends liked an ad increased their engagement with that ad, on average. But not all friends had equal influence. Friends with greater social status (measured by how many friends they had on WeChat) and greater product expertise in the ad product's category (measured by how many articles they read, for example, about cars or consumer electronics) had greater influence. In the Facebook voting experiments, those with closer ties had more influence than mere acquaintances.

The point is, because subgroup effects are so powerful, we must evaluate social media's impact with care. It's not enough to know the *average* effect of Russian misinformation on voting, or of antivax ads on vaccine hesitancy. We must understand the effects of these messages on specific subgroups and consider the totality of the varied and potentially countervailing effects on society as a whole. A perfect example is election manipulation. Though the average effect of digital ads on vote choices may be small or even nonexistent, if the right subgroups are targeted and influenced in the right geographies—in the right states or voting districts—the potential to move elections remains real.

CHAPTER 10

The Wisdom and Madness of Crowds

Paradoxically, the best way for a group to be smart is for each person in it to think and act as independently as possible.

—JAMES SUROWIECKI

Interdependence is and ought to be as much the ideal of man as self-sufficiency. Man is a social being.

—MOHANDAS GANDHI

In his influential book *The Wisdom of Crowds,* James Surowiecki described the power of collective judgment to solve many of humanity's most challenging problems, from prediction, to innovation, to governance, to strategic decision making, to more mundane matters like how to build a winning football or baseball team. The theory was originally proposed by Francis Galton a hundred years earlier to explain how a crowd of strangers could guess the weight of an ox to within a pound of its actual weight by averaging a sufficient number of individual guesses.

The idea was simple: a crowd with diverse, independent opinions of equal voice will outperform most if not all individual experts at a variety of tasks when their opinions are aggregated to harness their collective wisdom. It's an elegant theory that is, in large part, correct when you do the math of collective aggregation. But as Yogi Berra so eloquently opined, "In theory, there is no difference between theory and practice. But in practice, there is."

The only problem with Surowiecki's thesis is that his book was written in 2004, the same year Mark Zuckerberg founded Facebook. In the decade that followed, the Hype Machine systematically undercut the three fundamental assumptions of the wisdom of crowds. Crowd wisdom depends on having many diverse, independent opinions of equal voice. But as we know, the Hype Machine hypersocializes us, making our individual judgments systematically and algorithmically interdependent; polarizes us into homogeneous communities, like birds of a feather flocking together; and entrenches us in an unequal communication system that perpetuates the popularity of the popular and accelerates the creation of trends, in what is essentially an automated herding market, where people follow the behavior of others.

As a result, we're trending away from Surowiecki's vision of the wisdom of crowds, toward what his intellectual foil, Charles MacKay, called "the madness of crowds." How we design, use, and regulate the Hype Machine will determine whether it leads us toward wisdom or madness. The Hype Machine of today is built for madness, but it could be built for wisdom. My thinking about how to design it away from our collective pathologies was first sparked by a lunch I had in New York City.

Social Influence Bias

Before I taught at MIT, I was a professor at New York University, in the heart of Greenwich Village, which is a mecca of street jazz, beat poetry, and of course, food. The lunch options near my office, from Mario Batali's Babbo, to Mamoun's Falafel, to Thiru Kumar's dosa cart, were all exquisite. If you've ever eaten near Washington Square Park, you know what I mean. The smells and flavors are not easily forgotten. I frequently had lunch there with my students and colleagues, taking breaks from analysis and writing to eat and hash out new ideas.

One day a group of us went to a local eatery called Dojo, a staple of frugal student cuisine. It wasn't Babbo, but it wasn't street meat either—it was somewhere in between. After the meal, I felt compelled to share my experience by rating the restaurant online. With the taste of ginger dressing on my lips, I went back to my office and logged on to Yelp.

On this particular afternoon, the food was average, the service was average, the ambiance was average—the whole experience was, well, average. So I wanted to give the place a middling rating, three out of five stars. But as I went to input the three-star review, right next to where I would provide my own rating was a featured review written by a user named Shar H., with her bright-red five-star rating, waxing poetic about how "the prices here are amazing" and describing "their fresh and amazing, sweet and tart ginger dressing." I thought to myself, *You know . . . she has a point. For what they serve, the prices were truly amazing . . . and that sweet and tart ginger dressing was delicious!* So I gave the place four stars instead of three.

When I thought about it, I realized this wasn't good. Yelp and other ratings sites are supposed to aggregate the unbiased opinions of the crowd. They're supposed to convey true, population-level opinions about which restaurants or hotels are good or bad, so we can all make better choices. If I was swayed by the opinion of the last person who rated the restaurant, this would certainly introduce bias into the crowd's opinion. If everyone else was also swayed by the reviews that came before them, it would create the kind of herd behavior that could distort the wisdom of the crowd in profound ways. It was, for me, an aha moment.

I got out of my chair and walked next door to my postdoc Lev Muchnik's office. (He's now a professor at the Hebrew University of Jerusalem.) Lev's office door was always open, so I poked my head in and rapped on the open doorframe. When he looked up from his computer, I explained to him what had just happened, and we started talking through the implications. Could we build a model of these dynamics? Sure. But models of herd behavior had existed for decades. What we really wanted to know was, *does this happen often in real life, and if so, what does it mean for ratings and opinion dynamics online?*

These questions are important because ratings influence our choices. Ninety-two percent of consumers report reading reviews, of whom 46 percent say they are influenced to purchase, 43 percent say they are deterred from purchasing, and only 3 percent say their decisions are "unaffected" by reviews. Moreover, while 92 percent of consumers read reviews, only 6 percent write reviews, which means a vocal minority is influencing the opinions of the overwhelming majority. The potential consequences of ratings herding are significant because the 6 percent have an outsize impact on how the rest of us shop.

Sean Taylor, my PhD student at the time, who's now a senior data scientist at Lyft and the former head of the statistics team in Facebook's Core Data Science group, overheard my conversation with Lev and wandered across the hall. "Hey, what are you guys talking about?" This is how social science starts—it's sparked by everyday puzzles that evolve into investigations of how and why things happen.

Lev, Sean, and I took this nagging question about herd behavior and embarked on a research project to uncover the truth about population-scale opinion dynamics in the crowd. Did current ratings affect future ratings? If so, what did this mean for bias in crowdsourced opinions online? Finding a correlation between current ratings and future ratings wouldn't tell us much, because correlations in past and future ratings could just be driven by quality. High-quality restaurants (or shoes or hotels) will get high current ratings and high future ratings, while low-quality restaurants will get low ratings today and low ratings tomorrow. Although past ratings are correlated with future ratings, there was really only one way for us to determine if past ratings *influence* future ratings. We had to design an experiment that manipulated ratings.

So we worked with a social news aggregation website, similar to Reddit, to test the herding hypothesis at scale. The site allowed users to post and rate news items and comments. Rather than star ratings, it gave users the option to give thumbs-up or thumbs-down ratings, which made the experiment cleaner. Our experiment randomly gave items posted to the website a single thumbs-up or thumbs-down at the beginning of their ratings cycle; we also had a control group that had no change in ratings. We then watched the ratings for these three groups unfold. Each item typically had hundreds or thousands of ratings, so the introduction of a single random thumbs-up or thumbs-down was a minimal manipulation. We didn't want to put our thumb on the scale too hard (so to speak). But despite the subtlety of the experiment, the results were dramatic.

The positive manipulation shifted the entire ratings distribution to the right. (Compare the line with the up arrows, representing the thumbs-up group, to the line with the stars, representing the control group, in Figure 10.1.) A single positive thumbs-up vote at the beginning of the ratings life cycle increased the likelihood of positive ratings by 32 percent and caused a 25 percent increase in mean ratings. In fact, the effect was so powerful, it caused a "superstar effect" for some items, for which positive herding snowballed into ratings stardom. If we randomly assigned an item to get an extra thumbs-up, it was 30 percent more likely to exceed a score of 10, which was no small feat given the mean rating on the site was 1.9. So with a small random bump-up at the beginning of the ratings cycle, items were 30 percent more likely to shoot off into the stratosphere of ratings.

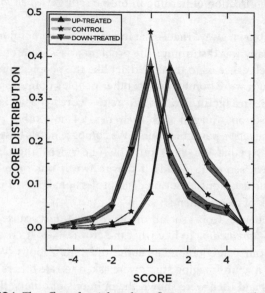

Figure 10.1 *The effect of social media influence on ratings. The graph shows the distributions of normalized ratings of three randomly selected groups of posts on a social news aggregation website similar to Reddit. In the "up-treated" group, posts were manipulated to display a single thumbs-up vote as the first rating on the post (the line with the up arrow). In the "down-treated" group, posts were manipulated to display a single thumbs-down vote as the first rating on the post (the line with the down arrow). In the control group, posts were not manipulated (the line with the star). Ninety-five percent confidence intervals are inferred from Bayesian logistic regression with commenter, rater, and commenter-rater random effects.*

We were also struck by another result in Figure 10.1: the herding was asymmetric. While the ratings of the thumbs-up group (the line with the up arrows) were shifted dramatically to the right (toward higher ratings), the ratings of the thumbs-down group (the line with the down arrows) weren't shifted as much to the left (toward lower ratings). While consumers increased their positive ratings in response to the thumbs-up, they reacted to the thumbs-down by giving a thumbs-up vote, perhaps to correct what they saw as an injustice. The negative manipulation was muted by this "correction effect," which pumped the breaks on negative herding. As we'll see, this has profound implications for the direction of herding in online ratings, *which favors positive herding.*

We were blown away. That social influence caused opinions to shift so dramatically was disturbing. The problem arises from our herd instincts, which cause us to think and act like the people around us. In the digital age, we're bombarded by other people's opinions every day on Facebook, Instagram, Twitter, and Yelp—we're hypersocialized. We browse books on Amazon with awareness of how other customers liked (or disliked) a particular tome. We compare hotels based on user ratings on Expedia. We check out YouTube videos' thumbs-up and thumbs-down scores to decide if they're worth our time. We even make serious decisions about medical professionals based in part on the feedback of prior patients.

Peer influence from social media doesn't just cause outward conformity—*pretending* to like what the crowd likes. It creates actual changes in our value judgments about different options. When participants in a neuroimaging study were asked to rate others' facial attractiveness and then were shown the opinions of others, their fMRI results showed not only that they were conforming to the crowd's opinion of attractiveness, but that the parts of their brains that code subjective value judgments were being activated, "suggesting that exposure to social norms affected participants' neural representations of value." In another study, participants were asked their opinions of music and then exposed to the opinions of experts and the crowd. Social influence changed the participants' expressed opinions about the music, and fMRI results showed that "social influence mediates the very basic value signals . . . [that] could contribute to the rapid learning and the swift spread of values through a population."

When we rate things online, our instincts to follow others combine with our greater susceptibility to positive social influence. Seeing that others have appreciated a certain book, hotel, restaurant, or doctor—and rewarded them with a high rating—causes us to provide a similarly high rating and to think more highly of them. Experiments have shown that we tend to herd on cultural choices, like which music to listen to and even what to pay attention to on the street corner. This abnormality in crowd opinions also helps explain the totally unexpected shape of the ubiquitous star ratings distributions on e-commerce websites like Amazon.

The *J*-Curve of Star Ratings

The shape of online star ratings distributions has always puzzled me. If we randomly polled a representative sample of verified purchasers of shoes or hotel packages, we'd expect their experiences to roughly follow a bell curve. A small group would have had wildly positive experiences. A similarly small group would have had terrible experiences. But the vast majority would have had average experiences—neither horrible nor amazing, just middling. Sure, the ratings distributions of great products would be shifted to the right and the ratings distributions of poor products would be shifted to the left. But if you aggregated the ratings of all the good and bad products over all the consumers who experienced them, you'd expect to see something approximating a normal distribution, or bell curve (Figure 10.2).

But when you aggregate online ratings over many products and consumers, across different categories and platforms, you instead get a curious distribution that looks like a *J*, with lots of 5s and 4s, a moderate number of 1s and 2s, and very few 3s. The *J*-curve of online star ratings is surprisingly consistent. If you're near a computer, head to Amazon and browse a few items at random. It doesn't usually matter which item or category you choose; the ratings are usually *J*-shaped. Highly rated products tend to have a flatter *J*, like a hockey stick with fewer 1s, while products with average ratings tend to have a sharper *J* with more 1s. But the *J*-shape is ubiquitous: lots of 5s and 4s, fewer 1s and 2s, and very few 3s. But why?

The evidence points to three potential explanations. First, there's a *purchasing bias*. Consumers who purchase products (and therefore can choose to leave verified reviews) are more favorably disposed to them in the first place, since they liked them enough to buy them. Second, there's a *reporting bias*. Consumers who have had either really good or really bad experiences are more motivated to provide ratings. People who have had average experiences aren't compelled to review

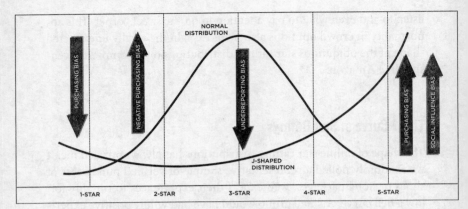

Figure 10.2 *The curious J-curve of online ratings. While we would expect consumers' experiences with products to be "bell-shaped," with the majority of them being average, online ratings typically follow a J-curve, with lots of 5s and 4s, a moderate number of 1s and 2s, and very few 3s. This can be explained by a purchasing bias, an underreporting bias, and a social influence bias.*

them. So ratings oversample good and bad experiences and sample good experiences at a higher rate than bad ones. Another contributing factor occurs when we agree to mutually beneficial outcomes with our transaction partners. For example, a simple trick enables riders and drivers on Uber and Lyft to collude to give each other good ratings. As you're leaving an Uber, you ask, "Five for five?" meaning "I'll give you five stars if you return the favor," a practice that contributes to ratings inflation. Finally, as we saw in our ratings experiment, *social influence bias* favors positive herding over negative herding. Together, these explanations drive ratings distributions toward the *J*-curve.

The positive herding in online opinions has implications for business strategy, fraud prevention, stock prices, and even elections. For example, one easy strategy among brands eager to strengthen their reputation is to encourage satisfied customers to rate and rate early. Encouraging consumers who had a positive experience to rate early will nudge future raters toward higher ratings and push opinion dynamics in a brand's favor. And it's not disinguous because the ratings are real.

Positive herding can also thwart fraud detection. A website like Reddit uses machine learning to detect fake reviews. When it finds one, it removes it. But removing the fake review does nothing to eliminate the influence the fake review had on all the legitimate reviews that came after it. The fraud seeps into the system, tainting the legitimate reviews as well.

Herding theories suggest that "cascades" of information, shared from person to person, create bubbles in markets, from stock prices to housing. The Dutch tulip craze is frequently cited as a historical example of such a bubble. But today the Hype Machine has institutionalized and automated social influence bias to such an extent that it's now ubiquitous. The implications are potentially far-reaching, and it's unclear whether we fully understand them.

Take elections, for example. We published our social influence bias experiment in the midst of the 2012 U.S. presidential election. While we were analyzing the dramatic positive herding in our experiment, I remember listening to radio reports of election polls tallying President Obama's approval rating, to tell us who was leading in the presidential race. With the results of our bias experiment fresh in my mind, I couldn't help but wonder, *Are these polls predicting the election results or are they driving them?* My colleagues in political science have shown that polls can affect voter turnout. If your candidate is ahead, you might think, *We can't possibly lose this election. So there's no need for me to vote.* Our results suggest that herding may drive not only whether people vote but also how they vote. While our study was not about voting per se, herding exists in many human behaviors. There is no reason to think that voting is immune, and Facebook's voting experiments suggest it isn't.

One solution is to make online ratings private, until the sites have enough ratings that they are stable. For example, several months after we published our study on social influence bias in *Science*, Reddit changed its policy to hide ratings until items had a chance to accumulate several hundred ratings in private. If a sufficient number of votes are cast in private, the independence of crowd opinions is maintained, at least until single votes are unlikely to influence the crowd. In a blog post, Reddit explained that it made the change to avoid social influence bias and discourage fraud. In 2019, Instagram began hiding likes on its platform for an entirely different reason. How will these policy changes affect society? We'll soon see.

Collective Intelligence in the Shadow of the Hype Machine

The Hype Machine is often described as a precursor to the hive mind. Its algorithms, when appropriately applied, can enhance our collective intelligence by rapidly aggregating the opinions of the crowd in smart ways. But when those algorithms bake our collective flaws into crowd behavior, they can derail our predictive capacity and send our collective judgment off the rails. A perfect example is found in our collective algorithmic attempts to predict pandemics.

During the 2020 coronavirus pandemic, several companies and research groups attempted to predict the virus's spread by analyzing mentions of its symptoms in social media and search queries. The approach was not new. In fact, it was popularized as a way to predict influenza (the flu) between 2009 and 2013. The flu is responsible for about a million deaths a year worldwide and, at the time I wrote this, the coronavirus had claimed over a hundred thousand lives in a few short months. But early detection, coupled with rapid response, can reduce the impact of pandemics on our health. Predicting virus outbreaks can improve the allocation of resources and response planning for organizations like the Centers for Disease Control (CDC) in the United States. Until 2009, the CDC used records of flu-related physician visits and other virological and clinical health data to report flu incidence on a weekly basis with a one- to two-week lag.

In February 2009, Google launched its own flu-detection system, called Google Flu Trends (GFT), which used hundreds of billions of individual Google searches for 50 million flu-related search queries to predict the weekly incidence of flu across the United States. The logic was simple: people with the flu typically search for flu symptoms and home remedies online before visiting the doctor. A model using these search queries might predict the flu more quickly than traditional surveillance systems. It was a bet on algorithmically enabled collective intelligence, and it turned out to be a good bet.

Google Flu Trends predicted the flu with a mean correlation of 0.97, and much more quickly than the CDC, with a one-day lag instead of the traditional one- to two-week lag. The results were astounding. The method was heralded as a milestone in collective intelligence for health surveillance. Using the crowd's wisdom, reflected in the billions of searches for flu symptoms (like headache, stuffy nose, and fever) and home remedies (like lozenges and hot compresses), vastly improved traditional surveillance methods—until it didn't.

From June 2009 to June 2011, Google's estimates tracked actual flu cases nearly perfectly. Then suddenly, beginning in June 2011, GFT's predictions went off the rails, overestimating the flu by more than 50 percent from 2011 to 2013, reporting overly high flu prevalence in 100 out of 108 weeks starting in August 2011. During the winter of 2012–13, Google's estimates were more than double the CDC's reports.

How did the wisdom of crowds so quickly turn into the madness of crowds? There are two main explanations. First, the GFT designers fell victim to what David Lazer, Ryan Kennedy, Gary King, and Alessandro Vespignani called "big data hubris." By throwing vast amounts of data (billions of searches for millions of terms) at a prediction task with relatively few objective flu records (thousands of observations of doctor's visits), the model suffered from what statisticians call overfitting and spurious correlation. Many of the 50 million search terms that correlated with the flu were related in time but had nothing to do with the flu itself. For example, the flu season roughly corresponds to basketball season. So basketball-related search terms were correlated with the flu, but only coincidentally. The same was true of search terms related to winter. As a result, GFT missed badly on nonseasonal flu predictions, like the off-season H1N1 pandemic of 2009. As Lazer and his colleagues wrote, "GFT was part flu detector, part winter detector."

Second, several small tweaks to Google's search algorithm eroded GFT's accuracy. In June 2011, Google began suggesting additional search terms related to users' search queries. In February 2012 it began returning potential diagnoses as additional suggested search terms when users searched for flu symptoms like fever or cough. These design choices baked bias into the Hype Machine's code, pushing Google users to search for flu-related terms more than they would have without the algorithmic nudges. These new suggestions resulted in more flu searches, leading GFT to think there was more flu than actually existed. It's a dramatic example of how software code determines the Hype Machine's impact. Small algorithm changes helped turn a leading example of the wisdom of crowds into madness by overturning one of the three pillars on which the wisdom of crowds rests—by injecting *interdependence* into what were previously independent opinions. Wise crowds, the theory goes, typically require three things:

independence, diversity, and equality. The problem is that the Hype Machine undermines all of them.

Independence

Crowds predict accurately because they cancel out individuals' errors. Recall Francis Galton's crowd guessing the ox's weight. No matter how experienced or perceptive individuals are about oxen weights, they will make mistakes. Some will overestimate the weight and some will underestimate it. But if these errors are uncorrelated (meaning they're unrelated to each other) and unbiased (meaning they don't *systematically* under- or overestimate the true weight), then given enough guesses, the over- and underestimates will cancel out and the average (or median) opinion will be close to the truth. In mathematical terms, when errors are uncorrelated, wisdom emerges from an increasing number of guesses.

Independence is important because it allows individuals to bring their own information to a collective guess without being tainted by others' opinions and without any one opinion pulling the crowd off course. Social influence, on the other hand, injects positive correlations into individual guesses because we mimic others' opinions, perhaps because we think they know something we don't or feel pressure to conform to the group. This creates a herding effect, which drags the crowd toward one guess or another, eliminating its ability to cancel out errors. Online rating bias and Google Flu Trends are potent examples of this pathology.

To his credit, James Surowiecki, the author of *The Wisdom of Crowds*, acknowledged that humans are "social beings." "We want to learn from each other and learning is a social process," he wrote. "The neighborhoods where we live, the schools we attend, and the corporations where we work shape the way we think and feel." But despite acknowledging social influence as a fact of life, he maintained his thesis that wisdom, generally, requires independence. "What I want to argue here," he wrote, "is that the more influence a group's members exert on each other, and the more personal contact they have with each other, the less likely it is that the group's decisions will be wise ones. The more influence we exert on each other, the more likely it is that we will believe the same things and make the same mistakes. That means it's possible that we could become individually smarter but collectively dumber."

But the Hype Machine makes social influence ubiquitous, and I'm not sure Surowiecki saw it coming. "Do cascades exist?" he wrote. "Without a doubt. They are less ubiquitous than the restaurant-going model suggests, since, as Yale economist Robert Shiller has suggested, people don't usually make decisions in sequence. 'In most cases,' Shiller writes, 'many people independently choose their action based on their own signals, without observing the actions of others.'" Clearly neither Surowiecki nor Shiller had experienced Instagram, Yelp, Twitter, hashtags, viral memes, trending topics, or social media influencers when they drew this conclusion.

Today we observe others' actions while making sequential decisions all the time. Exposure to others' opinions at the point of decision is the norm, not the exception. We don't have to seek out social influence. It finds us. Push notifications bombard us with other people's opinions all day long, whether we like it or not. In fact, if we were to revise Shiller's conclusion in the context of online ratings, reviews, tweets, shares, and referrals, we might say that today many people don't choose their action *without* observing the actions of others. But is that bad? Well, it depends, and I'll return to that in a minute.

Diversity

The second pillar of crowd wisdom is diversity. Crowds aren't wise when everyone has the same opinion or holds entrenched polarized opinions. Smart aggregations of collective judgment benefit from diverse ideas in problem solving and prediction. Why? Because diverse groups uncover multiple solutions and ways of applying those solutions effectively. The complex systems scientist Scott Page notes that diversity trumps homogeneity in problem-solving groups and, under the right conditions,* trumps ability as well. It turns out that cognitively diverse groups outperform groups with the best problem solvers

---

* The problem must be difficult, and the sets of problem solvers from which we form groups and the groups themselves must be sufficiently large.

precisely because top performers tend to think similarly, so they don't explore enough possible solutions to find better alternatives. In predicting election outcomes, stock prices, or the weight of an ox, crowd diversity is as important as the accuracy of the individuals that make up the crowd. And when you aggregate a crowd's prediction, it is always at least as good as the average prediction of a member of the crowd. These mathematical regularities rest, in large part, on the diversity of the crowd.

One hotly debated trend that can reduce diversity is polarization. Polarization is dangerous because it can create gridlock and cripple a society's ability to effectively process social information. It amplifies our biases as people prefer ideas that conform to their own beliefs. This "motivated reasoning" can push polarized factions into entrenched disagreements, even about basic facts. We saw that during Donald Trump's impeachment inquiry in the U.S. House of Representatives and impeachment trial in the Senate. Neither Democratic nor Republican arguments seemed to sway the other side; each party was entrenched in its own perspective. Chances are you saw the trial in one way or another, depending on your political leanings, and have a hard time believing that someone could hold an opposing view.

Our entrenched, polarized views are susceptible to "confirmation bias," the natural human tendency to more often believe facts and opinions that support rather than contradict our tightly held beliefs. From tension between Democrats and Republicans in the United States to those supporting "leave" or "remain" in the U.K.'s Brexit vote, to the right- and left-leaning parties in Brazil's latest presidential election, polarization seems to have swept the globe. . . . But has it, in fact?

The Polarization Paradox

When you dig into the data, the rise of polarization is not as clear-cut as it may seem, globally or even in the United States. On the one hand, when we compare the views of self-identified Republicans and Democrats across scales of political values, as the Pew Research Center has done since 1994, we see that a dramatic divide between the parties has emerged since 2004, the year Facebook was founded. The divide is even more pronounced among the "politically engaged" (Figure 10.3).

But when we examine party identification, ideology, and viewpoints on specific political issues, we see that nothing much has changed

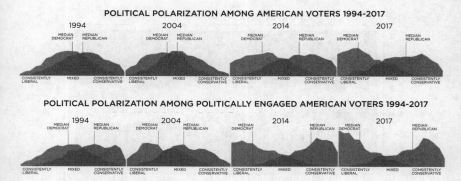

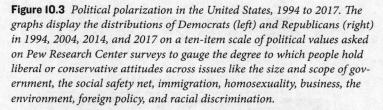

Figure 10.3 *Political polarization in the United States, 1994 to 2017. The graphs display the distributions of Democrats (left) and Republicans (right) in 1994, 2004, 2014, and 2017 on a ten-item scale of political values asked on Pew Research Center surveys to gauge the degree to which people hold liberal or conservative attitudes across issues like the size and scope of government, the social safety net, immigration, homosexuality, business, the environment, foreign policy, and racial discrimination.*

since the 1960s. As Matthew Gentzkow has noted, "We see no evidence whatsoever of growing polarization" in either party affiliation or liberal-conservative leanings among the American electorate over the last fifty years. "Very few Americans describe themselves as 'very' conservative or liberal. Of the rest, those calling themselves 'conservative,' 'liberal' or 'moderate' have remained remarkably stable, with no hint of a move toward the extremes in recent years" (Figure 10.4). If opinions about political issues were becoming polarized, we would expect to see widening distributions among American opinions across economic and social issues. But most Americans hold moderate views on most issues, with stable "single peaked" distributions of opinions across economic and social questions.

Yet the voting data "seem to scream increasing polarization." The share of American voters living in counties in which presidential candidates won by "landslide" vote margins of 20 percent or more has increased from 25 percent in 1976 to 60 percent in 2016; voters are less likely to split tickets across party lines in concurrent presidential and congressional races; and county-level vote shares have become more correlated over time, with voters more likely to vote for the same party in presidential and congressional races.

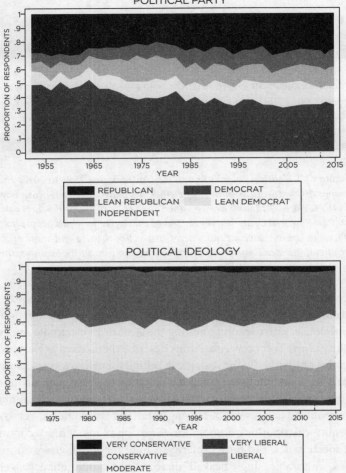

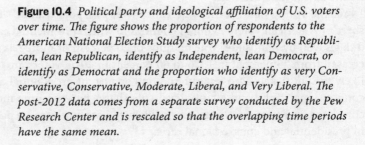

Figure 10.4 *Political party and ideological affiliation of U.S. voters over time. The figure shows the proportion of respondents to the American National Election Study survey who identify as Republican, lean Republican, identify as Independent, lean Democrat, or identify as Democrat and the proportion who identify as very Conservative, Conservative, Moderate, Liberal, and Very Liberal. The post-2012 data comes from a separate survey conducted by the Pew Research Center and is rescaled so that the overlapping time periods have the same mean.*

How can this be? How can it be that while the shares of Republicans and Democrats (party identity) and conservatives and liberals (political ideology) have remained stable for many decades, a dramatic divide has arisen among Democrats and Republicans along scales of political ideology and positions on prominent issues?

The answer is simple: the correlation of people's views with their party identification has skyrocketed. Americans have sorted into two camps with two homogeneous belief systems. Although most have maintained moderate views on most issues in the aggregate, they have realigned on issue- and candidate-specific views across party lines. While the overall fractions of Americans holding pro-immigration and anti-immigration views hasn't changed, "the fraction of Republicans holding pro-immigrant views, or Democrats holding anti-immigrant views, has decreased substantially." Voters' issue-specific views have clustered into divergent homogeneous viewpoints in line with a single party. This wasn't always the case. "It used to be more common for people to hold liberal views on some issues (say social policy) and conservative views on others (say economic policy)," Gentzkow writes. "Today, more people hold either liberal or conservative-leaning views across the board."

This divide has spilled out into American culture. When Suzanne Kapner and Dante Chinni analyzed the Simmons National Consumer Survey, a survey of consumers' brand preferences, from 2004 to 2018, they found that brands have become more associated either with the Republican or the Democratic Party in recent years. When you look at consumers' brand loyalty and purchasing patterns, you find that Republicans buy Wrangler jeans, while Democrats buy Levi's. Republicans buy cars from General Motors, while Democrats buy Volkswagens. And as we all know, Republicans watch Fox News, while Democrats watch CNN.

As much of this has been driven by branding, marketing, and targeting as it has by divergence in consumer tastes. Brands are beginning to take stances on social issues, perhaps as an expression of their leadership's social values or as an attempt to identify with certain groups of consumers. For example, Levi's has embraced liberal causes like gun control and pro-immigrant policies. Gillette created controversy with its ads questioning toxic masculinity and featuring a father teaching his transgender son to shave. And who could forget Nike's embrace of

Colin Kaepernick, the former San Francisco 49ers quarterback who took a knee during the national anthem to protest minority oppression? The fraction of Americans who say they would choose, switch, avoid, or boycott a brand based on its stand on societal issues jumped from 47 percent in 2017 to 60 percent in 2018. It may not be surprising to hear that in 2018, 46 percent of Nike customers identified as Democrats, while only 31 percent were Republicans.

As Republicans and Democrats sort into tight, homogeneous communities on the issues, and to some extent on their loyalty to certain brands, a related divide has emerged in how members of both parties see each other. "Affective polarization"— dislike, distrust, and animosity among political parties—has grown substantially since the mid- to late 1990s in U.S. "thermometer" ratings, which measure respondents' relative feelings for their own and the other political party on a hundred-point scale from warm to cold; in in-group and out-group ratings of whether members of one's own and the other party are "selfish" or "intelligent"; and in the proportion of those who would be displeased if their children married someone from the opposite political party. Affective polarization is now at its highest level in sixty years, and it corresponds to the political polarization Pew documented from 1994 to 2017.

The natural next question is, why? Why do we see this growing divide in America and, frankly, around the world, in Bangladesh, Brazil, Canada, Switzerland, Colombia, India, Indonesia, Kenya, Poland, Turkey, and elsewhere? The origins of polarization are complex, and the science of its causes is by no means settled. But we do have evidence for several contributing factors, many of which remain controversial. First, partisan sorting, or the realignment of ideologies and social identities, like race and religion, has coalesced along party lines. Evangelical Christians overwhelmingly vote Republican, while African-Americans overwhelming vote Democratic.

Second, the American electorate has been economically polarized over the last decade. Median household income increased 17 percent in Democratic districts, typically in cities and suburbs, with higher levels of education and greater availability of professional jobs; meanwhile it fell 3 percent in less-educated, working-class, rural Republican districts with agricultural and low-skilled manufacturing jobs that are more vulnerable to overseas competition.

Third, the partisan polarization of cable news media has likely reinforced political identities and increased affective polarization between the parties. That said, partisans also select into right- or left-leaning media audiences, making it difficult to determine whether the news media causes polarization or if an already-polarized public simply chooses which polarized media to watch.

Fourth, the Internet is frequently blamed for the rise of polarization, as personalization and targeting combine to create what legal scholar Cass Sunstein and activist and MoveOn.org director Eli Pariser describe as "filter bubbles" of polarized content, which allow various factions to consume completely different information and facts about the world. That said, there is conflicting evidence on the Internet's contribution to polarization. Some studies find small increases in polarization with Internet use, while others find that polarization is more prevalent among those with less Internet use.

Important evidence on diverging trends in affective polarization across countries is provided by one of the only longitudinal cross-cultural studies, by Levi Boxell, Matthew Gentzkow, and Jesse Shapiro. Their analysis across four decades and eight countries showed that while affective polarization has steadily increased in the United States, Canada, and Switzerland over the last forty years, it has consistently decreased in Australia, New Zealand, Britain, Sweden, Norway, and Germany.

As Internet access was high and rising in all these countries during that time, an Internet-based explanation of affective polarization is unlikely, although "the fact that in many countries polarization rose faster in the post-2000 period than the pre-2000 period is consistent with a role for digital media," as they note. These trends can't explain why polarization also rose in the 1990s and why it rose in some countries and fell in others after 2000. This suggests multiple factors contribute to the rise of affective polarization and that country-specific trends, like rising income inequality, growing racial divisions, and the rise of cable news in the United States, for example, could combine with digital and social media to create polarization.

In the last few years, many have wondered what the Hype Machine has to do with all this discord. Automated, personalized targeting and trending algorithms seem tailored to drive us toward greater homogeneity and polarization. The hypersocialization of society itself may reduce diversity because, as we coalesce or herd around others' opinions, we may be clustering into tight-knit thought bubbles with those like ourselves.

Could the Hype Machine combine with country-specific factors like income inequality, racial division, and increasing party affiliation to create online echo chambers that accelerate affective polarization? Do these factors make homogeneous, party-affiliated groups easier to target on Facebook and other social media? These are complicated questions. Newsfeed-ranking and friend-suggestion algorithms may well combine with our own choices to shape what we read and believe to further divide us. What does the science tell us about this possibility?

Is the Hype Machine Polarizing Us?

First, feed algorithms learn our preferences from what we click, engage with, and like, and they are trained to give us more of what engages us the most. The platforms claim that they don't just maximize clicks and that their algorithms include provisions to increase diversity. But my intuition is that the diversity-seeking provisions of the Hype Machine's algorithms probably explore our preferences only to improve their own accuracy, rather than to increase the diversity of our consumption. (It's difficult to know for sure because the platforms don't publish their algorithms.) By trying content that's different from what we normally like, the algorithms search our interests to make sure they haven't missed anything, or to make sure that our preferences haven't changed. But these diversity provisions are likely overwhelmed by the algorithms' overarching aim, which is to give us more of what engages us.

Second, the Hype Machine's content-curation algorithms reduce consumption diversity through a Hype Loop that nudges us toward polarization: Friend-suggestion algorithms connect us with people like ourselves. So the content shared by our contacts is biased toward our own perspectives. Newsfeed algorithms further reduce content diversity by narrowing our reading options to the items that most directly match our preferences. We then choose to read an even narrower subset of this content, feeding biased choices back into the machine intelligence that infers what we want, creating a cycle of polarization that draws us into factionalized information bubbles. It's a vicious Hype Loop, driven by algorithms and our own choices working in unison, leading us toward myopic, polarized views of the world.

In a widely cited paper published in *Science* in 2015, my colleagues at Facebook Eytan Bakshy, Solomon Messing, and Lada Adamic studied the extent to which our networks, the newsfeed algorithm, and our own choices affect our exposure to ideologically diverse news on Facebook. They analyzed how 10 million U.S. Facebook users interacted with socially shared news on their newsfeeds. They found a narrowing of content options at each successive phase of the content-curation process: curation by friends' sharing decisions, curation by the newsfeed algorithm, and curation by our own choices of what to read.

At each stage of the curation process, we have access to fewer and fewer ideologically diverse views. Because our social networks are polarized by friend recommendations and our individual connection preferences, both of which favor homophily, there is significant clustering by political affiliation on Facebook. The researchers observed that in line with the polarization in the network's structure, there is substantial polarization in the news content our friends share with us. Figure 10.5 compares the dramatic polarization of hard news content shared by our networks and the relative lack of polarization of shared soft news (sports, entertainment, or travel content). The newsfeed algorithm then further reduced exposure to diverse content by 8 percent for self-identified liberals and 5 percent for self-identified conservatives. Finally, individual choices among algorithmically curated newsfeed items resulted in exposure to 6 percent less diverse content for liberals and 17 percent less diverse content for conservatives.

The findings were clear: who we follow on Facebook (which as we know is strongly influenced by friend recommendations) limits our exposure to hard news about politics and world affairs featuring diverse points of view by structuring who we follow and thus the social content to which we are exposed. The newsfeed algorithm furthers this polarization, albeit more modestly. Finally, our individual choices limit what we read even more, feeding back into how the machine interprets what we want, in a reinforcing ideological cycle.

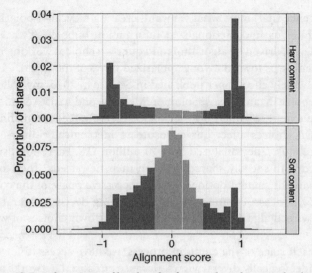

Figure 10.5 *Polarization of hard and soft news shared on Facebook. The graphs display the distributions of ideological alignment of the hard and soft news shared in the newsfeeds of 10 million U.S. Facebook users. Ideological alignment of left-leaning or right-leaning content was measured as the average affiliation of sharers weighted by the total number of shares. So if, for example, many left-leaning friends shared a piece of content, it would be labeled as left-leaning.*

The Engagement Diversity Trap

It's hard to conclude from Facebook's observational research that the algorithms or our choices *cause* polarization in our exposure to hard news, because the research is based on correlations rather than causation. But experimental evidence gathered by former MIT postdoc Ananya Sen provided the first causal evidence of the link between polarization and the algorithmic curation of news, in a study he conducted with Jörg Claussen and Christian Peukert at a major German news website from 2017 to 2018.

They ran a large experiment to test whether algorithmic curation causes filter bubbles by randomly assigning some users to receive news curated by an algorithm, and others to receive news curated by humans. Users in the control group were assigned to a page curated by human editors. Users in the experimental group saw content algorithmically curated, based on users' prior reading history, in the fourth slot (or news item entry) of the website's newsfeed. Everything else about the page was identical in the control and experimental groups. By comparing the human-curated fourth slot with the machine-curated fourth slot, they measured the extent to which algorithmic curation narrows news consumption.

The results of an analysis of 150 million user sessions confirmed three things about algorithmic curation.

First, algorithmic curation outperformed human curation in maximizing user engagement. After collecting data on just six visits, the algorithm was better at predicting what the reader wanted and consistently outperformed human editors in getting readers to click through.* This confirmed the effectiveness of algorithmic curation at maximizing engagement at scale. The more data the algorithm had, the more it engaged users, up to a point of diminishing returns.

Second, algorithmic curation caused a filter bubble that significantly reduced news diversity. Readers who came back to the website multiple times were randomly assigned to the algorithm or to the humans each time. When they were assigned to the algorithm, the filter bubble set in, and they read more narrowly. When they were assigned to the page edited by humans, they read more widely.

Third, algorithmic curation didn't just narrow readers' options for diverse content, it caused their reading choices to narrow as well. In other words, the filter bubble was not limited to the fourth slot in the newsfeed—it spilled over into consumption choices more generally. Users assigned to the algorithm not only read more narrowly in the fourth slot but also clicked on and read more narrowly in the other, human-curated slots as well. Ananya's study provided the first large-scale experimental evidence that algorithmic curation *causes* filter bubbles. It also suggested that algorithmic curation narrows what we read both by limiting our options and by narrowing the choices we make among those options, which could explain why the Facebook study found significant narrowing attributable to human choices.

My PhD student Dave Holtz and I found something similar in a

---

* Interestingly, the human editors outperformed the algorithm on days with fast-breaking news, suggesting humans may be better at predicting readers' tastes for newsworthy content.

large-scale experiment we conducted testing the effects of personalized recommendations on consumption diversity in collaboration with Ben Carterette, Henriette Cramer, Praveen Ravichandran, and Zahra Nazari at the music-streaming platform Spotify. In our experiment, some Spotify users were given podcast recommendations personalized by their prior listening history, while others were recommended the most popular podcasts in their demographic group. Algorithmic recommendations increased engagement, increasing the number of users streaming podcasts by 36.33 percent and the average podcast streams per user by 28.90 percent. But the treatment also created clusters of polarized consumption that were homogeneous within the clusters and diverse across them. The recommendations decreased the diversity of podcast streams to individuals by 11.51 percent, while increasing the aggregate diversity of podcast streams by 5.96 percent. Like Claussen, Peukert, and Sen, we found that algorithmic curation not only narrowed users' options—they caused users to narrow their choices too. User choices narrowed not only on the home page, where algorithmic recommendations were shown, but also in other areas of the platform, like in users' libraries and on radio station pages, where algorithmic recommendations were not shown.

In our experiment, the filter bubble effects of algorithmic curation did not persist absent that curation. When we turned algorithmic recommendations off, users' diversity of consumption returned to normal. That suggests that our preferences for diverse options are resilient and recover from the polarizing effects of algorithmic curation. This raises the possibility that automated algorithms designed to maximize engagement do not permanently alter our consumption patterns, and that better algorithm designs can restore diversity to the content we consume on social media.

But neither of these studies examined the effects of polarized media consumption on political polarization. To make a direct connection between social media and political polarization, we would need an experiment that randomized social media users' newsfeeds and measured the resulting changes in their news consumption and political attitudes. To make such a study as valid and generally applicable as possible, ideally it would be conducted on Facebook, which is by far the largest platform for social media news consumption in the world. Yale's Ro'ee Levy conducted just such an experiment.

Levy randomly nudged some American adult Facebook users to subscribe to either liberal or conservative news outlets. Half of the participants subscribed. Those treated with liberal subscriptions received more liberal news in their newsfeeds, and those treated with conservative subscriptions received more conservative news. Levy measured the effects of these random injections of liberal and conservative content on users' media diets and subsequent changes in their political opinions and attitudes. His experiment recorded four key findings.

First, the Facebook newsfeed substantially altered online news consumption in the experiment. Injecting liberal and conservative news items into their newsfeeds altered users' media diets toward the political leaning they were assigned to. In other words, conservatives assigned to receive more liberal news shifted their media diets toward the liberal end of the political spectrum, and liberals assigned to conservative news did the same in the other direction. This could be viewed as good or bad news in terms of polarization. On the one hand, it implies that Facebook could be an effective tool for increasing exposure to news that runs counter to one's ideology. On the other hand, if Facebook supplies users with news that reinforces their viewpoints, it will increase the polarization of media diets. It depends on how the algorithm is programmed.

Second, exposure to news that runs counter to one's beliefs decreases the antipathy one feels toward those that are not part of their political party. Levy used a classic "feeling thermometer" to measure the effects of such tweaks to the newsfeed. From 1996 to 2016, the "thermometer" of affective polarization—the antipathy toward Democrats by Republicans, or toward Republicans by Democrats—increased by 3.83 degrees overall. But Levy's experiment, in which his team injected random variation of attitudes into Facebook newsfeeds, decreased such polarization by 0.98 degrees. When he estimated what would happen if Facebook exposed users to "an equal share of pro- and counter-attitudinal news," Levy found that "the difference in their feeling toward parties would decrease by 3.76 degrees, almost the entire increase over the past two decades."

Third, the newsfeed manipulation had no measurable effect on political opinions. This is in line with the polarization paradox I discussed earlier. While the last twenty years have seen significant partisan division, the American electorate's political opinions have remained moderate and stable. In contrast, what it means to be a Democrat or a Republican has become more homogenized within the two parties.

Finally, Levy found that Facebook's newsfeed algorithm does create a filter bubble. The algorithm is less likely to supply people with news that runs counter to their preexisting attitudes. Even though the experiment inspired people to read opposing viewpoints, Facebook's algorithm continued to supply them with content that leaned toward their prior political views despite their having subscribed to counterattitudinal sources.

Those who claim the Hype Machine is polarizing argue that it creates filter bubbles that in turn polarize us. While no hard evidence directly confirms or denies the Hype Machine's role in polarization, evidence from multiple experimental studies shows that the machine's recommendation algorithms create filter bubbles of polarized content consumption. These results track with recent evidence that "Americans are polarized not only in their views on policy issues and attitudes towards government and society, but also in their *perceptions* of the same factual reality."

But it doesn't have to be this way. If we're careful with the code, we could encourage exposure to alternative views to our own. The designers of the Hype Machine's recommendation algorithms could use multiobjective optimization—the process of achieving multiple different goals with software code—to promote engagement and exposure to diverse content and viewpoints at the same time. Spotify's "discover weekly" recommendations are a good case in point. Discover weekly is intended to introduce listeners to new music they have never heard but would probably like based on what they have listened to in the past. I find it wildly engaging. And although it isn't about exposure to diverse political views or content, the same logic could be applied to our newsfeeds. I, for one, would welcome the diversity.

Equality

The wisdom of crowds is, at its core, a mathematical concept about patterns of collective or aggregated opinion, in teams, communities, and societies. But the math has evolved since Francis Galton first worked out our collective intelligence about ox weights. The most significant advance in our thinking about crowd wisdom in the last decade has been to realize (and formally consider) how crowds are organized into collectives by the networks that connect them. When we extended the wisdom of crowds to *networks,* we discovered the supreme importance of equality to wisdom. In the age of social media, maintaining equality and minority expression is essential, not just for their moral value but to realize the potential of collective intelligence. To understand why, we first have to consider how we learn from and structure our social interactions.

As we read books, listen to news, or observe events firsthand, we incorporate new information and update our beliefs about the world. We also learn socially, by incorporating the beliefs, opinions, and perspectives of our friends into our own perspectives. In fact, we engage in "social learning" every day, in nearly every aspect of our lives, as we discuss breaking news, fashion trends, and politics with the people we know.

Over the last decade, the Hype Machine has forcefully inserted itself into our social learning by curating social signals and promoting (or demoting) social feedback—for example, by displaying or hiding likes on shared content (as Instagram did in 2019), or by suppressing ratings until a sufficient number has accumulated (as Reddit did in 2013), or by limiting the number of times information can be shared (as WhatsApp did when it restricted users to five reshares in 2019 and then to one reshare in 2020 to prevent coronavirus misinformation). These algorithm design choices, combined with our own choices, change how we learn about the world.

Just as influential, however, is the social structure through which the opinions of others reach us. Since our worldviews depend, in part, on the information and opinions of those around us, the structure of the social ties that connect us impacts the flow of perspectives, opinions, and ideas in society. And the social structures most likely to support collective intelligence are characterized by equality.

The math was worked out by my colleague Matt Jackson at Stanford and his former student Ben Golub, now at Harvard. When they sat down to model Galton's theory in the context of networks, they kept running into the importance of equality.* Golub and Jackson asked the following question: assuming there is some truth we should all know, which some people know and some people don't, which social network structures will allow society to converge on that truth?† They called societies that did so "wise."

They found that a society's network has one simple and complete characterization of wisdom—one requirement for being able to arrive at the truth. And that is that it does not have, in modern vernacular, "influencers." As Golub and Jackson wrote, "Disproportionate popularity is the sole obstacle to wisdom. . . . Having agents who are prominent, causes learning to fail, since their influence on the limiting beliefs is excessive." Societies without wisdom lack "balance," meaning some groups have disproportionately more influence than others and may not pay sufficient attention to the rest of the world.

Sound familiar? This is the world we live in, where Barack Obama and Donald Trump have 110 million and 67 million Twitter followers, respectively. Where Kanye West has 30 million followers and follows 300 people. Where trending algorithms promote the most popular people and content, and where "preferential attachment" (the tendency for popular nodes in a network to attract more connections) makes the most popular more popular. Golub and Jackson found these types of societies are prone to madness.

It's an elegant theory, and the math is impeccable. But as an empiricist, I'm always curious whether our theories apply in real life. My colleague Damon Centola at the University of Pennsylvania and his team

---

* Golub and Jackson considered a model in which people update their beliefs by taking a weighted average of their own perspectives and those of the friends, family members, and co-workers they communicate with. While Galton was interested in whether an outside observer could aggregate the truth, collective intelligence, in its purest form, is about whether society can arrive at the truth by itself. When crowd wisdom is used to describe honeybees finding the best source of nectar, the metaphor applies to the hive's ability to search wisely, not the beekeeper's ability to aggregate bee choices to calculate their distance to the nectar.

† It's an important question that relates to the wisdom of crowd aggregation or the ability of an outside observer to develop an accurate estimate of the truth given what everyone knows. In this case, Golub and Jackson were interested in whether individuals in society would converge toward the truth, so they started with a scenario in which a central planner could aggregate the truth among the individuals' beliefs, which were equivalent to the true state of nature plus some noise.

tested the theory in a series of online experiments. I talked to Damon's student Devon Brackbill about it at the International Conference on Computational Social Science in Helsinki, in the summer of 2015. Devon told me he, Damon, and Josh Becker were working on a series of experiments testing the limits of crowd wisdom in the face of increasing social influence, and the impact of centralized versus equitable networks on collective intelligence.

They placed a thousand people in different online social networks, gave them tasks testing their crowd wisdom, and paid them for their accuracy. Some participants were randomly assigned to "equitable" networks in which everyone was equally connected, while others were assigned to "centralized" networks in which a central influencer had a disproportionate number of connections. A third control group had no connections, representing a truly "independent" crowd. They then gave the groups tasks designed to test the wisdom of crowds—for example, to estimate the calorie content of food or the number of candies in a jar. And they measured the differences in each group's ability to converge on the truth over several rounds of prediction, punctuated by communication between the participants within their social networks.

What they found validated Golub and Jackson's theory. The equitable networks, in which everyone was equally connected, increased their accuracy as they communicated, while the centralized networks were biased toward the beliefs of the most prominent influencers. The results taught us a lot about the wisdom of networked crowds. Social influence eliminated independence and reduced the diversity of the crowd's estimates, which corroborated the importance Galton and Surowiecki placed on independence and diversity.

But social influence and interdependence didn't necessarily undermine the wisdom of crowds. Crowds made interdependent by social influence could still exhibit wisdom—even *greater* wisdom—by either being interdependent but equal or, if unequal, by having wise influencers.

Becker, Brackbill, and Centola discovered two types of centralized networks in their experiment: those that were "centered toward truth" and those that were "centered away from truth." In networks that were centered toward truth, the influencers' estimates were on the opposite side of the truth from the group mean and therefore pulled the group average toward the truth and increased its accuracy. In networks that were centered away from truth, the group mean lay between the influencers' estimates and the truth, and so the influencers led their groups away from the truth and reduced the groups' accuracy.

Think about the following example. If there are 50 candies in the jar and the group mean estimate is 40, an influencer who estimates 55 (more accurate than the group mean) or 65 (less accurate) will pull the group toward the truth. But an influencer who estimates 35 will pull the group away from the truth. It all depends on how close the influencer is to the truth *relative* to the group.

All this suggests that whether hypersocialization will lead us toward collective intelligence or collective madness depends on several factors: the structure of the networks we create, the designs of systems that propagate social signals in society, the wisdom of our influencers, and our ability to learn from our social environments in productive rather than destructive ways. There are reasons to be hopeful, because the most recent thinking points us toward solutions for harnessing the wisdom of crowds for the collective good.

Long Live the Wisdom of Crowds

The Hype Machine's current design undercuts the three pillars of crowd wisdom, threatening our ability to achieve collective intelligence and pointing society toward polarization and inequality, elements associated with crowd madness. These trends suggest the Hype Machine will inhibit our ability to process social information to achieve optimal social outcomes, potentially disrupting our democracies, our markets, and our ability to predict contagious diseases. However, the newest research suggests avenues that could help us restore independence, diversity, and equality, or to achieve crowd wisdom without them. But these adaptations require a radical rethinking of the design and structure of the Hype Machine and our use of it. So why not engage in such radical rethinking, just for a few pages? Why not imagine a Hype Machine that harnesses, amplifies, and directs our collective intelligence for good?

One thing Damon Centola and his team learned while studying networked crowds was that crowd wisdom can be improved by social influence when the most influential individuals are also the most accurate. Networks that put more weight on the opinions of those with the greatest accuracy, reliability, or access to the truth can perform even better than independent crowds. (The call to "listen to the scientists" on climate change and pandemic responses comes to mind.) But how can we engineer the Hype Machine to put more emphasis or weight on these peers?

The Hype Machine is already replete with feedback mechanisms— they're just designed to feed back the wrong signals. Take likes, for example. The "like" button is the engine of the attention economy. It is designed to capture our attention, to elicit our approval or disapproval of the content we see, and to incentivize us to produce more content by giving us a dopamine rush. The more we like social media content, the more engaged we are and the more opportunity there is to serve us ads. Likes serve another purpose, however, because as we like more content, we signal our preferences to the Hype Machine, which en-ables the ads served in those impressions to be targeted at the right people.

Now imagine a world in which we went back to the invention of the "like" button and replaced it with a "truth" button (for content we think is true), or a "reliability" button (for content we think is from a reliable source), or a "wholesomeness" button (for content that is good for us), or an "educational" button (for content that taught us some-thing). The thought exercise forces us to rethink the feedback we see on social media and to consider how *code* changes could reengineer the Hype Machine toward positivity. In fact, we already use *norms* to participate in this reengineering effort. For example, we have, as a so-ciety, largely accepted that on Twitter "retweets do not necessarily mean endorsements," because we have adopted the ubiquitous "RT ≠ En-dorsement" tag to reengineer the meaning of a retweet. Research shows that feedback is essential to our ability to process social infor-mation in collectively useful ways. So how we formally and informally design that feedback will help shape how the Hype Machine shapes us.

What if every time we posted content to social media we were given the option to relate how "confident" we were in the material, or if we were asked whether we thought other people's posts were true? How long would it take before all Americans knew the correct capitals of all fifty states? How long would it take before everyone in the United States knew their Miranda rights?

Feedback is not just about weighting the information we receive in socially beneficial ways. It also allows us to adapt the network itself. Would we change who we are following on Twitter if their profiles displayed a "veracity" score that recorded the percentage of their posts that were fact-checked to be true or false? If decisions on who to follow were affected by how truthful people were, and if truth tellers amassed larger followings, would everyone be inspired to be more truthful? Would that limit the number of reshares of false information and the followers of false-news-peddling accounts?

Abdullah Almaatouq, my colleague at MIT, and his collaborators built an experiment similar to Centola's experiments at UPenn. They placed fifteen hundred people in different online social networks and gave them tasks testing their crowd wisdom. But in these experiments, they randomly varied feedback and plasticity (the ability for people to rewire who they follow).

In the first experiment, they varied plasticity and held feedback constant. Groups were randomly placed into a "solo" condition where they solved tasks in isolation; in a "static network" where the social networks were unchanging; or in a "dynamic network" in which they could rewire who they followed. In the second experiment, the researchers varied feedback and held plasticity constant. Groups were randomly placed into the solo condition with no performance feedback (feedback on how accurate their answers were); a "no feedback condition" in which people were in a social network but were not shown any performance feedback; a "self-feedback" condition in which people were in a social network but were only shown feedback on their own performance; and a "full feedback" condition in which people were placed in a social network and were shown performance feedback on all participants, including themselves.

These groups all played a game in which they guessed the correlations in scatter plots they were shown (Figure 10.6) and were paid for their accuracy. In some of the scatter plots, the correlations were easy to see while in others they were hard to see. Figure 10.6 shows two plots with the same correlation, but the amount of data in the left panel makes the correlation easier to see than in the right panel, with far less data or information.

The researchers asked the groups to record their correlation guesses upon seeing each scatter plot. In each successive round, the groups

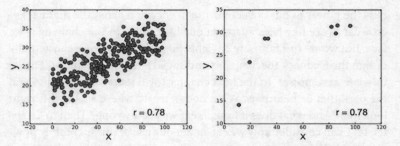

Figure 10.6 *The "guess the correlation" game. The graphs show examples of the scatter plots used in the "wisdom of networked crowds" experiment. For any given round, all participants saw plots that shared an identical true correlation, but were more (right) or less (left) difficult to discern by looking at the data.*

that received feedback were told how well they and their peers were doing, and the groups in the dynamic networks were allowed to change their networks in response to performance feedback. The researchers then recorded how well each of the groups did in moving toward the true correlation in the data.

What they found confirmed that adaptive networks that were able to rewire based on feedback attained crowd wisdom better than any other group. In other words, networked groups outperformed independent groups, confirming that interdependence can be productive under the right conditions. The dynamic networks that rewired in response to feedback adapted over time and achieved the lowest error rates across all the experiments.

The implications for the Hype Machine are clear. In the last decade, we have created a dynamic global network of over 3 billion people, with a tsunami of feedback in the likes, shares, retweets, and comments we post to social media every day. And this network is adaptive, in that we can choose who to follow or stop following at any moment. The most recent experiments on the wisdom of crowds show that this type of adaptive network can achieve crowd wisdom that outperforms independent groups and the best-performing individuals when it is provided with high-quality performance feedback. This means, under the right conditions, our increasing interdependence and hypersocialization can be *assets* for human civilization rather than liabilities.

The question now becomes: how can we design this system to harness the power of our collective intelligence and avoid the madness of crowds? We're like bees adapting our hive mind to the challenges we face. But we are in a far more enviable position because we can actually design the feedback mechanisms and social adaptations that will make us wiser as a species. In the next chapter I will sketch the promise and the peril that lie before us. What does a world where we get this right look like? And what does it look like if we get it wrong? Then in Chapter 12, I will consider how we can adapt our use of this incredibly powerful and disruptive technology to steer it toward the promise and away from the peril.

CHAPTER 11

Social Media's Promise Is Also Its Peril

*When people are connected, we can just do some great
things. They have the opportunity to get access to jobs,
education, health, communications. We have the
opportunity to bring the people we care about closer to us.
It really makes a big difference.*

—MARK ZUCKERBERG

*They have taken advantage of our trust, using
sophisticated techniques to prey on the weakest aspects of
human psychology, to gather and exploit private data,
and to craft business models that do not protect users
from harm.*

—ROGER MCNAMEE

Occasionally, the Hype Machine glimmers with flashes of life-affirming brilliance. April 2015 was one of those moments. Nepal experienced its worst natural disaster in a century. For billions of years, the Indian tectonic plate had been grinding under the Eurasia plate at the fault line that created the Himalayas. On April 25 an 8.1-magnitude earthquake at this fault line shook Nepal so forcefully that it triggered an avalanche on Mount Everest 140 miles away. Whole villages were destroyed, and hundreds of thousands of Nepalese were left homeless.

Within seconds of the earthquake hitting Nepal, Facebook's Safety Check triggered notifications to millions of users asking if they were safe. As telephone service was disrupted, calling was not an option. But Safety Check automatically located 8.5 million people and notified 150 million of their loved ones of their safety within minutes. Not only did these notifications help first responders know where to look for survivors, but Facebook also delivered one of the largest simultaneous experiences of relief in human history that day. After the feeling of relief subsided, the real relief work began.

The world flooded aid into the region. The European Union donated $3 million, Canada $4 million; the Chinese gave $9.9 million, and the United States donated $10 million. Facebook wanted to do its part, so it spun up a "donate" button to raise money for disaster relief. 770,000 people from 175 countries donated $15.5 million—more than the European Union and the United States combined. The money went to fund emergency medical facilities, disease control, sanitation, health programs, and women's safety initiatives for millions of people.

My point is that the Hype Machine can create tremendous value. But in this, perhaps its darkest hour, it's easy to lose sight of that value. I want to remind us of the awe-inspiring power of the Hype Machine to create positive change in our world. But I have to temper that optimism by noting that its sources of positivity are also the sources of the very ills we are trying to avoid. This crystallizes a simple argument central to this book: that the wellspring of positivity that the Hype Machine creates is the same well from which its dark side emerges. This dual nature makes managing social media difficult. Without a nuanced approach, as we turn up the value, we will unleash the darkness. And as we counter the darkness, we will diminish the value.

The Collective Action Problem

One of the fundamental impediments to human progress is our inability to coordinate large groups to act for the collective good. Simple features like Safety Check demonstrate that automated, population-scale communication platforms can facilitate such coordination. Political philosophers and social scientists have been discussing collective action as a broader problem of incentives and signaling for centuries. Everyone is better off cooperating, but worse off if they cooperate while others free ride. Achieving collective action requires communicating everyone's commitment to cooperate, as well as coordinating their joint action.

The collective action problem lies at the heart of many of today's most pressing global challenges. Addressing climate change requires large numbers of people (and businesses) to cooperate to reduce their carbon footprints, even when no one individual's action will move the needle. Vibrant democracies depend on large numbers of people voting, even though each person's vote is largely inconsequential. Combating contagious diseases requires enough people to remain socially distant or enough vaccinations to achieve herd immunity, even when misinformation erroneously convinces some people that the threat is exaggerated or some parents that their vaccination decisions will harm their kids.

I remember talking with Twitter co-founder Biz Stone about collective action the first time we met. We served on a panel together at an event on technological change organized by Oxford University and UCLA in February 2014. During lunch, while he was picking at his salad on a bright sunny day on the terrace of one of the picturesque buildings on UCLA's campus, he told me a story that I could never have predicted. It was the story of the moment he knew Twitter would be big. It was also a story of the Hype Machine's power to rapidly organize groups.

Biz told me that soon after they built the beta version of Twitter, some of the founders, early engineers, and their friends were at a bar blowing off steam after a hard day's work. The group was scattered throughout the venue. Some people were sitting at tables, some were at the bar in small groups, and others were talking just outside the entrance. Biz and a couple of his friends wanted to move to a place they knew down the street. But getting everyone's attention would have been difficult, especially if you wanted to do it discreetly. You couldn't just stand on a barstool and yell. You couldn't call everyone on the phone in some gigantic conference call. More important, coordinating collective action would have been nearly impossible amid the hustle and bustle of the bar. While they hadn't built Twitter for this purpose (it was designed as a real-time information network, not as an organizing tool), they realized, in that moment, that it was incredibly efficient at signaling group interests and coordinating collective action. The network was small back then, and everyone in their group followed each other on Twitter. So with a couple of tweets—"Hey, let's move to the Irish bar down the street," "Now?" "Yeah, now"—the group achieved consensus and coordinated a collective move without uttering a word. Biz told me, "That's when I knew Twitter would be big."

The Hype Machine's power to transform collective action is visible in social media's impact on protest demonstrations and social movements. We've seen the consequences repeat themselves in Egypt, Russia, Ukraine, and most recently Hong Kong. But the relationship between social media, protest demonstrations, and social movements is fraught with both promise and peril.

I Am *Charlie Hebdo*

On January 7, 2015, armed Al Qaeda gunmen attacked the Paris office of the French satirical newspaper *Charlie Hebdo,* killing twelve people and injuring eleven more. The gruesome attack, which was a reaction to a satirical political cartoon depicting the Prophet Muhammad published on the cover of the newspaper two months earlier, spurred large demonstrations against terrorism and in support of free speech around the world. On the evening of the attack, over 100,000 people demonstrated across France, 35,000 of them in Paris. The slogan *"Je suis Charlie"* (I am Charlie) was adopted globally as a symbol of solidarity with the demonstrations. It appeared on signs, websites, billboards, and T-shirts, and #jesuischarlie became the top-trending hashtag on Twitter after the attack. Over the next three days, demonstrations continued around the world, gathering 700,000 people in France on January 10 and culminating in a 2-million-person march in Paris on January 11. Just four days after the shooting, nearly 4 million people joined demonstrations in the largest public rallies in France since World War II.

Protests like these require signals of a group's commitment to cooperate and coordination of their efforts. The Hype Machine facilitates both the signaling and the coordination by rapidly disseminating information, support, and camaraderie, and by efficiently spreading news about when, where, and how a protest will take place. Symbols of solidarity abound in social media, from likes and reshares of hashtags, to the filters we display over our profile pictures in support of, for example, the Bataclan or Orlando nightclub shooting victims, LGBT rights, or our brave men and women in uniform. Before the Hype Machine, we communicated by email and phones and printed leaflets. Collective organizing certainly existed before social media. So does social media really make a difference? Biz Stone's anecdote about the bar is telling, but is there evidence that social media overcomes the collective action problem and facilitates the coordination and communication necessary to support mass organizing?

Political scientists Jennifer Larson, Jonathan Nagler, Jonathan Ronen, and Josh Tucker wanted to find out. So they collected data on 130 million Twitter users during the *Charlie Hebdo* protests and analyzed whether participation in the protests depended on exposure to other people's intentions and communication through Twitter. The key to their study was connecting detailed data on the social media communications of a large population with their geolocations during the protest. Geolocation indicated whether someone marched in a protest. By analyzing the correspondence between the communication network and protest participation, they tested whether social media enabled the protests.

Protest participation depends on peer influence. Someone should be more likely to protest if they are more strongly connected to others who are protesting on Twitter. So the researchers compared Twitter users located at the protests to users who were interested in the protest movement (as indicated by their use of *Charlie Hebdo* hashtags) and eligible to participate (they were located in Paris near enough to the protests) but did *not* take part in the protests. They analyzed protesters' and nonprotesters' Twitter networks by collecting data on their direct ties (who they followed and who followed them), as well as their ties' ties.

The analysis revealed that protesters had more exposure to social signals from others who were protesting and stronger ties to other protesters—they had more mutual friends in common with protesters, and their ties were reciprocated. Not only did they follow other protesters in greater proportions on Twitter, but those protesters followed them back at greater rates. This suggests that social media is instrumental in signaling, coordinating, and facilitating the mass mobilization of social protests.

But it doesn't prove beyond a reasonable doubt that social media *causes* protests. It could simply be that people who protest select into networks with others who protest, rather than their social media connections inspiring them to protest. The recurring challenge of analyzing the Hype Machine's impact on our world is one of cause and effect—what effects would not have occurred had social media not existed? The true test of the Hype Machine's contribution to the rise of social movements and protests in Egypt, Russia, Ukraine, Hong Kong, and elsewhere is whether those protests would have happened, would have been as large, and would have arisen as quickly without social media. But to understand whether social media enables protest movements, we have to first explore the intriguing cloak-and-dagger story of a lesser-known social media superstar whom some have dubbed "the Neo of Russia."

Russia's "Neo"

Pavel Durov has been called many things—"Russia's Mark Zuckerberg," a "social media star," and "the Neo of Russia" (a reference to the main character of the popular science fiction film *The Matrix*). If you've never heard of him, you might be surprised to learn that, together with his brother Nikolai, he built two of the largest social media platforms the world has ever seen, all while living a clandestine life, bouncing from hotel to hotel and continent to continent, eluding the surveillance of Vladimir Putin and others whose power he threatens.

The comparison to *The Matrix* is heightened by Durov's resemblance to the film's mythic hero, Neo: he has short dark hair, a sharp jawline, and a penchant for wearing all-black suits under long black trench coats, and with his libertarian political leanings, he eschews government control at every turn. Durov launched his first major social network, VKontakte (VK) ("in touch" in Russian), the year he graduated from St. Petersburg State University in 2006. The network is not a household name in the West, but with over 400 million registered users, it is one of the largest social media networks in the world. It is the most popular social media network in Russia, ahead of Facebook, Twitter, and all its Russian competitors. It also boasts staggering engagement metrics, with users spending an average of 27 minutes visiting 42 pages on every visit. (Users spend an average of 17 minutes visiting 16 pages per visit on Facebook, and 10 minutes visiting 7 pages on Twitter.) SimilarWeb (which excludes Chinese websites) ranks VK as the fourth most trafficked social media network in the world, just behind Facebook, Instagram, and Twitter and ahead of WhatsApp, LinkedIn, Pinterest, and Reddit.

The Russian government took a hands-off approach to VK when it first launched. Copying Facebook's design but with more liberal content policies, VK became a haven for Russia's youth and a cornerstone of Russian political and cultural life. But all that changed in December 2011. Following widespread claims of fraud during the 2011 parliamentary elections, Russians took to the streets in the largest protests the country had seen since the 1990s. The Snow Revolution, as it was called, was organized and supported on VK, Facebook, Twitter, and LiveJournal, and it grew in size through December in Moscow, St. Petersburg, Vladivostok, Kaliningrad, Tomsk, Omsk, and many other Russian cities.

As the protests grew, Putin's light touch on VK turned into an iron fist. The Federal Security Service (FSB) demanded that VK delete the pages of seven groups that were using the social network to spur and coordinate the protests. Durov refused. Adding insult to injury, he posted a satirical picture of a dog in a hoodie with its tongue sticking out next to a scan of the official FSB request. The refusal was not well received in Moscow. Soon afterward Durov awoke to armed Russian security forces threatening to break down the door to his St. Petersburg apartment. When he refused to let them in, they retreated only after an hour-long standoff in the hallway. The message was clear. Putin was not interested in letting a thousand flowers bloom online. The FSB upped its efforts to curb VK's online protest organizing, demanding Durov shutter a group supporting the opposition leader Alexei Navalny and the Ukrainian activists organizing the Maidan protests in Kiev. Durov continued to resist.

Eventually the Russian government orchestrated a hostile takeover of VK (pressuring Durov to sell), through its largest competitor, Mail.ru, and United Capital Partners, an investment fund with ties to Putin. The FSB raided VK's offices and Durov's home, but he eluded the authorities, all while posting pictures of hairy dogs and giving "Mail.ru and its attempts to take over VK" the middle finger on social media. Eventually, United Capital Partners bought a 48 percent stake in VK, and in January 2014, Durov was forced to sell his remaining 12 percent share to an ally of the owner of Mail.ru, which then bought UCP's stake, giving Mail.ru complete control of the company.

VK and the Snow Revolution

How instrumental was VK in enabling the Snow Revolution? While dramatic social protest movements accompany the rise of social media, from the Snow Revolution to Occupy Wall Street, and from Tahrir Square to the streets of Hong Kong, evidence of a correlation between social media and protest participation doesn't prove that social media triggers or enables social protests. But the way VK rolled out gave scientists the data they needed to sort out its impact.

Think back to the description of how Facebook beat MySpace. By virtue of its college launch strategy, Facebook had developed a network where everyone knew each other. As a result, you were more likely to already know more people when you joined Facebook than when you joined MySpace. The local network effects enabled by this rollout made Facebook more valuable to new users.

VK rolled out similarly. Pavel Durov began by posting an invitation to apply for VK membership to a St. Petersburg State University (SPSU) student online forum. As students requested access, Durov personally approved all new accounts. So the first VK users were Durov's SPSU classmates. As they invited their friends and family members from their hometowns, the launch strategy drove rapid VK adoption in those cities. But not in others. So the hometowns of Pavel Durov's classmates saw a long-lasting acceleration of VK penetration, compared to other Russian cities. This is what scientists call a "natural experiment."

A natural experiment allows us to measure the effect of VK on protest participation, in this case by comparing protest participation in cities where VK penetration was high to cities in which it was low. Ruben Enikolopov, Alexey Makarin, and Maria Petrova used this same method to estimate the effect of VK penetration on protest participation during the Snow Revolution. They painstakingly collected data on the city of residence for all VK users with public accounts who joined before 2011; the number of protests and protesters in each city from news sources, police reports, and official announcements by protest organizers; and the number of SPSU students coming from each city who were born within a certain number of years of Pavel Durov's birthday, for all 625 Russian cities in their data.

I was Maria's discussant when she presented this research to the U.S.

National Bureau of Economic Research (NBER) in the summer of 2015. *Finally, some causal evidence of the link between social media and collective action,* I thought. The rest of the NBER was equally impressed. Maria and her colleagues confirmed that the effects of social media on political protests and social movements are sizable. A 10 percent increase in the number of VK users in a city caused a 19 percent increase in the number of protesters, and a 4.6 percent increase in the likelihood of a protest taking place at all, controlling for the city's size and other factors.

The Hype Machine is the most effective tool ever built for enabling collective action. It connects billions of people in real time and helps large groups signal their commitment and coordinate their action. But there's a big difference between mounting a protest and creating a successful social movement. It turns out that the speed and scale of rapid organizing enabled by the Hype Machine is also the Achilles' heel of today's protest movements.

The Power and Fragility of Digital Collective Action*

Although social media helps us organize collective action, recent social-media-fueled protests in Russia, Ukraine, the United States, and Hong Kong demonstrate that it does not necessarily create successful social movements. Protests help initiate change but often fall short of achieving meaningful victories. There are two reasons for this "one step forward two steps back" tango of modern organizing: technology-enabled protest movements are fragile, and governments opposed to them can co-opt the very technology that enables them.

Zeynep Tufekci's book *Twitter and Tear Gas* provides a comprehensive deep dive into how social media has changed social movements. Her thesis, backed by stacks of research, suggests that protest movements enabled by technology rise rapidly but often sputter at their zenith. At the precise moment they make headway and capture the world's attention, they experience what Tufekci calls "tactical freeze"— an inability to adjust tactics, negotiate demands, and push for tangible policy changes. What causes tactical freeze? The rapid mobilization

---

* This is the subtitle of Zeynep Tufekci's book *Twitter and Tear Gas.*

that the Hype Machine enables is typically accompanied by leaderless, ad hoc decision making and a shallow organization that develops without much early planning.

Successful social movements—the civil rights movement of Martin Luther King, Jr., the Indian independence movement of Mahatma Gandhi—developed over many years. They were well planned, meticulously organized, and had clear, tangible policy demands. The speed and scale of modern networked organizing rapidly amps up protest movements before they have a chance to develop an organization or establish genuine leadership, a decision-making structure, or an effective tactical strategy.

At the same time, the very technology that enables protests can be co-opted by the governments they oppose. In 2019, for example, the Chinese government used disinformation on social media to disrupt the Hong Kong protests and to change the domestic and international perception of the protesters by exaggerating the harm caused to bystanders. The Chinese government is suspected of hiring as many as 2 million people to insert propaganda into social media; the political scientist and statistician Gary King and his colleagues at Harvard estimated that they fabricate and post about 448 million social media comments a year toward this end. In Russia, Putin's allies simply took over VK and squashed protesters' online presence. As the stories of modern protests make clear, the Hype Machine enables social mobilization but in a fragile way.

This doesn't mean that protests enabled by social media can't evolve into successful social movements. While historical social movements tend to build up, over time, through sustained protests that were the culmination of years of organizing, "it is not correct to label [modern social-media-enabled] movements as failures," Tufekci writes. "Their trajectories do not match those of past movements, and neither should our benchmarks of timelines for success or impact. . . . It should be looked at as the initial moment of the movement's bursting onto the scene, but only the first stage in a potentially long journey." So what will be the legacy of social movements enabled by the Hype Machine? It is being written as we speak. Sometimes it enables and propels progressive social movements fighting oppression. Sometimes it harbors and supports violent extremism.

Telegram

After Pavel Durov built the machine that enabled the Snow Revolution, he fled Russia with a handful of developers and opened a Swiss bank account, where he parked the $300 million he received from the sale of VK. He became a citizen of St. Kitts by donating $250,000 to the Caribbean island's sugar industry, which allowed him visa-free travel to Europe. He embraced a covert, nomadic lifestyle—his team bounces from country to country, hotel suite to hotel suite, working on their next big social platform. Armed with his massive bank account, his St. Kitts passport, and a team of developers, he and his brother Nikolai began building a lightweight, encrypted-messaging app called Telegram.

Telegram embodies Durov's political philosophy—an unconditional embrace of personal freedom and freedom from government surveillance. The brothers built Telegram to protect their own communications from the Russian government. Now they wanted to provide the same freedom from surveillance to the rest of the world. And the world eagerly embraced it. Telegram grew faster than WhatsApp, Facebook, Twitter, or any other social media platform in history, reaching 100 million monthly active users in two years and 500 million by 2020.

Although cryptography experts have questioned its encryption, Telegram's emphasis on privacy, combined with Durov's commitment to resisting government intrusion, have made it a bastion of private communication. It provides lightweight encryption and stores data in several different jurisdictions, making it difficult to access or subpoena. Its secret chat option allows users to send messages with self-destruct times, and its public channels allow administrators to publish messages to unlimited audiences. Protecting privacy and individual data has been Durov's sole priority in building Telegram. He has resisted governments' requests to hand over data or build back doors into Telegram's infrastructure.

In the wake of Edward Snowden, Cambridge Analytica, and the release of Netflix's *The Great Hack,* the reasons behind Telegram's meteoric rise seem obvious. Individuals around the world are clamoring for privacy, security, and freedom from surveillance. Tim Cook, the CEO of Apple, was applauded when he resisted the government's request to crack the San Bernardino shooter's private iPhone data, and there are certainly important values and protections that must be preserved in privacy rights and data security. But as we found out on November 13, 2015, unrestricted, private, and anonymous communication can aid and abet the darkness in social media as well.

Four months after I discussed Maria Petrova's paper on the role of social media in the Snow Revolution at the NBER, the band Eagles of Death Metal were playing a concert in the Bataclan nightclub in Paris. An hour into the show, shots rang out from four automatic rifles. Armed gunmen entered the club, firing off hundreds of rounds. They killed ninety people in a coordinated attack that, when combined with suicide bombings at the Stade de France and additional gunfire at several Paris cafés, took 130 souls in the bloodiest terrorist act on European soil since the Madrid train bombing of 2004. The Islamic State (ISIS) claimed responsibility for the carnage, in retaliation for French air strikes in Syria and Iraq.

The attacks had been planned in Syria and coordinated by a terrorist cell in Belgium. Much of the planning took place face-to-face and on recycled cell phones to avoid detection. But the Hype Machine also played its part. According to police reports, the terrorists downloaded Telegram to their mobile phones on the morning of the attack and used the bastion of private, secure communication to coordinate their activities. While there are detailed records of voice calls and text messages between the mobile phones of the terrorists in Belgium and the attackers in Paris, providing intelligence about ISIS operations, there are no records of the Telegram communications because the platform's encryption and timed self-destruct messages provided clandestine cover for the coordinated carnage.

A Conduit for Good and Evil

Social media's role in progressive anticorruption demonstrations in Egypt, Russia, and Hong Kong on the one hand, and its role in coordinating the Paris terror attacks on the other, makes clear that the Hype Machine is a conduit for both good and evil. Nowhere is this clash of good and evil more obvious than in the fight against terrorism. It is well known that Al Qaeda and the Islamic State use social media to spread terrorist propaganda, disseminating beheading videos to spread fear and recruitment videos to amass new members. But the same technology is being used, for example by Google, to disrupt the very terrorist recruiting networks the Hype Machine enables.

Google's Jigsaw uses technology to make the world safer. Its mission is to defend free speech and combat harassment, injustice, and violent extremism. One of its primary efforts in this regard has been the development of a counterterrorism technique called the Redirect Method. The Redirect Method was created to stop the recruitment of new terrorists before they commit atrocities.

The method uses AdWords targeting, and curated YouTube content to reverse online radicalization. ISIS videos recruit new users by describing their great governance, their military might, their religious legitimacy, the call to jihad, and the victimization of Muslims around the world. The Redirect Method developed two YouTube channels, one in English and one in Arabic, to counter these narratives head-on.

Jigsaw found persuasive videos of curated citizen testimonials, on-the-ground reports, and anti-ISIS religious appeals to counter ISIS's five established recruitment narratives. For example, it curated videos that documented ISIS's atrocities toward civilians and its failed efforts at governance, including long food lines, helpless elderly residents being harassed by ISIS fighters, and the failing ISIS healthcare system. It included videos featuring clerics refuting violent extremism and undercutting ISIS's religious legitimacy, as well as videos of ISIS defectors denouncing the senseless violence of the group. It avoided using any videos produced by Western media, like the BBC, because interviews with ISIS defectors revealed that would-be terrorists typically dismissed these sources.

The curated content was organized into YouTube channels and set to repeat in automated playlists. A playlist refuting the "good governance" narrative showed videos on food shortages, the lack of education in ISIS-controlled territories, and the paucity of healthcare. A playlist refuting the "military strength" narrative documented the military setbacks ISIS was suffering at the hands of the Kurdish forces, the Iraqi Army, and Coalition forces. The team targeted AdWords ads at individuals searching for information about how to join ISIS, redirecting them to the curated videos that refuted ISIS claims.

The text, image, and video ads had the look and feel of ISIS-created content, a neutral textual tone, and striking images but raised questions that potential ISIS recruits might be asking themselves. The ads were targeted at keywords that included ISIS supporter slogans, names of official ISIS media outlets, ISIS mentions of jihad or specific fatwas (rulings on Islamic law by recognized authorities), and even the names of hotels known to host new ISIS recruits on their journey to the caliphate.

During an eight-week pilot experiment in 2016, the project reached 320,000 potential ISIS recruits, who collectively watched over half a million minutes of anti-ISIS content. The campaign's click-through rates (CTRs) far exceeded those of benchmark ads for similar search terms in the twelve months prior to the pilot, achieving a 3.1 percent CTR for English ads (76 percent better than the 1.7 percent benchmark) and a 4.3 percent CTR for Arabic ads (79 percent better than the 2.4 percent benchmark). Since the pilot project, the Redirect Method has been used to fight suicide and to offer a countermeasure to the Ku Klux Klan, extremism, and hate speech online.

There are many examples of social media used for good. The Ice Bucket Challenge raised over $250 million in donations for ALS (or Lou Gehrig's disease) in two months in 2014. While there are 120,000 people waiting for organ donations in the United States and 20 die waiting every day, only 600 Americans a day registered as organ donors before 2012. When Facebook launched its organ donation program that same year, there were 13,000 new organ donor registrations on the first day, a twenty-one-fold increase from the daily average, and the program more than doubled the average number of daily organ donations. When Nigeria, Liberia, and Congo experienced deadly Ebola outbreaks in 2014, 2015, and 2018, respectively, social media improved disease prediction, detected geographic changes in the disease outbreaks, and scaled public health interventions to wider geographic regions with greater frequency, at a fraction of the cost. But with the promise comes the peril. Social media also spread misinformation about Ebola. In Nigeria, for example, a hoax meme suggested you could cure the disease by excessively drinking salt water, which led to several deaths. A similar pattern repeated itself during the COVID-19 pandemic. While social media delivered lifesaving information and provided human connection at a time of forced social distancing, misinformation and hoax cures also spread around the world, hindering public health efforts to contain the pandemic.

The Transparency Paradox

Immediately after the Cambridge Analytica scandal broke, in an interview by Martin Giles for the *MIT Technology Review,* I predicted the Hype Machine was about to face a dilemma that would pull it in competing directions. On the one hand, social media platforms would face pressure to be more open and transparent about their inner workings: how their trending and ad-targeting algorithms work, how misinformation diffuses through them, and whether recommendation engines increase polarization. The world wanted Facebook and Twitter to open the kimono and reveal how it all worked, so we could understand how to use and fix social media.

On the other hand, the Hype Machine would also be pushed to protect our privacy and security, to lock down consumer data, to stop sharing private information with third parties, and to protect us from data breaches like Cambridge Analytica's. The European General Data Protection Regulation (GDPR) and California's Consumer Privacy Act (the most aggressive state data privacy legislation in the United States) mandate much stricter controls on how the Hype Machine handles, retains, stores, and shares consumers' data. So on the one hand the world is demanding more transparency, and on the other we are insisting on privacy and security. These two demands are in conflict, creating the transparency paradox.

Privacy is essential in a free, democratic society. But transparency is essential to understanding and designing social media to harness its promise while avoiding its peril. We all—citizens, legislatures, and managers—want to know how these platforms operate, from the inside out, so we can understand how to curb the spread of hatred, protect democracy from manipulation, and shield our children from bullying and predation. Yet we want private data to remain private and secure. In the *MIT Technology Review* interview, I predicted the pendulum would first swing sharply toward privacy and security.

A month after my interview, Mark Zuckerberg began his keynote at

Facebook's annual developer conference F8 by arguing that "the future is private," explaining that "a private social platform will be even more important to our lives than our digital town squares" and outlining an about-face from "connecting the world" to "a privacy-focused vision for social networking." Facebook announced it would be unifying its messaging services, from WhatsApp to Messenger to Instagram, and embracing private, secure, end-to-end encryption. "In the history of Facebook, there have been four major versions of the product so far and this is the fifth," Zuckerberg said. "So we're calling this FB 5." Facebook was locking down and going private.

Two shocks to the system forced this shift. First, Cambridge Analytica highlighted the dangers of freely sharing the Hype Machine's private data for behavioral targeting, election manipulation, and the broader threat to democracy. But a second threat also contributed to the shift—the world wanted to hold the Hype Machine accountable for all the harmful content on its platforms, like the livestream of the horrific massacre in Christchurch, New Zealand.

On March 15, 2019, three days before Carole Cadwalladr and whistleblower Christopher Wiley broke the Cambridge Analytica story in *The Guardian,* a sick, racist gunman livestreamed his vicious mosque attack in Christchurch on Facebook. The world saw a gory, firsthand account of his crimes in a video eerily reminiscent of a first-person-shooter video game. The attack and the video were made to go viral. The killer posted a seventy-four-page manifesto filled with racist rants and links to the forthcoming livestream on social media, and subsequently posted the video to his Facebook page. Several thousand people saw the original live feed, and 1.5 million others tried to share it on Facebook in the hours after the attack. Facebook blocked 1.2 million of these uploads, but 300,000 slipped through its content moderation.

In the fall of 2019, both Elizabeth Warren and Joe Biden derided Facebook for allowing Donald Trump to promote known falsehoods about Biden in political ads. Facebook refused to take down the ads because they "did not violate Facebook policy." The Christchurch video and false political advertising posted during the 2020 U.S. election highlight a critical dilemma in dealing with the Hype Machine. There is demand for the grotesque and incendiary. There are child pornographers and consumers of child pornography. There are violent extremists and those who seek out violent extremism. There are those who would perpetuate lies for political gain and those who are attracted to and willing to share those lies. So how do we address this new conduit for good and evil? Should Facebook, Twitter, Instagram, and WhatsApp be responsible for policing speech? Do we want to entrust them with that responsibility?

In October 2019, U.S. attorney general William Barr, U.K. secretary of state for the Home Department Priti Patel, and Australian minister of home affairs Peter Dutton sent a letter to Mark Zuckerberg asking him to halt plans for end-to-end encryption and requesting backdoor access for their governments to root out criminals on Facebook. A few days later FBI director Christopher Wray condemned the encryption plan, calling it "a dream come true for predators and child pornographers," adding that making Facebook private and encrypted would produce "a lawless space created not by the American people or their representatives but by the owners of one big company." "We're going to lose the ability to find those kids who need to be rescued," Wray said. "We're going to lose the ability to find the bad guys."

Privacy advocates and security experts balked at the implications. The Electronic Frontier Foundation claimed the governments' descriptions of encryption's threat to public safety were exaggerated, that access to criminals' data existed without programming back doors into the social media platforms, and that "encryption protects us all, including preserving not just digital but physical security for the most vulnerable users." The debate ties directly to Pavel Durov's philosophy holding privacy and security sacrosanct.

After Robert Mueller indicted Russia for interfering in the 2016 U.S. presidential election, the data science community mobilized to seek answers. Studies were launched quantifying the breadth, scale, and impact of misinformation and election manipulation efforts around the world. Scientists understood that democracy was under attack and that they were qualified to help defend it. They could measure and suggest how to curb its effects. Gary King at Harvard and Nate Persily at Stanford teamed up to launch Social Science One, a novel industry-academic partnership designed to facilitate scientific access to the social media data needed to understand the Hype Machine's effects on democracy and society. It is a noble endeavor. Funded by multiple foundations, supported by the Social Science Research Council, and in direct collaboration with Facebook, it set out on an ambitious plan to provide data and funding for research to understand the Hype Machine's impact on our world.

But the initiative ran into problems when Facebook recoiled from the transparency required. The push to be private and secure made it difficult to comply with the access to data to which it had originally agreed. My friend and colleague Solomon Messing was responsible for the data releases at Facebook. As he described it, Facebook wanted to release the data, but they were having problems releasing it while protecting users' privacy and security. Facebook had run head-on into the transparency paradox.

Where is the appropriate line between protecting public safety on the one hand and our right to secure, private communications on the other? Surely the answer can't be that there is no legitimate public safety interest in what is said on social media, or that the government should be allowed to freely snoop on any conversations it wishes without probable cause.

I believe there is a third way. To thread the needle through the transparency paradox, social media platforms must become both more transparent and more secure at the same time. They must allow transparency while preserving privacy, for example by achieving "differential privacy." Differential privacy is a standard for making individuals' data anonymous, so that it can be examined to understand patterns of election manipulation and crime, while guaranteeing individual consumers' anonymity. (I'll return to this third way, the question of where business and government should draw the line between privacy and security and how Facebook handled the transparency paradox in fulfilling its commitments to Social Science One in Chapter 12.)

Welfare at a Cost

In addition to enabling (fragile) social movements, being a conduit for good and evil, and sitting on a knife's edge between transparency and privacy, the Hype Machine also creates tremendous economic benefits—but at a cost. While the harmful effects of social media have stolen the spotlight in recent years, it's worth reminding ourselves that the Hype Machine gives us free access to news and knowledge, coordinates connections with people with whom we can build businesses, connects us with economic and social opportunities, facilitates the acquisition of new skills, provides us with social support, and more. The economic value created by the Hype Machine is potentially massive. But with all these potential benefits and harms to balance, how do we measure the benefits and costs of social media?

While commonly used measures of economic activity, like gross domestic product (GDP) and productivity, tell us about an economy's "performance," they don't tell us much about its citizens' well-being. Some economists have tried to measure welfare with subjective assessments like life satisfaction or happiness. But these measures are imprecise. In the end, our best measure of the economic welfare of a nation is its economic "surplus."

Surplus is the economic value created by transactions that are priced at less than what consumers would be willing to pay for them (consumer surplus) and more than what producers would be willing to sell them for (producer surplus). Since consumers typically capture 98 percent of the welfare gains from innovation, consumer surplus is the primary component of economic welfare. If I'm willing to pay $800 for the new iPhone but only have to pay $600, I stand to gain $200 of consumer surplus by buying it. When we add up all the differences between what consumers pay for goods and what they would be willing to pay, we have a measure of the economy's total consumer surplus—consumers' welfare gains from all economic transactions.

But what consumers would pay and what producers would sell social media for is tough to measure because it's free. The Hype Machine's business model (which I dissected in Chapter 9) sells targeted ads to brands and political campaigns and offers its services to consumers for free. And the fact that it's free also complicates antitrust regulation of social media (as I will discuss in Chapter 12). So how do we measure surpluses when a product is free? It's a critical question facing economists in today's digital age, because a growing share of our economy is made up of free digital goods like Spotify, YouTube, Wikipedia, and the entire Hype Machine, including Facebook, Twitter, Instagram, and the rest.

My friend, mentor, and MIT colleague Erik Brynjolfsson, in collaboration with Avi Collis and Felix Eggers, recently had an epiphany about how we might measure the Hype Machine's welfare effects.

While we can't directly measure the differences in what people would be willing to pay for Facebook and what they actually pay, because no one pays for Facebook, we can measure Facebook's welfare contributions by instead seeing how much people *would have to be paid to give it up*. And that's exactly what Erik, Avi, and Felix did in a series of massive online choice experiments between 2016 and 2018: they paid people to give up Facebook, then added up how much they'd paid.

They first asked people how much they'd have to be paid to give up Facebook for a month, then paid them upon verifying the inactivity of their Facebook accounts (which participants consented to in order to be paid). They then asked people how much they would need to give up Twitter, Instagram, Snapchat, LinkedIn, and WhatsApp for a month. They asked about other free digital services too, like Web search, email, maps, messaging, and video and music streaming, as well as some costly nondigital services, like having "no breakfast cereal for a year," "no TV for a year," and "no toilets in my home for a year." (They couldn't verify participants' abstinence from these other services, as they did from the Hype Machine, but no study is perfect.) These experiments allowed them "to estimate demand curves for any good using data from thousands of consumers that are representative of the national population."

In 2016 and 2017 the median consumer was willing to give up Facebook for a month for about $48, meaning U.S. consumers derive about $48 a month in consumer surplus from Facebook. These estimates correlated with usage. The more consumers used Facebook, posted status updates, liked content, shared pictures and news, played games, and made friends, the more they valued Facebook, and the more they had to be paid to give it up.

Using similar choice experiments, Hunt Allcott, Luca Braghieri, Sarah Eichmeyer, and Matthew Gentzkow demonstrated that Facebook generates about $31 billion a month in consumer surplus in the United States, which amounts to $370 billion a year in economic welfare gains. Now imagine that number globally, not just for Facebook but also for Instagram, Twitter, Snapchat, WeChat, WhatsApp, VK, and Telegram. The Hype Machine clearly creates massive economic welfare benefits. But at what cost?

The costs of social media don't accumulate in dollars, rupees, lire, or euros, but rather in hard-to-measure consumer harms that are difficult to price in. I'm sure you've heard the saying, "If you're not paying for a product, then you're the product." The idea is that free products usually sell advertisers access to consumers' attention. The "cost" of the service to the consumer is borne not in a price but in what they give up in exchange for the service instead of money. In the case of social media, the "cost" to consumers is borne in its potential harmful effects, from the effect of fake news on democracy, to the negative consequences for our mental and physical health, to the most-talked-about cost after the Cambridge Analytica scandal—our loss of privacy and the vulnerability of our consumer data.

At the individual level, social media use correlates with negative effects on well-being and mental health. The rise of social media and smartphone use corresponds with sharp increases in depression and suicide, although there is little direct evidence of a causal link between the two to date. At the societal level, there's the impact of fake news on democracy and the rise of echo chambers and political polarization.

Unfortunately, these costs are difficult to price into calculations of economic welfare. First, consumers don't recognize the negative individual effects. For example, while Allcott, Gentzkow, and their colleagues estimated that Facebook use reduced face-to-face time socializing with friends and family and well-being, users recognized these costs only *after* giving up Facebook during the experiment. After a period off the platform, users valued Facebook less than while using it, perhaps because they substituted time they spent on Facebook for other, more worthwhile activities that they discovered they liked more.

Second, we're not that good at accurately subtracting societal harm from the individual benefits of the products we consume. For example, we don't typically desire to pay less for Facebook because of its effects on democracy, or for our cars because of their effects on the environment (although some of us do value societal harms to some degree, when we pay a premium for hybrid or electric vehicles).

No study has ever convincingly measured the net benefits of the Hype Machine, and it is unlikely any study ever will, because the costs of the societal-level negative effects on well-being and mental health are difficult to measure. How, for example, how would you put a price on the cost of social media's disruption of democracy?

(Unequal) Opportunity

Social networks create economic opportunity and social mobility, but
for some more than others. One theory we discussed in Chapter 3 is
that social media networks create opportunity through the "strength of
weak ties." The theory argues that economic opportunity comes to us
disproportionately through our weak ties—who are less well connected
to the rest of our friends, make our networks "diverse," and tend to swim
in pools of opportunity that our other contacts don't see. They are the
conduits of novel opportunities—for example, job opportunities.

Nathan Eagle, Michael Macy, and Rob Claxton tested this theory on
an entire country. They collected data on mobile phone and landline
calls for the entire U.K. and connected them with national census data
on social and economic development. They captured 90 percent of all
mobile phones and 99 percent of all residential and commercial land-
lines, and analyzed calling patterns for 68 million people. They tested
whether people with weaker, more diverse ties in their communication networks had higher socioeconomic status. And that's exactly
what they found: the greater the diversity of someone's communication network, the greater their socioeconomic status (Figure 11.1).

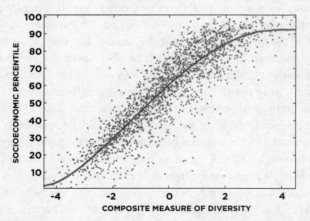

Figure 11.1 *The graph displays the relationship between social network diversity and socioeconomic rank.*

But as you know by now, I'm a stickler for distinguishing correlation
from causation. In this case, it's important, because if people with more

economic opportunity tend to develop more diverse networks (rather than the networks providing the opportunity), then the Hype Machine is more likely to *reflect* economic opportunity than to *create* it. How important is the machine in all this? Do we just replicate our existing social networks on social media, or do the Hype Machine's recommendation engines provide us with new economic opportunities?

Erik Brynjolfsson and I collaborated with Ya Xu and Guillaume Saint-Jacques of LinkedIn to find out. Guillaume was our PhD student at MIT before going to work for Ya, LinkedIn's director of data science. The collaboration allowed us to test the cause and effect relationship between weak ties and job mobility. We used data from sixty randomized experiments conducted on LinkedIn's "people you may know" (PYMK) algorithm, which recommends new connections to LinkedIn users. The experiments randomly varied the number of weak ties in the networks of 80 million people by suggesting more or fewer weak ties as contacts. This allowed us to test the extent to which weak ties cause job mobility. The results proved, for the first time, that weak ties *create* job opportunities and that PYMK algorithms can create weak ties. Depending on how we design it, the Hype Machine has the power to create job mobility and economic opportunity and to affect the distribution of those economic opportunities across its users.

More recently, Luis Armona, an economics PhD student at Stanford University, analyzed a natural experiment to measure the effect of Facebook on economic opportunity and wages. Think back to Jimmy Fallon's conversation with Sean Parker about Facebook's go-to-market strategy. Facebook entered the market through college campuses. But not every college went online at the same time. The 760 colleges that joined Facebook between February 2004 and May 2005 did so at different times, which meant that some college students had access to Facebook while others didn't. By comparing the wage growth of those with access to Facebook to those without it over time, Armona was able to measure how wiring into the Hype Machine affects economic opportunities and wages. He found that access to Facebook for four years of college caused a nearly 3 percent increase in average earnings. That's a meaningful effect. Armona also showed, through analysis of students' LinkedIn and other data, that the boost in wages caused by Facebook came through increased social ties to former classmates, which strengthened employment networks between college alumni.

Lynn Wu at Wharton (our former MIT PhD student) analyzed a natural experiment that corroborated these results. She studied the introduction of enterprise social media in a company and analyzed how it affected economic opportunities at work. The social media tool enabled employees to search for new contacts in the organization by their expertise. Her analysis revealed that its introduction made employees' social network connections more diverse (which she measured using email communications), increased their productivity, and decreased their likelihood of being fired.

More recently, Sydnee Caldwell, a graduate of the MIT PhD program in economics, applied this thinking to an analysis of wages and job mobility in Denmark. Analyzing detailed data on co-worker networks, wages, job mobility, and labor demand at co-workers' new firms, Caldwell and Nikolaj Harmon measured whether job openings at former co-workers' new firms correlated with wage increases and job opportunities for the study's subjects. They asked whether, among equally productive workers, workers with networks that provided better information about opportunities at other firms could negotiate higher salaries at their current firms. The answer was a definitive yes. Workers with better information networks negotiated higher wages and experienced greater job mobility and income.

But when Caldwell and Harmon analyzed whether everyone experienced the information benefits of social networks, they discovered inequality. Impacts on earnings were concentrated among highly skilled workers. Workers with specialized skills experienced double the effect on wages compared to middle-skill workers and nearly five times that of the least skilled workers. Since skilled workers also had higher baseline earnings, these impacts translated to substantially larger effects on total earnings. In fact, social network information had no impact on the earnings of the least skilled workers—assembly workers, manual-skilled workers, and craftsmen—and women benefited less than men across the board. While the Hype Machine creates economic opportunity through greater job mobility, higher wages, stronger productivity, and more job security, men and the more educated and skilled benefit disproportionately from this opportunity, meaning the rich get richer.

Three forces create unequal access to the opportunities created by the Hype Machine. First, there are disparities in access to the Hype

Machine across geography, socioeconomic status, and gender. Developing countries lag behind advanced economies in Internet, social media, and smartphone access. But beyond the digital divide in access to social media, there is a digital divide between what my friend and colleague Eszter Hargittai calls "capacity enhancing" and recreational uses of social media. The economically advantaged tend to use social media in ways that offer "opportunities for upward mobility," including relationship and reputation building, information seeking, collaboration, mobilization, and other "activities that may lead to more informed political participation, career advancement, or information seeking about financial and health services." Although research has found positive effects of activities that lead to self-improvement for those from less advantaged backgrounds, Hargittai found they tend to engage in these activities less, exacerbating inequality in the distribution of social media's benefits.

Second, the Hype Machine's network helps the rich get richer. As people make connections on social media, they connect to other people like themselves (that's homophily). So new connections reinforce existing disparities. Friend-recommendation algorithms are based in part on the user's current connections. Since mutual friends guide "people you may know" recommendations on social media, the tendency to connect with people like ourselves keeps social media networks segregated and divided among the rich and the poor.

Finally, the Hype Machine provides greater returns for highly skilled workers whose jobs depend more on acquiring and processing the information, knowledge, and skills that social media provides, exacerbating inequality.*

The Hype Machine holds the potential for tremendous promise and significant peril. It enables broad, rapid collective action, but action that is fragile. It spreads both positive and harmful content and behavior. When it is programmed for privacy and security, it forgoes trans-

---

* It's important to note that, in his study of Facebook, Luis Armona found that wage increases caused by Facebook were larger for female students and students from lower-middle-class families, suggesting the potential for the Hype Machine to reduce gender and income disparities. However, Armona's sample was limited to 760 selective four-year universities, the graduates of which are likely drawn from the high end of the skills distribution. Low-skilled workers studied by Caldwell, Harmon, and Hargittai were mostly excluded from Armona's analysis as a consequence of his sample.

parency. It supports broad increases in economic welfare and costly harms that are not priced in. It creates social and economic opportunity, but with unequal access. To achieve the promise and avoid the peril we will need scalpels, not broadswords.

Scalpels, Not Broadswords

One lesson I learned at the Kennedy School of Government at Harvard is that sometimes markets fail. While there, I analyzed how, when, and why they fail and how to remedy market failures. These lessons come in handy when thinking about social media because the Hype Machine is ripe for market failure. When technology exacerbates the spread of misinformation, terrorism, election manipulation, disruptions of public health, and the loss of privacy, and those harms are not priced into the market, sensible government regulation becomes necessary.

But there's a real danger that ill-conceived legislation will shackle innovation, free speech, productivity, growth, consumer surpluses, and the social and economic benefits of social technologies. When we understand that the sources of social media's promise are also the sources of the ills we are trying to avoid, it becomes clear that blunt attempts at regulation are likely to fail. Social media regulation must be carefully thought through to preserve the promise while avoiding the peril. Several recent examples of how not to regulate social media make clear why we need scalpels, not broadswords.

The struggling Ugandan economy inspired Ugandan citizens and businesses to move online in an effort to leapfrog the antiquated telecommunications infrastructure there. But in July 2018, following protests against his rule, Yoweri Museveni imposed a five-cents-per-day tax on social media and increased taxes on mobile money by 5 percent to curb antigovernment sentiment and increase tax revenue. Unfortunately, this broadsword approach had devastating unintended consequences for Uganda.

For many Ugandans, social media is the on-ramp to the Internet, and apps like Facebook and WhatsApp are essential for business, education, news, social support, and access to emergency services. Six months after the tax was imposed, Ugandan Internet usage fell 26 percent as the economic burden of the tax sent Ugandans fleeing offline. The Alliance for Affordable Internet estimated that while the tax increased Internet connection costs by 1 percent for the richest Ugandans, it increased these costs by 10 percent for the country's poorest. One gigabyte of data cost them 40 percent of their average monthly income. The chilling effect on social media also reduced growth, employment, and business revenue. One study estimated the tax will cost the Ugandan economy $750 million, or 3 percent of its GDP, and reduce tax revenue by $109 million as a result. In an effort to quell government opposition, Museveni's broadsword cut sinew and muscle in the Ugandan economy and denied his citizens access to social media's promise.

Russia's attempt to regulate Telegram is another example of a broadsword that backfired. Telegram was banned in Russia in April 2018 after Durov resisted the Russian government's attempts to gain access to encrypted messages. In 2016, Russia's Yarovaya, or "Big Brother," law required social media and messaging apps to build back doors to their infrastructure so the FSB could investigate terrorism and have broad access to encrypted messages. When Durov refused, claiming the laws were "incompatible with Telegram's privacy policy," Telegram was banned.

Enforcing the ban, however, proved harder than imposing it. The Roskomnadzor, Russia's version of the Federal Communications Commission (FCC) in the United States, moved to block IP addresses hosting the service and asked Google and Apple to remove Telegram from their app stores. But Durov migrated Telegram's hosting to third-party cloud providers, like Amazon and Google, to maintain availability, and Apple and Google refused to remove Telegram. So Russia clamped down on Google's and Amazon's clouds, blocking at least 19 million IP addresses.

But Telegram remained available. Many Russians began using virtual private networks (VPNs) to access the service, and Telegram's daily active users (DAUs) grew from 3.7 million in April 2018, when it was banned, to 4.4 million in February 2019. It's still the third most popular messaging app in Russia, just behind WhatsApp and Viber. While Russia's attempts to snuff out Telegram failed, they succeeded in suffocating many of the country's "legitimate" online services. Since the block wasn't sophisticated enough to target Telegram alone, many retailers, major online banking services, e-commerce websites, and messaging apps, like Viber and TamTam (state-sponsored media's suggested alternative to Telegram), were all disrupted. Even the website that hosted Roskomnadzor-blacklisted companies went down.

These examples illustrate that regulating the Hype Machine requires nuance. Even though the Ugandan and Russian regulations lacked good faith, these blunt policies demonstrate that social media regulations can shore up authoritarian power and create unintended consequences. In some sense, these are obvious examples of how not to regulate social media. But the nuanced choices we must make are sometimes not so obvious. This will become apparent when I consider how we must adapt to the Hype Machine in the final chapter.

CHAPTER 12

Rescuing the New Social Age

Privacy, Free Speech, and Antitrust in the New Social Age

It has become appallingly obvious that our technology has exceeded our humanity.

—ALBERT EINSTEIN

Today we're at a crossroads of privacy and security, free speech and hate speech, truth and falsity, democracy and authoritarianism, inclusion and polarization. While the Hype Machine is not solely responsible for any of these outcomes, it plays a role in all of them. Coming to terms with social media's influence on our democracy, our economy, and the very fabric of civil society leads to inevitable questions: How can we adapt? How can we navigate the design, regulation, and use of new social technologies to realize their potential and avoid their peril? These complex questions have no easy answers, but I believe there are paths to a brighter future.

In this chapter, I will explore solutions for innovation and antitrust, privacy and data protection, misinformation and fake news, election integrity, free speech, and building a healthier communications ecosystem. To do so, I will rely on the four levers I've outlined throughout this book (money, code, norms, and laws) and address the three main stakeholders (social media platforms, policy makers, and ordinary citizens) who collectively control our digital future. Let me begin with perhaps the most popular question facing social media regulation today: should Facebook and other social media be broken up?

Competition, Innovation, and Antitrust

In March 2019, senator and then presidential candidate Elizabeth Warren declared war on Facebook. "Today's big tech companies have too much power," she said, "too much power over our economy, our society, and our democracy. They've bulldozed competition, used our private information for profit, and tilted the playing field against everyone else." As she called to break up the company, she seemed genuinely angry. And she wasn't alone. Facebook co-founder Chris Hughes revealed in a *New York Times* op-ed that he felt "a sense of anger and responsibility" for the havoc Facebook has wreaked on our world. He added, "Mark [Zuckerberg]'s power is unprecedented and un-American. It's time to break up Facebook." Their anger and the anger of millions of Facebook users around the world is understandable. I've spilled a lot of ink in this book on how the Hype Machine has failed us on privacy, misinformation, hate speech, and election integrity. I'm angry too. But anger doesn't lead to great policy. To understand how to best rein in and harness the Hype Machine, I believe we have to be both rigorous and nuanced.

Warren and Hughes are right about one thing: competition is the foundation of a brighter Social Age. It underpins all the other adaptations we must undertake. Competition checks market power and enables societal values to lead corporate values. The suppression of competition in the social media marketplace creates a cascade of market failures that prevents us from protecting privacy, innovation, truth, and democracy. "Imagine Facebook and Instagram trying to outdo each other to protect your privacy and keep misinformation out of your feed," Warren said in a tweet, "instead of working together to sell your data, inundate you with misinformation, and undermine our election security. That's why we need to #BreakUpBigTech."

But while Warren and Hughes correctly diagnosed the problem, I believe they miscalculated on the solution. Warren's presidential campaign neatly combined rhetoric against the unbridled power of big corporations with personal attacks against Mark Zuckerberg's extraordinary wealth and Facebook's erosion of democracy and privacy. "The monopolists will make less monopoly money, boo hoo," she said of her plan to break up big tech. But touting trust-busting as the solution to our social media dilemma is a false promise. At some point the campaign banners will come down, the political confetti will be swept away, and we'll be left with the unenviable task of actually cleaning up the New Social Age. Breaking up Facebook will not solve any of the major challenges facing social media, and packaging these challenges into neat political slogans will only make them harder to overcome.

The antitrust case against Facebook ignores the economic conditions that tip social media markets toward concentration. And it does nothing to directly protect privacy, distinguish free speech from hate speech, ensure election integrity, or reduce fake news. It addresses symptoms, not causes. While competition can help force platforms to compete for our attention with designs that protect our social values, the market forces that tip the New Social Age toward monopolies will remain even if Facebook is dismantled. We need more fundamental solutions.

Evidence of Facebook's monopoly and monopolization is tenuous. But more important, focusing on breaking up Facebook will distract us from developing more lasting solutions that address our societal concerns, like comprehensive federal privacy reform, data portability legislation to ensure open markets, and regulation of political advertising and harmful speech on social media. We would do better to attack these regulatory challenges head-on than to pursue a potentially decade-long antitrust case against Facebook that is ultimately likely to fail.

The Antitrust Case Against Facebook

In his op-ed, Facebook co-founder Chris Hughes argued that "the Sherman Antitrust Act of 1890 outlawed monopolies." That's not exactly right. Under U.S. antitrust law, it's not illegal to be a monopoly. It's illegal to become a monopoly, or to leverage monopoly power for market dominance in adjacent markets, through anticompetitive practices that stifle competition. The point of antitrust is to protect consumers from harms created by uncompetitive markets, not to punish big companies for being big. If a company gets big by innovating and competing, its harms emanate not from being a monopoly but from practices that themselves deserve our regulatory attention. If we focus on breaking up Facebook as a cure-all, we will distract ourselves from legislating and regulating the root causes of the harms created by the Hype Machine.

Since the 1970s, U.S. antitrust law has been dominated by a "consumer welfare" perspective—defined by Yale law professor and appellate judge Robert Bork and promoted by the Chicago School of Economics—that narrowly interprets consumer harm from uncompetitive markets as the result of higher prices (and secondarily from restricted output and reduced quality). But this narrow view misses Facebook entirely. Facebook is free. Consumers aren't harmed by Facebook's ability to charge higher prices because Facebook doesn't charge consumers to begin with. Consumers are, however, harmed by inadequate competition in social media because, without robust alternatives, Facebook can lock us into draconian policies about its use of our data in a network tainted with fake news, misinformation, and hate speech. This side effect of a lack of competition is real.

Today Bork's narrow view of consumer harm is being challenged by an evolving vision of antitrust. While a law student at Yale, Lina Khan wrote an article titled "Amazon's Antitrust Paradox" (a play on Bork's seminal book *The Antitrust Paradox*) that laid out a legal argument for updating antitrust regulation for the platform era. Her point was that platforms like Amazon, which control the rules and algorithms that run digital marketplaces, have a conflict of interest when they sell their own products in those markets. Tim O'Reilly, founder of O'Reilly Media, and Elizabeth Warren have made similar arguments about Amazon and Google. Since Amazon controls the rules of the road for which products are seen and promoted by algorithms on its platform, it can promote its own products over those of competitors. Google Shopping is being investigated by antitrust authorities in Europe for a similar conflict of interest. As Senator Warren put it, "You don't get to be the umpire and have a team in the game." It's an important argument. Prices aren't everything. Amazon's products are frequently cheaper than those of its competitors, but a loss of choice reduces the platform's incentive to innovate. And of course, if Amazon's lower prices drive some competitors out of the market, it can later raise its prices to enhance its profits.

The antitrust arguments made by politicians, pundits, and the media against Google, Amazon, Apple, and Facebook are often grouped together under the banner of "breaking up big tech." But the antitrust considerations against each are quite different. The markets, anticompetitive practices, and potential for consumer harm are all different. The antitrust implications of running a platform in which you sell your own products, as Amazon does, are, in some respects, more compelling. The antitrust argument against Facebook is weaker. While several prominent thinkers have articulated reasons to break up Facebook, it's hard to see any of them holding up in antitrust litigation.

Robert Reich, former secretary of labor under President Clinton and professor of public policy at UC Berkeley, argues that "Facebook and Twitter spread Trump's lies, so we must break them up." "The reason," he argues, "that 45% of Americans rely on Facebook for news and Trump's tweets reach 66 million [people] is because these platforms are near monopolies." Putting aside the inherent problem of naming two competitors—Facebook and Twitter—as monopolies in the same sentence, Twitter has only 300 million users, and is twelfth in global social networking. The 45 percent Reich points to hardly constitutes a monopoly in news, and that number describes users getting *some* news from Facebook, not relying on it exclusively. Moreover, it's simply not true that Trump's tweets reach 66 million people. While 66 million people may follow Donald Trump, Twitter's algorithm distributes his tweets to a fraction of those followers. Measuring reach this way is like attributing Fox News's viewership to everyone who owns a TV and subscribes to a channel package that includes Fox. More important, spreading lies, while hardly a virtue, is not, in itself, anticompetitive. It's a harm that deserves legislative scrutiny, not a justification for antitrust action.

That's not to say Reich is wrong to be concerned about political lies or the effects of unregulated streams of misinformation on democracy. But attempting to break up Facebook on this legal basis alone will fail in the courtrooms, or it will destabilize antitrust regulation if it succeeds. Strong legislation regulating political speech on social media, on the other hand, would apply to all social media—Facebook, Twitter, and any future social media platform of any size—not just any one company that antitrust litigation managed to break up.

A second argument, articulated by Open Markets Institute fellow Matt Stoller, is that Google and Facebook's monopolization of advertising has been killing newspapers around the world. But the decline of newspapers, newspaper employment, and newspaper circulation all began in the late 1980s, the decline of newspaper advertising revenue began at the turn of the century with the advent of the Internet, online news circulation and digital advertising revenue have increased for the last ten years, and experimental evidence suggests that Google, for example, increases news readership rather than reducing it.

In 2014, Spain enacted copyright reforms that allowed newspapers to charge Google News for linking to its news snippets. When Google shut down Spanish Google News in response to the reform, it reduced overall news consumption by 20 percent and reduced pageviews on publishers' websites other than Google News by 10 percent, a reduction that was concentrated among small publishers. Although this ignores the appropriation of advertising dollars or euros in the news industry, it suggests that news aggregators like Google complement, rather than compete with, traditional news publishers, especially the small ones. Furthermore, the targeted advertising enabled by Google and Facebook lifts publisher revenue. When users opt out of targeted ads, it costs them and the exchanges about $9 per consumer. So while I too lament the loss of my hometown newspaper, Google and Facebook didn't kill the news, and the decline of newspapers is not a reason to break up Google or Facebook.

A more measured antitrust case against Facebook was developed by Dina Srinivasan in 2019 while she was a law student at Yale. She argues that Facebook gained monopoly power by promising to protect users' privacy, then broke those promises once it gained a dominant market position. Srinivasan's argument articulates a specific anticompetitive practice—the disingenuous promotion of false privacy protections—as the source of Facebook's monopoly and identifies a specific harm from monopolization: the eventual dissolution of privacy, which would not, Srinivasan argues, be possible in a competitive market.

The problem with this argument is that while there is evidence that Facebook reduced its privacy protections over time, there is no real evidence that its promise to protect privacy is what drove its user growth. While consumers express privacy concerns in surveys, the evidence strongly suggests they do not read privacy policies or choose products and services based on privacy. It's much more likely (as I described in Chapter 5) that Facebook's strong local network effects combined with its college launch strategy drove its growth and created its market dominance.

Another argument in favor of breaking up Facebook is that its acquisitions of WhatsApp and Instagram were anticompetitive practices and created monopoly power. But sustaining this argument in court would require a complex and perhaps overly broad definition of the market for social media. Facebook is a social network focused on friends and family. WhatsApp is a private messaging service, and Instagram is a public photo-sharing application. They operate in distinct markets with multiple competitors. A successful argument for unwinding these acquisitions would have to rely on complex market definitions and Facebook's anticompetitive monopolization of adjacent photo-sharing and messaging markets, which are less concentrated than the narrower market for social networking. The litigation would be costly, and although it might succeed, its success would take a long time and would by no means be guaranteed.

Finally, some argue that Facebook has too much political clout. But antitrust regulation is ill-equipped to rein in corporate political influence. While the Sherman Act was passed partly to address the political power of big business, antitrust economist and former DOJ and Council of Economic Advisers expert Carl Shapiro has noted, "Antitrust institutions are poorly suited to address problems associated with the excessive political power of large corporations." Though the antitrust authorities and courts know how to measure the economic effects of monopolization, there are no reliable methods for measuring the political power of companies. Legitimizing antitrust enforcement based on political power would politicize the process and invite corruption by "allowing the executive branch to punish its enemies and reward its allies through the antitrust cases brought." As Shapiro has noted, "Asking the courts to approve or block mergers based on the political power of the merging firms would undermine the rule of law while inevitably drawing the judicial branch into deeply political considerations." If we want to deal with the power of corporate money in politics—whether it's spent on Facebook ads or in lobbying politicians—we're better off passing meaningful campaign finance and anticorruption legislation. Breaking up Facebook is not a solution to this problem.

From the perspective of economic regulation, breaking up Facebook is like putting a Band-Aid on a tumor. It does nothing to promote the market conditions needed to sustain competition, because network effects inherent in social media will simply tip the next Facebook-like company into dominance. The problem in this market is one of interoperability—of access to a level playing field on which different social media services can fairly compete for customers. Social media markets tip toward monopolies when network effects combine with the high-tech construction of walled gardens that limit our freedom to choose among social technologies. Breaking up one company won't change the underlying economics of the market. Structural reform of social media—through a commitment to making data and social graphs (social media contact networks) portable, allowing consumers to take their data to competing companies the way we do in the tele-communications industry, and forward-looking merger oversight—offers a more comprehensive, long-term solution.

Social Graph and Data Portability

When Mark Zuckerberg testified before the U.S. Congress in 2018, Sen. John Kennedy asked him, "Are you willing to give me the right to take my data on Facebook and move it to another social media plat-form?" The senator was concerned that Facebook's lack of data porta-bility was locking customers into its network. If users could take their data to other services, it might spur competition and allow new social networks to flourish. Zuckerberg replied, "Senator, you can already do that. We have a 'Download Your Information' tool where you can go get a file of all the content there, and then do whatever you want with it."

That answer sounds like data portability, but to anyone in the know, it's laughable. The Download Your Information tool and other current versions of data portability, on Facebook and other social media, allow users to access simple document files with text data on their profile entries, lists of their posts, and accounts they have liked. This data is not usable with other providers. And that's exactly what Facebook wants, because genuine interoperability would threaten its competi-tive advantage and undermine the power of its network effects.

When you try to download your social graph from Facebook, you don't get a portable database of contacts that can easily operate with other networks. Instead, you get a text file of your friends' names and the dates that they joined Facebook, which is nowhere near as useful.

True interoperability, on the other hand, is essential to ensuring that new networks are able to grow and compete. If we hope to maintain innovation in social media and social networking, we need to be able to take our social networks to a competitor, if we choose. We should be allowed to use multiple different services. How can we bring this about? One way to ensure data portability and competition is to mandate, by law, that technology platforms make their data, and specifically their social networks, portable.

Luigi Zingales and Guy Rolnik of the University of Chicago proposed such a solution in the summer of 2017. They argued that consumers should own their social graphs and that graphs from different platforms should be interoperable, meaning messages from one network should be instantly rerouted to other networks. The idea is analogous to "number portability" in the telecommunications industry. In 1996 the FCC mandated number portability to promote competition between mobile and fixed landline providers in the United States. The idea is that if consumers own their mobile numbers, they can easily switch between carriers while retaining their call networks (the people who associate them with those numbers), fostering competition between operators and reducing prices. ·

Think back to the chat wars of the late 1990s. Microsoft and Yahoo! were trying to make the AIM network interoperable so that users could switch, for example, from AIM to MSN Messenger, take their connections with them, and be able to easily message friends from one network to the other. When consumers on one network can easily connect with consumers on another network, the value from network effects is diminished and competition is enhanced, giving more opportunity to new entrants and stripping away power from incumbents.

The idea behind social graph portability is that consumers would own their social graphs. When they switched to a new social networking service, their connections and their friends' identities could be transferred to facilitate exchanges on the new network as well as across networks. That said, a number of technical difficulties arise when you attempt to apply the logic of telephone number portability to social graph portability.

First, social graphs and phone numbers are different. A social graph is a complex web of interconnections over which property rights are difficult to assign. Defining the property right at the level of the graph makes its management complex and, in a dynamic environment in which social graph connections change, difficult to maintain over time. Joshua Gans, at the University of Toronto, has proposed a variant of social graph portability to deal with these complexities. Rather than assigning consumers the right to their social graphs, he argues that rights should be assigned at the level of identities and coupled with permissions that delineate how consumers want their messages routed across networks. Rather than social graph portability, Gans calls this "identity portability."

The idea is that consumers would own their identities and could freely switch from one network to another with permissions outlining who they would exchange messages with across the networks. As a result, "the network effects insulating digital platforms from competitive pressure will be mitigated. . . . Individuals could switch between platforms based on their tastes and preferences as well as the innovations devised by different platforms. . . . The point is that the ability to earn money from a user's attention will become more contestable as a result of identity portability."

Second, social media services differ from phone calls. Text and voice exchanges are standardized and therefore easier to make interoperable. But messages on Facebook, WhatsApp, Twitter, and Snapchat are harder to seamlessly exchange across the different networks. Messages on Snapchat disappear, while messages on Facebook persist. Messages on Twitter are public and limited to 240 characters, while messages on WhatsApp are private and unlimited in length. While protocols for distinct message types could be developed, the complexity of interoperability in this context certainly exceeds that of the exchange of voice calls and text messages on mobile phones.

Which brings me to a third problem. Conformity to message standards reduces differentiation, which is precisely the type of innovation that social graph portability would aim to support. If every new social network conformed to the messaging formats of incumbents, just to gain access to their network effects, innovation and new ways of interacting would be stifled.

Though the technical aspects of network interoperability are challenging, it's a crucial dimension of competition that will play an outsize role in our approach to innovation and antitrust. If the platforms faced legislation with teeth, they would innovate ways to interoperate.

They've solved far more difficult technical challenges in the past. I could imagine platforms accepting different message formats and not having a monopoly on any format. In this scenario, the market for messaging and social media would become contestable.

Do these solutions seem heavy-handed? You may be surprised to learn that the precedent for such government intervention already exists. AT&T was barred from preventing competitors from making and selling handsets in 1968; Microsoft was prevented from locking consumers into Explorer, its on-ramp to the Internet, in 2001; and when local telephone carriers were deregulated in the 1980s and 1990s, they were required to make their networks interoperable so consumers could make calls from one network to another. Even the chat wars of the late 1990s ended with a similar intervention. When the FCC approved the merger of AOL and Time Warner in 2002, it forced AOL to make AIM interoperable with Yahoo!, MSN Messenger, and others. As a result, AOL's market share in instant messaging fell from 65 percent before the merger, to 59 percent one year later, to just over 50 percent three years after that. In 2018, AIM ceded the entire chat market to new entrants like Apple, Facebook, Snapchat, and Google. Given this history, it's more surprising that these new entrants *haven't* been made interoperable than it is to suggest they should be.

Finally, data and social graph portability alone may not be enough to ensure competition. The ability to process such data requires systems that scale. Any solution that enables scalable alternatives to market leaders will need not only to make the data available but also to make the systems that can process that data available. Such access is not unprecedented. The U.S. Telecommunications Act of 1996 provides new entrants unbundled access to elements of the telecommunications infrastructure, such as telephone lines or switches, owned and operated by existing telecommunications companies, at a regulated rate. While this levels the playing field for new entrants to compete with incumbents, it may also reduce an incumbent's incentive to invest in the infrastructure itself. The analogy to Facebook is simple: to allow new entrants a level playing field, it may be beneficial to require incumbents, like Facebook, to provide access to unbundled elements of their data-processing infrastructure. In fact, Facebook makes some of these elements available through open-source code already.

Policy makers are taking small steps toward data and social graph portability. For example, the bipartisan ACCESS Act, introduced by Democrats Mark Warner and Richard Blumenthal and Republican Josh Hawley, attempts to make social media networks interoperable. The bill would force platforms with over 100 million users, like Facebook, Twitter, and Pinterest, to make their social networks interoperable and give consumers the right to export their data.

The platforms are moving toward data and social graph portability too. Since the time Senator Kennedy asked Mark Zuckerberg about data portability, Facebook has joined Google, Twitter, Microsoft, and Apple in supporting the Data Transfer Project, an industry collaboration committed to "building a common framework with open-source code that can connect any two online service providers, enabling a seamless, direct, user initiated portability of data between the two platforms." In December 2019, Jack Dorsey, CEO of Twitter, announced a new research team, called Bluesky, dedicated to creating open and decentralized technical standards for social media platforms to share and manage content.

How well these industry-led efforts will achieve interoperability remains to be seen. If industry efforts revert to "standards wars" over who controls the right to define interoperability, it may be essential for policy makers to mandate strict, open interoperability standards that enforce market contestability and guarantee consumers control of their data. Part of the problem (as I foreshadowed in Chapter 11) is that interoperability requires platforms to allow third parties to access consumer data. But that very access threatens privacy and led to the Cambridge Analytica scandal of 2018. So policy makers and platforms will need to work together to thread the needle of the transparency paradox—the pressure to be more open and secure at the same time. Solutions will need to include privacy-preserving techniques for data sharing, secure interoperable protocols, and strict monitoring of the custodial third parties that facilitate interoperability, as is mandated in the ACCESS Act.

Breaking up social media *without* ensuring interoperability is perhaps the worst of all possible approaches. As I described in Chapter 11, social media creates a tremendous amount of consumer welfare. That welfare derives in large part from the value created by local network effects—our connections to people who matter to us, both personally and professionally. As we discussed in Chapter 5, the larger a network grows, the greater its direct and local network effects. So breaking social media into smaller and smaller networks without ensuring that consumers can easily connect to one another across those networks will destroy much of the economic and social value created by social media without solving any of the problems it can create.

The regulation of competition in social media must be forward-looking. The market moves fast, and new innovations emerge every day. The rise of Telegram in messaging and TikTok in video sharing is evidence of this rapid innovation. Humans are lousy predictors of nonlinear innovation, and the market for social media is likely to evolve in ways we can't currently see. Video is already eating images. Augmented reality could eat video. And virtual reality and automated virtual beings may supplant both. It's hard to tell where innovation will come from or where it's going. Rather than looking backward toward breaking up what already exists, I believe we should focus our attention on forward-looking oversight of competition by, for example, evaluating the competitive effects of mergers and acquisitions before they happen. Attempting to break up Facebook through the courts could take ten years. By the time that happens, Facebook and the landscape of social media will look nothing like they do today. Forward-looking legislation that ensures competition, open markets, and a level playing field will chart a more productive path than looking backward to unwind networks and companies that already exist.

Privacy and Data Protection

The potential abuses of personal data can be seen in the Cambridge Analytica scandal, predatory loans targeting low-income minorities, gender discrimination in employment advertising, and foreign election interference. The need for comprehensive privacy and data protection legislation should, by now, be obvious. But blind adherence to privacy absolutism risks endangering investigative journalism, diabetes and Alzheimer's research, competitive advantages from machine learning, audits of election integrity, and the economic surplus generated by the advertising economy. We can create enforceable privacy legislation that protects our rights and minimizes harm from data breaches like Cambridge Analytica's. But to do so while balancing other interests requires thoughtfulness and nuance. The devil is in the details.

Three global privacy approaches have emerged over the last decade. China has erected a surveillance state, embracing the government's unfettered access to granular data about all Chinese citizens and empowering private companies to collect such data, almost without limits. Nearly everything is digitally monitored, and citizens have few to no rights in their personal information or protections against its use by government or private entities. On the other side of the spectrum is the European approach, codified by the General Data Protection Regulation (GDPR), which establishes strict protections of consumer data, illuminates citizens' rights regarding its use, and imposes weighty penalties for violations of those rights. All EU countries have established national laws enacting the original Data Protection Directive (which the GDPR updated), and several countries outside the EU, like Australia, New Zealand, and Japan, have laws loosely following the GDPR in establishing privacy and data protection. Somewhere in the middle is the United States, which is still crafting its position on privacy and data protection at the state and federal levels. Though comprehensive privacy reform has yet to be passed at the federal level, states, led by California's Consumer Privacy Act (CCPA), are beginning to create a patchwork of privacy legislation across the country.

America's laissez-faire approach to privacy has enabled unprecedented innovation and the growth of data-driven businesses like Google and Facebook. But it has also wrought significant harm to American democracy and the rights of its citizens. To establish the most productive approach to privacy legislation, the United States would be wise to learn from the other global privacy regimes and to consider how each is impacting its citizens.

Our privacy is essential for moral, practical, and utilitarian reasons. The right to private spaces, private conversations, and private behavior is a bulwark against repression. Governments with the ability to root out individuals' beliefs and behaviors can identify and punish dissent. Repressive regimes surveil their opposition under the cover of weak privacy laws. Companies can use private data to discriminate based on behaviors, beliefs, or economic and social circumstances. Protecting the privacy of individuals' political beliefs and health conditions can help prevent discrimination. Privacy is also a foundation of free speech, not only in the freedom from retaliation but also because the possibility of surveillance has a chilling effect. As Michel Foucault has described, using eighteenth-century British philosopher Jeremy Bentham's panoptic prison as a metaphor, a panoptic system that could be watching us at any moment will systematically change the way we behave and speak in every moment. As Columbia law professor and author Tim Wu has noted, "Mass privacy is the freedom to act without being watched and thus, in a sense, to be who we really are—not who we want others to think we are. At stake, then, is something akin to the soul."

But while comprehensive privacy reform is essential, privacy absolutism will derail other societal interests. For example, the GDPR is currently bringing some international medical research to a grinding halt. Since May 2018 several European countries have stopped sharing data with the U.S. National Institutes of Health for important research on diabetes and Alzheimer's disease due to a lack of harmonization of privacy protections. Since the research involves the collection of DNA samples from subjects in the United States and Europe, many European countries are now effectively prohibited by law from pursuing such research.

While one could argue that medical research is a reason to quickly harmonize U.S. privacy standards with those of the EU, GDPR prohibitions against data retention and use could also prevent election audits and research into the impact of the Hype Machine on society. In designing legislation, we must think systematically about the trade-offs, for example, between election integrity and privacy. As Dean Eckles and I pointed out in *Science,* "Well-intentioned privacy regulations, while important, may also impede assessments" of election interference by complicating or even outlawing the routine retention of data necessary to audit election manipulation. I'm an advocate for privacy legislation. But overbroad legislation delegitimizing data retention will make auditing social platforms difficult. As we regulate privacy, we must not limit our ability to audit, study, and understand the Hype Machine's role in society. There are privacy-preserving ways to protect our data and our elections at the same time (which I will address in more detail later in this chapter). To take advantage of them, Congress must acknowledge these multiple goals and consult with experts to avoid their trade-offs.

Privacy reform could also conflict with the public's right to know. In

Romania in 2018 an investigative journalism project received incriminating evidence of a massive fraud by senior Romanian official Liviu Dragnea. When the team of journalists published the story along with all the evidence, including emails, photos, videos, and screenshots, given to them by an anonymous tipster, the Romanian Data Protection Authority pounced on them, claiming they had violated Romanian data protection laws by revealing Dragnea's private information. The Romanian authorities demanded the journalists reveal the identity of the tipster, how they received the information, how it was stored, and whether they had more personal data on Dragnea or other Romanian politicians. In other words, the GDPR was weaponized for political retaliation and media suppression. The journalists were threatened with a 20-million-euro fine, which undoubtedly will have a chilling effect on their future investigations as well as on other journalists in Romania.

Privacy legislation could also interfere with commercial advances from machine learning and data processing, which increasingly comprise a greater portion of the U.S., European, and global economies. The GDPR, for example, technically prohibits automated decision making (and thus machine-learning models) without a human in the loop to oversee the machine. (See the GDPR's Article 22.) This provision seems to ban machine learning altogether for applications as broad-based as recommendation systems (like Amazon's "people who liked this also liked this" feature), advertising systems, social networks, ratings, and assessment models. But exceptions for cases where processing is necessary for contractual reasons or is separately authorized by law, or when the data subject has explicitly consented, make machine learning feasible in Europe, though with a significantly increased cost of compliance. Furthermore, there is debate as to whether the GDPR requires machine-learning decisions to be explainable to the subjects of those decisions. If such a requirement is enforced, many machine-learning models, like deep learning, support vector machines, and random forests, which are inherently difficult to explain, could become more difficult to use.

The most absurd example of the unintended consequences of data privacy I've heard concerns the great U.S. chicken price-fixing scheme. From 2008 to 2016, chicken prices in the United States rose 50 percent while key chicken-breeding costs and pork and beef prices were all falling significantly. A class action lawsuit against the "big chicken" companies, including Tyson Foods and Pilgrim's Pride, alleges they manipulated chicken prices by coordinating the destruction of flocks of breeder hens who laid the eggs. The lawsuit claims the firms were conspiring under the veil of a privacy-preserving anonymous app called Agri Stats, which enabled them to clandestinely share detailed information about their operating profits and the size and age of their breeder flocks, allowing "industry leaders to deduce how many birds their competitors were hatching and reduce their own production rates accordingly." The anonymous app enabled a level of data sharing that could never have taken place out in the open, providing cover for big chicken's collusion.

Finally, the GDPR has had a negative effect on Europe's advertising economy, costing publishers and advertising firms significant revenues and jobs. In the days leading up to and immediately after the GDPR went into effect, European ad exchanges saw ad demand volumes plummet by 25 to 40 percent. As privacy legislation increases the costs of collecting consumer data, it hinders targeted advertising and makes personalizing website experiences more difficult. Garrett Johnson and his colleague Scott Shriver have estimated that publisher readership and ad revenues fell by 10 percent for EU users due to GDPR implementation. Further research by Johnson and Shriver with Shaoyin Du shows that when publishers and exchanges are not able to target advertising because users opt out, publishers and exchanges earn 52 percent less revenue than comparable ads for users who allow behavioral targeting. A large-scale randomized experiment by Deepak Ravichandran and Nitish Korula at Google found the same 52 percent reduction in ad revenue when they disabled cookies for a randomly selected group of the top five hundred global publishers, suggesting that the targeted advertising enabled by the Hype Machine contributes significantly to publisher and brand revenue.* Furthermore, privacy laws can affect employment. Research by Jian Jia, Ginger Zhe Jin, and Liad

---

* Critics of targeting typically point to a paper by my friend and colleague Alessandro Acquisti and his colleagues, which found only a 4 percent reduction in publisher revenue, rather than the more typical ~50 percent reduction. However, this paper has been criticized for masking much of the true effect by controlling for firm-level variation, which captures firms' quality of data and skills with targeted advertising.

Wagman suggests that the GDPR cost Europe up to forty thousand jobs in the technology startup sector alone in the first four months after its implementation.

While none of these are reasons to avoid enacting federal privacy legislation in the United States, they are reasons to write new laws that, while protecting privacy and harmonizing with the EU, also minimize the social, economic, and democratic trade-offs inherent in implementing sweeping privacy reform.

The right to privacy was established by the Supreme Court in *Griswold v. Connecticut,* in which Justice William Douglas wrote for the majority that the right emanated, by implication, from "penumbras" of other rights explicitly protected in the Constitution. While there is no federal law protecting digital privacy in the United States, the first state law, California's Consumer Privacy Act, went into effect on January 1, 2020, while I was writing this book.

Though the CCPA is similar to the GDPR, in many ways it's less stringent, even though it has a broader definition of personal data that includes household information. The GDPR gives EU citizens the right to know what information a company has collected on them, the right to an explanation of how automated decisions, like ad targeting or recommendations, are made using their data, the right to object to profiling, and the "right to be forgotten," which requires data collectors to delete certain information at a user's request. The GDPR also requires the establishment of a dedicated data protection authority or agency in each EU country to inform citizens about their rights, protect their privacy, and handle grievances.

The CCPA, on the other hand, allows consumers to opt out of having their data shared with or sold to third parties and gives businesses the ability to offer discounts to people who are willing to have their data shared or sold to third parties. The California law gives customers the right to find out what information a company collects about them. After a request, companies have forty-five days to provide customers a comprehensive report about the information they have, and to which third parties it was sold over the preceding twelve months.

The exact provisions of a federal privacy law will need to be debated and considered, but it's hard to imagine such legislation without a new federal agency to administer and enforce it, the creation of which will likely change the landscape of data collection and processing in the United States in dramatic ways.

Fake News and Misinformation

The annexation of Crimea, election and stock manipulation, and the recent coronavirus pandemic and measles resurgence highlight the potential consequences of the spread of fake news online. But fake news is a complex problem without a simple solution. While competition and privacy can and should be regulated, misinformation presents a unique challenge because it requires choosing an arbiter of truth—assigning rights to define what's true and false—which is not typically an appropriate role for governments (except in extreme cases of the protection of health and safety, like yelling "fire" in a crowded theater). For this reason alone, the fight against misinformation will (and should) be won not by policy makers but by platforms and people. While there is no silver bullet, a combination of approaches can, together, dampen the spread of false news and lessen its impact on society.

The first approach is labeling. Think of it this way: When we buy food at the grocery store, it's extensively labeled. We know how many calories it has, how much fat it contains, and even if it was produced in a facility that processes wheat or peanuts (for those consumers with allergies). These nutrition labels are mandated by law. But when we read news online, we don't have any labels about the provenance or veracity of the information we are consuming. What's contained in this information? Is the source credible? How was the information collected? What is the editorial policy of the journal? How many independent sources must verify a claim before they publish it? How often does this source publish information that is fact-checked to be true or false? While we are extensively informed about the food we consume, we have almost no data about the information we consume.

Research suggests that labeling could dampen the spread of misinformation. For example, my colleagues Dave Rand and Gordon Pennycook have found that, when it comes to fake news, consumers are "lazy, not biased." When they think analytically about the news, they are better able to tell truth from falsity. "People fall for fake news because they fail to think; not because they think in a motivated or identity-protective way." Prompting people to think about the information they consume can change whether they believe and share it. The finding corroborates work by Adrien Friggeri, Lada Adamic, Dean Eckles, and Justin Cheng that found that debunking false social media rumors inspires people to delete their reshares of the false information on Facebook.

Pennycook, Rand, and Eckles recently teamed up with Ziv Epstein, Mohsen Mosleh, and Antonio Arechar to put this approach to the test in a series of experiments reducing the spread of misinformation online. They found that subtly nudging people to think about the accuracy of what they read can increase the quality of the information they share. A separate experiment by Brendan Nyhan and his colleagues showed that fake news labels reduced the perceived accuracy of false headlines. Taken together, these results suggest that subtle cognitive nudges to think about accuracy and veracity can dampen the spread of untrustworthy information in social media. That is good news, because labeling and nudges to consider accuracy are unobtrusive solutions that scale. But the solution is not perfect. In the study by Nyhan and colleagues, fake news labels also decreased the belief in true news, suggesting the labels created a general distrust in news, which mirrors what happened when the SEC outed the fake news circulating on stock market news sites (as I described in Chapter 2). Furthermore, labeling fake news can create an "implied truth effect" whereby consumers assume news that isn't labeled must be true simply because it has avoided being debunked. As we pursue labeling, we must ensure that it counters fake news effectively while avoiding known difficulties in its implementation.

I advocated strongly for labeling fake news in my 2018 TEDx Talk at CERN in Geneva. Since then, the major platforms have adopted labeling as a proactive approach to routing out misinformation. Twitter began labeling "manipulated media" in March 2020, including sophisticated deepfakes and simple, deceptively edited video and audio that is either fabricated or altered to the point that it changes the meaning of the content. While Facebook moved to label false posts more clearly in October 2019, they have so far refused to do so for political advertising or content. When Twitter applied its new manipulated media label to a video of Joe Biden edited to make him look like he was conceding that he couldn't win the presidency, Facebook was blasted by the Biden campaign for failing to label the manipulated video. These judgment calls and the details of misinformation labeling policies will be the front lines of the fight to transparently distinguish truth from falsity. It's important that we make these policies as effective as possible while avoiding some of their documented shortcomings.

Second, we must address the economic incentives behind creating and spreading false information. During the 2016 U.S. presidential election, a wave of misinformation from Macedonia was created to make money from ads that ran next to fake content. There was no political motive. Since fake news travels so much farther, faster, deeper, and more broadly than the truth, and (as our research shows) is 70 percent more likely to be reshared, we need to cut off the financial returns to spreading misinformation and reduce the economic incentive to create it in the first place.

YouTube pursued this approach in an effort to fight the spread of antivaccine misinformation. In February 2019 it removed ads from all videos advocating against vaccinations and demonetized antivaccine accounts, making it impossible for them to earn ad revenues. YouTube community guidelines now state that "content that promotes harmful or dangerous acts that result in serious physical, emotional, or psychological injury is not suitable for advertising." That includes "promoting or advocating for harmful health or medical claims or practices," such as "anti-vaccination, or AIDS denialist movements . . . and content which implies serious medical conditions do not exist or are an elaborate hoax." Pinterest has blocked searches for antivaccine content. When social media platforms like YouTube and Pinterest do both—stop paying advertising dollars for misinformation, while blocking searches and banning harmful content—they are more likely to be successful in starving the market for misinformation.

Third, while research on the efficacy of media literacy in combating fake news is still in its infancy, it could be an important avenue toward inoculating people against bias and falsity. Media literacy is designed to teach people, through primary and secondary education, to think critically about the information they consume and share. It includes teaching the ability to distinguish fact from opinion, to spot fake news, and to understand the use of media in persuasion.

Several programs are currently being developed and tested, including Google's Be Internet Awesome, which teaches kids "how to avoid a phishing attack, what bots are, how to verify that information is credible, how to evaluate sources, how to identify disinformation online and spot fake URLs." The University of Cambridge launched a game in 2018 called Bad News that teaches Internet users to spot fake news by creating it themselves. In the browser game, players use Twitter bots, create Photoshop evidence, and spread conspiracy theories to attract followers, while trying to maintain a high "credibility score" for persuasiveness. Sander van der Linden, director of the Cambridge Social Decision-Making Lab, says, "Our game work[s] like a psychological vaccination," inoculating users by exposing them to a small dose of falsity. A study with fifteen thousand participants found that the game reduced the perceived reliability of fake news by an average of 21 percent and did not impact how users perceived real news. Moreover, those who were assessed as more susceptible to fake news headlines at the outset benefited more from the game.

Fourth, we should pursue technological solutions to the spread of misinformation. Although not a cure-all, machine-learning algorithms can root out false information online. The best algorithms use features of the content, such as the language, structure, and claims of false information, and also consider characteristics of how information spreads as signals of falsity. For example, our former student and now Dartmouth professor Soroush Vosoughi built a rumor predictor in 2015 that was able to correctly predict the veracity of 75 percent of rumors spreading on Twitter faster than any other public source, including journalists and law enforcement officials. Technology moves fast, and the state-of-the-art algorithms used by the major platforms are likely more effective today. Data sets used to train new algorithms have been made available, for example, on the data science competition website Kaggle. But technology is not a silver bullet; human beings must remain in the loop of this technology. The scale of the problem is too large for humans to address alone, but we cannot abdicate our responsibility to judge the legitimacy of information. Human labels are essential for training machine-learning algorithms and to ensure that human judgment leads algorithmic judgment in defining truth and falsity.

Fifth, platform policies also help. All the social media platforms use algorithms to curate the information we see. Building reliability metrics into those algorithms could help reduce the spread of low-quality and false information online. We know repetition can increase belief in false news, so policies that dampen the spread of information can help tip the balance toward truth. In 2019, WhatsApp limited the number of times people can forward messages to five, worldwide. Since WhatsApp chat groups support a maximum of 256 people, the five reshare limit effectively constrained the number of people one can reach with any given piece of content to 1,280 (5 times 260). WhatsApp announced the reshare limit as part of its fight against "misinformation and rumors" in the hope that slowing down the spread of information would allow true information to catch up with false news. In April 2020, it strengthened this restriction by limiting forwarding of highly shared messages to a single reshare in an effort to crack down on coronavirus misinformation during the pandemic, which reduced viral message forwarding by 70 percent.

For all the talk of regulation and technology solutions, one thing we can't escape in dealing with fake news is the core problem of defining truth and falsity. How should we, as a society, decide what's true and what's false? And who should decide that? Technology is no solution for this problem. Ethics and philosophy will provide the solutions. As we decide how to manage falsity in the era of reality distortion, we should elevate the importance of ethics and philosophy in guiding the decisions we make. And (as we'll see when we discuss free speech) these questions are at the intersection of ethics and policy, where philosophical and practical considerations meet to determine, for example, how we draw lines between true and false, between free and harmful speech, and who should draw them.

Election Integrity

In the 2020 election, for example, the United States must be aware of manipulation attempts not just by Russia but also by China, Iran, and others. Liberal democracies around the world are at risk as unanswered questions remain about the role of misinformation in elections in the United Kingdom, Sweden, Germany, Brazil, and India. If our elections lack integrity, no amount of free speech or inclusion can save our democracies because voting protects all other rights. Unfortunately, in the United States, too little is being done. Most of the legislation designed to protect elections has been blocked in the U.S. Senate, and the social media platforms have resisted research into election interference.

We know Russia orchestrated a "sweeping and systematic" attack on the 2016 U.S. presidential election, spreading misinformation to at least 126 million people on Facebook and 20 million people on Instagram, and posting 10 million tweets from accounts with more than 6 million followers on Twitter. We know at least 44 percent of voting-age Americans visited a fake news source in the final weeks before the election. We also know that Russia targeted misinformation at swing states and attacked voting systems in all fifty states. What we don't know is whether these efforts tipped the 2016 election, or if they are affecting the current election in 2020. We don't know because we're not measuring it. To harden our democracies to the threat of digital manipulation, we need research and legislation: research to understand the threat, and legislation to neutralize it. Today the threat remains unchecked.

As Dean Eckles and I wrote in *Science* in August 2019, research on election interference is scarce and underdeveloped, creating a vacuum filled by speculation. So we outlined a four-step blueprint for understanding how, when, and to what extent online misinformation affects elections, by cataloging exposure to manipulative media, combining that exposure data with data on voting behavior, assessing the causal effect of manipulative messages on voting, and assessing the consequences of changes in voting behavior for elections. I believe that by pursuing this agenda and parallel work on the hacking of voting systems, we will learn how to protect democracy. Without it, democracies will remain vulnerable to foreign and domestic attacks worldwide.

Social media platforms must collaborate more openly with independent researchers to understand the threat. Jack Dorsey made an impressive commitment to our decade-long study of the spread of fake news on Twitter. His support was public-minded and remained consistent despite the potential for negative press. Similarly, Facebook has at times facilitated important scientific studies of political communication and misinformation. Unfortunately, these have typically been one-off endeavors. Even the most systematic initiatives, like Social Science One, have at times found their access to data on election manipulation choked off by the social platforms.

Social Science One is an industry-academic partnership created by Gary King at Harvard and Nate Persily at Stanford, working to provide funding and data to study the effects of social media on democracy. Facebook signed on to this partnership in an effort to be more transparent about its role in democracy. But after promising to deliver data to researchers, it delayed the data's release, and the funders of Social Science One threatened to pull out if Facebook abandoned its commitments. Facebook claimed it was struggling to release the data in ways that ensured both privacy and security.

I know the researchers responsible for the partnership at Facebook, and they seemed genuinely committed to following through. So at the time, I went on TV to defend their public statements describing the difficulty of resolving the transparency paradox. But five months later they still hadn't delivered the data, and the funders of Social Science One began to withdraw. The "eternal delays and barriers from both within and beyond [Facebook]" led the leadership of Social Science One to declare that "the current situation is untenable. . . . We are mostly left in the dark, lacking appropriate data to assess potential risks and benefits. This is not an acceptable situation. . . . The consequences of failure—again, for both scientific knowledge specifically, and for our democratic societies more generally—are too dire."

Then in February 2020 my colleague Solomon Messing, who led the effort to anonymize and release the Facebook data to Social Science One, demonstrated that my faith in Facebook's efforts was not unfounded. He announced the release of "one of the largest social science data sets ever constructed—a compact summary of nearly an exabyte of data . . . meant to facilitate research on misinformation from across the web, shared on Facebook." Social Science One announced that the data summarized "38 million URLs . . . [and included] the types of people who viewed, shared, liked, reacted to, shared without viewing, and otherwise interacted with these links." When Social Science One began, it had thought securing this data would take "about two months of work." It took nearly two years. Releasing data of this scale and scope in privacy-preserving ways is challenging. So while this data release is positive, we still have work to do.

I believe several steps can reinvigorate scientific research into the effects of the Hype Machine on elections and democracy. First, we need technical solutions to the transparency paradox that enable the platforms to become more transparent and more secure at the same time. Anonymizing data before it's released to researchers can help ensure privacy while enabling the science we need to harden our democracy. Part of what enabled Facebook's unprecedented data release was a commitment to action-level differential privacy, a data obfuscation technique that can guarantee privacy. But to release data anonymously, you have to add noise to it. And the more noise you add, the further from ground truth you get. To manage this trade-off, Daniel Kifer and Solomon Messing worked with computer scientist Aaron Roth, co-author (with Michael Kearns) of *The Ethical Algorithm,* and his team to develop guidelines for implementing differentially private systems that "maximize the utility of the data for research while protecting privacy." More research implementing differential privacy in both the scientific community and in companies like Facebook, Google, and Twitter is needed to make the methods more efficient, secure, and scalable, especially now that differential privacy is being applied to data, for example, from the U.S. census, which is used to make consequential policy decisions on voting rights, fund allocations, and political apportionment.

There is a risk that differentially private census data could unfairly impact minority groups and exacerbate inequality by adding noise that obfuscates the need for minority representation. For instance, if data from a community with a sufficient minority population to warrant funding or qualification for dual language social services is smoothed over or obfuscated to the point of erasing these qualifying differences, the cost of privacy could exceed its benefits. More work is needed to ensure that the benefits of differential privacy can be achieved while avoiding its pitfalls.

Second, I believe research "safe harbors," in which scientists can access and analyze sensitive data, should be created and supported by policy makers and social media platforms. Such safe harbors, which are commonly used in research on sensitive public administration, health, and medical data, set limits on the type and amount of data that can be accessed and analyzed, as well as the analysis that can be performed. A similar model is used by the U.S. Census Bureau, which "deputizes" scientists, after the necessary background checks, to analyze its data on Census Bureau premises, without the ability to remove data from the bureau's control.

Third, the social media platforms must make a firm, verifiable, and enforceable commitment to "make accurate and representative data available for scientific research into the most pressing issues of public concern." The companies must include Facebook, Twitter, YouTube, and others. Perhaps only mounting pressure from legislators and the public will ensure that experts have the access they need to do the work that is required. Research collaborations with social media platforms, like that being undertaken by Social Science One, can facilitate access to important data for understanding democracy's vulnerability to social media manipulation. I hope the realization that research is essential to protecting our democracies worldwide will overcome partisanship and myopic commercial interests in making the necessary data available in ways that also preserve privacy. Currently, the science on these important questions is nonexistent, so we are flying blind. If the social media platforms cannot proactively commit to supporting science to secure democracy, Congress must step in to enforce compliance, in the national interest.

Unfortunately, legislation protecting democracy from election manipulation is also nearly nonexistent. Senate majority leader Mitch McConnell agreed to provide $250 million in election funding in 2019 to "help states improve their defenses and shore up their voting systems." But the measure included less than half of the funding requested in the Secure America's Federal Elections Act and no meaningful legislative reforms to protect elections. As Minority Leader Chuck Schumer put it, "There are multiple, bipartisan pieces of legislation awaiting action on the floor that would counter foreign influence operations against our democracy, safeguard our elections, and deter foreign adversaries from attempting to interfere." He added that if we don't do more, "the job will remain incomplete and our democracy vulnerable." Congress must act quickly and prudently. If sweeping electoral reform bills like HR 1 are too contentious, surely we can achieve a bipartisan commitment to more targeted legislation like the FIRE Act, the SECURE Our Democracy Act, and the Voting System Cybersecurity Act. The release of extra federal funding would help states defend elections and voting systems, and risk-limiting audits could preserve the integrity of the vote itself.

Unfortunately, misinformation is becoming more insidious. We have already seen a bigger role for doctored images and video. As I described in Chapter 2, rapid innovation in generative adversarial networks (GANs) is making deepfakes more convincing and harder to detect. If foreign governments can successfully manipulate elections—or appear to do so—the foundations of our system of government are almost certain to erode. Only a coordinated legislative, commercial, and scientific effort can harden our elections and preserve our democracy. I believe lawmakers (whether Republican or Democrat), the platforms themselves, and scientists who resist this endeavor will find themselves on the wrong side of history.

Free Speech and Harmful Speech

Another vital dilemma complicating the Hype Machine's role in society is the tension between free speech and harmful speech. On the one hand, free speech is a cornerstone of liberal democracy and a free society. On the other, we obviously want to prevent the livestreaming of mass murders and terrorist attacks on Facebook. How do we inhibit one without choking the other?

The tension between free expression and harm existed long before the Hype Machine. In America, we've wrestled with it since our founding. The First Amendment prohibits Congress from passing laws abridging the freedom of speech, but the Fourteenth Amendment guarantees all citizens equal protection under the law. These ideals are in tension when one person's speech abridges the rights of another. They are in conflict when racist threats silence minorities, when bigotry begets violence, and when sexist language and behavior threaten women in the workplace. The tension between free speech and harmful speech raises the questions: Where do we draw the line? Where does free speech end and freedom from harm begin online?

Free speech absolutism is untenable. We all agree that terrorist attacks and mass murders are not speech. Even the Supreme Court agrees that not all content should be protected by the First Amendment. We regulate child pornography, incitements to violence, libel, and defamation. There are clear cases where speech should be limited to protect the safety, security, and rights of others. But the other end of the spectrum is equally problematic. Blanket censorship makes a free and open society impossible and leads down a slippery slope to repression and authoritarianism. China's surveillance of social media is not the only extreme case.

Prime Minister Narendra Modi's government in India is pursuing sweeping legislation to force social media platforms to remove content it deems libelous, hateful, or false. Singapore has enacted anti-fake-news legislation that forces search engines, social media companies, and messaging apps to keep records of what users view and to take down or label content the government deems false or misleading. Russia has criminalized fake news. Publishers who spread what the Russian government considers "disrespect for society, government, state symbols, the constitution and government institutions" can be fined and jailed. These examples of government speech regulation are antithetical to the principles of liberal democracy. So how should the lines be drawn?

In 2017 the German Network Enforcement Act required social media companies to delete posts that violate German speech laws banning hatred, child pornography, blasphemy, and many other forms of regulated speech. It was the first broad-scale law holding social media companies responsible for content on their platforms. After the law passed, the journalist and writer Virginia Heffernan posted a tweet that claimed, "For anyone beset by Nazi and brownshirt bots: I changed my Twitter address to Germany at the suggestion of a shrewd friend, and they vanished. Germany has stricter hate-speech laws." Snopes determined that claim was "mostly true," because "certain national socialist, white nationalist and Nazi Twitter profiles are 'withheld' when viewed by a Twitter user whose country is set to Germany." When governments regulate speech, trolls are forced back into their caves.

But when social media platforms moderate speech, it appears as if the same thing happens. In 2015, Reddit closed multiple subreddits for violating its antiharassment policies. My colleague Eric Gilbert, Eshwar Chandrasekharan, and their team found that after the ban, Reddit experienced an 80 percent reduction in hate speech by users who had frequented the banned subreddits. And while users of the banned subreddits migrated to other subreddits, "the migrants did not bring hate speech with them to their new communities, nor did the longtime residents [of those communities] pick it up from them. Reddit did not 'spread the infection.'"

Both legislation and content moderation by the platforms seem to work. So how can we incentivize the appropriate actors to act?

Much of the discussion in the United States centers on Section 230 of the Communications Decency Act (CDA). Section 230 establishes broad immunity for social media platforms and other "interactive computer services" from civil prosecution based on what users post. Some advocates incorrectly interpret this law as absolving social media platforms of a responsibility to moderate user-generated content. But to the contrary, the law was established to do the exact opposite. In the early days of the Internet, the courts gave CompuServe, a community-based communication platform, immunity from prosecution precisely because it did *not* moderate the content on its platform. At the same time, the courts found its competitor Prodigy liable for the content-moderation decisions it was making. This created a perverse incentive for platforms to avoid moderating content to escape the liability that accompanied content moderation decisions. Recognizing the need to incentivize platforms to moderate content, Section 230 provided platforms the protections they needed to make tough content-moderation decisions without the fear of civil prosecution.

When we understand this history, it becomes clear how Section 230 helps maintain free speech and the quality of our communication ecosystem. If the platforms were liable for the harm done by any of their 3 billion users across trillions of daily messages, then social media and many other Internet services, including Wikipedia, and the commenting sections of many newspapers would likely become unworkable overnight. In this sense, Section 230 makes social media platforms, commenting on online newspapers, and even Wikipedia possible.

Today perspectives on Section 230 range from a view that the platforms moderate too much by showing bias against conservative voices, to a view that the platforms moderate too little in the face of fake news, propaganda, and false political advertising. However, the debate about where the line should be drawn obscures a more important question: who should draw the line in the first place?

To address a perceived bias against conservative voices on social media, Republican Josh Hawley of Missouri has proposed a bill in the U.S. Senate that would require the Federal Trade Commission, a five-person commission of presidential appointees, to certify the political neutrality of a platform before it received Section 230 protections under the CDA. Such a measure would impose government oversight over social media moderation by requiring platforms to appease the speech requirements of the commission to avoid the civil litigation that Section 230 shields them from. If the Congress does not act to reform Section 230 to protect conservative voices, President Trump has signaled he will impose an executive order to have the Federal Communications Commission clarify when Section 230 applies in an attempt to police social media moderation and curb this perceived anticonservative bias. These approaches would directly insert the executive branch and associated commissions into the regulation of speech online.

An alternative approach would impose discrete limits on Section 230 with case-by-case congressional legislation as implemented, for example, by the Fight Online Sex Trafficking Act and the Stop Enabling Sex Traffickers Act, or Fosta-Sesta, which removes 230 protections for services that "promote and facilitate prostitution." While the appropriateness of a specific limitation can be debated (Fosta-Sesta was controversial as some sex workers said it made their lives more, not less, dangerous), that's the point of a legislative approach—it's deliberative.

A perfect example of the need for deliberation is the regulation of political speech on social media. The use of targeted social media ads during Russia's interference in the 2016 U.S. presidential election, and the specter of false political advertising so keenly highlighted by Alexandria Ocasio-Cortez (AOC) in her questioning of Mark Zuckerberg before the U.S. Congress, highlight the potential for unregulated political speech to disrupt free and fair elections. In response to Russian manipulation, Sens. Mark Warner, Amy Klobuchar, and John McCain introduced the Honest Ads Act, which would require social media platforms to disclose who buys political ads, how much they spend, and how they are targeted, as well as to make "reasonable efforts" to ensure ads are not purchased by foreign actors. There have also been calls to force social media platforms to fact-check political ads to maintain truth during elections and issue-specific campaigns. Facebook has refused to fact-check political advertising, while Twitter banned political ads altogether.

Free speech advocates suggest, however, that laws such as the Honest Ads Act would unduly burden political speech. In fact, when Maryland and Washington implemented similar restrictions, Google stopped political advertising in those states altogether, and Facebook stopped taking political ads in Washington. A district court has already ruled the Maryland law unconstitutional on First Amendment grounds. If the burden of policing political speech makes social media platforms eliminate paid political speech altogether to avoid liability, it could quell speech beyond acceptable limits. The point of AOC's questioning of Mark Zuckerberg, however, was to suggest that the platforms self-regulate. If Facebook were to fact-check ads and limit foreign political advertising on its own, there might be less need for regulation. But this simply shifts the burden of speech regulation to the platforms—a shift Zuckerberg has been fighting tooth and nail to avoid.

The key question that these debates raise is not which speech should be regulated, though that is obviously important. It is, rather, *who* should decide which speech is legitimate and which speech should be curtailed. That brings me back to the point of this discussion: more important than deciding which speech to allow and which speech to curtail is deciding how these lines should be drawn and who should draw them. Should the platforms decide the limits of free speech? A five-person commission of presidential appointees? An executive order? The legislatures?

When we think about how to balance free speech and harmful speech on the Hype Machine, we should consider the process *before* the outcome. Limiting free speech raises important ethical and constitutional questions. The case-by-case nature of speech decisions and the fact that society's norms and circumstances will likely change as technology changes suggest the importance of a deliberative process that defaults to the broad protection of free speech and leaves to the courts the task of defining free speech and to the legislatures the task of circumscribing protections from civil litigation over harmful speech. Where limits to speech make sense due to the egregious nature of its potential harm in specific circumstances, the process for deciding those limits should be deliberative and representative, rather than swiftly enacted by a select few. Deliberative processes make change deliberate, as it should be for limitations imposed on free speech.

A National Commission on Technology and Democracy

In researching this book, I watched hours of congressional testimony by tech executives like Mark Zuckerberg, Jack Dorsey, Sundar Pichai, and Susan Wojcicki. I watched testimony on privacy, antitrust, election manipulation, data protection, algorithmic bias, and the role of social media in vaccine hesitancy, free speech, political bias, filter bubbles, and fake news. I got one overwhelming feeling from watching congressmen and -women question tech executives: we need more experts leading the way. Charting our technological future will be complex, technical, and nuanced. Our approach to free speech will affect data protection. Privacy legislation will affect election integrity. Antitrust policy will affect privacy and democracy.

We need a diverse set of experts to lead us out of the social media morass we find ourselves in. We need a bipartisan National Commission on Technology and Democracy, staffed with scientists, industry representatives, and policy makers who understand the issues and how they interrelate. National commissions have, at times, served a valuable role in navigating complicated crises. The idea is not new. In fact, others have proposed it for this very crisis. Now is the time to empower and bring the most meaningful and relevant expertise to bear on building a healthier social ecosystem.

Building a Healthier Social Ecosystem

So how can we build a healthier social ecosystem? That's the key question I've raised throughout this book. The answer brings us back to the Hype Loop—the feedback loop of machine intelligence and human agency. Focusing on just one side of the loop is only half the story. Some see design and engineering as the key drivers of our digital future. But the machine's design is nothing without human choices. And while others believe our choices got us into this mess, they underestimate the power of technology to structure our world. To succeed, we'll need to address both, as well as the social, economic, and regulatory environments in which our design choices and use of social media take place.

Network effects tip social media toward concentration. Concentration stifles choice. And a lack of choice allows platforms to pursue purely financial goals. When consumers have no alternatives, business models focus on delivering lifetime value to the platforms. It's only when platforms have to *compete* for our business and our attention that they will focus on the value they deliver to us. By encouraging competition, we have a shot at shifting the economic incentives that guide the design of the Hype Machine from a focus on the value that platforms *extract from* consumers to a focus on the value they should *deliver to* consumers. The best way to encourage social media competition is to enforce interoperability, data and social graph portability, and an ability for consumers to seamlessly move from one service to another.

But all this only sets the stage for change. After a restoration of competition, consumers will need to define the values they want the platforms to deliver, and to enforce those values by doing business only with platforms that make good on them. In a competitive market, platforms will be forced to provide us with the most desirable social media experiences—experiences that don't make us anxious, depressed, angry, and regretful but instead make us confident in what we read, teach us something new, or introduce us to people who expand our thinking and add value to our professional and social lives. Take the "like" button, for example. Liking is, in a Pavlovian sense, the most basic expression of our reactions to social content. It tells platforms what we like so they can give us more of it, and so that popularity is flagged for the crowd to consume.

But there are more creative ways to label content that could help us get more out of our social media experiences and potentially inform Facebook, Instagram, and Twitter, in more nuanced ways, how to provide content that is of value to us. What if there was a "truth" button, or a "trust" button, or a "knowledge" button? What if users gained in reputation not through popularity but as being influencers who connected us to the most valuable new ideas and people, or who taught us something new, or who provided us with the most social support, or corrected our mistakes, or saved us from our own bad habits?

What if the Hype Machine's design wasn't geared toward likes that give us a fleeting dopamine rush to induce us to produce more of the most popular content, but instead incentivized us to produce the most valuable, uplifting, motivating, or thought-provoking content? In a competitive market, platforms may be more likely to move from information-poor to information-rich designs, with metadata about the provenance of the content they offer, the veracity of its sources, and the context in which it is produced. Such information could go a long way toward informing our choices of what to believe and share.

This is just one hypothetical example, but it stresses the importance of thinking about what we want to promote in the world. Do we really want a world dominated by popularity? (Such worlds tip toward madness and away from wisdom, as we learned.) Or would we rather promote those who uplift our spirit, enhance our knowledge, and deepen our emotional stability?

The "time well spent" movement is admirable, but design alone cannot achieve its goals. Yes, we need social software designed to support the values we want to promote, but we need to advocate for those values through our own collective behavior as well. The #deletefacebook movement is an expression of that desire. Even without real alternatives, society is pushing back on the Hype Machine's current designs. We need to lean into that feeling and back it up with action. Software code design is only one of the four levers we have at our disposal.

If regulators can create and enforce competition and mitigate market failures, in privacy and speech, through *laws,* the environment will enable realistic choices that can lead us away from the Hype Machine's current design. If designers think carefully about the software *code* that can support the values we espouse rather than the ones we are forced into today, we will have real alternatives to choose from. If we develop and enforce the *norms* that transform human agency into collective action, we will make those choices a reality at a societal level. If all these levers are pulled in unison to create the future we want, it will force the business models that direct the *money* in today's social media economy to change, because the money follows our attention. In this way, we are the architects of our own future. We control the Hype Machine's destiny because it depends on us for its survival.

Social media is not going to be cleaned up with a simple slogan or a three-step action plan. It's a complex system. Improving it will require a coordinated set of approaches. And because it is so new, there's a great deal of uncertainty. One path may seem like the right approach, only to backfire and create the very outcomes we're trying to avoid. But with a coordinated campaign of money, code, norms, and laws, I believe we can successfully adapt the Hype Machine to a brighter future that achieves its thrilling promise while avoiding its perils.

As we attempt to steer social media in the right direction, we'll need to test different approaches, guided by theory and validated by experiment. The social media platforms, the policy makers, and the people will need to work together, drawing on the data and analyses of the scientists who study social media. With the right goals, experimentation, and a little determination we can start to move in a positive direction, creating incremental victories and building something that will promote the best values of human civilization. I, for one, look forward to collaborating with the brilliant, conscientious engineers, executives, policy makers, and scientists who are working on changing the Hype Machine's destiny. Our path to a brighter Social Age starts now.

Acknowledgments

No intellectual endeavor is accomplished alone. We are social thinkers. That's part of the point of this book and one reason the Hype Machine is so singularly important to humankind. We are influenced, taught, improved, and pushed further by the input of those around us, intellectually, emotionally, and spiritually. This is certainly true for me. I work in teams in everything I do. And this book was made possible by the contributions of so many. I'd like to thank some of them here. While this list is long, it's far from comprehensive. I'm so appreciative to so many for so much.

First and foremost, thank you to my parents, for every conversation, every opportunity, and every hug. You are my two best friends, and you are responsible for who I am today (sorry). I sincerely appreciate everything you do and have done for me and for instilling in me the principles that guide me every day. I love you. Thank you, Kaya, for being my inspiration and the most important thing in my life. Everything I do, I do for you. I feel blessed to be your father and I cannot wait to watch you grow into yourself. It's an honor to learn from you, to think with you, and to laugh like silly kids with you. Thank you also to Meissa for helping me raise the best kid on earth. Thank you to Miles Daniel and Paul Falzone for the lifetime of trusted brotherhood. Your spiritual and intellectual guidance has been essential, calming, and enlightening.

Thank you to Erik Brynjolfsson, who helped me understand what it means to dissect a puzzle until it reveals its essence. You taught me the art of intellectual prioritization, how to find the core and to not let the rest clutter it up. You also taught me about our responsibility to knowledge. I am immensely grateful. To Peter Weill and Marshall Van Alstyne, thank you both for shaping my thought process, for the emphasis on precision and communication and how useless one is without the other.

This book was the result of twenty years of research. Some have been my co-conspirators in science. Others contributed directly to the words in this text. Some did both. Let me start with those who directly shaped this manuscript and helped make sure I didn't make any egregious errors along the way. Duncan Watts: I have so much respect for you and your approach to ideas. You've taught me so much and there is no one I'd rather disagree with, though our disagreements are rare. Thank you specifically for keeping my arguments about the wisdom of crowds and collective intelligence rigorous and compelling. Thank you to Dean Eckles and Brendan Nyhan for helping me think about the rise of falsity and to Dean for thinking with me about causal inference and helping me guide the Social Analytics Lab at MIT. Thank you to Emily Falk for being my Sherpa through the neuroscience of social media and for making sure I understood it before I wrote about it. Thank you to Abdullah Almaatouq for making sure my arguments about the wisdom of crowds were current, cogent, and consistent with every aspect of the theory. Thank you to Adam Grant for making time to read the book and providing the most insightful comments, not just about the text, but about the broader art of communicating with books like this one.

The Hype Machine was checked and rechecked by so many. I'm glad some of your oversight rubbed off on me. Thank you to Bronwyn Fryer for early conversations. Thank you to Roger Scholl and Kevin Doughten for masterful editing. The two of you not only helped make this manuscript great, you make me a better writer. You are both so smart. Thank you to Joanna Kosmides Edwards for combining your artistic genius with your intense precision in creating all of the illustrations for the book. Your talent is unparalleled and I'm honored to work with you.

Thank you to all of the students and postdoctoral fellows who I have had the privilege of working with over the years. I tried my best to communicate our science as accurately and effectively as possible. This book is yours as much as it is mine, because everything in it is based on research we did together over the last twenty years and that we will hopefully do for the next twenty and beyond. Thank you to Sean Taylor, Lev Muchnik, and Dylan Walker, who formed the core team in the early years and who are repeatedly mentioned throughout this book. All three of you are brilliant and helped me learn as we learned. Thank you to Paramveer Dhillon and Christos Nicolaides, and to Naghmeh Momeni, Lynn Wu, Shan Huang, Michael Zhao, Jeremy Yang, Dave

Holtz, Madhav Kumar, Cathy Cao, Dan Rock, Guillaume Saint-Jacques, and Soroush Vosoughi for getting into the trenches with me and digging deep to make sure all of it was rigorous and meaningful every step of the way. I know you are all going to shine so brightly in the years to come. I can't wait to watch it happen with a big smile on my face.

Thank you to Tom Malone, Wanda Olikowski, and Ezra Zuckerman for teaching me how to do it, then having faith enough in me to welcome me back to do it some more, and to Dave Schmittlein for your continued faith in me. Thank you to Foster Provost and Vasant Dhar for invaluable friendship, intellectual mentorship, personal guidance, and support and the laughter that makes it all worthwhile. Thank you to Arun Sundararajan, Anindya Ghose, Natalia Levina, Panos Ipeirotis, and Roy Radner, among others, for being the best colleagues a young assistant professor could have had, and to John Horton, Catherine Tucker, Drazen Prelec, Juanjuan Zhang, Duncan Simester, Dave Rand, Birger Wernerfelt, John Little, and Glen Urban for being the best colleagues an old hand could have. Thank you to Ron Burt, Matthew Jackson, Jon Kleinberg, Sanjeev Goyal, Michael Kearns, Bin Yu, Nicholas Christakis, László Barabási, David Lazer, Alex Vespignani, Ray Reagans, Noshir Contractor, and Brian Uzzi for your mentorship and friendship throughout my career. Thank you to Sandy Pentland and Deb Roy for tremendous collaborations. It's an honor to work with you. Thank you to Claudia Perlich, Hillary Mason, Tina Eliassi-Rad, and Branden Fitelson for meaningful interactions that sparked many ideas.

Thank you to everyone at CISR, including Jeanne Ross, Chris Foglia, Stephanie Warner, Nils Fonstad, George Westerman, and many more, who nurtured me as I grew. Thank you to everyone at the MIT Initiative on the Digital Economy, who supported me when I was a student, and who now have to put up with me as the initiative's director. Thank you to David Verrill for all that you do and have done. Thank you to Christie Ko, Susan Young, Shannon Farrelly, Tammy Buzzell, Paula Klein, Devin Cook, Jovi Koene, Carrie Reynolds, and Joanne Batziotegos for keeping us moving in the right direction in such a professional and polished way. Thank you to the IDE's exceptionally creative and insightful co-director Andy McAfee. It's a real pleasure to flow with you. I'm looking forward to building what's next.

There are so many in industry who have taught me so much. Thank you to Teddy Milos for keeping Paul and me in line. Thank you to Alex Collmer, Jason Donnell, Joline McGoldrick, James Kupernik, Tom Coburn, Jonathan Lacoste, Yael Avidan, Alex Chang, Matt Sunbulli, Ankur Jain, Gustav Praekelt, Leetha Fiderman, Moran Cerf, Andrew Zolli, Matt Mason, and Matthew Williams for your friendship and insight.

Thank you to Rafe Sagalyn for your expert stewardship of this idea. You are truly a master of your craft. Last but not least, thank you to Black Brick Coffee in Williamsburg, Brooklyn, where most of this book was written, for keeping me caffeinated during the long days and to Maison Premiere next door for feeding me immediately afterward.

For those of you who I will regret not mentioning, please know that I truly appreciate you and that Kevin won't let me write another word.

Notes

Preface: Social Media's Time of Reckoning

x **Demand for social media skyrocketed:** Mike Isaac and Sheera Frenkel, "Facebook Is 'Just Trying to Keep the Lights On' as Traffic Soars in Pandemic," *New York Times,* March 24, 2020.

x **new downloads of Netflix jumped:** Daisuke Wakabayashi, Jack Nicas, Steve Lohr, and Mike Isaac, "Big Tech Could Emerge from Coronavirus Crisis Stronger Than Ever," *New York Times,* March 23, 2020.

xi **Slack CEO Stewart Butterfield tweeted:** Stewart Butterfield, tweet, March 25, 2020, https://twitter.com/stewart/status/1243000497566441472.

xi **Describing their attempts to cope with the surge:** Alex Schultz and Jay Parikh, "Keeping Our Services Stable and Reliable During the COVID-19 Outbreak," Facebook About blog, March 24, 2020, https://about.fb.com/news/2020/03/keeping-our-apps-stable-during-covid-19/.

xi **Mark Zuckerberg was blunter:** Isaac and Frenkel, "Facebook Is 'Just Trying to Keep the Lights On.'"

xi **Facebook used aggregate anonymous mobility data:** Tony Romm, Elizabeth Dwoskin, and Craig Timberg, "U.S. Government, Tech Industry Discussing Ways to Use Smartphone Location Data to Combat Coronavirus," *Washington Post,* March 17, 2020; Issie Lapowsky, "Facebook Data Can Help Measure Social Distancing in California," *Protocol,* March 17, 2020.

xii **Our analysis suggested that the social communication happening over Facebook:** David Holtz et al., "Interdependence and the Cost of Uncoordinated Responses to COVID-19," *Proceedings of the National Academy of Sciences (PNAS),* August 2020, https://www.pnas.org/content/117/33/19837.

xii **People's distancing behaviors in response to lockdowns in one state:** Michael Zhao, David Holtz, and Sinan Aral, "Interdependent Program Evaluation: Geographic and Social Spillovers in COVID-19 Closures and Reopenings in the U.S.," MIT Initiative on the Digital Economy Working Paper, 2021.

xii **We immediately called publicly:** Sinan Aral, "If States Don't Coordinate Lockdown Procedures Immediately, Our Future Is Grim," *Los Angeles Times,* August 9, 2020, https://www.latimes.com/opinion/story/2020-08-09/coronavirus-spread-patterns-social-influence.

xii **We also collaborated with Facebook and the World Health Organization (WHO) to create:** Avinash Collis et al., "Global Survey on COVID-19 Beliefs, Behaviors, and Norms," MIT Sloan School of Management, Technical Report, 2020, https://covidsurvey.mit.edu/covid_survey_files/COVID_BBN_survey_report.pdf.

xiii **As of this printing:** "COVID-19 Beliefs, Behaviors & Norms Survey," MIT, https://covidsurvey.mit.edu/.

xiii **In one experiment, we found:** Alex Moehring et al., "Surfacing Norms to Increase Vaccine Acceptance," Proceedings of the National Academy of Sciences, MIT Initiative on the Digital Economy, Working Paper, 2020, https://psyarxiv.com/srv6t/.

xiii **When we released the study:** Sinan Aral and Dean Eckles, "Why Public Health Messaging Should Emphasize Vaccine Acceptance, Not Hesitancy," *Los Angeles Times,* February 23, 2021, https://www.latimes.com/opinion/story/2021-02-23/vaccine-hesitancy-public-health-message.

xiv **COVIDConnect had become the official engine of the global WHO WhatsApp channel:** Antony Sguazzin, "WhatsApp Service in S. Africa Goes Global in WHO Virus Fight," Bloomberg, March 25, 2020.

xiv **Facebook even set up a $100 million small-business relief fund:** Thomas Kouloupoulos, "Facebook Is Giving Out $100 Million in Small-Business Grants. Here's What to Know—and What the Rest of Big Tech Should Learn," Inc.com, March 19, 2020.

xiv **In October 2020, a plot to kidnap and kill:** Charlie Warzel, "Facebook and the Group That Planned to Kidnap Gretchen Whitmer," *New York Times,* October 8, 2020, https://www.nytimes.com/2020/10/08/opinion/facebook-gretchen-whitmer.html.

xiv **In January 2021, misinformation spreading over social media legitimized, mobilized, and organized:** Sophie Bushwick, "What the Capitol Riot Data Download Shows about Social Media Vulnerabilities," *Scientific American,* January 27, 2021, https://www.scientificamerican.com/article/what-the-capitol-riot-data-download-shows-about-social-media-vulnerabilities/.

xv **Sacha Baron Cohen called social media:** Sacha Baron Cohen, "Read Sacha Baron Cohen's Scathing Attack on Facebook in Full: 'Greatest Propaganda Machine in History,'" *Guardian,* November 22, 2019.

xv **The study Baron Cohen was referring to was one I published:** Soroush Vosoughi, Deb Roy, and Sinan Aral, "The Spread of True and False News Online," *Science* 359, no. 6380 (2018): 1146–51.

xv **cauldron of misinformation:** Zeke Miller and Colleen Long, "US Officials: Foreign Disinformation Is Stoking Virus Fears," *US News,* March 16, 2020; Brooke Singman and Gillian Turner, "Foreign Disinformation Campaign on Fake National Quarantine Trying to Cause Panic, Trump Admin. Officials Say," Fox News, March 16, 2020.

xv **Google, Apple, and MIT developed Bluetooth-based contact tracing systems:** Mark Gurman, "Apple, Google Bring Covid-19 Contact-Tracing to 3 Billion People," Bloomberg, April 10, 2020; Kylie Foy, "Bluetooth Signals from Your Smartphone Could Automate Covid-19 Contact Tracing While Preserving Privacy," MIT News, April 8, 2020, http://news.mit.edu/2020/bluetooth-covid-19-contact-tracing-0409.

Chapter I: The New Social Age

5 **"marked the first time":** Madeleine Albright, former U.S. Secretary of State, testimony at hearing before the U.S. Senate Armed Services Committee, January 29, 2015, https://www.armed-services.senate.gov/imo/media/doc/Albright_01-29-15.pdf.

6 **longitudinal study of the spread of fake news:** Soroush Vosoughi, Deb Roy, and Sinan Aral, "The Spread of True and False News Online," *Science* 359, no. 6380 (2018): 1146–51.

8 **the Q&A took place in a moderately sized room:** You can watch the Town Hall here: https://www.facebook.com/qawithmark/videos/929895810401528/.

9 **that of several investigative journalists:** Adrian Chen, "The Agency," *New York Times Magazine,* June 7, 2005.

9 **Russia's Internet Research Agency:** *United States of America v. Internet Research Agency LLC,* 18 U.S.C. §§ 2, 371, 1349, 1028A, https://www.justice.gov/file/1035477/download.

10 **"vowing that Jews in Odessa":** "Analysis of Russia's Information Campaign Against Ukraine," *NATO StratCom Centre of Excellence Report,* https://www.act.nato.int/images/stories/events/2015/sfpdpe/sfpdpe15_rr03.pdf.

10 **"we all know well who created":** Sergey Lavrov, Russian foreign minister, speech during the high-level segment of the twenty-fifth session of the UN Human Rights Council, Geneva, March 3, 2014, https://www.mid.ru/en/web/guest/vistupleniya_ministra/-/asset_publisher/MCZ7HQuMdqBY/content/id/72642.

11 **77 percent of Crimeans report Russian:** State Statistics Committee of Ukraine, 2001 Census, http://2001.ukrcensus.gov.ua/eng/results/. A more recent Crimean census, conducted by Russia in 2014 after the annexation, is disputed.

21 **Cambridge Analytica controversy:** Carole Cadwalladr, " 'I Made Steve Bannon's Psychological Warfare Tool': Meet the Data War Whistleblower," *Guardian,* March 18, 2018.

21 **Mark Zuckerberg to testify:** Mark Zuckerberg, chairman and chief executive officer of Facebook, testimony at hearing before the U.S. Senate Committee on the Judiciary and Committee on Commerce, Science, and Transportation, April 10, 2018, https://en.wikisource.org/wiki/Zuckerberg_Senate_Transcript_2018; Mark Zuckerberg, testimony at hearing before the U.S. House of Representatives Committee on Energy and Commerce, April 11, 2018, https://docs.house.gov/meetings/IF/IF00/20180411/108090/HHRG-115-IF00-Transcript-20180411.pdf; Mark Zuckerberg, testimony at meeting of the Conference of Presidents of the European Parliament, Brussels, May 22, 2018, https://www.c-span.org/video/?446000-1/facebook-ceo-mark-zuckerberg-testifies-eu-lawmakers.

21 **a public tirade:** Marc Pritchard, chief brand officer of Procter & Gamble, "Better Advertising Enabled by Media Transparency," speech at the Internet Advertising Bureau's Annual Leadership Meeting, January 29, 2017, https://www.youtube.com/watch?v=NEUCOsphoI0.

21 **cut P&G's digital advertising budget by $200 million:** Jack Neff, "Procter &

Gamble's Best Sales in a Decade Come Despite Drop in Ad Spending," *AdAge,* July 30, 2019.

21 **Unilever followed suit:** Gurjit Degun, "Unilever and Sky Adspend Dropped 30% in 2018," *Campaign US,* February 12, 2019, https://www.campaignlive .com/article/unilever-sky-adspend-dropped-30-2018/1525590.

21 **P&G reported a 7.5 percent *increase*:** Ellen Hammett, "P&G Puts Focus on Reach: It's a More Important Measure Than Spend," *MarketingWeek,* June 17, 2019; Neff, "Procter & Gamble's Best Sales"; Dianna Christe, "P&G's Sales Jump as Ad Spending Shrinks, Data-Driven Marketing Ramps Up," *Marketing Dive,* July 31, 2019.

21 **Unilever posted a 3.8 percent gain in organic sales in the same period:** "Third Quarter Results Show Improved Growth Across All Our Divisions," Unilever press release, October 10, 2018, https://www.unilever.com/news/ press-releases/2018/third-quarter-results-show-improved-growth-across -all-our-divisions.html.

Chapter 2: The End of Reality

24 **"Breaking: Two Explosions":** Tero Karppi and Kate Crawford, "Social Media, Financial Algorithms and the Hack Crash," *Theory, Culture and Society* 33, no. 1 (2016): 73–92.

24 **there have only ever been four breaches:** "White House Security Breaches Fast Facts," CNN, updated March 25, 2020, https://www.cnn.com/2017/ 06/14/us/white-house-security-breaches-fast-facts/index.html.

25 **the Dow fell instantly:** Karppi and Crawford, "Social Media, Financial Algorithms," 73–92.

25 **rushed to stockpile gas:** Patti Domm, "Gasoline Prices at Pump Spike on Fears of Spot Shortages, as Biggest U.S. Refinery Shuts," CNBC, August 31, 2017.

26 **manic stockpiling, driven by social media:** David Schechter and Marjorie Owens, "Railroad Commissioner: There's No Fuel Crisis in Texas," WFAA, Dallas, August 31, 2017, https://www.wfaa.com/article/news/local/texas -news/railroad-commissioner-theres-no-fuel-crisis-in-texas/287-469658632.

26 **a list of "hot 50" rumors:** Sinan Aral, "Truth, Disrupted," *Harvard Business Review,* July 2018.

27 **Lidingo was a fake news factory:** *Securities and Exchange Commission v. Lidingo Holdings, LLC, Kamilla Bjorlin, Andrew Hodge, Brian Nichols, and Vincent Cassano,* Case no. 17-2540, filed April 10, 2017, U.S. District Court, Southern District of New York.

27 **"social media relations, marketing":** "Order Instituting Cease-and-Desist Proceedings . . . ," *In the Matter of Michael A. McCarthy, The Dreamteam Group, LLC, Mission Investor Relations, LLC, and Qualitystocks, LLC,* Administrative Proceeding File no. 3-17917, April 10, 2017, https://www.sec .gov/litigation/admin/2017/33-10343.pdf.

27 **"leveraged its extensive online social network to maximize exposure":** Ibid.

28 **study of the relationship between fake news and financial markets:** Shimon Kogan, Tobias J. Moskowitz, and Marina Niessner, "Fake News: Evidence from Financial Markets," April 22, 2019, https://ssrn.com/abstract=3237763.

29 **Fake articles had, on average, nearly three times the impact:** These results suggest that fake news moves markets, especially for smaller firms with a greater fraction of retail investors. But they should also be taken with a grain of salt. This is not a randomized experiment. Although the timing of price movements is suggestive, it is not clear from this data that prices are moved only by fake news. Kogan et al., "Fake News," analyzed a selected sample of fake news articles identified by the SEC as having the express purpose of manipulating stock prices. In the larger, noisier sample of fake news articles identified by their linguistic style (rather than those verified by the SEC), the researchers found significant effects on trading volume for small firms with more retail ownership but no detectable effects on price volatility. This could be because the SEC data is a selected sample or because the linguistic method for identifying fake news is unreliable. A contemporaneous study of fake financial news on Seeking Alpha by my friend and collaborator Jeffrey Hu and his colleagues Jonathan Clarke, Hailiang Chen, and Ding Du, corroborated that fake news attracts more clicks than real news but found no effect of fake news on trading volume or price volatility compared to a matched sample of real news. In contrast to Kogan et al., they concluded that "the stock market appears to price fake news correctly." Jonathan Clarke et al., "Fake News, Investor Attention, and Market Reaction," Georgia Tech Scheller College of Business Research Paper no. 18–29 (2019), https://ssrn.com/abstract=3213024.

30 **When the Mueller report was released in April 2019:** Special Counsel Robert S. Mueller III, *Report on the Investigation into Russian Interference in the 2016 Presidential Election,* Submitted Pursuant to 28 C.F.R. § 600.8(c), Washington, D.C., March 2019, https://www.justice.gov/storage/report.pdf.

30 **one led by New Knowledge:** Renee DiResta et al., *The Tactics and Tropes of the Internet Research Agency,* Investigation of Russian Interference prepared for the U.S. Senate Select Committee on Intelligence (New Knowledge, 2019), https://int.nyt.com/data/documenthelper/533-read-report-internet-research-agency/7871ea6d5b7bedafbf19/optimized/full.pdf.

30 **John Kelly, founder and CEO of Graphika:** Philip N. Howard et al., *The IRA, Social Media and Political Polarization in the United States, 2012–2018,* Investigation of Russian Interference prepared for the U.S. Senate Select Committee on Intelligence (Graphika, 2019), https://int.nyt.com/data/documenthelper/534-oxford-russia-internet-research-agency/c6588b4a7b940c551c38/optimized/full.pdf.

31 *source* **accounts, which posted fake content:** Gillian Cleary, "Twitterbots: Anatomy of a Propaganda Campaign," *Symantec Threat Intelligence Blog,* June 5, 2019, https://symantec-blogs.broadcom.com/blogs/threat-intelligence/twitterbots-propaganda-disinformation.

32 **were shared more and received:** Craig Silverman, "This Analysis Shows

How Viral Fake Election News Stories Outperformed Real News on Facebook," *BuzzFeed*, November 16, 2016.

32 **42 percent of visits to fake news websites:** Hunt Allcott and Matthew Gentzkow, "Social Media and Fake News in the 2016 Election," *Journal of Economic Perspectives* 31, no. 2 (2017): 211–36.

32 **while 44 percent of Americans visited fake news websites in the weeks before the election:** Andrew Guess, Brendan Nyhan, and Jason Reifler, "Selective Exposure to Misinformation: Evidence from the Consumption of Fake News During the 2016 US Presidential Campaign," *European Research Council* (2018), 9.

32 **Lazer and his colleagues found:** Nir Grinberg et al., "Fake News on Twitter During the 2016 US Presidential Election," *Science* 363, no. 6425 (2019): 374–78.

32 **"one or several" fake news stories:** Allcott and Gentzkow, "Social Media and Fake News."

33 **110 million voting-age Americans visited:** Calculated as 44 percent of approximately 250 million voting-age Americans in 2016. "Estimates of the Voting Age Population for 2016," *Federal Register*, n.d., https://www.federal register.gov/documents/2017/01/30/2017-01890/estimates-of-the-voting -age-population-for-2016.

33 **10 percent of respondents shared fake news:** Guess, Nyhan, and Reifler, "Selective Exposure to Misinformation."

33 **"superspreaders" and "superconsumers":** Chengsheng Shao et al., "The Spread of Low-Credibility Content by Social Bots," *Nature Communications* 9, no. 1 (2018): 4787; Emilio Ferrara et al., "The Rise of Social Bots," *Communications of the ACM* 59, no. 7 (2016): 96–104.

34 **"the proportion of misinformation":** Philip N. Howard et al., "Social Media, News and Political Information During the US Election: Was Polarizing Content Concentrated in Swing States?," *arXiv:1802.03573* (2018).

34 **12 of 16 swing states were above the average:** While Iowa, Wisconsin, Minnesota, and Maine were the swing states below the national average concentration of polarizing political content from Russian, WikiLeaks, and junk news sources, Colorado, Ohio, Michigan, Georgia, New Hampshire, Pennsylvania, North Carolina, Virginia, Florida, Nevada, Missouri, and Arizona were all above it. States were classified as swing states in November 2016 by the National Constitution Center.

34 **effectively decided the election:** Ed Kilgore, "The Final, Final, Final Results for the Presidential Popular Vote Are In," *New York*, December 20, 2016.

35 **"overt suppression narratives":** DiResta et al., *The Tactics and Tropes of the Internet Research Agency*.

35 **Konstantin Kilimnik:** Jon Swaine, "Manafort Shared Polling Data on 2016 Election with Elusive Russian—Mueller," *Guardian*, January 8, 2019; Mueller, *Report on the Investigation Into Russian Interference in the 2016 Presidential Election*.

36 **a 61-million-person experiment:** Robert M. Bond et al., "A 61-Million-Person Experiment in Social Influence and Political Mobilization," *Nature* 489, no. 7415 (2012): 295.

36 **a follow-up experiment by Facebook:** Jason J. Jones et al., "Social Influence and Political Mobilization: Further Evidence from a Randomized Experiment in the 2012 US Presidential Election," *PloS One* 12, no. 4 (2017): e0173851.

36 **the substantial research on the effects:** At the time this book went to print, there were also two unpublished studies of social media's effects on vote choice. The first relies on postelection surveys, rather than on verified voting data, which are prone to recall error and self-reporting bias. Richard Gunther, Paul A. Beck, and Erik C. Nisbet, "Fake News Did Have a Significant Impact on the Vote in the 2016 Election: Original Full-Length Version with Methodological Appendix" (Ohio State University, 2018), https://cpb-us-w2.wpmucdn.com/u.osu.edu/dist/d/12059/files/2015/03/Fake-News-Piece-for-The-Conversation-with-methodological-appendix-11d0ni9.pdf. The second study used validated data on voter turnout and polling of vote choice, and exploited temporal variation and conditions on past turnout and vote choice, but also excluded undecideds. Guess, Nyhan, and Reifler, "Selective Exposure to Misinformation." Both studies lack any good-as-random variation or other formal method of causal inference.

36 **Chris Bail and his team found:** Christopher A. Bail, Brian Guay, Emily Maloney, Aidan Combs, D. Sunshine Hillygus, Friedolin Merhout, Deen Freelon, and Alexander Volfovsky, "Assessing the Russian Internet Research Agency's Impact on the Political Attitudes and Behaviors of American Twitter Users in Late 2017," *Proceedings of the National Academy of Sciences* 117, no. 1 (2020): 243–50.

37 **"the best estimate of the size of persuasive":** Joshua L. Kalla and David E. Broockman, "The Minimal Persuasive Effects of Campaign Contact in General Elections: Evidence from 49 Field Experiments," *American Political Science Review* 112, no. 1 (2018): 148–66.

37 **informing voters in favor of abortion rights:** Todd Rogers and David Nickerson, "Can Inaccurate Beliefs About Incumbents Be Changed? And Can Reframing Change Votes?," Harvard Kennedy School, Working Paper no. RWP13-018, 2013, http://scholar.harvard.edu/files/todd_rogers/files/can_inaccurate_beliefs_about_incumbents_be_changed_ssrn.pdf.

37 **a randomized experiment by Katherine Haenschen and Jay Jennings:** Katherine Haenschen and Jay Jennings, "Mobilizing Millennial Voters with Targeted Internet Advertisements: A Field Experiment," *Political Communication* 36, no. 3 (2019): 357–75.

37 **Research by Andrew Guess:** Andrew M. Guess, Dominique Lockett, Benjamin Lyons, Jacob M. Montgomery, Brendan Nyhan, and Jason Reifler, " 'Fake News' May Have Limited Effects Beyond Increasing Beliefs in False Claims," *Harvard Kennedy School Misinformation Review* 1, no. 1 (2020).

38 **direct mailings, combined with social pressure:** Donald P. Green, Mary C.

McGrath, and Peter M. Aronow, "Field Experiments and the Study of Voter Turnout," *Journal of Elections, Public Opinion and Parties* 23, no. 1 (2013): 27–48.

38 **the effect of text messages:** Allison Dale and Aaron Strauss, "Don't Forget to Vote: Text Message Reminders as a Mobilization Tool," *American Journal of Political Science* 53, no. 4 (2009): 787–804.

38 **personalized emails have a similar impact:** N. Malhotra, M. R. Michelson, and A. A. Valenzuela, "Emails from Official Sources Can Increase Turnout," *Quarterly Journal of Political Science* 7 (2012): 321–32; T. C. Davenport, "Unsubscribe: The Effects of Peer-to-Peer Email on Voter Turnout—Results from a Field Experiment in the June 6, 2006, California Primary Election," unpublished manuscript (Yale University, 2012).

38 **We should all have been alarmed:** Dan Mangan, "Read Robert Mueller's Opening Statement: Russian Interference Among 'Most Serious' Challenges to American Democracy," CNBC, July 24, 2019.

38 **FBI director Christopher Wray is warning:** Todd Ruger, "FBI Director Wants to 'Up Our Game' on Election Interference," *Roll Call,* May 7, 2019.

38 **the 2020 election is being targeted:** Adam Goldman, Julian E. Barnes, Maggie Haberman, and Nicholas Fandos, "Lawmakers Are Warned That Russia Is Meddling to Re-elect Trump," *New York Times,* February 20, 2020.

39 **Russian hackers successfully infiltrated:** Nicole Perlroth and Matthew Rosenberg, "Russians Hacked Ukrainian Gas Company at Center of Impeachment," *New York Times,* January 13, 2020.

40 **the 2018 Swedish general election:** Freja Hedman et al., "News and Political Information Consumption in Sweden: Mapping the 2018 Swedish General Election on Twitter," Comprop Data Memo no. 2018.3, September 6, 2018.

40 **the 2018 Brazilian national elections:** Cristina Tardáguila, Fabrício Benevenuto, and Pablo Ortellado, "Fake News Is Poisoning Brazilian Politics. WhatsApp Can Stop It," *New York Times,* October 17, 2018.

40 **Indian elections in 2019:** Samir Patil, "India Has a Public Health Crisis. It's Called Fake News," *New York Times,* April 29, 2019.

40 **In India, where 52 percent of people report getting news from WhatsApp:** Zeenab Aneez et al., *Reuters Institute India Digital News Report* (Oxford University, 2019), https://reutersinstitute.politics.ox.ac.uk/our-research/india -digital-news-report.

40 **"Concealed threats and outrages":** Donald L. Horowitz, *The Deadly Ethnic Riot* (Berkeley: University of California Press, 2001), 74–75.

41 **over 1,100 cases were reported:** "National Update on Measles Cases and Outbreaks—United States, January 1–October 1, 2019," *Morbidity and Mortality Weekly Report,* U.S. Centers for Disease Control and Prevention, October 11, 2019, https://www.cdc.gov/mmwr/volumes/68/wr/pdfs/ mm6840e2-H.pdf.

41 **It typically starts as a:** Peter J. Hotez, "You Are Unvaccinated and Got Sick. These Are Your Odds," *New York Times,* January 9, 2020.

42 **Measles is one of the world's most contagious viruses:** Deborah Balzer interview with Dr. Nipunie Rajapsakse, "Infectious Diseases A–Z: Why the Measles Virus Is So Contagious," Mayo Clinic, April 9, 2019, https://newsnetwork.mayoclinic.org/discussion/infectious-diseases-a-z-why-the-measles-virus-is-so-contagious/.

42 **the R0 of measles is 15:** Fiona M. Guerra, "The Basic Reproduction Number (R0) of Measles: A Systematic Review," *Lancet Infectious Diseases* 17, no. 12 (2017): e420–28; Ed Yong, "The Deceptively Simple Number Sparking Coronavirus Fears," *Atlantic,* January 28, 2020.

42 **develop herd immunity by vaccinating:** Manish Sadarangani, "Herd Immunity: How Does it Work?," Oxford Vaccine Group, Oxford University, April 26, 2016, https://www.ovg.ox.ac.uk/news/herd-immunity-how-does-it-work.

42 **Wakefield had been paid to falsify the evidence:** Gardiner Harris, "Journal Retracts 1998 Paper Linking Autism to Vaccines," *New York Times,* February 2, 2010.

43 **"social media and the amplification":** "Senate Hearing on Vaccines and Public Health," U.S. Senate Committee on Health, Education, Labor and Pensions, March 5, 2019, https://www.c-span.org/video/?458472-1/physicians-advocates-warn-senate-committee-vaccine-hesitancy-implications.

43 **Stop Mandatory Vaccination:** Julia Arciga, "Anti-vaxxer Larry Cook Has Weaponized Facebook Ads in War Against Science," *Daily Beast,* February 19, 2019.

43 **bought 54 percent of the antivaccine ads:** Amelia M. Jamison, "Vaccine-Related Advertising in the Facebook Ad Archive," *Vaccine* 38, no. 3 (2020): 512–20; Lena Sun, "Majority of Anti-vaccine Ads on Facebook Were Funded by Two Groups," *Washington Post,* November 15, 2019.

43 **More than 150 such posts:** Arciga, "Anti-vaxxer Larry Cook."

44 **"from fact-based medical information":** Julia Carrie Wong, "How Facebook and YouTube Help Spread Anti-vaxxer Propaganda," *Guardian,* February 1, 2019.

44 **"75% of Pinterest posts":** Nat Gyenes and An Xiao Mina, "How Misinfodemics Spread Disease," *Atlantic,* August 30, 2018.

44 **Russian Twitter bots were posting:** David A. Broniatowski et al., "Weaponized Health Communication: Twitter Bots and Russian Trolls Amplify the Vaccine Debate," *American Journal of Public Health* 108, no. 10 (2018): 1378–84.

44 **the top 50 vaccine pages on Facebook:** Alexis Madrigal, "The Small, Small World of Facebook's Anti-vaxxers," *Atlantic,* February 27, 2019.

44 **"the consumption of content about vaccines":** Ana Lucía Schmidt et al., "Polarization of the Vaccination Debate on Facebook," *Vaccine* 36, no. 25 (2018): 3606–12.

45 **decade-long study of the spread of false news online:** Soroush Vosoughi, Deb Roy, and Sinan Aral, "The Spread of True and False News Online," *Science* 359, no. 6380 (2018): 1146–51.

48 **how social bots spread fake news:** Chengsheng Shao et al., "The Spread of

Low-Credibility Content by Social Bots," *Nature Communications* 9, no. 1 (2018): 4787.

49 **Novelty attracts human attention:** Laurent Itti and Pierre Baldi, "Bayesian Surprise Attracts Human Attention," *Vision Research* 49, no. 10 (2009): 1295–306.

49 **It updates our understanding of the world:** Sinan Aral and Marshall Van Alstyne, "The Diversity-Bandwidth Trade-Off," *American Journal of Sociology* 117, no. 1 (2011): 90–171.

49 **"in the know" or who has access to "inside information":** Jonah Berger and K. L. Milkman, "What Makes Online Content Viral?," *Journal of Marketing Research* 49, no. 2 (2012): 192–205.

50 **novelty attracts our scarce attention:** Fang Wu and Bernardo A. Huberman, "Novelty and Collective Attention," *Proceedings of the National Academy of Sciences* 104, no. 45 (2007): 17599–601.

50 **We found that false rumors:** While we found false news to be more novel and that novel information was more likely to be retweeted, we don't know if novelty causes retweeting or if it is the only reason why false news is retweeted more often than the truth.

50 **what types of people were better able to recognize fake news:** Gordon Pennycook and David G. Rand, "Lazy, Not Biased: Susceptibility to Partisan Fake News Is Better Explained by Lack of Reasoning Than by Motivated Reasoning," *Cognition* 188 (2019): 39–50.

51 But **repetition causes belief:** Raymond S. Nickerson, "Confirmation Bias: A Ubiquitous Phenomenon in Many Guises," *Review of General Psychology* 2, no. 2 (1998): 175–220.

51 **"illusory truth effect":** Lynn Hasher, David Goldstein, and Thomas Toppino, "Frequency and the Conference of Referential Validity," *Journal of Verbal Learning and Verbal Behavior* 16, no. 1 (1977): 107–12.

51 **"no evidence of backlash, even under theoretically favorable conditions":** Andrew Guess and Alexander Coppock, "Does Counter-Attitudinal Information Cause Backlash? Results from Three Large Survey Experiments," *British Journal of Political Science* (2018): 1–19.

52 **its unemployed teen population:** Samanth Subramanian, "Inside the Macedonian Fake-News Complex," *Wired*, February 15, 2017.

52 **In 2019 fake news websites:** Global Disinformation Index, *The Quarter Billion Dollar Question: How Is Disinformation Gaming Ad Tech?*, September 2019, https://disinformationindex.org/wp-content/uploads/2019/09/GDI _Ad-tech_Report_Screen_AW16.pdf.

52 **"end of reality":** Franklin Foer, "The Era of Fake Video Begins," *Atlantic*, May 2018.

53 **"complete and total dipshit":** David Mack, "This PSA About Fake News from Barack Obama Is Not What It Appears," *BuzzFeed*, April 17, 2018. Video: "You Won't Believe What Obama Says in This Video!," *BuzzFeed-Video*, April 17, 2018, https://youtu.be/cQ54GDm1eL0.

53 **generative adversarial networks, or GANs:** Cade Metz, "Google's Duel-

ing Neural Networks Spar to Get Smarter, No Humans Required," *Wired,* April 11, 2017.

53 **"the coolest idea in deep learning":** Ibid.

54 **"One can easily imagine":** Daniel Benjamin and Steven Simon, "How Fake News Could Lead to Real War," *Politico,* July 5, 2019.

54 **deepfaked audio attacks against several of its clients:** Hugh Thompson, "Symantec Discusses the Financial Implications of Deepfakes," CNBC, July 18, 2019.

Chapter 3: The Hype Machine

56 **So he asked Facebook for $60,000:** Nick Bilton, "Facebook Graffiti Artist Could Be Worth $500 Million," *New York Times,* February 7, 2012.

56 **an artist-in-residence program:** Cade Metz, "The Amazing Murals Created by Facebook's Artists-in-Residence," *Wired,* November 24, 2014.

63 **Over an eight- to ten-year period, digital:** Andrew Perrin, "Social Networking Usage: 2005–2015," Pew Research Center, October 2015, http://www.pewinternet.org/2015/10/08/2015/Social-Networking-Usage-2005-2015/.

63 **global Facebook network:** Original illustration by Paul Butler; re-creation by Joanna Kosmides Edwards, https://paulbutler.org/2010/visualizing-facebook-friends/.

63 **the social graph:** Many great books by scientists have explored the structure and power of human networks. See Duncan J. Watts, *Six Degrees: The Science of a Connected Age* (New York: W. W. Norton, 2004); Albert-László Barabási, *Linked: The New Science of Networks* (Cambridge, Mass.: Perseus, 2002), esp. 409–10; Nicholas A. Christakis and James H. Fowler, *Connected: The Surprising Power of Our Social Networks and How They Shape Our Lives* (Boston: Little, Brown Spark, 2009); Sanjeev Goyal, *Connections: An Introduction to the Economics of Networks* (Princeton: Princeton University Press, 2012); and Matthew O. Jackson, *The Human Network: How Your Social Position Determines Your Power, Beliefs, and Behaviors* (New York: Pantheon, 2019).

64 **friendship paradox:** Scott L. Feld, "Why Your Friends Have More Friends Than You Do," *American Journal of Sociology* 96, no. 6 (1991): 1464–77.

65 **"forbidden triad":** Mark Granovetter, "The Strength of Weak Ties," *American Journal of Sociology* 78 (1973): 1360–80.

66 **"small worlds":** Duncan J. Watts and Steven H. Strogatz, "Collective Dynamics of 'Small-World' Networks," *Nature* 393, no. 6684 (1998): 440.

67 **six degrees of separation:** J. Travers and Stanley Milgram, "An Experimental Study of the Small World Problem," *Sociometry* 32 (1969); Duncan J. Watts, "Networks, Dynamics, and the Small World Phenomenon," *American Journal of Sociology* 105, no. 2 (1999): 493–527.

67 **Facebook recruited users within:** This "group-based targeting," incidentally, is the same go-to-market strategy advocated by Jeffrey Rohlfs in his seminal paper on network effects published in 1974 and reiterated onstage

by Sean Parker in conversation with Jimmy Fallon, in reference to Facebook's go-to-market strategy, at the NextWork Conference in 2011 (see footnote in Chapter 5).

67 **Individuals with access to scarce, novel:** Ronald Burt, *Structural Holes: The Social Structure of Competition* (Cambridge, Mass.: Harvard University Press, 1992); Ronald Burt, "Structural Holes and Good Ideas," *American Journal of Sociology* 110 (2004): 349–99; A. Hargadon and R. Sutton, "Technology Brokering and Innovation in a Product Development Firm," *Administrative Science Quarterly* 42 (1997): 716–49; R. Reagans and E. Zuckerman, "Networks, Diversity, and Productivity: The Social Capital of Corporate R&D Teams," *Organization Science* 12, no. 4 (2001): 502–17; Sinan Aral and Marshall Van Alstyne, "The Diversity-Bandwidth Trade-Off," *American Journal of Sociology* 117, no. 1 (2011): 90–171.

67 **they're also homophilous, meaning birds of a feather:** Miller McPherson, Lynn Smith-Lovin, and James M. Cook, "Birds of a Feather: Homophily in Social Networks," *Annual Review of Sociology* 27, no. 1 (2001): 415–44.

67 **People tend to make friends:** Gueorgi Kossinets and Duncan J. Watts, "Origins of Homophily in an Evolving Social Network," *American Journal of Sociology* 115, no. 2 (2009): 405–450.

68 **dual drivers of "choice" and "chance" in network evolution:** Sergio Currarini, Matthew O. Jackson, and Paolo Pin, "Identifying the Roles of Race-Based Choice and Chance in High School Friendship Network Formation," *Proceedings of the National Academy of Sciences* 107, no. 11 (2010): 4857–61.

68 **"choice homophily" and "induced homophily":** Kossinets and Watts, "Origins of Homophily."

68 **romantic relationships formed through online algorithms:** Michael J. Rosenfeld, Reuben J. Thomas, and Sonia Hausen, "Disintermediating Your Friends: How Online Dating in the United States Displaces Other Ways of Meeting," *Proceedings of the National Academy of Sciences* 116, no. 36 (2019): 17753–58.

69 **"the entire social network":** Johan Ugander et al., "The Anatomy of the Facebook Social Graph," *arXiv:1111.4503* (2011).

71 **Later studies have confirmed homophily in Facebook:** For a review of that literature and more primary evidence, see Andreas Wimmer and Kevin Lewis, "Beyond and Below Racial Homophily: ERG Models of a Friendship Network Documented on Facebook," *American Journal of Sociology* 116, no. 2 (2010): 583–642.

71 **"still in the range":** Seth A. Myers et al., "Information Network or Social Network? The Structure of the Twitter Follow Graph," in *Proceedings of the 23rd International Conference on World Wide Web* (New York: ACM, 2014), 493–98.

71 **The average path lengths between people:** Data compiled from and compared across Ugander et al., "Anatomy of Facebook Social Graph," and Myers et al., "Information Network or Social Network?"

72 **"AI is a fundamental risk":** "Elon Musk Talks Cars—and Humanity's Fate—with Governors," CNBC, July 17, 2017.

72 **Experts have testified that bots:** Clint Watts, testimony before U.S. Senate Select Committee on Intelligence, March 30, 2017, https://www.intelligence .senate.gov/sites/default/files/documents/os-cwatts-033017.pdf.

72 **rooted in and supported by research:** Wanda J. Orlikowski, "The Duality of Technology: Rethinking the Concept of Technology in Organizations," *Organization Science* 3, no. 3 (1992): 398–427; Anthony Giddens, *The Constitution of Society: Outline of the Theory of Structuration* (Berkeley: University of California Press, 1984).

73 **"a wealth of information creates a poverty of attention":** Herbert A. Simon, "Designing Organizations for an Information-Rich World," in *Computers, Communication, and the Public Interest,* ed. Martin Greenberger (Baltimore: Johns Hopkins University Press, 1971), 40–41.

74 **an artificial intelligence (AI) deep learning algorithm:** "Norman: World's First Psychopath AI," n.d., http://norman-ai.mit.edu/.

75 **Tay, the AI-powered chatbot:** James Vincent, "Twitter Taught Microsoft's AI Chatbot to Be a Racist Asshole in Less Than a Day," *Guardian,* March 24, 2016; Elle Hunt, "Tay, Microsoft's AI Chatbot, Gets a Crash Course in Racism from Twitter," *Guardian,* March 24, 2016.

76 **the same technology in China without any of these problems:** Peter Bright, "Tay, the Neo-Nazi Millennial Chatbot, Gets Autopsied," *Ars Technica,* March 25, 2016, https://arstechnica.com/information-technology/2016/03/ tay-the-neo-nazi-millennial-chatbot-gets-autopsied.

76 **Facebook's machine intelligence executes 200 trillion predictions per day:** Yann LeCun speaking with Bloomberg's Jeremy Kahn at Bloomberg's "Sooner Than You Think" conference in Paris, May 29, 2018, https://www .youtube.com/watch?v=dzQRCZyE4v0.

78 **we spend 100 million hours watching 8 billion Facebook videos:** Jenn Chen, "15 Facebook Stats Every Marketer Should Know for 2019," *Sprout Social* (2019), https://sproutsocial.com/insights/facebook-stats-for-marketers/.

78 **Video accounts for 80 percent of all consumer Internet traffic:** Mary Lister, "37 Staggering Video Marketing Statistics for 2018," *Wordstream Blog,* June 9, 2019, https://www.wordstream.com/blog/ws/2017/03/08/video -marketing-statistics.

79 **Facebook's "visual cortex":** Manohar Paluri, manager of Facebook's Computer Vision Group, speaking at the LDV Capital "Vision Summit" in 2017, https://www.ldv.co/blog/2018/4/4/facebook-is-building-a-visual-cortex-to -better-understand-content-and-people.

80 **"We've pushed computer vision to the next stage":** Joaquin Quiñonero Candela, "Building Scalable Systems to Understand Content," *Facebook Engineering Blog,* February 2, 2017, https://engineering.fb.com/ml-applications/ building-scalable-systems-to-understand-content/.

80 **Facebook filed a patent for making friend suggestions:** Elise Thomas, "A Creepy Facebook Idea Suggests Friends by Sensing Other People's Phones," *Wired UK,* November 4, 2018, https://www.wired.co.uk/article/facebook -phone-tracking-patent.

81 **In 2015 it filed another patent for a process:** Kashmir Hill, " 'People You

May Know': A Controversial Facebook Feature's 10-Year History," *Gizmodo,* August 8, 2018, https://gizmodo.com/people-you-may-know-a-controversial -facebook-features-1827981959.

81 **Facebook and Google now account for 65 percent:** Kurt Wagner, "Digital Advertising in the US Is Finally Bigger Than Print and Television," *Vox Recode,* February 20, 2019, https://www.vox.com/2019/2/20/18232433/ digital-advertising-facebook-google-growth-tv-print-emarketer-2019; "Digital Advertising Stats You Need for 2018," AppNexus White Paper, https:// www.appnexus.com/sites/default/files/whitepapers/guide-2018stats_2.pdf.

82 **92 percent of new friendships on Facebook are friends of friends:** Lars Backstrom, VP of engineering, "People You May Know," slides, presented by Facebook, July 12, 2010.

82 **friend-of-friend suggestions create connections five times:** See Jure Leskovec, "Dynamics of Large Networks," PhD diss., Carnegie Mellon University, School of Computer Science, Machine Learning Department, 2008, particularly the sections on "triangle closing models" and "the locality of edge attachment."

82 **back-of-the-envelope math on the computational complexity:** Backstrom, "People You May Know."

83 **The algorithms are able to hum through the data more efficiently:** PYMK algorithms don't necessarily restrict their suggestions to two-hop connections, but they dramatically favor them.

83 **though some platforms, like Twitter, now allow us to opt out:** Interestingly, Twitter enabled users to opt out of algorithmic curation a few weeks after Jack Dorsey faced pressure in congressional hearings regarding accusations that Twitter was biased when it "shadow banned" or "downranked" almost a million people due to the harmful content they or their followers had posted. Stan Horaczek, "Twitter Will Let You See Your Feed in Chronological Order Again—Here's How and Why," *Popular Science,* September 18, 2019, https://www.popsci.com/twitter-chronological-feed/.

84 **Those engagement probabilities are aggregated into a single relevance score:** Will Oremus, "Who Controls Your Facebook Feed," *Slate,* January 3, 2016.

85 **"time well spent":** Casey Newton, "'Time Well Spent' Is Shaping Up to Be Tech's Next Big Debate," *Verge,* January 17, 2018; Laura Hazard Owen, "Facebook Drastically Changes News Feed to Make It 'Good for People' (and Bad for Most Publishers)," *NiemanLab,* January 11, 2018, https://www .niemanlab.org/2018/01/facebook-drastically-changes-news-feed-to-make -it-good-for-people-and-bad-for-most-publishers/.

85 **"meaningful interactions":** Laura Hazard Owen, "One Year In, Facebook's Big Algorithm Change Has Spurred an Angry, Fox News–Dominated—and Very Engaged!—News Feed," *NiemanLab,* March 15, 2019, https://www .niemanlab.org/2019/03/one-year-in-facebooks-big-algorithm-change-has -spurred-an-angry-fox-news-dominated-and-very-engaged-news-feed/.

87 **"community rules":** J. Nathan Matias, "Preventing Harassment and Increasing Group Participation Through Social Norms in 2,190 Online Sci-

ence Discussions," *Proceedings of the National Academy of Sciences* 116, no. 20 (2019): 9785–89.

87 **So when should we follow the Hype Machine's recommendations:** Vasant Dhar, "When to Trust Robots with Decisions, and When Not To," *Harvard Business Review,* May 17, 2016, https://hbr.org/2016/05/when-to-trust-robots-with-decisions-and-when-not-to.

88 **people with higher cognitive reflection:** Renee Gosline and Heather Yang, "Consider the Source: How Cognitive Style Predisposes Preferences for Algorithmic or Human Input," MIT Initiative on the Digital Economy Working Paper, 2020.

89 **Facebook was blindsided by the transition:** Kurt Wagner, "Facebook Almost Missed the Mobile Revolution. It Can't Afford to Miss the Next Big Thing," *Vox,* April 29, 2019.

90 **These data are widely shared:** Stuart Thompson and Charlie Warzel, "Smartphones Are Spies. Here's Whom They Report To," *New York Times,* December 20, 2019.

90 **new augmented reality glasses:** Josh Constine, "Facebook Is Building an Operating System So It Can Ditch Android," *TechCrunch,* December 19, 2019, https://techcrunch.com/2019/12/19/facebook-operating-system/.

91 **"It's not about decoding random thoughts":** Olivia Solon, "Facebook Has 60 People Working on How to Read Your Mind," *Guardian,* April 19, 2017.

Chapter 4: Your Brain on Social Media

95 **the neural pain of loneliness inspires mice to be social:** Gillian A. Matthews et al., "Dorsal Raphe Dopamine Neurons Represent the Experience of Social Isolation," *Cell* 164, no. 4 (2016): 617–31.

95 **Isolation is aversive and unsafe for social species:** John T. Cacioppo, Stephanie Cacioppo, and Dorret I. Boomsma, "Evolutionary Mechanisms for Loneliness," *Cognition and Emotion* 28, no. 1 (2014): 3–21.

95 **It decreases the life span of fruit flies:** Hongyu Ruan and Chun-Fang Wu, "Social Interaction–Mediated Lifespan Extension of *Drosophila* Cu/Zn Superoxide Dismutase Mutants," *Proceedings of the National Academy of Sciences* 105, no. 21 (2008): 7506–10.

95 **It promotes obesity and Type II diabetes:** Katsunori Nonogaki, Kana Nozue, and Yoshitomo Oka, "Social Isolation Affects the Development of Obesity and Type 2 Diabetes in Mice," *Endocrinology* 148, no. 10 (2007): 4658–66.

95 **It increases stress responses:** Alexis M. Stranahan, David Khalil, and Elizabeth Gould, "Social Isolation Delays the Positive Effects of Running on Adult Neurogenesis," *Nature Neuroscience* 9, no. 4 (2006): 526–33.

95 **increases levels of the stress hormone cortisol in monkeys, pigs, and humans:** David M. Lyons, Chae M. G. Ha, and Seymour Levine, "Social Effects and Circadian Rhythms in Squirrel Monkey Pituitary-Adrenal Activity," *Hormones and Behavior* 29, no. 2 (1995): 177–90.

95 **it increases oxidative stress in rabbits:** Daniel A. Nation et al., "The Effect

of Social Environment on Markers of Vascular Oxidative Stress and Inflammation in the Watanabe Heritable Hyperlipidemic Rabbit," *Psychosomatic Medicine* 70, no. 3 (2008): 269–75.

95 **loneliness persists because it provides an evolutionary benefit:** John T. Cacioppo and William Patrick, *Loneliness: Human Nature and the Need for Social Connection* (New York: W. W. Norton, 2008).

95 **"chronic disease without redeeming features":** R. S. Weiss, *Loneliness: The Experience of Emotional and Social Isolation* (Cambridge, Mass.: MIT Press, 1973).

95 **loneliness motivates us to create, repair, and maintain our social relationships:** John T. Cacioppo and Stephanie Cacioppo, "The Phenotype of Loneliness," *European Journal of Developmental Psychology* 9, no. 4 (2012): 446–52.

95 **It modulates the dopamine reward system in our brains:** Naomi I. Eisenberger, Matthew D. Lieberman, and Kipling D. Williams, "Does Rejection Hurt? An fMRI Study of Social Exclusion," *Science* 302, no. 5643 (2003): 290–92.

95 **it creates neural pain, which we seek to remedy by socializing:** Naomi I. Eisenberger, "The Pain of Social Disconnection: Examining the Shared Neural Underpinnings of Physical and Social Pain," *Nature Reviews Neuroscience* 13, no. 6 (2012): 421–34.

95 **Our ventral striatum:** Arthur Aron et al., "Reward, Motivation, and Emotion Systems Associated with Early-Stage Intense Romantic Love," *Journal of Neurophysiology* 94, no. 1 (2005): 327–37.

95 **our cooperative relationships:** James K. Rilling et al., "A Neural Basis for Social Cooperation," *Neuron* 35, no. 2 (2002): 395–405.

95 **in social comparisons:** Klaus Fliessbach et al., "Social Comparison Affects Reward-Related Brain Activity in the Human Ventral Striatum," *Science* 318, no. 5854 (2007): 1305–8.

95 **and when we are being altruistic:** Dominique J. F. De Quervain et al., "The Neural Basis of Altruistic Punishment," *Science* 305, no. 5688 (2004): 1254.

96 **In 2005, only 7 percent:** Aaron Smith and Monica Anderson, "Social Media Use in 2018," Pew Research Center Survey, March 1, 2018, https://www.pewresearch.org/internet/2018/03/01/social-media-use-in-2018/.

96 **Today 7.7 billion people inhabit:** Laura Dolan, "55 Social Media Engagement Statistics for 2020," *Keap Business Success Blog*, February 10, 2020, https://keap.com/business-success-blog/marketing/social-media/best-social-media-marketing-stats-and-facts.

97 **the size of the human brain has doubled:** Rachael Rettner, "Why Are Human Brains So Big?," *Live Science*, July 13, 2009: https://www.livescience.com/5540-human-brains-big.html.

98 **primates' intelligence was driven primarily:** Alison Jolly, "Lemur Social Behavior and Primate Intelligence," *Science* 153, no. 3735 (1966): 501–6.

99 **"primate society, thus, could develop without":** Ibid.

99 **the more social a species, the larger its brain:** Robin I. M. Dunbar, "The

Social Brain Hypothesis," *Evolutionary Anthropology: Issues, News, and Reviews* 6, no. 5 (1998): 178–90.

100 **"more or less any measure of brain size one cares to use":** Robin I. M. Dunbar, "The Social Brain Hypothesis and Human Evolution," in *Oxford Research Encyclopedia of Psychology* (2016), 1, https://doi.org/10.1093/acrefore/9780190236557.013.44.

100 **the neocortex ratio is strongly correlated with group size:** Robin I. M. Dunbar, "Neocortex Size as a Constraint on Group Size in Primates," *Journal of Human Evolution* 22, no. 6 (1992): 469–93; Robin I. M. Dunbar, "Evolutionary Basis of the Social Brain," *Oxford Handbook of Social Neuroscience* (2011): 28–38.

101 **"think about other people's minds":** Matthew D. Lieberman, *Social: Why Our Brains Are Wired to Connect* (New York: Oxford University Press, 2013).

102 **The false belief test:** Daniel C. Dennett, *Brainstorms: Philosophical Essay on Mind and Psychology* (Montgomery, Ala.: Harvester Press, 1978).

102 **Sally-Anne task:** Simon Baron-Cohen, Alan M. Leslie, and Uta Frith, "Does the Autistic Child Have a 'Theory of Mind'?," *Cognition* 21, no. 1 (1985): 37–46.

103 **"varied parametrically with both":** Penelope A. Lewis et al., "Ventromedial Prefrontal Volume Predicts Understanding of Others and Social Network Size," *Neuroimage* 57, no. 4 (2011): 1624–29.

104 **recorded which regions of their brains lit up:** Lauren E. Sherman et al., "The Power of the Like in Adolescence: Effects of Peer Influence on Neural and Behavioral Responses to Social Media," *Psychological Science* 27, no. 7 (2016): 1027–35.

105 **They've since corroborated their results in young adults:** Lauren E. Sherman et al., "Peer Influence via Instagram: Effects on Brain and Behavior in Adolescence and Young Adulthood," *Child Development* 89, no. 1 (2018): 37–47.

105 **and for *giving* as well as receiving likes:** Lauren E. Sherman et al., "What the Brain 'Likes': Neural Correlates of Providing Feedback on Social Media," *Social Cognitive and Affective Neuroscience* 13, no. 7 (2018): 699–707.

106 **the rats would drop everything:** James Olds and Peter Milner, "Positive Reinforcement Produced by Electrical Stimulation of Septal Area and Other Regions of Rat Brain," *Journal of Comparative and Physiological Psychology* 47, no. 6 (1954): 419.

106 **he could condition dogs to associate a reward:** Ivan P. Pavlov, *Conditioned Reflexes: An Investigation of the Physiological Activity of the Cerebral Cortex,* trans. and ed. G. V. Anrep (Oxford: Oxford University Press, 1927), 1960.

106 **"The thought process was all about":** Mike Allen, "Sean Parker Unloads on Facebook: 'God Only Knows What It's Doing to Our Children's Brains,'" *Axios,* November 9, 2017; Erica Pandey, "Sean Parker: Facebook Was Designed to Exploit Human 'Vulnerability,'" *Axios,* November 9, 2017.

107 **brain responses to increases in reputation:** Dar Meshi, Carmen Morawetz,

and Hauke R. Heekeren, "Nucleus Accumbens Response to Gains in Reputation for the Self Relative to Gains for Others Predicts Social Media Use," *Frontiers in Human Neuroscience* 7 (2013): 439.

107 **But when Dean Eckles, Christos Nicolaides, and I studied running:** D. Eckles, C. Nicolaides, and S. Aral, "Social Influence, Habits, and Disrupted Performance Environments," Advances in Consumer Research Abstracts, Association for Consumer Research, 2017.

108 **use sunscreen:** Emily B. Falk et al., "Predicting Persuasion-Induced Behavior Change from the Brain," *Journal of Neuroscience* 30, no. 25 (2010): 8421–24.

108 **or quit smoking:** Emily B. Falk et al., "Neural Activity During Health Messaging Predicts Reductions in Smoking Above and Beyond Self-Report," *Health Psychology* 30, no. 2 (2011): 177.

108 **the National Cancer Institute's 1-800-QUIT-NOW smoking hotline:** Emily B. Falk, Elliot T. Berkman, and Matthew D. Lieberman, "From Neural Responses to Population Behavior: Neural Focus Group Predicts Population-Level Media Effects," *Psychological Science* 23, no. 5 (2012): 439–45.

108 **consider whether to green-light hypothetical TV pilots:** Emily B. Falk et al., "Creating Buzz: The Neural Correlates of Effective Message Propagation," *Psychological Science* 24, no. 7 (2013): 1234–42.

108 **"This suggests that even":** Lieberman, *Social,* 125.

109 **activation of signals associated with self-enhancement:** Christin Scholz et al., "A Neural Model of Valuation and Information Virality," *Proceedings of the National Academy of Sciences* 114, no. 11 (2017): 2881–86.

109 **"the anxiety generated by the mismatch":** Gregory S. Berns et al., "Neural Mechanisms of the Influence of Popularity on Adolescent Ratings of Music," *Neuroimage* 49, no. 3 (2010): 2687–96.

110 **adolescents could donate money to their peer group:** Jorien van Hoorn et al., "Peer Influence on Prosocial Behavior in Adolescence," *Journal of Research on Adolescence* 26, no. 1 (2016): 90–100.

Chapter 5: A Network's Gravity Is Proportional to Its Mass

112 **"Facebook . . . was built to accomplish":** Mark Zuckerberg, United States Securities and Exchange Commission, Form S-1 Registration Statement Under The Securities Act of 1933, Facebook, Inc., February 1, 2012.

112 **"a telephone—without a connection":** *Annual Report of the Directors of the American Telephone and Telegraph Company to the Stock Holders, for the Year Ending December 31, 1908* (Boston: Geo. H. Ellis Co., 1909), https://beatriceco.com/bti/porticus/bell/pdf/1908ATTar_Complete.pdf.

114 **"Understanding Network Effects":** This example is drawn from a class that I co-developed and co-taught with Arun Sundararajan, Anindya Ghose, Panos Ipeirotis, and others while a professor at the NYU Stern School of Business. Credit for this example is shared among these colleagues, espe-

cially Arun Sundararajan, who was responsible for revamping this class in the mid-2000s.

117 **Microsoft was paying developers over $100,000:** Casey Johnston, "Microsoft Pays '$100,000 or More' to Get Devs Coding for Windows Phone," *Ars Technica*, June 14, 2013, https://arstechnica.com/information-technology/2013/06/microsoft-pays-100000-or-more-to-get-devs-coding-for-windows-phone/.

117 **Apple owns 47.4 percent:** S. O'Dea, "Subscriber Share Held by Smartphone Operating Systems in the United States from 2012 to 2019," *Statistica*, February 28, 2020, https://www.statista.com/statistics/266572/market-share-held-by-smartphone-platforms-in-the-united-states/.

117 **Apple owns about 25 percent of the market:** "Mobile Operating System Market Share Worldwide, February 2019–February 2020," *Statcounter*, n.d., https://gs.statcounter.com/os-market-share/mobile/worldwide.

118 **NextWork conference:** You can see Jimmy Fallon's interview with Sean Parker here: https://www.youtube.com/watch?v=yCyMz-u-HcQ. Their discussion of network effects and Facebook's go-to-market strategy starts at about minute 20:00. You can see my talk at NextWork here: https://www.youtube.com/watch?v=0GjgFHrXHAc&t=819s.

120 **Network effects were introduced:** Jeffrey Rohlfs, "A Theory of Interdependent Demand for a Communications Service," *Bell Journal of Economics and Management Science* 5, no. 1 (1974): 16–37.

121 **Rohlfs's paper proposed an extended model:** Richard Schmalensee, "Jeffrey Rohlfs' 1974 Model of Facebook: An Introduction," *Competition and Policy International* 7, no. 1 (2011). My friend and colleague Arun Sundararajan extended this thinking in 2007 to the case of a group of consumers connected in a complex social network like Facebook, Twitter, and all the other social networks in the market today. Arun Sundararajan, "Local Network Effects and Complex Network Structure," *BE Journal of Theoretical Economics* 7, no. 1 (2007).

121 **It increased the value users got out of the connections:** The most recent research confirms that Facebook's value comes, in large part, from local network effects—the economic value of the specific people we connect with there. When Seth Benzell and Avi Collis asked people how much they would have to be paid to unfriend specific friends on Facebook, they found tremendous variability in how people value others on social media. For example, people over 65 valued connections to younger users more than the other way around; men aged 45 to 54 valued women aged 25 to 54 more than the women valued the men; and almost everybody valued men aged 25 to 34 more than those men valued others. Seth G. Benzell and Avinash Collis, "Multi-sided Platform Strategy, Taxation, and Regulation: A Quantitative Model and Application to Facebook," MIT Working Paper, 2019, https://pdfs.semanticscholar.org/9d69/1d88bd56c09006d903255129f858d0109ec6.pdf.

122 **"Orkut . . . is considered a close-knit community":** Yong-Yeol Ahn et al.,

"Analysis of Topological Characteristics of Huge Online Social Networking Services," in *Proceedings of the 16th International Conference on World Wide Web* (New York: ACM, 2007), 835–44.

122 **"an individual's demand may depend"**: Rohlfs, "Theory of Interdependent Demand," section 5.

126 **the rotund yellow mascot of AOL Instant Messenger**: Aja Romano, "Saying Goodbye to AIM, the Instant Messenger That Changed How We Communicate," *Vox*, December 15, 2017.

126 **In 1999, Microsoft and Yahoo! wrote code**: Saul Hansell, "In Cyberspace, Rivals Skirmish over Messaging," *New York Times*, July 24, 1999.

127 **AOL had used a security vulnerability in its code**: Matthew Nelson, "AOL's AIM Gets Bugged," CNN, August 20, 1999.

Chapter 6: Personalized Mass Persuasion

133 **The IRA registered as a commercial business in Russia in July 2013**: *United States of America v. Internet Research Agency LLC*, 18 U.S.C. §§ 2, 371, 1349, 1028A, https://www.justice.gov/file/1035477/download.

134 **It employed sophisticated ad targeting**: Philip N. Howard et al., "Social Media, News and Political Information During the US Election: Was Polarizing Content Concentrated in Swing States?," *arXiv:1802.03573* (2018).

134 **targeting left- and right-leaning Americans**: Renee DiResta et al., *The Tactics and Tropes of the Internet Research Agency*, Investigation of Russian Interference prepared for the U.S. Senate Select Committee on Intelligence (New Knowledge, 2019), https://int.nyt.com/data/documenthelper/533 -read-report-internet-research-agency/7871ea6d5b7bedafbf19/optimized/ full.pdf.

137 **The business was sold in 2017 for $630 million**: Catherine Shu, "Online Coupon Site RetailMeNot Acquired for $630 Million," *TechCrunch*, April 11, 2017, https://techcrunch.com/2017/04/10/online-coupon-site-retailmenot -acquired-for-630-million/.

139 **Two studies released by the Senate Intelligence Committee**: DiResta et al., *Tactics and Tropes of the Internet Research Agency*; Philip N. Howard et al., *The IRA, Social Media and Political Polarization in the United States, 2012– 2018*, Investigation of Russian Interference prepared for the U.S. Senate Select Committee on Intelligence (Graphika, 2019), https://int.nyt.com/data/ documenthelper/534-oxford-russia-internet-research-agency/c6588b4a7b 940c551c38/optimized/full.pdf.

139 **"if you wrote out a list of the most important factors"**: Nate Silver, tweet, December 17, 2018, https://twitter.com/natesilver538/status/107483371493 1224582?lang=en.

139 **"Russia-sponsored content on social media likely"**: John Sides, Michael Tesler, and Lynn Vavreck, *Identity Crisis: The 2016 Presidential Campaign and the Battle for the Meaning of America* (Princeton: Princeton University Press, 2018).

140 **Russian-linked spending and exposure to fake news:** Hunt Allcott and Matthew Gentzkow, "Social Media and Fake News in the 2016 Election," *Journal of Economic Perspectives* 31, no. 2 (2017): 211–36; Andrew Guess, Brendan Nyhan, and Jason Reifler, "Selective Exposure to Misinformation: Evidence from the Consumption of Fake News During the 2016 US Presidential Campaign," *European Research Council* (2018), 9; N. Grinberg et al., "Fake News on Twitter During the 2016 US Presidential Election," *Science* 363, no. 6425 (2019): 374–78.

140 **a combination of Russian trolls and hacking:** Kathleen Hall Jamieson, *Cyberwar: How Russian Hackers and Trolls Helped Elect a President* (New York: Oxford University Press, 2018).

140 **observational estimates of the effects of Facebook advertising campaigns:** Brett R. Gordon et al., "A Comparison of Approaches to Advertising Measurement: Evidence from Big Field Experiments at Facebook," *Marketing Science* 38, no. 2 (2019): 193–225.

140 **Our own estimates of social media influence were off:** Sinan Aral, Lev Muchnik, and Arun Sundararajan, "Distinguishing Influence-Based Contagion from Homophily-Driven Diffusion in Dynamic Networks," *Proceedings of the National Academy of Sciences* 106, no. 51 (2009): 21544–49; Dean Eckles and Eytan Bakshy, "Bias and High-Dimensional Adjustment in Observational Studies of Peer Effects," *arXiv:1706.04692* (2017).

140 **effectiveness of Cambridge Analytica's voter targeting on inferred personality traits:** Sandra C. Matz et al., "Psychological Targeting as an Effective Approach to Digital Mass Persuasion," *Proceedings of the National Academy of Sciences* 114, no. 48 (2017): 12714–19.

140 **is not estimated from randomized experiments and thus plausibly suffers from similar biases:** Dean Eckles, Brett R. Gordon, and Garrett A. Johnson, "Field Studies of Psychologically Targeted Ads Face Threats to Internal Validity," *Proceedings of the National Academy of Sciences* 115, no. 23 (2018): E5254–55.

143 **draft lottery imposed on U.S. citizens:** Joshua D. Angrist, "Lifetime Earnings and the Vietnam Era Draft Lottery: Evidence from Social Security Administrative Records," *American Economic Review* 80, no. 3 (1990): 313–36.

144 **consumers exposed to a display ad conduct 5 to 25 percent:** Panagiotis Papadimitriou et al., "Display Advertising Impact: Search Lift and Social Influence," in *Proceedings of the 17th ACM SIGKDD International Conference on Knowledge Discovery and Data Mining* (New York: ACM, 2011), 1019–27.

144 **That $1 invested in search and display returns $1.24 for display and $1.75 for search:** Pavel Kireyev, Koen Pauwels, and Sunil Gupta, "Do Display Ads Influence Search? Attribution and Dynamics in Online Advertising," *International Journal of Research in Marketing* 33, no. 3 (2016): 475–90.

145 **the past four decades of consumer engagement:** Rob Cain, framework slide shared with Ravi Bapna as part of his executive teaching at the Carlson School of Management at the University of Minnesota.

149 **actual overestimates of ad effectiveness found in a large-scale study at eBay:** Thomas Blake, Chris Nosko, and Steven Tadelis, "Consumer Heterogeneity and Paid Search Effectiveness: A Large-Scale Field Experiment," *Econometrica* 83, no. 1 (2015): 155–74.

149 **brand search ad effectiveness was overestimated:** Ibid.

149 **ROI inflation of 300 percent:** Randall A. Lewis and David H. Reiley, "Online Ads and Offline Sales: Measuring the Effect of Retail Advertising via a Controlled Experiment on Yahoo!," *Quantitative Marketing and Economics* 12, no. 3 (2014): 235–66.

149 **overestimates up to 1,600 percent:** Garrett A. Johnson, Randall A. Lewis, and Elmar I. Nubbemeyer, "Ghost Ads: Improving the Economics of Measuring Online Ad Effectiveness," *Journal of Marketing Research* 54, no. 6 (2017): 867–84.

149 **overestimated the lift from Facebook ads by up to 4,000 percent:** Gordon et al., "A Comparison of Approaches to Advertising Measurement: Evidence from Big Field Experiments at Facebook," 193–225.

150 **the ratio of the standard deviation to the mean of sales:** Randall A. Lewis and Justin M. Rao, "The Unfavorable Economics of Measuring the Returns to Advertising," *Quarterly Journal of Economics* 130, no. 4 (2015): 1941–73.

150 **"The variance of individual purchases":** Lewis and Reiley, "Online Ads and Offline Sales," 244.

151 **"consumers who have completed several eBay transactions":** Blake et al., "Consumer Heterogeneity and Paid Search Effectiveness," 159.

153 **an address that the digital marketing industry is still talking about today:** Marc Pritchard, chief brand officer, Procter & Gamble, "Better Advertising Enabled by Media Transparency," speech at the Internet Advertising Bureau's annual leadership meeting, January 29, 2017, https://www.youtube.com/watch?v=NEUCOsphoI0.

154 **P&G then put its money:** J. Neff, "Procter & Gamble's Best Sales in a Decade Come Despite Drop in Ad Spending," *AdAge,* July 2019.

154 **P&G delivered 7.5 percent organic sales growth:** D. Christe, "P&G's Sales Jump as Ad Spending Shrinks, Data-Driven Marketing Ramps Up," *Marketing Dive,* July 2019.

154 **First, P&G shifted its media spend from a focus on frequency:** E. Hammett, "P&G Puts Focus on Reach: It's a More Important Measure Than Spend," *MarketingWeek,* June 2019.

155 **"very targeted audiences":** Neff, "Procter & Gamble's Best Sales in a Decade."

155 **reducing the number of agencies:** Erica Sweeney, "P&G Tweaks Media Model as In-Housing Shift Continues Apace," *Marketing Dive,* January 17, 2019, https://www.marketingdive.com/news/pg-tweaks-media-model-as-in-housing-shift-continues-apace/546265/.

155 **media consumption soared:** Sarah Vizard and Molly Fleming, "P&G 'Doubles Down' on Marketing as Demand Soars," *MarketingWeek,* April 17, 2020.

Chapter 7: Hypersocialization

157 **In June 2020, Facebook announced:** Mark Zuckerberg, "Historic Facebook Campaign Will Boost Voter Registration, Turnout and Voices," *USA Today*, June 16, 2020.

157 **It validated its findings in public voting records:** Robert M. Bond et al., "A 61-Million-Person Experiment in Social Influence and Political Mobilization," *Nature* 489, no. 7415 (2012): 295.

157 **Facebook replicated the experiment in the 2012 U.S. presidential election:** Jason J. Jones et al., "Social Influence and Political Mobilization: Further Evidence from a Randomized Experiment in the 2012 US Presidential Election," *PloS One* 12, no. 4 (2017): e0173851.

159 **a social exercise app called Strava:** Jen See, "This Is What a Gold Medal Strava File Looks Like," *Men's Journal*, n.d., https://www.mensjournal.com/sports/this-is-what-a-gold-medal-strava-file-looks-like-w433826/.

159 **In 2018 Strava athletes gave 3.6 billion kudos:** Strava, "Year in Sport 2018," November 28, 2018, https://blog.strava.com/press/2018-year-in-sport/.

161 **daily exercise patterns of 1.1 million runners:** Sinan Aral and Christos Nicolaides, "Exercise Contagion in a Global Social Network," *Nature Communications* 8 (2017): 14753.

163 **social sharing of *Times* articles in one city:** Sinan Aral and Michael Zhao, "Social Media Sharing and Online News Consumption," February 4, 2019, https://ssrn.com/abstract=3328864.

163 **More romantic partners have been introduced online:** Michael J. Rosenfeld, Reuben J. Thomas, and Sonia Hausen, "Disintermediating Your Friends: How Online Dating in the United States Displaces Other Ways of Meeting," *Proceedings of the National Academy of Sciences* 116, no. 36 (2019): 17753–58.

164 **how the digital breadcrumbs we leave on social dating sites:** Ravi Bapna et al., "One-Way Mirrors in Online Dating: A Randomized Field Experiment," *Management Science* 62, no. 11 (2016): 3100–122.

166 **gifting of Chinese Red Packets on WeChat:** Yuan Yuan et al., "Social Contagion of Gift Exchange in Online Groups," *arXiv:1906.09698v2* (2019).

167 **"emotional contagion":** Adam D. I. Kramer, Jamie E. Guillory, and Jeffrey T. Hancock, "Experimental Evidence of Massive-Scale Emotional Contagion Through Social Networks," *Proceedings of the National Academy of Sciences* 111, no. 24 (2014): 8788–90.

Chapter 8: Strategies for a Hypersocialized World

170 **landmark "network neighbors" study:** Shawndra Hill, Foster Provost, and Chris Volinsky, "Network-Based Marketing: Identifying Likely Adopters via Consumer Networks," *Statistical Science* 21, no. 2 (2006): 256–76.

172 **word-of-mouth opinions of friends:** "Global Trust in Advertising Report," Nielsen, September 2015, https://www.nielsen.com/wp-content/uploads/sites/3/2019/04/global-trust-in-advertising-report-sept-2015-1.pdf.

173 **Joseph Ziyaee earned in a six-month period:** "Joseph Ziyaee: 5 Fast Facts You Need to Know," https://heavy.com/news/2016/02/joseph-ziyaee-king -of-uber-90k-how-to-make-money-uber-driver-referral-code-rules-photos -reddit/.

174 **the effect of adding a viral incentive to the promotion:** Sinan Aral and Sean Taylor, "Viral Incentive Systems: A Randomized Field Experiment," Work-shop on Information Systems Economics, Shanghai, China, 2011.

174 **"turn your friends into Benjamins":** You can see the DirecTV ad cam-paign I am referring to here: http://www.directv.com/DTVAPP/referral/ referralProgram.jsp.

177 **During our longitudinal study of Go's adoption:** Sinan Aral, Lev Muchnik, and Arun Sundararajan, "Distinguishing Influence-Based Contagion from Homophily-Driven Diffusion in Dynamic Networks," *Proceedings of the Na-tional Academy of Sciences* 106, no. 51 (2009): 21544–49.

177 **a seminal method developed by Paul Rosenbaum and Don Rubin two de-cades earlier:** Paul R. Rosenbaum and Donald B. Rubin, "Constructing a Control Group Using Multivariate Matched Sampling Methods That Incor-porate the Propensity Score," *American Statistician* 39, no. 1 (1985): 33–38; Dean Eckles and Eytan Bakshy, "Bias and High-Dimensional Adjustment in Observational Studies of Peer Effects," *arXiv:1706.04692* (2017).

181 **two experiments on random samples of 6 million and 23 million Face-book users:** Eytan Bakshy et al., "Social Influence in Social Advertising: Evidence from Field Experiments," in *Proceedings of the 13th ACM Confer-ence on Electronic Commerce* (New York: ACM, 2012), 146–61.

183 **experiment in collaboration with WeChat:** Shan Huang et al., "Social Ad-vertising Effectiveness Across Products: A Large-Scale Field Experiment," *Marketing Science,* forthcoming.

187 *viral characteristics***:** Jonah Berger, *Contagious: Why Things Catch On* (New York: Simon & Schuster, 2013).

187 **content that evokes emotional arousal:** Jonah Berger and Katherine L. Milkman, "What Makes Online Content Viral?," *Journal of Marketing Re-search* 49, no. 2 (2012): 192–205.

188 **"We were amazed at how quickly Hotmail spread":** Steve Jurvetson, "What Exactly Is Viral Marketing?," *Red Herring* 78 (2000): 110–12.

188 **a large-scale randomized experiment on Facebook:** Sinan Aral and Dylan Walker, "Creating Social Contagion Through Viral Product Design: A Ran-domized Trial of Peer Influence in Networks," *Management Science* 57, no. 9 (2011): 1623–39.

191 **"$527,000 in a month or almost $6.4 million in a year":** Rachel Strugatz, "Bloggers and Digital Influencers Are Reshaping the Fashion and Beauty Landscape," *Los Angeles Times,* August 10, 2016.

191 **Her second crashed Nordstrom's website:** Lisa Lockwood, "Something Navy Crashes Site, Beats Expectations at Nordstrom," *WWD,* September 25, 2018, https://wwd.com/fashion-news/fashion-scoops/something-navy -crashes-site-beats-expectations-nordstrom-1202845078/; Merin Curotto, "Something Navy's Arielle Charnas Is More Successful Than Ever—but at

What Price?," *Observer,* December 12, 2018, https://observer.com/2018/12/something-navy-star-arielle-charnas-launching-nordstrom-holiday-line/.

191 **"Social media is everything for me":** Tyler McCall, "How Arielle Charnas Turned Her Blog, 'Something Navy,' Into a Lifestyle Brand," *Fashionista,* September 24, 2018, https://fashionista.com/2018/09/something-navy-arielle-charnas-career.

191 **"one in ten" influencers drive behavior change:** Elihu Katz and Paul F. Lazarsfeld, *Personal Influence: The Part Played by People in the Flow of Mass Communications* (New York: Free Press, 1955).

191 **it was popularized for general readers:** Malcolm Gladwell, *The Tipping Point: How Little Things Can Make a Big Difference* (Boston: Little, Brown, 2000).

192 **Influencer marketing will be a $10 billion industry by 2021:** "Influencing Set to Become $10B Industry by 2020," *Yahoo! Finance,* September 27, 2019, https://www.msn.com/en-us/money/topstocks/influencing-set-to-become-dollar10b-industry-by-2020/vi-AAHWrRc.

192 **To understand Obama's influence, we'd have to know:** Gregory Ferenstein, "Dear Klout, This Is How You Measure Influence," *TechCrunch,* June 6, 2012, http://techcrunch.com/2012/06/21/science-social-contagion-klout/.

193 **This means thinking about behavior change rather than behavioral tendencies:** Sinan Aral, "Commentary—Identifying Social Influence: A Comment on Opinion Leadership and Social Contagion in New Product Diffusion," *Marketing Science* 30, no. 2 (2011): 217–23, http://mktsci.journal.informs.org/content/30/2/217.abstract.

193 **Dylan Walker and I wanted to untangle that hair ball:** Sinan Aral and Dylan Walker, "Identifying Influential and Susceptible Members of Social Networks," *Science* 337, no. 6092 (2012): 337–41, http://www.sciencemag.org/content/337/6092/337.

195 **Third, we learned how clustering and influence are related:** Sinan Aral and Dylan Walker, "Tie Strength, Embeddedness, and Social Influence: A Large-Scale Networked Experiment," *Management Science* 60, no. 6 (2014): 1352–70.

196 **The problem was first formalized:** Pedro Domingos and Matt Richardson, "Mining the Network Value of Customers," in *Proceedings of the Seventh ACM SIGKDD International Conference on Knowledge Discovery and Data Mining* (New York: ACM, 2001), 57–66.

196 **Kim Kardashian charges up to $500,000 for an Instagram post:** Kate Taylor, "Kim Kardashian Revealed in a Lawsuit That She Demands up to Half a Million Dollars for a Single Instagram Post and Other Details About How Much She Charges for Endorsement Deals," *Business Insider,* May 9, 2019.

197 **people with more friends are more likely to be connected to others:** Scott L. Feld, "Why Your Friends Have More Friends Than You Do," *American Journal of Sociology* 96, no. 6 (1991): 1464–77.

197 **spread adoption of multivitamins:** David A. Kim et al., "Social Network Targeting to Maximise Population Behaviour Change: A Cluster Randomised Controlled Trial," *Lancet* 386, no. 9989 (2015): 145–53.

198 **Instagram influencers with more followers get fewer likes per follower:** "Influencer Marketing Benchmarks Report," *InfluencerDB*, 2019, https://cdn2.hubspot.net/hubfs/4030790/MARKETING/Resources/Education/E-Books/Influencer%20Marketing%20Benchmarks%20Report%202019/InfluencerDB_Influencer-Marketing-Benchmarks-Report-2019.pdf.

198 **"ordinary influencers":** Eytan Bakshy et al., "Everyone's an Influencer: Quantifying Influence on Twitter," in *Proceedings of the Fourth ACM International Conference on Web Search and Data Mining* (New York: ACM, 2011), 65–74.

198 **"optimal seeds . . . are relatively":** Sinan Aral and Paramveer S. Dhillon, "Social Influence Maximization Under Empirical Influence Models," *Nature Human Behaviour* 2, no. 6 (2018): 375–82.

Chapter 9: The Attention Economy and the Tyranny of Trends

200 **"the power of big data in global elections":** Alexander Nix, "Cambridge Analytica—the Power of Big Data and Psychographics," Concordia Annual Summit, New York, 2016, https://www.youtube.com/watch?v=n8Dd5aVXLCc.

200 **Nix would be caught in an undercover video:** "Exposed: Undercover Secrets of Trump's Data Firm," Channel 4 News, March 20, 2018, https://www.channel4.com/news/exposed-undercover-secrets-of-donald-trump-data-firm-cambridge-analytica.

207 **cleverly exploited this change in European privacy laws to measure the effectiveness of microtargeting:** Avi Goldfarb and Catherine E. Tucker, "Privacy Regulation and Online Advertising," *Management Science* 57, no. 1 (2011): 57–71.

209 **Dstillery's original targeting system and its performance:** Claudia Perlich et al., "Machine Learning for Targeted Display Advertising: Transfer Learning in Action," *Machine Learning* 95, no. 1 (2014): 103–27.

209 **personalized ads were two to four times more effective:** Alexander Bleier and Maik Eisenbeiss, "Personalized Online Advertising Effectiveness: The Interplay of What, When, and Where," *Marketing Science* 34, no. 5 (2015): 669–88.

209 **ads targeted based on consumers' online search and shopping behavior:** Christopher A. Summers, Robert W. Smith, and Rebecca Walker Reczek, "An Audience of One: Behaviorally Targeted Ads as Implied Social Labels," *Journal of Consumer Research* 43, no. 1 (2016): 156–78.

210 **accuracy of the microtargeting audiences created by many different data brokers:** Nico Neumann, Catherine E. Tucker, and Timothy Whitfield, "Frontiers: How Effective Is Third-Party Consumer Profiling? Evidence from Field Studies," *Marketing Science* 38, no. 6 (2019): 918–26.

210 **Microtargeting is a $20 billion industry in the United States alone:** "The State of Data," Interactive Advertising Bureau and Winterberry Group, 2018, https://www.iab.com/insights/the-state-of-data-2018/.

212 **the largest public study of psychological profiling ever conducted on Facebook:** Sandra C. Matz et al., "Psychological Targeting as an Effective

Approach to Digital Mass Persuasion," *Proceedings of the National Academy of Sciences* 114, no. 48 (2017): 12714–19.

213 **"influencing elections"**: Hannes Grassegger and Mikael Krogerus, "The Data That Turned the World Upside Down," Motherboard, Vice.com, January 28, 2017, https://www.vice.com/en_us/article/mg9vvn/how-our-likes -helped-trump-win.

213 **"has had no dealings"**: John Morgan, "Michal Kosinski: Enemy of Privacy or Just a Whistleblower?," *Times Higher Education,* March 22, 2018, https:// www.timeshighereducation.com/features/michal-kosinski-enemy-privacy -or-just-whistleblower.

214 **"comparison of Facebook ad campaigns does not"**: Dean Eckles, Brett R. Gordon, and Garrett A. Johnson, "Field Studies of Psychologically Targeted Ads Face Threats to Internal Validity," *Proceedings of the National Academy of Sciences* 115, no. 23 (2018): E5254–55.

216 **what's popular, engaging, or "trending"**: "Trending on Instagram," *Instagram Engineering,* July 6, 2015, https://instagram-engineering.com/trending-on -instagram-b749450e6d93.

217 **Twitter was charging them $200,000 per day**: Seth Fiegerman, "Report: Twitter Now Charges $200,000 for Promoted Trends," *TechCrunch,* February 11, 2013: https://mashable.com/2013/02/11/report-twitter-now-charges -200000-for-promoted-trends/.

218 **Russian operatives then went to work**: Molly McKew, "How Twitter Bots and Trump Fans Made #ReleaseTheMemo Go Viral," *Politico,* February 4, 2018.

220 **"preferential attachment"**: Albert-László Barabási and Réka Albert, "Emergence of Scaling in Random Networks," *Science* 286, no. 5439 (1999): 509–12.

220 **"The vast majority of users do not"**: Linhong Zhu and Kristina Lerman, "Attention Inequality in Social Media," *arXiv:1601.07200* (2016).

221 **novel information was the most valuable for enhancing work productivity**: Sinan Aral and Marshall Van Alstyne, "The Diversity-Bandwidth Trade-Off," *American Journal of Sociology* 117, no. 1 (2011): 90–171.

221 **a second company in a completely different industry**: Sinan Aral and Paramveer S. Dhillon, "Social Influence Maximization Under Empirical Influence Models," *Nature Human Behaviour* 2, no. 6 (2018): 375–82.

221 **Local network effects are strongest for strong ties, not weak ties**: Lynn Wu et al., "Mining Face-to-Face Interaction Networks Using Sociometric Badges: Predicting Productivity in an IT Configuration Task," in *Proceedings of the 29th Annual International Conference on Information Systems* (Paris, 2008).

222 **the effects of anonymity on social media behavior**: Sean J. Taylor, Lev Muchnik, and Sinan Aral, "What's in a Username? Identity Cue Effects in Social Media," MIT Working Paper, July 23, 2019, http://dx.doi.org/10.2139/ ssrn.2538130.

223 **our study of digital exercise contagion**: Sinan Aral and Christos Nicolaides, "Exercise Contagion in a Global Social Network," *Nature Communications* 8, no. 1 (2017): 1–8.

223 **We tend to evaluate our own exercise performance in comparison to others':** Leon Festinger, "A Theory of Social Comparison Processes," *Human Relations* 7, no. 2 (1954): 117–40.

223 **what inspires us to run more—comparisons to those performing better:** 223 Tesser, "Toward a Self-Evaluation Maintenance Model of Human Behavior," *Advances in Experimental Social Psychology* 21 (1988).

223 **or comparisons to those performing worse than us:** Stephen M. Garcia, Avishalom Tor, and Richard Gonzalez, "Ranks and Rivals: A Theory of Competition," *Personality and Social Psychology Bulletin* 32, no. 7 (2006): 970–82.

223 **"competitive behavior to protect one's superiority":** Festinger, "A Theory of Social Comparison Processes," 126.

224 **men report being more influenced by social support in their decision:** Nelli Hankonen et al., "Gender Differences in Social Cognitive Determinants of Exercise Adoption," *Psychology and Health* 25, no. 1 (2010): 55–69.

224 **At WeChat, we found that showing a user:** Shan Huang et al., "Social Advertising Effectiveness Across Products: A Large-Scale Field Experiment," *Marketing Science,* forthcoming.

224 **those with closer ties had more influence than mere acquaintances:** Robert M. Bond et al., "A 61-Million-Person Experiment in Social Influence and Political Mobilization," *Nature* 489, no. 7415 (2012): 295.

Chapter 10: The Wisdom and Madness of Crowds

225 **power of collective judgment to solve:** James Surowiecki, *The Wisdom of Crowds* (New York: Anchor, 2005).

225 **The theory was originally proposed:** Francis Galton, "Vox Populi," *Nature* 75, no. 7 (1907): 450–51.

227 **Ninety-two percent of consumers report reading reviews:** "Through the Eyes of the Consumer," Consumer Shopping Habits Survey, Channel Advisor, 2010, http://docplayer.net/18410379-Channeladvisor-white-paper-through-the-eyes-of-the-consumer-2010-consumer-shopping-habits-survey.html; "Study Shows 97% of People Buy from Local Businesses They Discover on Yelp," Nielsen Survey Commissioned by Yelp, October 11, 2019, https://blog.yelp.com/2019/10/study-shows-97-of-people-buy-from-local-businesses-they-discover-on-yelp.

228 **population-scale opinion dynamics in the crowd:** Lev Muchnik, Sinan Aral, and Sean J. Taylor, "Social Influence Bias: A Randomized Experiment," *Science* 341, no. 6146 (2013): 647–51; Sinan Aral, "The Problem with Online Ratings," *MIT Sloan Management Review* 55, no. 2 (2014): 47.

230 **"suggesting that exposure to social norms":** Jamil Zaki, Jessica Schirmer, and Jason P. Mitchell, "Social Influence Modulates the Neural Computation of Value," *Psychological Science* 22, no. 7 (2011): 894–900.

230 **"social influence mediates the very basic value signals":** Daniel K. Campbell-Meiklejohn et al., "How the Opinion of Others Affects Our Valuation of Objects," *Current Biology* 20, no. 13 (2010): 1165.

230 **we tend to herd on cultural choices, like which music to listen:** Matthew J. Salganik, Peter Sheridan Dodds, and Duncan J. Watts, "Experimental Study of Inequality and Unpredictability in an Artificial Cultural Market," *Science* 311, no. 5762 (2006): 854–56; Duncan J. Watts, *Everything Is Obvious* (*Once You Know the Answer)* (New York: Crown Business, 2011).

231 **and even what to pay attention to on the street corner:** Stanley Milgram, Leonard Bickman, and Lawrence Berkowitz, "Note on the Drawing Power of Crowds of Different Size," *Journal of Personality and Social Psychology* 13, no. 2 (1969): 79.

231 **The J-curve of online star ratings is surprisingly consistent:** Nan Hu, Paul A. Pavlou, and Jie Jennifer Zhang, "Why Do Online Product Reviews Have a J-Shaped Distribution? Overcoming Biases in Online Word-of-Mouth Communication," *Communications of the ACM* 52, no. 10 (2009): 144–47; Nan Hu, Paul A. Pavlou, and Jennifer Zhang, "Can Online Reviews Reveal a Product's True Quality? Empirical Findings and Analytical Modeling of Online Word-of-Mouth Communication," in *Proceedings of the 7th ACM Conference on Electronic Commerce* (New York: ACM, 2006), 324–30.

234 **Google Flu Trends predicted the flu:** Jeremy Ginsberg et al., "Detecting Influenza Epidemics Using Search Engine Query Data," *Nature* 457, no. 7232 (2009): 1012.

235 **"big data hubris":** David Lazer et al., "The Parable of Google Flu: Traps in Big Data Analysis," *Science* 343, no. 6176 (2014): 1203–5.

236 **"We want to learn from each other":** Surowiecki, *Wisdom of Crowds,* 55.

237 **The complex systems scientist Scott Page notes that diversity:** Lu Hong and Scott E. Page, "Groups of Diverse Problem Solvers Can Outperform Groups of High-Ability Problem Solvers," *Proceedings of the National Academy of Sciences* 101, no. 46 (2004): 16385–89; Scott E. Page, *The Difference: How the Power of Diversity Creates Better Groups, Firms, Schools, and Societies,* rev. ed. (Princeton: Princeton University Press, 2008).

238 **we see that a dramatic divide between the parties:** "Political Polarization, 1994–2017," Pew Research Center, October 20, 2017, https://www.people-press.org/interactives/political-polarization-1994-2017/.

239 **"We see no evidence whatsoever of growing polarization":** Matthew Gentzkow, "Polarization in 2016," Toulouse Network for Information Technology white paper (2016), http://web.stanford.edu/~gentzkow/research/PolarizationIn2016.pdf.

239 **"landslide" vote margins of 20 percent or more:** Bill Bishop, *The Big Sort: Why the Clustering of Like-Minded America Is Tearing Us Apart* (New York: Houghton Mifflin, 2008); Bill Bishop, "Caught in a Landslide—County-Level Voting Shows Increased 'Sorting,'" *Daily Yonder,* November 21, 2016, https://www.dailyyonder.com/caught-in-a-landslide-county-level-voting-shows-increased-sorting/2016/11/21/16361/.

239 **voters are less likely to split tickets across party lines:** Marc J. Hetherington, "Resurgent Mass Partisanship: The Role of Elite Polarization," *American Political Science Review* 95, no. 3 (2001): 619–31; William G. Mayer,

"Mass Partisanship, 1946–1996," in *Partisan Approaches to Postwar American Politics*, ed. Byron E. Shafer (New York: Chatham House, 1998).

239 **county-level vote shares have become more correlated:** Larry Bartels, "Electoral Continuity and Change, 1868–1996," *Electoral Studies* 17, no. 3 (1998): 301–26.

239 **voters more likely to vote for the same party in presidential and congressional races:** Richard Fleisher and John R. Bond, "The Shrinking Middle in the US Congress," *British Journal of Political Science* 34, no. 3 (2004): 429–51; Gary C. Jacobson, "Partisan Polarization in Presidential Support: The Electoral Connection," *Congress and the Presidency* 30, no. 1 (2003): 1–36.

241 **the correlation of people's views with their party identification:** Gentzkow, "Polarization in 2016."

241 **"It used to be more common":** Ibid., 12.

241 **Simmons National Consumer Survey:** Suzanne Kapner and Dante Chinni, "Are Your Jeans Red or Blue? Shopping America's Partisan Divide," *Wall Street Journal*, November 19, 2019.

242 **"Affective polarization":** Shanto Iyengar et al., "The Origins and Consequences of Affective Polarization in the United States," *Annual Review of Political Science* 22 (2019): 129–46.

242 **American electorate has been economically polarized:** Mark Muro and Jacob Whiton, "America Has Two Economies—and They're Diverging Fast," Brookings Institution, September 19, 2019, https://www.brookings.edu/blog/the-avenue/2019/09/10/america-has-two-economies-and-theyre-diverging-fast/?mod=article_inline; Aaron Zitner and Dante Chinni, "Democrats and Republicans Live in Different Worlds," *Wall Street Journal*, September 20, 2019.

243 **partisans also select into right- or left-leaning media audiences:** Kevin Arceneaux and Martin Johnson, *Changing Minds or Changing Channels? Partisan News in an Age of Choice* (Chicago: University of Chicago Press, 2013).

243 **"filter bubbles" of polarized content:** Cass R. Sunstein, *Republic.com* (Princeton: Princeton University Press, 2001); Eli Pariser, *The Filter Bubble: What the Internet Is Hiding from You* (London: Penguin UK, 2011).

243 **Some studies find small increases in polarization with Internet use:** Yphtach Lelkes, Gaurav Sood, and Shanto Iyengar, "The Hostile Audience: The Effect of Access to Broadband Internet on Partisan Affect," *American Journal of Political Science* 61, no. 1 (2017): 5–20.

243 **others find that polarization is more prevalent among those with less Internet use:** Levi Boxell, Matthew Gentzkow, and Jesse M. Shapiro, "Greater Internet Use Is Not Associated with Faster Growth in Political Polarization Among US Demographic Groups," *Proceedings of the National Academy of Sciences* 114, no. 40 (2017): 10612–17; Matthew Gentzkow and Jesse M. Shapiro, "Ideological Segregation Online and Offline," *Quarterly Journal of Economics* 126, no. 4 (2011): 1799–839.

243 **diverging trends in affective polarization across countries:** Levi Boxell,

Matthew Gentzkow, and Jesse M. Shapiro, "Cross-Country Trends in Affective Polarization," National Bureau of Economic Research, Working Paper no. 26669, January 2020, https://www.nber.org/papers/w26669.

243 **"the fact that in many countries":** Ibid.

245 **the extent to which our networks, the newsfeed algorithm:** Eytan Bakshy, Solomon Messing, and Lada A. Adamic, "Exposure to Ideologically Diverse News and Opinion on Facebook," *Science* 348, no. 6239 (2015): 1130–32.

246 **the link between polarization and the algorithmic curation of news:** Jörg Claussen, Christian Peukert, and Ananya Sen, "The Editor vs. the Algorithm: Economic Returns to Data and Externalities in Online News," November 12, 2019, https://papers.ssrn.com/sol3/papers.cfm?abstract_id=3479854.

248 **at the music-streaming platform Spotify:** David Holtz, Ben Carterette, and Sinan Aral, "The Engagement-Diversity Trade-Off: Evidence from a Field Experiment on Spotify," MIT Sloan Working Paper, 2020.

248 **just such an experiment:** Ro'ee Levy, "Social Media, News Consumption, and Polarization: Evidence from a Field Experiment," Yale Working Paper, 2020, https://levyroee.github.io/Papers/Social_Media_and_Polarization .pdf.

250 **"Americans are polarized not only":** Alberto F. Alesina, Armando Miano, and Stefanie Stantcheva, "The Polarization of Reality," National Bureau of Economic Research, Working Paper no. 26675, January 2020, https://www .nber.org/papers/w26675.

251 **We also learn socially, by incorporating:** Morris H. DeGroot, "Reaching a Consensus," *Journal of the American Statistical Association* 69, no. 345 (1974): 118–21.

251 **as WhatsApp did when it restricted users to five reshares in 2019:** "Facebook's WhatsApp Limits Users to Five Text Forwards to Curb Rumors," Reuters, January 21, 2019.

251 **The math was worked out:** Benjamin Golub and Matthew O. Jackson, "Naive Learning in Social Networks and the Wisdom of Crowds," *American Economic Journal: Microeconomics* 2, no. 1 (2010): 112–49.

252 **"Disproportionate popularity is the sole":** Ibid., 114–15.

252 **these types of societies are prone to madness:** Golub and Jackson were motivated by prior work, like Bala Venkatesh and Sanjeev Goyal, "Learning from Neighbors," *Review of Economic Studies* 65 (1998): 595–621; Daron Acemoglu et al., "Bayesian Learning in Social Networks," *Review of Economic Studies* 78, no. 4 (2011): 1201–36.

253 **They placed a thousand people:** Joshua Becker, Devon Brackbill, and Damon Centola, "Network Dynamics of Social Influence in the Wisdom of Crowds," *Proceedings of the National Academy of Sciences* 114, no. 26 (2017): E5070–76.

256 **an experiment similar to Centola's experiments at UPenn:** Abdullah Almaatouq et al., "Adaptive Social Networks Promote the Wisdom of Crowds," *Proceedings of the National Academy of Sciences,* forthcoming.

Chapter II: Social Media's Promise Is Also Its Peril

259 **an 8.1-magnitude earthquake at this fault line:** Thomas Fuller and Chris Buckley, "Earthquake Aftershocks Jolt Nepal as Death Toll Rises Above 3,400," *New York Times,* April 26, 2015.

259 **Facebook's Safety Check triggered:** Ken Yeung, "Over 770K Facebook Users Donated $15M to Support Nepal Earthquake Relief," *Venture Beat,* September 28, 2015, https://venturebeat.com/2015/09/28/over-770k-facebook -users-donated-15m-to-support-nepal-earthquake-relief/.

262 **a 2-million-person march in Paris on January 11:** Anthony Faiola and Griff Witte, "Massive Crowds Join March for Solidarity in Paris," *Washington Post,* January 11, 2015.

263 **data on 130 million Twitter users during the *Charlie Hebdo* protests:** Jennifer M. Larson et al., "Social Networks and Protest Participation: Evidence from 130 Million Twitter Users," *American Journal of Political Science* 63, no. 3 (2019): 690–705.

264 **Pavel Durov:** V. Walt, "With Telegram, a Reclusive Social Media Star Rises Again," *Fortune,* February 23, 2016.

264 **staggering engagement metrics:** "Top Websites Ranking," SimilarWeb, https://www.similarweb.com/top-websites/category/internet-and-telecom/ social-network.

265 **a satirical picture of a dog in a hoodie:** E. Hartog, "How Telegram Became the Durov Brothers' Weapon Against Surveillance," *Moscow Times,* March 3, 2016, https://www.themoscowtimes.com/2016/03/03/how-telegram-became -the-durov-brothers-weapon-against-surveillance-a52042.

265 **armed Russian security forces threatening:** D. Hakim, "Once Celebrated in Russia, the Programmer Pavel Durov Chooses Exile," *New York Times,* December 2, 2014.

265 **a hostile takeover of VK:** I. Lunden, "Pavel Durov Resigns as Head of Russian Social Network VK.com, Ukraine Conflict Was the Tipping Point," *TechCrunch,* April 1, 2014, https://techcrunch.com/2014/04/01/founder -pavel-durov-says-hes-stepped-down-as-head-of-russias-top-social-network -vk-com/.

266 **the effect of VK penetration on protest participation:** Ruben Enikolopov, Alexey Makarin, and Maria Petrova, "Social Media and Protest Participation: Evidence from Russia," *Econometrica,* November 15, 2019, https:// ssrn.com/abstract=2696236.

267 **"tactical freeze":** Zeynep Tufekci, *Twitter and Tear Gas: The Power and Fragility of Networked Protest* (New Haven, Conn.: Yale University Press, 2017).

268 **the Chinese government used disinformation on social media:** Steven Lee Myers and Paul Mozur, "China Is Waging a Disinformation War Against Hong Kong Protesters," *New York Times,* August 13, 2019.

268 **suspected of hiring as many as 2 million people:** Gary King, Jennifer Pan, and Margaret E. Roberts, "How the Chinese Government Fabricates Social Media Posts for Strategic Distraction, Not Engaged Argument," *American Political Science Review* 111, no. 3 (2017): 484–501.

268 **"it is not correct to label":** Tufekci, *Twitter and Tear Gas,* xiv.

269 **Telegram grew faster:** Andrew Neiman, "Telegram Users Growth Compared to Other IM Services," *Telegram Geeks,* March 1, 2016, https://telegramgeeks .com/2016/03/telegram-users-growth-compared/.

269 **and 500 million by 2020:** Mansoor Iqbal, "Telegram Revenue and Usage Statistics (2019)," *Business of Apps,* November 6, 2019, https://www.business ofapps.com/data/telegram-statistics/.

269 **the reasons behind Telegram's meteoric rise:** Karim Amer and Jehane Noujaim, *The Great Hack* (documentary film), Netflix (2019).

270 **terrorists downloaded Telegram:** Paul Cruickshank, "The Inside Story of the Paris and Brussels Attacks," CNN, October 30, 2017.

271 **the Redirect Method:** "The Redirect Method: A Blueprint for Bypassing Extremism," The Redirect Method, https://redirectmethod.org/downloads/ RedirectMethod-FullMethod-PDF.pdf.

272 **used to fight suicide:** Patrick Berlinquette, "I Used Google Ads for Social Engineering. It Worked," *New York Times,* July 7, 2019.

272 **a countermeasure to the Ku Klux Klan:** Edward C. Baig, "Redirecting Hate: ADL Hopes Googling KKK or Jihad Will Take You Down a Different Path," *USA Today,* June 24, 2019.

272 **The Ice Bucket Challenge:** "Ice Bucket Challenge," Wikipedia, https:// en.wikipedia.org/wiki/Ice_Bucket_Challenge.

272 **organ donation program:** Michelle Castillo, "Study: Allowing Organ Donation Status on Facebook Increased Number of Donors," CBS News, June 18, 2013; Andrew M. Cameron et al., "Social Media and Organ Donor Registration: The Facebook Effect," *American Journal of Transplantation* 13, no. 8 (2013): 2059–65.

272 **When Nigeria, Liberia, and Congo experienced deadly Ebola:** Tom Risen, "Mobile Phones, Social Media Aiding Ebola Fight," *US News,* October 10, 2014.

272 **In Nigeria, for example, a hoax meme:** Meg Carter, "How Twitter May Have Helped Nigeria Contain Ebola," *British Medical Journal* 349 (2014).

273 **a dilemma that would pull it in competing directions:** Martin Giles, "The Cambridge Analytica Affair Reveals Facebook's 'Transparency Paradox,'" *MIT Technology Review,* March 19, 2018, https://www.technologyreview.com/ s/610577/the-cambridge-analytica-affair-reveals-facebooks-transparency -paradox/.

274 **"the future is private":** Nick Statt, "Facebook CEO Mark Zuckerberg Says the 'Future Is Private,'" *Verge,* April 30, 2019.

274 **a seventy-four-page manifesto filled with racist rants:** Daniel Victor, "In Christchurch, Signs Point to a Gunman Steeped in Internet Trolling," *New York Times,* March 15, 2019.

275 **asking him to halt plans for end-to-end encryption:** Julia Carrie Wong, "US, UK and Australia Urge Facebook to Create Backdoor Access to Encrypted Messages," *Guardian,* October 3, 2019.

275 **"a dream come true for predators and child pornographers":** "FBI Director Warns Facebook Could Become Platform of 'Child Pornographers,'" Reuters, October 4, 2019.

276 **Facebook recoiled from the transparency required:** Craig Silverman, "Facebook Said It Would Give Detailed Data to Academics. They're Still Waiting," *BuzzFeed*, August 22, 2019; Craig Silverman, "Funders Have Given Facebook a Deadline to Share Data with Researchers or They're Pulling Out," *BuzzFeed*, August 27, 2019.

277 **consumer surplus is the primary component:** William D. Nordhaus, "Schumpeterian Profits in the American Economy: Theory and Measurement," National Bureau of Economic Research, Working Paper no. 10433, 2004.

278 **they paid people to give up Facebook, then added up:** Erik Brynjolfsson, Avinash Collis, and Felix Eggers, "Using Massive Online Choice Experiments to Measure Changes in Well-Being," *Proceedings of the National Academy of Sciences* 116, no. 15 (2019): 7250–55.

278 **Facebook generates about $31 billion a month:** Hunt Allcott et al., "The Welfare Effects of Social Media," National Bureau of Economic Research, Working Paper no. 25514, 2019. The $370 billion estimate of annual welfare contributions is an extrapolation of their monthly estimate.

280 **One theory we discussed:** Mark Granovetter, "The Strength of Weak Ties," *American Journal of Sociology* 78 (1973): 1360–80.

280 **tested this theory on an entire country:** Nathan Eagle, Michael Macy, and Rob Claxton, "Network Diversity and Economic Development," *Science* 328, no. 5981 (2010): 1029–31.

281 **The collaboration allowed us to test the cause and effect relationship:** Guillaume Saint-Jacques, Erik Brynjolfsson, and Sinan Aral, "A Causal Test of the Strength of Weak Ties," MIT Initiative on the Digital Economy Working Paper, February 2020.

281 **measure the effect of Facebook on economic opportunity and wages:** Luis Armona, "Online Social Network Effects in Labor Markets," Stanford University, Department of Economics Working Paper, 2018.

282 **the introduction of enterprise social media:** Lynn Wu, "Social Network Effects on Productivity and Job Security: Evidence from the Adoption of a Social Networking Tool," *Information Systems Research* 24, no. 1 (2013): 30–51.

282 **whether job openings at former co-workers' new firms correlated:** Sydnee Caldwell and Nikolaj Harmon, "Outside Options, Bargaining, and Wages: Evidence from Coworker Networks," University of Copenhagen Working Paper, 2019.

283 **"capacity enhancing":** Eszter Hargittai and Amanda Hinnant, "Digital Inequality: Differences in Young Adults' Use of the Internet," *Communication Research* 35, no. 5 (2008): 602–21.

283 **"activities that may lead to more informed":** Ibid., 606–7.

283 **the Hype Machine provides greater returns for highly skilled workers:** Daron Acemoglu, "Why Do New Technologies Complement Skills? Directed Technical Change and Wage Inequality," *Quarterly Journal of Economics* 113, no. 4 (1998): 1055–89; David H. Autor, Lawrence F. Katz, and Alan B. Krueger, "Computing Inequality: Have Computers Changed the Labor Market?," *Quarterly Journal of Economics* 113, no. 4 (1998): 1169–213.

284 **Ugandan Internet usage fell 26 percent:** Abdi Latif Dahir, "Uganda's Social Media Tax Has Led to a Drop in Internet and Mobile Money Users," *Quartz,* February 19, 2019, https://qz.com/africa/1553468/uganda-social-media-tax -decrease-internet-users-revenues/.

285 **tax increased Internet connection costs by 1 percent:** Juliet Nanfuka, "Social Media Tax Cuts Ugandan Internet Users by Five Million, Penetration Down from 47% to 35%," Collaboration on International ICT Policy in East and Southern Africa, January 31, 2019, https://cipesa.org/2019/01/ %EF%BB%BFsocial-media-tax-cuts-ugandan-internet-users-by-five-million -penetration-down-from-47-to-35/.

285 **the tax will cost the Ugandan economy $750 million:** Abdi Latif Dahir, "Uganda's 'Regressive' Social Media Tax May Cost Its Economy Hundreds of Millions of Dollars," *Quartz,* September 1, 2018, https://qz.com/africa/ 1375795/ugandas-regressive-social-media-tax-may-cost-its-economy-hundreds -of-millions-of-dollars/.

285 **"incompatible with Telegram's privacy policy":** "One Year After Ban, Telegram Still Accessible from Russia with Growing Audience," East West Digital News, *BNE Intellinews,* May 1, 2019, https://www.intellinews.com/one -year-after-ban-telegram-still-accessible-from-russia-with-growing-audience -160502/.

285 **Many Russians began using virtual private networks (VPNs):** Matt Burgess, "This Is Why Russia's Attempts to Block Telegram Have Failed," *Wired UK,* April 28, 2018, https://www.wired.co.uk/article/telegram-in-russia -blocked-web-app-ban-facebook-twitter-google; "One Year After Ban."

285 **they succeeded in suffocating many of the country's "legitimate" online services:** Vlad Savov, "Russia's Telegram Ban Is a Big, Convoluted Mess," *Verge,* April 17, 2018.

Chapter 12: Rescuing the New Social Age

288 **"Today's big tech companies have too much power":** Elizabeth Warren, "Breaking Up Big Tech," blog post, 2019, https://2020.elizabethwarren.com/ toolkit/break-up-big-tech.

288 **"a sense of anger and responsibility":** Chris Hughes, "It's Time to Break Up Facebook," *New York Times,* May 9, 2019.

288 **"Imagine Facebook and Instagram trying":** Elizabeth Warren, tweet, October 1, 2019, https://twitter.com/ewarren/status/1179118108633636865.

290 **a legal argument for updating antitrust regulation:** Lina M. Khan, "Amazon's Antitrust Paradox," *Yale Law Journal* 126, no. 3 (2016): 710.

290 **similar arguments about Amazon and Google:** Tim O'Reilly, "Antitrust Regulators Are Using the Wrong Tools to Break Up Big Tech," *Quartz,* July 17, 2019, https://qz.com/1666863/why-big-tech-keeps-outsmarting-antitrust -regulators/.

291 **"Facebook and Twitter spread Trump's lies":** Robert Reich, "Facebook and Twitter Spread Trump's Lies, So We Must Break Them Up," *Guardian,* November 3, 2019.

291 **Google and Facebook's monopolization of advertising:** Matt Stoller, "Tech Companies Are Destroying Democracy and the Free Press," *New York Times,* October 17, 2019; Matt Stoller, "The Great Breakup of Big Tech Is Finally Beginning," *Guardian,* September 9, 2019.

291 **the decline of newspapers, newspaper employment:** "Employment Trends in Newspaper Publishing and Other Media, 1990–2016," U.S. Bureau of Labor Statistics, June 2, 2016, https://www.bls.gov/opub/ted/2016/employment -trends-in-newspaper-publishing-and-other-media-1990-2016.htm; "Number of Daily Newspapers in the U.S. 1970–2016," *Statistica,* https://www .statista.com/statistics/183408/number-of-us-daily-newspapers-since-1975/.

292 **the decline of newspaper advertising revenue began:** Mark J. Perry, "Free Fall: Adjusted for Inflation, Print Newspaper Advertising Revenue in 2012 Lower Than in 1950," Seeking Alpha, August 8, 2013, https://seekingalpha .com/article/1327381-free-fall-adjusted-for-inflation-print-newspaper -advertising-revenue-in-2012-lower-than-in-1950; data from the Newspaper Association of America.

292 **online news circulation and digital advertising revenue have increased:** "Newspapers Fact Sheet," Pew Research Center—Journalism and Media, July 9, 2019, https://www.journalism.org/fact-sheet/newspapers/.

292 **When Google shut down Spanish Google News:** Susan Athey, Markus Mobius, and Jeno Pal, "The Impact of Aggregators on Internet News Consumption," Stanford Graduate School of Business, Working Paper no. 3353, January 11, 2017, https://www.gsb.stanford.edu/faculty-research/working -papers/impact-news-aggregators-internet-news-consumption-case-local ization.

292 **When users opt out of targeted ads:** Garrett A. Johnson, Scott K. Shriver, and Shaoyin Du, "Consumer Privacy Choice in Online Advertising: Who Opts Out and at What Cost to Industry?," Simon Business School, Working Paper no. FR 17–19, June 19, 2019, https://papers.ssrn.com/sol3/papers .cfm?abstract_id=3020503.

292 **A more measured antitrust case against Facebook:** Dina Srinivasan, "The Antitrust Case Against Facebook: A Monopolist's Journey Towards Pervasive Surveillance in Spite of Consumers' Preference for Privacy," *Berkeley Business Law Journal* 16, no. 1 (2019): 39.

293 **"Antitrust institutions are poorly suited":** Carl Shapiro, "Antitrust in a Time of Populism," *International Journal of Industrial Organization* 61 (2018): 714–48.

295 **argued that consumers should own their social graphs:** Luigi Zingales and Guy Rolnik, "A Way to Own Your Social-Media Data," *New York Times,* June 30, 2017.

296 **"identity portability":** Joshua Gans, "Enhancing Competition with Data and Identity Portability," Brookings Institution, Hamilton Project Policy Proposal 2018–10, June 2018, 1–23, https://www.hamiltonproject.org/ assets/files/Gans_20180611.pdf.

296 **"the network effects insulating digital platforms":** Ibid., 13.

297 **AOL's market share in instant messaging:** Ibid.

298 **the bipartisan ACCESS Act:** Augmenting Compatibility and Competition by Enabling Service Switching Act of 2019 (S. 2658), 116th Congress (2019–20), https://www.congress.gov/bill/116th-congress/senate-bill/2658/text.

298 **"building a common framework with open-source code":** For a description of the project and its collaborators, see: https://datatransferproject.dev/.

298 **Bluesky, dedicated to creating open and decentralized technical standards:** Annie Palmer, "Twitter CEO Jack Dorsey Has an Idealistic Vision for the Future of Social Media and Is Funding a Small Team to Chase It," CNBC, December 11, 2019.

301 **a panoptic system that could be watching us:** Michel Foucault, *Surveiller et punir: Naissance de la prison* (Paris: Gallimard, 1975).

301 **"Mass privacy is the freedom to act without being watched":** Tim Wu, "How Capitalism Betrayed Privacy," *New York Times,* April 10, 2019.

301 **several European countries have stopped sharing data:** Tania Rabesandratana, "European Data Law Is Impeding Studies on Diabetes and Alzheimer's, Researchers Warn," *Science News,* November 20, 2019.

301 **"Well-intentioned privacy regulations, while important":** Sinan Aral and Dean Eckles, "Protecting Elections from Social Media Manipulation," *Science* 365, no. 6456 (2019): 858–61.

302 **claiming they had violated Romanian data protection laws:** Bernhard Warner, "Online-Privacy Laws Come with a Downside," *Atlantic,* June 3, 2019.

303 **"industry leaders to deduce":** David Yaffe-Bellany, "Why Chicken Producers Are Under Investigation for Price Fixing," *New York Times,* June 25, 2019.

303 **European ad exchanges saw ad demand:** Jessica Davies, "GDPR Mayhem: Programmatic Ad Buying Plummets in Europe," *Digiday,* May 25, 2018, https://digiday.com/media/gdpr-mayhem-programmatic-ad-buying-plummets-europe/.

303 **publisher readership and ad revenues fell by 10 percent for EU users:** Garrett A. Johnson and Scott K. Shriver, "Privacy and Market Concentration: Intended and Unintended Consequences of the GDPR," Questrom School of Business Working Paper, November 6, 2019, https://ssrn.com/abstract=3477686.

303 **when publishers and exchanges are not able to target advertising:** Johnson et al., "Consumer Privacy Choice in Online Advertising: Who Opts Out and at What Cost to Industry?"

303 **found the same 52 percent reduction in ad revenue when:** Deepak Ravichandran and Nitish Korula, "The Effect of Disabling Third-Party Cookies on Publisher Revenue," Google Working Paper, 2019, https://services.google.com/fh/files/misc/disabling_third-party_cookies_publisher_revenue.pdf.

303 **Critics of targeting:** Veronica Marotta, Vihanshu Abhishek, and Alessandro Acquisti, "Online Tracking and Publisher's Revenue: An Empirical Analysis," Carnegie Mellon University Working Paper, 2019.

304 **the GDPR cost Europe up to forty thousand jobs:** Jian Jia, Ginger Zhe Jin, and Liad Wagman, "The Short-Run Effects of GDPR on Technology Ven-

ture Investment," National Bureau of Economic Research, Working Paper no. 25248, November 2018, https://www.nber.org/papers/w25248.

305 **"lazy, not biased":** Gordon Pennycook and David G. Rand, "Lazy, Not Biased: Susceptibility to Partisan Fake News Is Better Explained by Lack of Reasoning Than by Motivated Reasoning," *Cognition* 188 (2019): 39–50.

306 **debunking false social media rumors inspires people:** Adrien Friggeri et al., "Rumor Cascades," in *Eighth International AAAI Conference on Weblogs and Social Media* (2014), https://www.aaai.org/ocs/index.php/ICWSM/ICWSM14/paper/viewFile/8122/8110.

306 **experiments reducing the spread of misinformation online:** Gordon Pennycook et al., "Understanding and Reducing the Spread of Misinformation Online," MIT Sloan Working Paper, 2019.

306 **fake news labels reduced the perceived accuracy of false headlines:** Katherine Clayton et al., "Real Solutions for Fake News? Measuring the Effectiveness of General Warnings and Fact-Check Tags in Reducing Belief in False Stories on Social Media," *Political Behavior* (2019): 1–23.

306 **"implied truth effect":** Gordon Pennycook, Adam Bear, Evan T. Collins, and David G. Rand, "The Implied Truth Effect: Attaching Warnings to a Subset of Fake News Headlines Increases Perceived Accuracy of Headlines Without Warnings," *Management Science,* February 21, 2020, https://doi.org/10.1287/mnsc.2019.3478.

306 **I advocated strongly for labeling fake news:** Sinan Aral, "How We Can Protect Truth in the Age of Misinformation," TEDxCERN, https://www.ted.com/talks/sinan_aral_how_we_can_protect_truth_in_the_age_of_misinformation.

308 **"how to avoid a phishing attack, what bots are":** Sarah Perez, @sarahintampa, "Google's New Media Literacy Program Teaches Kids How to Spot Disinformation and Fake News," *TechCrunch,* June 24, 2019, https://techcrunch.com/2019/06/24/googles-new-media-literacy-program-teaches-kids-how-to-spot-disinformation-and-fake-news/; Google's "Be Internet Awesome," https://beinternetawesome.withgoogle.com/en_us/.

308 **Bad News:** "Fake News 'Vaccine' Works: 'Pre-Bunking' Game Reduces Susceptibility to Disinformation," *Science Daily,* June 24, 2019, https://www.sciencedaily.com/releases/2019/06/190624204800.htm.

308 **the game reduced the perceived reliability of fake news:** Jon Roozenbeek and Sander van der Linden, "Fake News Game Confers Psychological Resistance Against Online Misinformation," *Palgrave Communications* 5, no. 1 (2019): 12.

308 **able to correctly predict the veracity of 75 percent of rumors:** Soroush Vosoughi, "Automatic Detection and Verification of Rumors on Twitter," PhD diss., Massachusetts Institute of Technology, 2015.

309 **"misinformation and rumors":** "Facebook's WhatsApp Limits Users to Five Text Forwards to Curb Rumors," Reuters, January 21, 2019.

309 **reduced viral message forwarding by 70 percent:** Isabel Togoh, "WhatsApp Viral Message Forwarding Drops 70% After New Limits to Stop Coronavirus Misinformation," *Forbes,* April 27, 2020.

310 **research on election interference is scarce and underdeveloped:** Aral and Eckles, "Protecting Elections from Social Media Manipulation."

311 **it delayed the data's release, and the funders of Social Science One:** Craig Silverman, "Facebook Said It Would Give Detailed Data to Academics. They're Still Waiting," *BuzzFeed,* August 22, 2019; Craig Silverman, "Funders Have Given Facebook a Deadline to Share Data with Researchers or They're Pulling Out," *BuzzFeed,* August 27, 2019.

311 **"eternal delays and barriers from both within":** "Public Statement from the Co-chairs and European Advisory Committee of Social Science One," December 11, 2019, https://socialscience.one/blog/public-statement-european -advisory-committee-social-science-one.

311 **"one of the largest social science data sets ever constructed":** Solomon Messing (@SolomonMg), "IT'S OUT—On January 17, we launched one of the largest social science data sets ever constructed," Twitter, February 13, 2020.

311 **"38 million URLs . . . [and included] the types of people":** Gary King and Nathaniel Persily, "Unprecedented Facebook URLs Dataset Now Available for Academic Research Through Social Science One," *Social Science One Blog,* February 13, 2020, https://socialscience.one/blog/unprecedented -facebook-urls-dataset-now-available-research-through-social-science -one.

312 **"maximize the utility of the data for research":** Daniel Kifer et al., "Guidelines for Implementing and Auditing Differentially Private Systems," *arXiv:2002.04049* [cs.CR], February 10, 2020, https://arxiv.org/abs/2002.04049.

313 **"help states improve their defenses and shore up":** Dan Desai Martin, "Mitch McConnell Caves After Months of Blocking Vote on Election Security," *American Independent,* September 16, 2019, https://americanindependent .com/mitch-mcconnell-senate-election-security-funding-moscow-mitch/.

313 **"There are multiple, bipartisan pieces of legislation":** "Schumer Remarks After Sen. McConnell, Senate GOP Relent on Election Security Funding," Sen. Charles Schumer press release, September 19, 2019, https://www .democrats.senate.gov/news/press-releases/schumer-remarks-after-sen -mcconnell-senate-gop-relent-on-election-security-funding.

315 **Modi's government in India is pursuing sweeping legislation:** Vindu Goel, "India Proposes Chinese-Style Internet Censorship," *New York Times,* February 14, 2019.

315 **Singapore has enacted anti-fake-news legislation:** Jennifer Daskal, "This 'Fake News' Law Threatens Free Speech. But It Doesn't Stop There," *New York Times,* May 30, 2019.

315 **"disrespect for society, government, state symbols":** Shannon Van Sant, "Russia Criminalizes the Spread of Online News Which 'Disrespects' the Government," NPR News, March 18, 2019.

315 **"mostly true," because "certain national socialist":** Dan MacGuill, "Does Switching Your Twitter Location to Germany Block Nazi Content?," *Snopes,* December 6, 2017, https://www.snopes.com/fact-check/twitter-germany -nazis/.

315 **Reddit experienced an 80 percent reduction:** Eshwar Chandrasekharan et al., "You Can't Stay Here: The Efficacy of Reddit's 2015 Ban Examined Through Hate Speech," *Proceedings of the ACM on Human-Computer Interaction* 1, no. 2 (2017): 1–22, http://comp.social.gatech.edu/papers/cscw18 -chand-hate.pdf.

315 **"the migrants did not bring hate speech":** Ibid., 16.

316 **Section 230 provided platforms the protections they needed:** Jeff Kosseff, *The Twenty-six Words That Created the Internet* (Ithaca, N.Y.: Cornell University Press, 2019).

317 **a bill in the U.S. Senate:** Matt Laslo, "The Fight over Section 203—and the Internet as We Know It," *Wired,* August 13, 2019.

317 **an executive order to have the Federal Communications Commission clarify:** Adi Robertson, "Trump's Anti-Bias Order Sounds Like a Nonsensical Warning Shot Against Facebook," *Verge,* August 12, 2019.

317 **"reasonable efforts":** Honest Ads Act (S.1356), 116th Congress (2019–20), https://www.congress.gov/bill/116th-congress/senate-bill/1356/text.

319 **others have proposed it for this very crisis:** Jeff Berman, "Big Tech Needs Regulation, but DC Must Go to School Before It Goes to Work," *Recode,* June 14, 2019, https://www.vox.com/recode/2019/6/14/18679675/big-tech -regulation-national-commission-technology-democracy.

Illustration Sources

119 **Figure 5.2:** Facebook, Inc. and MySpace, Inc. quarterly earnings reports from Statistica.com.

146 **Figure 6.2:** "Precision and Recall," Wikipedia, https://en.wikipedia.org/wiki/Precision_and_recall; redrawn by Joanna Kosmides Edwards.

160 **Figure 7.1:** Strava, "Year in Sport 2018," November 28, 2018, https://blog.strava.com/press/2018-year-in-sport/; redrawn by Joanna Kosmides Edwards.

171 **Figure 8.1:** Shawndra Hill, Foster Provost, and Chris Volinsky, "Network-Based Marketing: Identifying Likely Adopters via Consumer Networks," *Statistical Science* 21, no. 2 (2006): 256–76; and slides created by Hill, Provost, and Volinsky; redrawn by Joanna Kosmides Edwards.

182 **Figure 8.4:** Eytan Bakshy et al., "Social Influence in Social Advertising: Evidence from Field Experiments," in *Proceedings of the 13th ACM Conference on Electronic Commerce* (ACM, 2012), 146–61.

186 **Figure 8.5:** Shan Huang et al., "Social Advertising Effectiveness Across Products: A Large-Scale Field Experiment," *Marketing Science,* forthcoming.

229 **Figure 10.1:** Lev Muchnik, Sinan Aral, and Sean J. Taylor, "Social Influence Bias: A Randomized Experiment," *Science* 341, no. 6146 (2013): 647–51.

232 **Figure 10.2:** Nan Hu, Paul A. Pavlou, and Jie Jennifer Zhang, "Why Do Online Product Reviews Have a J-Shaped Distribution? Overcoming Biases in Online Word-of-Mouth Communication," *Communications of the ACM* 52, no. 10 (2009): 144–47; redrawn by Joanna Kosmides Edwards.

239 **Figure 10.3:** "The Partisan Divide on Political Values Grows Even Wider," Pew Research Center, October 5, 2017, https://www.people-press.org/2017/10/05/the-partisan-divide-on-political-values-grows-even-wider/.

240 **Figure 10.4:** Matthew Gentzkow, "Polarization in 2016," Toulouse Network for Information Technology white paper (2016), http://web.stanford.edu/~gentzkow/research/PolarizationIn2016.pdf.

246 **Figure 10.5:** Eytan Bakshy, Solomon Messing, and Lada A. Adamic, "Exposure to Ideologically Diverse News and Opinion on Facebook," *Science* 348, no. 6239 (2015): 1130–32.

257 **Figure 10.6:** Abdullah Almaatouq et al., "Adaptive Social Networks Promote the Wisdom of Crowds," *Proceedings of the National Academy of Sciences,* forthcoming.

280 **Figure 11.1:** Nathan Eagle, Michael Macy, and Rob Claxton, "Network Diversity and Economic Development," *Science* 328, no. 5981 (2010): 1029–31.

Index

SINAN ARAL is the David Austin Professor of Management, Marketing, IT, and Data Science at MIT, director of the MIT Initiative on the Digital Economy, and head of MIT's Social Analytics Lab. He is an active entrepreneur and venture capitalist who served as chief scientist at several startups; co-founded Manifest Capital, a VC fund that grows startups into the Hype Machine; and worked closely with Facebook, Yahoo!, Twitter, LinkedIn, Snapchat, WeChat, and *The New York Times,* among other companies. He currently serves on the advisory boards of the Alan Turing Institute, the British national institute for data science, in London; the Centre for Responsible Media Technology and Innovation in Norway; and C6 Bank, Brazil's first all-digital bank.

Twitter: @sinanaral
Instagram: @professorsinan

ABOUT THE TYPE

This book was set in Minion, a 1990 Adobe Originals typeface by Robert Slimbach. Minion is inspired by classical, old-style typefaces of the late Renaissance, a period of elegant and beautiful type designs. Created primarily for text setting, Minion combines the aesthetic and functional qualities that make text type highly readable with the versatility of digital technology.